JOHN–GHATAK–TARKOVSKY

JOHN–GHATAK–TARKOVSKY
CITIZENS FILMMAKERS HACKERS

ASHISH RAJADHYAKSHA

FOREWORD BY
SAEED AKHTAR MIRZA

SHER-GIL SUNDARAM
ARTS FOUNDATION

TULIKA
BOOKS

First published in India in 2023 by
SSAF–Tulika Books

Sher-Gil Sundaram Arts Foundation (SSAF)
3/9 (first floor), Shanti Niketan, New Delhi 110 021, India | ssaf.in

Tulika Books
44 (first floor) Shahpur Jat, New Delhi 110 049, India | tulikabooks.in

ISBN: 978-81-950559-7-5

Design: Kinshuk Rawat

Printed at Lustra Print Process Pvt. Ltd., New Delhi

CONTENTS

FOREWORD

It starts, almost innocuously, with a students' strike in 2015 at the prestigious Film and Television Institute of India in Pune. They are protesting against what they perceive as the government's nonchalant attitude in appointing a Chairman of the Governing Council of the Institute. The students believe that he does not have the academic or philosophical credentials for the post, and therefore his appointment is an insult to the history and prestige of this centre of learning.

That is the beginning of this book, but slowly it reveals its real intentions over a thoroughly researched 328 pages.

Yes, Ashish Rajadhyaksha's book, *John–Ghatak–Tarkovsky*, is an analysis of the very nature of cinema that makes it such a threat in the eyes of the state. It is about the right to freedom of expression and dissent at one end, and the counter-strategy to control and regulate it at the other.

This clash of ideas forms the main thrust of the book. And that is why it begins with the strike. The students realized it was not just the selection of the candidate that was offensive, but rather the arrogance of the state to ram down a decision that, at its core, was contemptuous of the nature of the medium.

Ever since its inception, cinema has been in the forefront of all kinds of debates around the world. The most famous one in India, as the author discovers, was between Mahatma Gandhi and K.A. Abbas. Gandhi saw cinema almost as a pathway to hell as, according to him, it catered to base human instincts; Abbas countered this argument. In fact, he took his battle against censorship right up to the Supreme Court of India, and echoes of that debate resonate till today.

However, the book wants to lead us elsewhere. This is a meticulously documented tale of the journey of a means of communication that had within it the seeds of rebellion, resistance and dissent. It had the capacity to question accepted narratives and ways of seeing. It had the capacity to shock. And this is why most regimes were extremely wary of this 'power', why it had to be regulated.

But, as they say, 'the genie was out of the bottle'.

Most importantly, the book covers the debates that occurred within the country and all the commissions of enquiry that were set up to somehow try to understand the exact nature of the medium. The debates centred around the need to allow for freedoms that were guaranteed in the Constitution, and yet to regulate this medium that could, at times, unleash forces not necessarily healthy for the smooth running of the government. The cast of characters in this detailed documentation covers politicians, bureaucrats, filmmakers, judges, and a host of people who chipped in with their opinions. Everybody had a stake in the outcome of this exercise.

This is a journey that is still on, as countries and governments are enacting newer and harsher laws to control the spread of ideas, subverting or circumventing laws that protect human rights. This is a cautionary tale about an impending digital future. Where will the newer battles lie, how will they be waged, and what laws and strategies will regimes use to keep things under control?

And, this brings me to the title of the book. It is taken from one of the many banners that the striking students of the film school defiantly held up to make their case. This particular one says it all. John Abraham, Ritwik Ghatak and Andrei Tarkovsky were three filmmakers, iconoclasts really, from the past who were free spirits, and they could not be regulated.

SAEED AKHTAR MIRZA
September 2022

Facing page
Protest banner with images of film stills, roses and solidarity notes on a memorial altar created outside the Kala Akademi, Mandovi, Goa. From Prateek Vats' **Retracing Freedom – Goa** (2015).

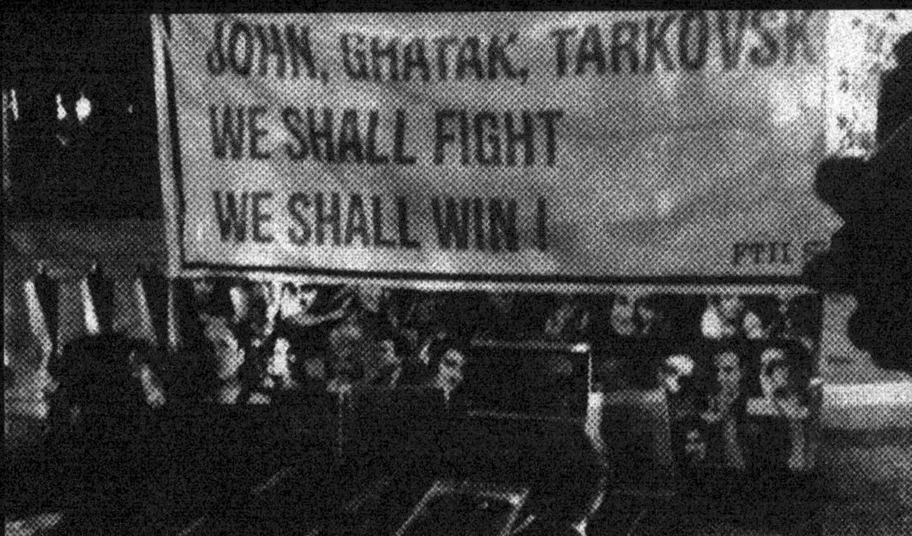
JOHN, GHATAK, TARKOVSK
WE SHALL FIGHT
WE SHALL WIN !

1960-61
F. UGC → University Film Council — Marie Seton as adviser

Children's Film Society — Pt. Hriday Nath Kunzru

Mahendra Nath

RR Diwakar
Chairman of UGC

Sapru House

Kedar Sharma
films made

Societies set up
11 societies Agra / Allahabad / Saugor / Lucknow

Secretary of UFC

Mrs. Gandhi
Usha Bhagat

Agra self

Mrs. Vijaya Mulay
UFC

S.R. Chakravarti — book on AV

about a year or more

Seminar at Sapru House

wound up.

1981 — Fiasco of UFC again

1981 → Yashpal

UFC set up

at

Archive

Fund actually remitted to Archive

Dr. S.N. Pewari appointed coordinator — SB as Tech. Adviser

Problem of Poona University — H.G. Bhide (V.C.)

Training programme in Pune University

fizzle out due to some anomaly

Check with P.K. Nair for details

Film Studies at Jadavpur & Rasgram. address & Basotharo Bengali

GHATAK 2 ... history

INTRODUCTION

In 2015, students of the venerable Pune-based Film and Television Institute of India (FTII) re-ignited several longstanding paranoias about both the teaching and the studying of cinema in India. Mainly, they were protesting the nomination of several individuals to the Institute's Governing Council whose only qualification to govern India's premier film school seemed to be their direct affiliation with the ruling Bharatiya Janata Party and its allied formations. But then, they went further.

A Cinema Beyond Itself

They had a strike that lasted 139 days, but the story didn't end there. As the 2015 action shaded, and then fragmented, into multiple sequel actions on and off campus, it grew a long tail. Many of its consequences were practical in nature, but some were more opaque. In a way the strike itself ended in failure, for the authorities were unrelenting. It became a difficult, painful, often dramatic, sometimes deadly and always complex negotiation as students encountered an utterly intransigent state apparatus, violence, police intimidation and legal harassment.

In 2021, at the moment of writing, there are almost no students physically present at the FTII (they have been sent home under the Covid protocol to do online learning), but there is palpable fear of what might happen as and when they do come back. Even as the campus finds itself increasingly patrolled by a discipline-driven, law-and-order-obsessed regime of control terrified of creativity and enveloped by a cynicism no longer capable of pedagogic ambition, it appears as though an ideal has got extinguished that was once incarnated by the cinema, by the filmmaker, the campus and (as other university agitations that shortly followed defined it) the *campus-nation*.

Failure is often just another word for absence of narrative closure, and all of this is only one half of an ever-larger story. An entirely other side to it arose when, in 2015, the students claimed for their agitation something resembling national significance. Their protest was specific, targeted against specific individuals,

Facing page
Professor Satish Bahadur's spontaneously produced chart of the genesis of the FTII, the history of film teaching in India, and the several persons and institutions involved. Made for the author in 2003.

and essentially a fight against political interference. They framed it, however, around the right to see, to study, to make and to show cinema, and then placed this somewhat niche struggle alongside and sometimes even *within* other protest movements erupting just then across the country's universities. This was the more amorphous side of the story, and it was given a startling new visibility through innovative moves – conceptual as well as tactical – of protesting, creating unified fronts and coalitions, and sometimes, of making art.

Stories without closure tend to become larger than themselves. In one way the FTII, whatever its issues, has historically been marginal to India's academic behemoths dominated by the major universities in Delhi, Hyderabad and Kolkata that led the protests that year. And yet, with only a slight twist of the kaleidoscope, the right to the cinema found itself becoming central to a very large struggle indeed.

Framing the Cinema

As the strike grew and expanded to eventually take on a life of its own, we were reminded yet again that, as an idealized *cause célèbre*, cinema in India has historically been larger than itself, has repeatedly exceeded the spaces to which it has been designated. It has spilled out of the film frame, gone beyond the movie theatre, overwhelmed the reformist purpose of cinematic realism, and refused to be constrained by institutional pedagogy.

Inevitably, then, the cinema has featured from the time of late colonialism not so much to make art or provide entertainment as to become an instrument in the regulation of public order. Given that its popularity was viewed as an ever-present danger to that order, the right to the cinema has come alongside specific public conditionalities of finding a cinematic protocol that could reproduce, in the process of making as well as showing films, precisely the eight specific 'reasonable restrictions' to free speech defined in the Constitution.[1]

For such a regulatory cinema (as the state apparatus saw it) to work, trained crews were needed who possessed specific skills that Indians, it was often suspected, lacked: how to shoot, to edit and to process footage so as to induct spectators into that protocol, and keep interpretative misuse in check. The task of the filmmaker–

-1

These are: 1. interests of the sovereignty and integrity of India, 2. the security of the State, 3. friendly relations with foreign States, 4. public order, 5. decency or morality or 6. in relation to contempt of court, 7. defamation or 8. incitement to an offence. As Justice Nariman said, these are the 'eight subjects' covered in Article 19(2), and no other. #5, in Supreme Court of India, *Shreya Singhal vs UOI* on 24 March 2015.

auteur was, to take only one example, to frame such control within cinematic realism, and to produce narrative guarantees for an effective and functioning system of regulatory protocols – ensuring no mis- or overinterpretation of texts such as might lead to incitement or disaffection. The filmmaker's right to freedom of speech was always thus conditional rather than absolute. The Censor Board was charged with overseeing this narrative contract, and diverse extra-censorial 'political society'-type groupings were brought in to further manage spectatorial excess just in case the auteur fell short of his reformist–realist contractual obligations. When all else failed, there was always the judiciary. And, of course, the police.

Given the clutch of rights and responsibilities involved in this essentially colonial arrangement, and given their multifarious links to Article 19 of the Constitution (and its cinematic avatar, Sections 5 and 6 of the Indian Cinematograph Act, 1952), the cinema has posed before the modern state several of the same administrative complexities as the modern public itself has done – to the point where an expansive idea of cinema has sometimes been rendered indistinguishable from the amorphous publics it serviced. For, like them, its political danger stems from its sheer obscene existence – as a perennial threat arising from its disruptive incapability, some might say refusal, to learn how to meet its institutional–pedagogic responsibilities.

It has thus found itself, in ways that its practitioners haven't always been able to comprehend, at the very centre of historical tensions between India's judiciary and executive over the very large question of maintaining public order: what it involved, where the threat to such order came from, and what rights people, especially filmmakers – and now film students – could claim when charged with disturbing that order.

Fear of the Apparatus

In the 2000s, a new and profoundly postcolonial era dawned on this history. A few months before the strike was announced, a famous Supreme Court judgment struck down a key clause in the Information Technology Act, 2000, on the grounds that it was violative of the right to free speech.[2] In his argument for why that clause (the notorious 66-A) was essential for governance, India's

-2

Supreme Court of India, *Shreya Singhal vs UOI* on 24 March 2015.

Attorney General attributed a magnified version of several of these very cinematic fears to the *internet*.

The internet was, in his fevered description, cinema on speed. It realized every one of the anxieties of the old cinephobic colonial establishment, of a cinema running riot in Indian hands. For unlike print, or even old-fashioned celluloid which was still susceptible to regulation, the internet 'has no [state] boundaries'. It is, said the Attorney General, accessible to 'literate and illiterate both', all of whom can download with 'one click' an 'objectionable post or video'. It is 'immune to pre-censorship' since everybody has become 'publisher, printer, producer, director and broadcaster ... without any statutory regulation'. Everybody is now a filmmaker, and this everybody is essentially 'anonymous'. 'Morphing of images, change of voices and many other technologically advanced methods' are now in people's hands. It is 'easily possible' now to 'outrage the modesty of anyone, use unacceptable filthy language and evoke communal frenzy which would lead to serious social disorder'. Worst of all, there is no public domain left to regulate since offence can occur 'at any place [and] at the time of his choice'.

Over the late 1990s and in the early decades of this century, the cinema's technological transition from celluloid to digital platforms has gone in lockstep with a digital arsenal put together by the Indian state. It has sometimes participated in, and at other times fought, the totalitarian impulses of digital governance. What this transition has also done is once again put filmmakers – or what was once the hypervisible filmmaker and is now, this book will argue, perhaps closer to the invisible digital hacker – as well as their illiterate publics back in the eye of the storm, on an entirely new firing line.

The problem has once more to do with public order. It is yet another battle between India's executive and its judiciary. The digital era has also become a new staging ground for an old cinematic problem.

Cinema and the Campus

The 2016 'winter of discontent' started early, perhaps in late 2014 with Jadavpur University's *hokkolorob* agitation. Over the next sixteen months campus protests spread across India. Many began as local incidents that escalated into battles for academic autonomy.

Several went further into defending the physical autonomy of the perimeter. In almost all instances, whatever the original cause, the agitation took its essential political form the moment the police, or other self-appointed lawmakers, entered the campus – as they did at Jadavpur University on the night of 17 September 2014; at FTII on the night of 18 August 2015 and at Jawaharlal Nehru University (JNU) on 12 February 2016; and most vividly perhaps when paramilitary forces attacked the Jamia Millia Islamia and Aligarh Muslim University campuses on 16 December 2019.

In every instance, this was a direct attack as much on the physical space itself as on the academic freedom it stood for. Safety on the campus came to signify – and the police to directly threaten – the basic rights of life and liberty, in addition to those of free speech, unfettered thinking and equality before the law. As several historians speaking at JNU's famous Freedom Square in January 2016 asserted, it was the university that demonstrated, at that difficult moment, many of the basic associational rights of modernity, in a way the nation had apparently forgotten how to do.[3] In October 2016, when the University Grants Commission (UGC) announced higher boundary walls, barbed wire, police presence on the campus, biometric attendance and the patrolling of student hostels,[4] it escalated into a direct attack on citizenship itself – as would be graphically revealed in the protests against the Citizenship Amendment Act of 2019, and the arrest of several students from JNU and Jamia Millia Islamia, including the 'Pinjra Tod' activists of Delhi University, under the amended Unlawful Activities Prevention Act (UAPA).

Campus freedom in this time often came to be defined by the right to make and to show film. At the *velivada* created in Hyderabad Central University following the suicide of the Ambedkar Students' Association member Rohith Vemula in January 2016, this right lay alongside the right to debate, to make art, to think and to speak freely. Its privileged form was the documentary, as it mutated into numerous moving-image experiments, often livestreamed on dedicated YouTube channels enabled by the proliferation of recording devices across the campus. There were surveillance cameras and related digital security devices. There were various kinds of informal filmmaking to record what was happening – sometimes as a measure of self-defence, at other times to produce public evidence.

-3

See Janaki Nair, 'A teach-in for a JNU Spring', in JNUTA, *What the Nation Really Needs to Know: The JNU Nationalism Lectures*, Noida: Harper Collins, 2016.

-4

'UGC sets new norms to boost campus security', *Security Today*, 9 October 2015.

As the agitations took to the streets in processions and occupy movements, they also brought into India what has come to be known worldwide as the networked protest, and by a term originally coined in Argentina in December 2001 as *horizontalidad* or horizontalism. Seeking to overcome the traditional hierarchies of organized, leader-driven political action, the effort to create new democratic social spaces was enabled by new technologies permitting horizontal peer-to-peer circulation, authorless memes, and the rapid movement – or what the 2019 Hong Kong protesters described as 'being water' – of data, ideas and human action.

The history of student agitations in India from 2014, or when the Narendra Modi government's reign began, through to 2020, when the pandemic allowed a major crackdown on protesters, is still being written. When it is done, the FTII strike of 2015 will feature as both a central presence and a curious anomaly. It happened at a film school with a miniscule student population even by the standards of an average college, let alone a university, with no established student union, no hypervisible leadership, and, despite a long history of agitation, no real culture of political debate or dissent. The story can only be told in bold strokes as one of transition, of the state, of technology and the technologies of protest – and of the cinema.

An Institution Beyond Itself

Some time during the great Wisdom Tree Festival of 2003, Satish Bahadur drew a spontaneous 'map' for this author of the genesis of the FTII and the history of film-teaching in India. It is a strange and unusual document that is as much about individuals as about the institutions they started. Bahadur traces the origins of film pedagogy to the UGC through to the FTII, and notes, as though an afterthought, the birth of film studies and Jadavpur University (directing me to Jasodhara Bagchi for more). Essentially, the trajectory is defined by names – Marie Seton, parliamentarian H.N. Kunzru, Indira Gandhi and her secretary Usha Bhagat, Vijaya Mulay, Yash Pal – and there is the occasional filmmaker, like Kidar Sharma when he was made Chairman of the Children's Film Society. On the bottom right side in a little box is the name GHATAK with a question mark, and beneath it barely decipherable words that read like 'prodn history'. Paralleling these individuals and their vision as reflected in seminars at Sapru House is an institutional story told using terms like 'fiasco' (when outlining the unfortunate career of the University Film Council, first set up by the UGC and then sought to be revived by Yash Pal in 1981) and 'fizzling out' (when referring to an attempted affiliation to Pune University).

Contradictions, between visionary projects and institutional failures inherent to the Indian cinema, appear as though written into the founding of the FTII. Its very conception – in the S.K. Patil Film Inquiry Committee set up to outline a central role for the state in administering cinema – was sandwiched between two major events. Published in October 1951, the Patil Committee Report came eight months after the launch of a brand-new post-Independence Central Censor Board (in January 1951) and nine months before the passing of the Indian Cinematograph Act (July 1952).

The overarching state project that the Patil Inquiry Committee conceived, a few months after the First Five Year Economic Plan had been announced in the first flush of state developmentalism, reveals both its ambition for and its innate fear of the cinema. The 'training school in the art of cinematography' was conceived in tandem with a slew of institutions as part of a gargantuan apparatus for a wholly government-owned and government-run film industry. Patil's centrepiece was a Film Finance Corporation (FFC) that would, for a start, fund the *entire* film industry.[5] One half of the Indian cinema's total production budget would come directly from the state, and the other half would be raised from public subscription and Entertainment Tax. This would, Patil said, put a 'check on futile productions'.[6] Documentary would of course be entirely state-run. Patil then added a censorship mechanism patterned on the notorious Production Code Administration of Hollywood.[7] This Code would charge the Film Finance Corporation with the further responsibilities of providing, in addition to the finance, 'experts' who would scrutinize 'the full shooting script, lyrics, particulars of the cast etc.'.[8]

All this would be run by an apex Film Council of India, an Indian equivalent of the British Film Institute. Film education taken as a whole – from using film as a teaching aid in schools to technical training for the industry – would be placed under a body

-5

Its genesis was a National Film Finance Corporation set up in Britain in 1949, followed by the Eady Levy (in 1950) to create a production fund from a levy on tickets. The ancestry of the FFC may even go back to the Lord Moyne Committee on Cinematograph Films (1936), which recommended an organization 'created by financial interests to finance the film production industry in this country, in approved cases, on reasonably cheap terms but nevertheless on a commercial basis' (Moyne Committee 1936, p. 13).

-6

India was making 275 films every year at an average cost of Rs 3.25 lakhs each. The Committee felt that 200 films for Rs 1 lakh each was enough for India. *Report of the Film Inquiry Committee* (Chair: S.K. Patil), 1951 (hereafter S.K. Patil Report), p. 103.

-7

Commonly known as 'The Code', it was introduced in the USA in 1934 under pressure from the Protestant Church, civic and women's organizations, and in direct response to threats of economic boycott from the Legion of Decency.

-8

S.K. Patil Report, p. 105.

that would superintend and regulate the film industry, and act as its 'guide, friend and philosopher'.[9]

Little of this actually happened. The 'encouragement and promotion of Film Libraries, Clubs and Societies' led to the Federation of Film Societies of India in 1960; its plan to 'award annual prizes ... [and] selection of films for exhibition in India or abroad at festivals of cinematic art' became the future Directorate of Film Festivals; and the Central Film Library was obviously the origin of the National Film Archive of India. Most other ideas remained either unrealized or, like the FFC (later NFDC), took a very different turn.[10] The 'fiasco' of the UGC's University Film Council too had a short life.

What did remain, like a miasma, was Patil's true contribution: an overdetermined vision, a bureaucratic fantasy of a pliant cinema that would at once cater to state development, return its investment in the market, *and* get recognized internationally as art. The imagination was part-Soviet, part-Hollywood, part-European arthouse, all yoked to the Five Year Plan ideology – an unreachable star, described in this book as state modernism, against which everything that actually happened would be perennially pre-programmed to fall short.

It is this bureaucratic ideal, which has dogged the institution and its diploma holders alike, that the events of 2015 may well have unintentionally buried. Originally the FII, later the FTII when television was added, was initially a Department under the Ministry of Information and Broadcasting, and after 1971 an autonomous Society with its own Governing Council – autonomous yet under direct control of the I&B Ministry. It has remained torn between being an instrument for technical training,[11] state development, catering to an unruly, unreconstructed and (as many saw it) near-criminal film industry, and producing an auteur cinema capable of global (read European film festival) recognition in the field of 'cinema art'.

As a result the FTII has – depending on whom you ask – both spectacularly succeeded and utterly failed in this endeavour. Many of Bollywood's leading producers, directors and stars are its graduates, as are its big-name cinematographers, editors and sound designers, as are most of the celebrated auteurs of the regional cinemas, as are most of India's avant-garde directors. Teaching, on the other hand

-9

S.K. Patil Report, p. 187.

-10

Among the myriad recommendations, to take only a few random examples, was to start a journal along the lines of *Sight & Sound*, to produce annual reports by the industry, and to conduct a 'quinquennial survey of the film industry'. It is interesting to imagine, in hindsight, Federation of Film Societies of India (FFSI) periodicals such as *Indian Film Culture* and *IFSON* (*Indian Film Society News*), or even the NFDC's short-lived *Cinema in India*, as long-term legatees of the S.K. Patil Report.

-11

Girish Karnad writes in his autobiography of his opposition to the television wing when he was Director of FTII. It was to be 'a place to train technicians and administrators'. If FTII ever taught television, it had to do so 'just as it taught film – as a creative medium'. See Girish Karnad, *This Life at Play: Memoirs*, Noida: Harper Collins, 2021, p. 272.

– barring iconic figures – is widely viewed as poor; the pedagogy is commonly described as peer-to-peer, batch-driven or handed down senior to junior; the bureaucracy is uniformly seen as stifling. All its students, almost without exception, remember FTII as a formative and career-defining experience. Its astonishing success has always been as though despite itself.

It was, in the end (until the arrival of the internet), the proximity of the National Film Archive, and thus an untrammelled and unguarded gateway to world cinema, that truly opened the floodgates, replacing the state ideal with an often largely unauthorized cinematic alter-ego received as though directly from Europe. This alter-ego was what allowed the forbidding apparatus of the cinema to be challenged, and it soon further extended to a corresponding ability to occupy the campus and make it one's own. It was all, in that tradition of cinema, part of the process of learning to become a filmmaker.

The Vision of Patil

Cinematic excess, the spillover of the cinema into an uncensorable everyday superfluity, has haunted the Indian state – as though Patil's original vision uncorked a genie that has ever since refused to be bottled.

In 1952, the original Cinematograph Act had defined the cinematograph to mean 'any apparatus for the representation of moving pictures or series of pictures'. Seven years later came a curious little amendment to that definition, a line clarifying that '"film" means a cinematograph film'. Why this little addition was needed isn't clear, nor what other kind of film there was at the time. Decades later it did help the Karnataka High Court to conclude, in a seminal 1990 judgment, that live telecasts on Doordarshan did not qualify as films.[12]

In 2013, the Mukul Mudgal Committee, set up to make recommendations for a new Cinematograph Act, widened this ambit. The cinema, Mudgal said, had 'undergone a radical change since 1952', its 'tools and technology ... and even its cherished audience have metamorphosed through time'.[13] He now wanted the definition of 'film' to include its video versions, its songs and their lyrics, its advertising material, its item numbers, and even

-12

Responding to the submission that 'programmes of Door Darshan are nothing but telecast of the films, therefore, the exclusion of Door Darshan amounts to discrimination', the Karnataka High Court said that 'It (was) not possible to accept this contention' since 'the word "film" means a cinematograph film as defined under Clause (dd) of Section 2 of the (Cinematograph) Act'. Karnataka High Court, *K.M. Shankarappa vs Union of India* on 2 April 1990.

-13

Justice Mukul Mudgal (Chair), 'Report of The Committee of Experts to Examine Issues of Certification Under the Cinematograph Act 1952', 28 September 2013, chapter 1, n. 2.

its posters. In his own sense of expanded cinema, Mudgal was gesturing towards a social space in which film reproduced itself – as a kind of cinema-effect – outside of the movie theatre, and wanted this effect to also be controlled by a revamped and vastly expanded Censor Board.

Since Independence, more significantly since the Emergency, there has been a cinepolitics that has impacted almost every major political development in India, where virtually every major technological change in the cinema is presented alongside basic transformations in the political public sphere.[14] The present book is pivoted on 2015, but it tells a longer story. It effectively begins in 1975 and leaves it, unfinished, in 2018 – bookended thus by the Emergency and the Bhima Koregaon crackdown on several of India's academics, intellectuals and lawyers. It is a political history intrinsically linked to major changes in the practice of the moving image. We see 16 mm and the portable projector in the New Cinema as directly enabling late 1960s' political agitations followed by the Emergency. We see satellite and terrestrial television define the early era of liberalization, video and the independent documentary similarly frame globalization, and digitization and social media directly impact the 1990s' neoliberal turn.

A central focus of this book is on the last of these many turns – namely, the arrival of the digital era. The transformation of the moving image has gone hand in hand with a major digital arsenal being put together by the Indian state. The abstraction, and segregation, of what was once a public into 'targeted beneficiaries' with different economic definitions (as well as its direct corollary, potential targets for state surveillance) has grown in tandem with new laws that trace back in some form to the old colonial Sedition Act. These laws use several phrases that merge into a single identikit, enabling another kind of targeting. The 'interest of the sovereignty or integrity of India, defence of India, security of the State, friendly relations with foreign States' now merges into 'disloyalty to the Constitution' (Citizenship Act, 1955), and then into 'public order or for preventing incitement to the commission of any cognizable offence' (Information Technology Act, 2000), 'disaffection towards the Government established by law' (124A, Indian Penal Code), 'causes or is intended to cause disaffection against India' (Unlawful

-14

The term 'cinepolitics' was coined by Madhava Prasad to discuss movie stars and state politics in South India. See Madhava Prasad, *Cine Politics: Film Stars and Political Existence in South India*, Hyderabad: Orient Blackswan, 2014. It is used rather differently here.

Activities Prevention Act), the 'sovereignty and integrity of India, and the security of the State, friendly relations with foreign States, public order' (Personal Data Protection Bill, 2019). As the days go by these terms increasingly appear to run into each other, and anyone can be accused of any or all of these unbailable offences practically at whim.

A widespread use of the concept of expanded cinema in art is to produce (quoting the Tate Gallery) something of an immersive experience that challenges the 'boundaries of cinema and rejects the traditional one-way relationship between the audience and the screen'.[15] When a larger-than-life Indian cinema takes to the streets, that sounds like a very limited definition.

-15 Art term definition of 'Expanded Cinema', Tate Gallery.

—

Nevertheless, as the film students actually took to the streets between June and September of 2015, and as they gathered around the Wisdom Tree with Macbooks buzzing even as across the road lay a graveyard to the cinema itself, there was a connection between the way expanded cinema was originally theorized by Gene Youngblood to describe a *synaesthetic* cinema and several elements of film that rapidly grew into a key apparatus of protest.[16] A new *condition of consciousness* appears to have emerged attached to a new mode of making, showing and circulating the expanded moving image in India in this time.

-16 Gene Youngblood, *Expanded Cinema*, New York: P. Dutton & Co., 1970.

Each of the technologies of the moving image – 16 mm, VHS/UMatic, Beta, Digibeta, digital video and now purely digital – defined the filmmaker–auteur differently. Each has to be located in its political moment to conceive the impact of the free speech doctrine and the 'reasonable restrictions' clause on moving-image practice. Filmmakers once accused of indecency and immorality are now being increasingly targeted with preventive detention rather than the criminal justice system. The link between documentary and the arrival of tactical media is explored, as is the transformation in the career of the filmmaker, from the awe-inspiring *regisseur* of the 1980s to the invisible hacker of the 2010s.

This is a live story. At the time of writing, the Intermediary Guidelines and Digital Media Ethics Code of 2021 have been announced. The draft amendments to the Cinematograph Act of 1952 are also in the public domain. On 2 June 2020, an 'Expert Committee on Rationalization of Film Media Units and Review of Autonomous Bodies' recommended 'specific roadmaps' for the development of nearly all the institutions started under the old Patil Committee Report: the 'National Film Development Corporation, Films Division, Children's Film Society of India, Satyajit Ray Film and Television Institute, Directorate of Film Festivals, and National Film Archives of India'. The Expert Committee suggested that all these be either merged, restructured or summarily scrapped. Instead, 'an umbrella configuration with 4 broad verticals' should be created – the new verticals, named 'Production, Festival, Heritage and Knowledge', to be headed by 'professionals' presumably of corporate vintage.[17] This report, I&B Minister Prakash Javdekar promised, 'will not remain on the shelf'.

The cinema, and with it the larger expanded domain of the moving image, is gearing up for yet another battle. It could be another chapter in the history of that old cinematic ideal which gathered so many people around it. It may also be, truly and finally, its end.

-17

Press Information Bureau, Press Note: 'Expert Committees on Rationalization of Film Media Units and Review of Autonomous Bodies submit report', 2 June 2020.

CHAPTER 1

THE CAMPUS IN EXPANDED CINEMA

> '*Eisenstein–Pudovkin – We Shall Fight, We Shall Win.*' Students' slogan in 2015

Nobody is entirely sure who thought up the slogan or when it was first used. Made famous during the four-month-long strike of 2015 by students of the Film and Television Institute of India, it soon became a popular addition to *Awaaz do, Halla bol, Ek dhakka aur* and other lines familiar to Indian political sloganeering. Vikas Urs, core committee member of the 2015 strike, is reasonably sure he heard Eisenstein and Pudovkin's names on the street when he as a young fresher found himself unexpectedly in the middle of the major 'Hewitt' strike that engulfed the campus in 2010. On the other hand Naveen Padmanabha, who was general secretary of the FTII Students Association in 2010, is equally sure that both this

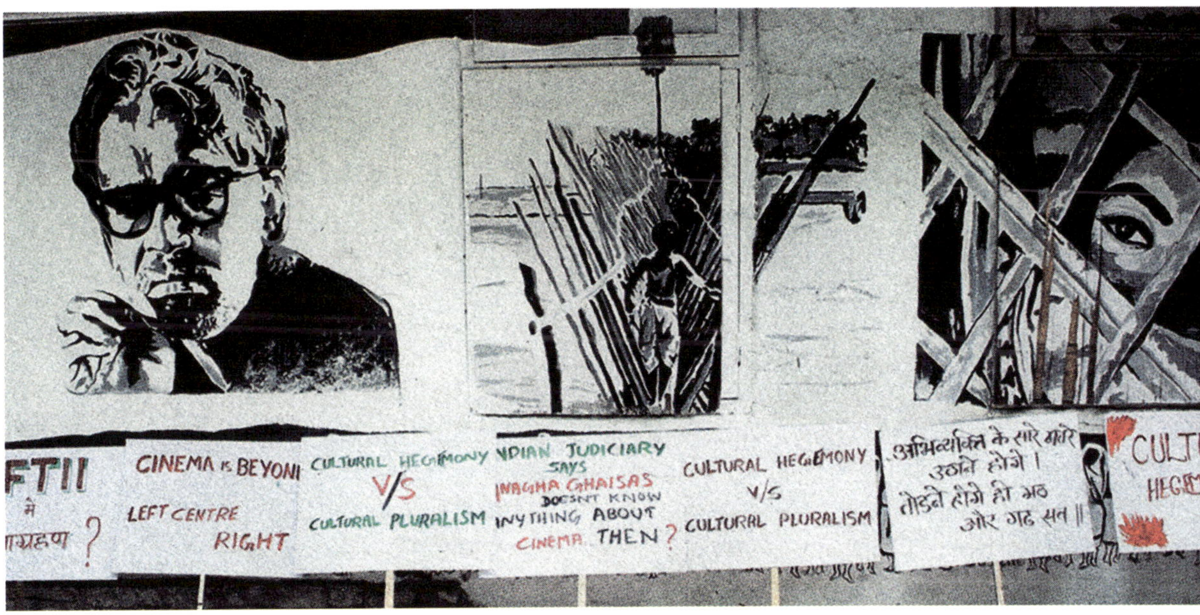

Ritwik Ghatak on the FTII campus wall. Images from his films oversee several placards used during the early days of the 2015 strike.

and the rather less rhymed dedication to 'John (Abraham)–(Ritwik) Ghatak–(Andrei) Tarkovsky' are of more recent vintage.[1]

The masters of the cinema, whenever they were first evoked, are certainly among those present on Tuesday, 9 June 2015, when Naveen, Nachi (Harishankar Nachimuthu) and Ajayan (Adat) sit in the Institute's canteen and look at the space in front marked out for a spanking new classroom theatre (or CRT). Across the road is the famous old CRT. It still has ancient 35-mm carbon arc projectors that are no longer used, and an old-fashioned tiled roof over rooms that go back to the era of the Prabhat Film Company. Even as they speak, it is probably screening a celluloid classic at the annual Film Appreciation Course taking place just then. A gigantic image of Ritwik Ghatak glowers down from the wall outside the Main Theatre in a blown-up reproduction from *Jukti Takko aar Gappo*, while John Abraham with his flowing mane looks down from another, alongside the words 'Strike. Down. Fascism.'

They are discussing trees. Specifically, the trees marked for uprooting to make way for the new CRT. Trees are no small issue, being in addition to everything else a rapidly disappearing presence on a campus that is also a permanent movie set for student exercises. The main Prabhat campus isn't large, and it has grown around an oddity – a straight road cutting right through it, like a spine. On one side are the legendary Prabhat Studio floors, now listed by INTACH as Grade II Heritage architecture. On the other side, part of the once open spaces increasingly being encroached, a mass of buildings in the *sarkari* PWD style of urban brutalism. The place thus splits open into a homage to institutional history on the right and amnesia on the left. As the road goes up the hill it enters a small, endangered patch of green, itself seeped in cinematic history. There is a 'Shantaram pond', originally constructed, it is said, in the early 1930s by S. Fattelal to shoot the flood sequences of the film *Sant Dnyaneshwar* (1940). To cinematographer Prabhati Gharat, who joined the Institute in 2011 and now specializes in deep-sea underwater photography, those trees were among the pivotal issues of her entire stay there. 'Next to the canteen ... that entire stretch ... like, don't take away our trees please.' 'You feel so disoriented. It just doesn't feel like your campus any more. Honestly, that was one of the reasons why I became a part of the strike.'[2]

-1

WhatsApp messages to the author from Vikas Urs and Naveen Padmanabha, 21 August 2020.

You can however actually hear the slogan at one moment in the documentary footage of the 13 September 2010 demonstration during the Hewitt strike. Kislay further clarifies that the original slogan, devised in 2010, was a variant of 'Ho Ho Ho Chi Minh – We shall fight, We shall win.' Conversation with Kislay, 25 June 2022.

-2

Conversation with Prabhati Gharat, 12 December 2018, Porvorim, Goa.

The morning's topic is to put together the agenda of a general body meeting of all students.[3] As they talk, Ajayan's mobile pings with strange news. Someone called Gajendra Chauhan has been named the Chairman of FTII's Governing Council. 'Gajendra who?' goes the uniform initial reaction. 'Yudhishthir', says one bright spark, recalling the patriarch Chauhan had played in B.R. Chopra's late 1980s' television epic *Mahabharata*.

A GBM did take place that night, but there are multiple versions of what exactly was discussed and agreed to. It began with around '30–35 of us', Nachi recalls, but attendance then gradually swelled. Television wing students arrived when Vibhu Puri, who was conducting a workshop, cancelled a class and urged them to attend. Scriptwriting course participants too rolled up. Eventually there were around sixty people, a 'big number for Institute'.[4]

Naveen, who had graduated in 2012, was on campus to guest-direct a playback exercise.[5] He heard that the meeting was at times fractious, eventually inconclusive. He was told that they would reconvene more publicly at 11 the next morning under the Wisdom Tree. Kislay remembers the day rather more vividly. He had been general secretary two terms earlier, and many still saw him as the public face of the student body. He phoned Nachi to ask him what was going on. They had been in conversation earlier. A controversy had erupted at the Indian Institute of Technology, Madras (in Chennai), when an Ambedkar–Periyar Study Circle was banned following the alleged receipt of an anonymous letter by the Ministry of Human Resource Development.[6] Nachi wanted the FTII to join several other universities in extending support, but had difficulty getting a consensus. Both Kislay and Ajayan supported Nachi on this, and now Kislay wanted to know how the GBM was going. It was a confusing agenda with trees and the 'Ambedkar–Periyar thing' merging into this news of a nothing actor that nobody knew very much about. The only thing everyone was agreed upon was that some kind of action was necessary, although nobody quite knew what.

The news of an impending strike caught many by surprise. Among those unprepared for it was the influential alumni body GraFTII comprising (mostly Mumbai-based) ex-students. Although functioning largely as an old boys' network, GraFTII has developed over the years several direct and indirect interests over the Institute.

-3

Events of 9 June 2015, reconstructed mainly from the recollections of Naveen, Nachi and Kislay.

-4

Conversation with Nachi, 2/3 March 2019, Chennai.

-5

This was Naveen's remarkable science fiction film, *Amateurs* (2016), a dialogue exercise for the 2012 batch, showing ham-radio amateurs tune in and eavesdrop on interstellar space conversations.

-6

The entire history of the Ambedkar–Periyar Study Circle controversy at IIT Madras is summarized, with key documents, in 'Ambedkar–Periyar Study Circle Ban in IIT Madras – The Real Story', *Vinavu*, 30 May 2015.

Also see Divya Rajagopal, 'After IIT Madras ban, Ambedkar–Periyar Study ircle spreads to other campuses', *The Economic Times*, 1 June 2015.

It exists as a mediation mechanism, a conduit to the government and sometimes to the industry. It thus has limited appetite for any radical action that might disrupt its settled ways, and so the students' stand rang multiple alarm bells. Kislay's phone was flooded with questions asking him what was going on. Nachi was 'getting calls from everywhere, seniors asking what's happening'. By 10, journalists began phoning in. Gajendra Chauhan had begun trending on national television.

Vikas too appeared uncertain about the way forward when Kislay called him. He knew that a response had to be put together but hadn't worked out what it might be. Opinion was veering round to a token one-day action, but there were practical problems – the Film Appreciation Course was going on with sixty participants from across the country attending lectures at the CRT. Should that be closed down? The most important issue was, really, how big was this Chauhan business? Was the problem just that he was some kind of B-actor? 'Naseeruddin Shah has also done a lot of bad films', Kislay says. 'Did that disqualify a person?'[7] Vinod Khanna's positive role as Chairman during the 2000 strike was still remembered.

It was generally agreed that a second and more 'proper' GBM be organized immediately. The difficulty was the news cycle, where the Chauhan report had taken on a life of its own. As his early career in soft porn was unearthed, his Yudhishthir persona too shifted: clips from films like *Khuli Khidki* (1989) and *Vaasna* (1991) began dominating social media. It was rumoured that the Information and Broadcasting Ministry was 'panicking' that their decision to reward a low-end party hack was beginning to backfire on them. Might they reconsider their decision? Best, all things considered, to organize something of a token nature and let the weekend play itself out. The weekend was anyway coming up.[8]

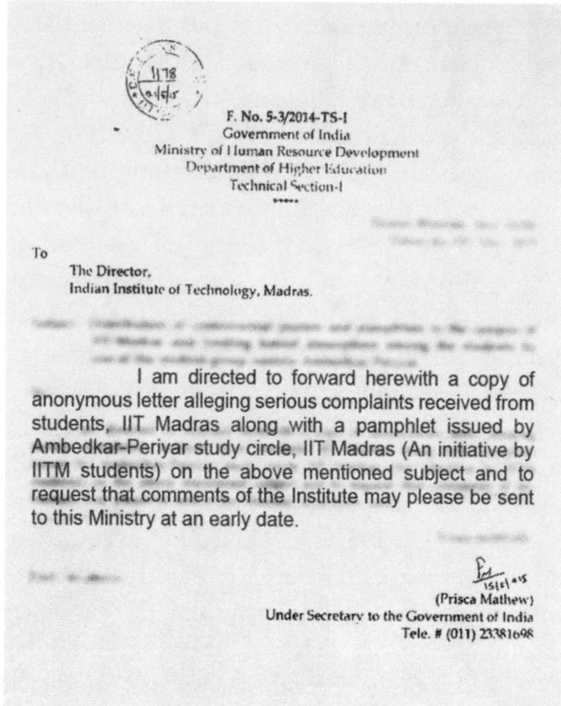

F. No. 5-3/2014-TS-I
Government of India
Ministry of Human Resource Development
Department of Higher Education
Technical Section-I

To

The Director,
Indian Institute of Technology, Madras.

I am directed to forward herewith a copy of anonymous letter alleging serious complaints received from students, IIT Madras along with a pamphlet issued by Ambedkar-Periyar study circle, IIT Madras (An initiative by IITM students) on the above mentioned subject and to request that comments of the Institute may please be sent to this Ministry at an early date.

(Prisca Mathew)
Under Secretary to the Government of India
Tele. # (011) 23381698

Summary and mash-up of 15 May 2015 letter from the Ministry of Human Resource Development to IIT Madras. This has been adapted from 'Ambedkar–Periyar Study Circle Ban in IIT Madras – The Real Story', *Vinavu*, 30 May 2015.

-7

Conversation with Kislay, 19 September 2018, New Delhi.

-8

The week launched an enduring feature of the entire strike: marathon GBMs in which 'anything and everything' was discussed. Conversations moved from routine moral policing to large political questions. 'We knew that we needed to build the capacity to bring forward our concerns, and not just make this into one [event that showed] our capacity to shout outside the gate with a placard.' Verbatim conversation with Vikas Urs, 21 October 2021, Mumbai.

Then the official notice from the Press Information Bureau arrived. The details came out – and the news was not good. If Chauhan's reputation had been a matter of confusion, there was none about the other names nominated to the Governing Council. As the penny dropped it fell like an explosion.

Narendra Pathak, president of the Maharashtra wing of the Akhil Bharatiya Vidyarthi Parishad (ABVP) that had attacked FTII students at a screening on 22 August 2013. *Shailesh Gupta*, Institute alumnus, known for a film titled *Shapath Modi Ki*. *Anagha Ghaisas*, a documentary filmmaker and producer whose best-known works were *Ram Mandir: Adalat aur Aastha* and *Shri Narendra Modi: Gatha Asamanya Netrutva ki*, and the person Pune-based documentary filmmaker (and much-liked Institute alumnus) Nandan Kudhyadi had sued for not paying him and for taking away his directorial credit for a 'patriotic' film on the National Defence Academy that she had commissioned. The Pune High Court ruling had observed that Ghaisas 'had not taken education in film shooting, editing and directing', 'does not know the difference between fiction and documentary', and 'does not have technical knowledge regarding film-making'.[9]

The other names listed were of actors Vidya Balan, Pallavi Joshi and Pranjal Saikia; author and theatre personality Urmil Kumar Thapalyal; and filmmakers Jahnu Barua, Santosh Sivan, Raju Hirani and Imo Singh. Clearly, none of FTII Director D.J. Narain's nominees of the previous December – A.R. Rahman, Javed Akhtar, Naseeruddin Shah, Resul Pookutty – had been considered.[10] Jahnu Barua and Santosh Sivan soon submitted letters declining their nomination.

—

In the event, the FTII strike was not to be a token – it lasted, as is well known now, a staggering 139 days. As a fight for academic autonomy that directly took on India's central government, it became an early and eventually key intervention in a larger history of political agitation at a pivotal moment for the Indian state. The longest and most substantial student agitation in an institution famous for a tradition of campus actions, it was also the first FTII

-9 See Ardhra Nair, 'Despite court order, FTII society member won't pay up director who shot docu for her', *The Indian Express*, 23 June 2015.

-10 See Atikh Rasheed, 'Narendra Pathak for Resul Pookutty: How FTII list was chopped and changed', *The Indian Express*, 17 August 2015.

strike to go beyond campus specifics and take on issues of significant national interest.

The 'national' into which this action was inserted may still be too recent to allow for historical certitudes. You could see it as a pivotal half-way mark between *hokkolorob*-2014 and Jamia-2019. You could also bookend the era with 2009, when digital governance took root in India with Aadhar, and 2020, the onset of the pandemic. However you define it, a central presence in the story was the period bracketing the first term of the Narendra Modi-led central government.

In the early hours of 17 September 2014, police entered Jadavpur University's campus in Kolkata. Students were conducting a *gherao* of the Vice Chancellor to protest his inaction over a sexual harassment issue. That night, as the police along with vandals (allegedly) affiliated to Bengal's Trinamool Congress entered at the invitation of the Vice Chancellor, a small and localized protest took on a national dimension. Named *hokkolorob* ('let there be noise', in reference to a Bangladeshi song), which soon became a hashtag,[11] the protest escalated across the city, ending only after a 150-hour hunger strike and the Vice Chancellor's eventual resignation. Five years later, on 15 December 2019, police would enter the Jamia Millia university, attack its students and vandalize its library, in the wake of protest marches against the Citizenship Amendment Act of 2019 over the previous two days.[12]

There was a dim awareness that the torch that this tiny campus in Pune now carried had already been lit. Students actively sought common cause with agitations going on in the academic behemoths of Delhi, Kolkata and Hyderabad, as much as with smaller universities as diverse as IIT Madras and Pondicherry University. A month after the strike was called off, in November 2015, the Occupy UGC movement began in Delhi.[13] Three months later the Hyderabad Central University saw a major student uprising after the suicide of Rohith Vemula, a member of the Ambedkar Students' Association, and a month after that was the arrest of students on the JNU campus in the wake of the 'sedition row'.

As the instruments for suppressing dissent got sharper, the bludgeon of choice for an increasingly authoritarian regime became Section 124A of the Indian Penal Code – the notorious 'sedition'

-11

See Devjyot Ghoshal, 'A brief history of #Hokkolorob, the hashtag that shook Kolkata', *Quartz India*, 9 October 2014.

-12

People's Union of Democratic Rights report, *Bloody Sunday 2019, Police Brutalities at Jamia Millia Islamia 13–15 December, 2019.*

Karwan-e-Mohabbat and India Cultural Forum, 'The Siege of Aligarh Muslim University: A fact finding report', *India Cultural Forum*, 24 December 2019.

-13

Occupy UGC: see Kavita Krishnan, 'Govt vs Students: Brutal Crackdown on #OCCUPYUGC Protest Sparks Nationwide Condemnation', *The Citizen*, 28 October 2015.

and Shehla Rashid Shora, '#OCCUPY UGC# A struggle for inclusion', *The Companion*, 20 December 2015.

Facing page and overleaf
Pune High Court, 2009: *Nandan Kudhyadi versus Anagha Ghaisas, Suit for Recovery of unpaid dues.*

Instituted on 27/07/2009
Registered on 27/07/2009
Decided on 15/11/2014
Duration 05Y 4 M12 D

In The Court of 35th Jt. Civil Judge Junior Division Pune, At Pune.
(Presided Over by **Shailesh U. Kanthe**)

Reg.Civ.Suit No 4701/2012.
Exh. No.95

Shri. Nandan Prabhakar Kudhyadi, Age: 56, Occu: Professor and Producer-Director, R/o.:- 4- Kanchan Apartment, Girija Society, Paud Road, Pune-38.	**Plaintiff**

VERSUS

Ms. Anagha Ashok Ghaisas, Age : 42, Occu: Sole proprietor of Creations Entertainment, R/o. : Shree Apartment, Behind Balshikshan School,Dhamanka Path, Mayur Colony, Pune -39.	**Defendant**

SUIT FOR RECOVERY RS.4,45,000/-

APPEARANCE :-
Learned **Advocate Shri R.B.Jagtap** for Plaintiff.
Learned **Advocate Shri M.P. Patil** for Defendant.

documentary. He admitted that, Rs. 32 lack was only given to the documentary.

26] In cross-examination of plaintiff, it has came on record that there was no any written agreement of the film production and payment. Plaintiff also admitted that there was no any writing in between plaintiff and defendant regarding permitting for plaintiff to script writing. Plaintiff also do not remember the exact number of tapes he recorded. Plaintiff also admitted that Dabake had also done some work of direction. Defendant had also conducted and additional shooting. Plaintiff denied the story put up by the defendant in the cross-examination.

27] In cross-examination of defendant at Exh.71 it is came in evidence that film production is only her occupation. she had not taken education in film shooting, editing and directing. She doesn't know the difference between fiction and documentary. Defendant do not have technical knowledge regarding making of the film. In the year 2009-2010 she obtained donation of about 25 lakhs from Ideal Road Builders(IRB)They paid Rs.13 lakhs towards NDA film but she don't have separate receipt to show the same. She had also maintained accounts as to expenditure for NDA film and will produce the accounts. IRB had not issued any letter stating out of 25 lakhs the amount of 13 lakhs were to be utilized for NDA

law targeted against 'any action that brings or attempts to bring hatred or contempt towards the government of India'. In 2019, the Unlawful Activities Prevention Act (UAPA) was added to the arsenal with the arrest of political 'dissidents', first with the Bhima Koregaon crackdown and then after the 2020 Delhi riots.

How to characterize the alarming speed with which state totalitarianism rose in those years? Was the first Modi regime historically unprecedented in India? Might it be seen as bearing resemblance to the national Emergency of 1975, or perhaps other domestic precedents? This question, and the growing theory that it was a kind of 'new normal' with Emergency-like consequences but none of its basic legal self-definition as a temporary ('emergency') measure, proved more complicated than it appeared. Ideologically, Hindutva majoritarianism was certainly not new to India. Nevertheless, its weaponization had taken the Modi government into areas where even the Vajpayee-led NDA's majoritarian excesses had never dared enter. If Vajpayee's interventions had been political-ideological, Modi's were much more into the *apparatus* of the state than merely its ideological armature. Several of Modi's instruments of choice, including the amended UAPA, the Citizenship Amendment Act, the National Population Register and the Aadhar biometric system of tagging state 'benefit', had actually been dreamed up by the earlier, seemingly ideologically opposed UPA-II regime and its Home Minister P. Chidambaram, whose inclinations were no less totalitarian than those of his successors. 2014–19 thus saw a long history of technological normalization of hierarchy reach its pinnacle, alongside an ever-expanding apparatus of digital surveillance that, together with labour automation, might be best described as (what political theorist Partha Chatterjee calls) the 'tactically extended state',[14] attributable thus as much to its *neoliberal* as its Hindutva character.

The tactics of protest in this time may also thus be usefully seen as directed as much towards the larger apparatus of the state as to any specific ruling ideologies of the government. They were no longer geared merely to replacing one entity in power with another. By 2015 the crisis had become more systemic than ideological, as the apparatus of state totalitarianism normalized and even institutionalized a complex technological system of targeted discrimination. As 'people'

-14
Chatterjee speaks of such a state as one where 'government must selectively extend benefits, suspend normal legal regulations, and treat (all) populations as exceptional cases', since benefit has to happen 'without ... jeopardizing the structure of law and property that prevails in civil society'. 'The zones of exception' in which rights and benefits are extended to people are 'declared and revoked tactically, based on political and usually short-term calculations of expected costs and benefits'. Partha Chatterjee, 'Passive Revolution: The Tactically Extended State', in *I Am the People: Reflections on Popular Sovereignty Today*, New York: Columbia University Press, 2020, p. 86.

gradually turned into digital data-producing machines, citizenship found itself transformed – and with it, its key representations such as leadership and authorship. New ethical principles saw new fundamental rights being created, born under a vastly expanded Article 21.[15] As these rights began being accorded selectively rather than universally, citizens too found themselves segregated according to whatever 'targeted benefits' they qualified for, delivered directly to an assigned, hierarchically ordered beneficiary status in return for data over which they seldom had control.

Like the political authority they challenged, the protests were both new and not new. They carried the memory of India's traditions of student action that went back to 1969–71, the Emergency, the 1980s' anti-fee-rise agitations and the 1990s' battles over 'reservations'. Equally clearly, *hokkolorob* brought into India in 2014 a mode that British Labour historian Paul Mason – speaking of movements that have engulfed much of the second decade of the twenty-first century, from Tahrir Square to Spain's *Indignados* and from Greece to Hong Kong – names the *networked protest*. Such a protest departed radically from classical modes, using methods that, says Mason, did not seem 'archaic or at odds with the modern contemporary world', but were 'more in tune with modernity than the methods of their rulers'.[16] Kahn-Harris discovers a new era of movements 'without a name', better seen as a

> trend, a direction, an idea-virus, a meme, a source of energy that can be traced through a large number of spaces and projects ... a way of thinking and acting: an agility, an adaptability, a refusal to accept the world as is ... to get stuck into fixed patterns of thought.

A central departure of the networked protest is its abandonment of leadership- and representation-driven action, and its replacement of the full-time political activist with amorphous and 'multiple' identities and a 'pick-and-mix attitude to commitment, a kind of learned mercuriality'.[17] A second departure is in its ability to fuse diverse kinds of informational flows to enable *sudden* action. The 'networked' public space combines 'the internet, the mobile phone, pre-existing social networks, street demonstrations, occupations of public squares and Friday gatherings around the mosques', says Manuel Castells, speaking about Tahrir Square.[18] Its primary purpose is reset to '*create community* to overcome fear'.

-15

Niraja Jayal writes, 'In its pronouncements since the 1980s, India's Supreme Court has read a variety of unenumerated rights into the Constitution through an expansive interpretation of Article 21 that guarantees the right to life. These include the right to live with human dignity, the right to livelihood, the right to shelter, the right to a pollution-free environment, the right to privacy, the right not to be subjected to bonded labour, and the right to medical aid.' It was all part of an 'incomplete – some might say incipient – project of social citizenship in India before and after the economic reforms of the 1990s'. Niraja Gopal Jayal, *Citizenship and Its Discontents: An Indian History*, Cambridge, Mass.: Harvard University Press, 2013, p. 166.

-16

Paul Mason, *Why It's Still Kicking Off Everywhere: The New Global Revolutions*, London: Verso, 2013, pp. 68–69.

-17

Ibid., p. 85.

-18

Manuel Castells, *Networks of Outrage and Hope: Social Movements in the Internet Age*, Cambridge: Polity Press, 2015, pp. 10, 57.

In both modes and techniques of organization, and in the ways they chose to define their cause, campus protests found themselves repeatedly overwhelmed by an experimental 'frontline' that went beyond any immediate agenda to produce new protocols for action and occupation. The activists were rarely full-time. Most possessed multiple and even 'gig' identities as they entered and exited protest spaces. If a part of the project was explicitly historical, recouping past histories of independent India, another part was equally dedicated to emphasizing the unprecedentedness of the present moment. In both, FTII-2015 found itself with a specific role to play. For the first time, a campus whose history of agitation has been both too small and too *outré* to have been part of any history of national student politics, not only became central to a larger narrative but was forced, literally as a survival strategy, to rewrite that narrative.

On the morning of 9 June 2015, in contrast to issues that the GBM was meant to be discussing – trees, dogs, the International Student Film Festival – and as their debate assumed unprecedented public purpose, a student strength of under three hundred effectively took on the nation's ruling establishment. It had no political unions nor any visible leadership – no student activists described themselves as political fulltimers although some had individual affiliations, and of course everybody had, for what they were worth, strong political views of one kind or other. As an SFI (Students Federation of India) leader mused, it was organizational inexperience writ large, an inability to know when to call it off, that took the strike to such extremes.

Something new needs figuring out here. A something that reveals itself, unsurprisingly, as being about the *cinema*. This will be the story of how a relatively unknown cinematic history cracked open an institutional shell, challenging contained pedagogy, to set a new kind of agenda for India's liberal university. It would speak to how the cinema contributed to a new generation of mediatized protests as they spread to several of India's campuses, and eventually to 'Occupy' movements across multiple Indian cities.

The Right to the Cinema

By Indian standards the numbers were miniscule; the dramatis personae – the students themselves, their teachers and mentors, their forebears, those who inspired them and those who were accused of having instigated them – were a small enough number for this author to discover a one- or two-degree separation from almost everyone involved. How such a number could have had the impact they did remains a question. It appeared to be linked to a mode of collectivity directly enabled by a digital ecosystem – a *digital unconscious*, so to say – that worked directly on the symbolic order, made tangible by the open-source protocols of networked protest.

The change in the apparatus of organization redefined authorship in artmaking. It would also fundamentally transform what we have understood as 'filmmaking' into something else that many consider to be entirely removed from the cinema as we have known it. An 'ancient, anarchist principle, usually betrayed in history' saw a seismic shift, not ideologically as much as it found itself manifested by the 'experience of Internet networks' where 'horizontality [became] the norm'.[19] There was 'little need for leadership because the coordination functions can be exercised by the network itself through interaction between its nodes'. Originality became anathema here. Shared footage and collaborative work extended into projects no longer made from scratch, nor ever completed. The filmmaker began working, like the hacker, in an informational relay – receiving audiovisual data from various sources, taking up from where someone had left off, and putting film data back into the public domain for future use by others.

Central to this gigantic process was the digital transformation of the cinema itself. Both in making and showing 'film', the political transformation of the neoliberal state was directly paralleled by the transformation of celluloid into digital. While digitization affected all artmaking, the cinema queered digitization as no other art form appeared to be able to – from data subjectivity to digital governance, from authorship and copyright to unauthorized and post-authorial production, and from censorship to circulation.

Photography, Walter Benjamin once said, possesses an 'optical unconscious'.[20] The cinema brought an additional feature, a collective body (*Kollektivleib*), to such an unconscious.[21] It challenged an old truth: that everybody who is awake has a world in common, while those who sleep, sleep alone. It instead produced a collective dream world peopled by collective dream figures. Benjamin's well-known example of such dream-figures was the profoundly

Facing page and overleaf
13 June 2015: Jawaharlal Nehru University Students Union (JNUSU) solidarity poster; first press release by the FTII Students Association on the appointment of Gajendra Chauhan and their refusal to 'take the bait'.

-19

Manuel Castells, 'A Rhizomatic Revolution: Indignadas in Spain', in *Networks of Outrage and Hope*, p. 132.

-20

'Photography, with its aids (slow-motion sequences, close-ups) ... can show him the optical unconscious, just as it is only through psychoanalysis that he learns of the compulsive unconscious.' Walter Benjamin, 'A Brief History of Photography', in *One-way Street and Other Writings*, tr. J.A. Underwood, Penguin, 2009, p. 273.

-21

'The collective reception of film ... introduces the possibility of organizing, through film's technological nature, a collective body, exposing the audience to a technology that does not embody an instrumentalist logic', for it is a 'procreation between humanity and the cosmos in technology', writes Daniel Mourenza (in *Walter Benjamin and the Aesthetics of Film*, Amsterdam: Amsterdam University Press, 2020, p. 37). Also see 'Mickey Mouse: Utopian and Barbarian', ibid., p. 195.

FTII Appointments:

Another Shameless Move by the Modi Govt to Saffronise and Downgrade Institutions!

Support FTII students' Protests against Appointment of Gajendra Chauhan as FTII Chairman!

JNUSU congratulates the students of FTII for their spirited protests against the appointment of Gajendra Singh as Chairman of FTII. JNUSU extends support and solidarity with FTII students, as they boycott classes and all academic activity in FTII to protest the saffronisation of FTII by the Modi government.

The recent appointments of Gajendra Chauhan as the Chairman, Anagha Ghaisas and Shailesh Gupta as Governing Council members of FTII have been made not on the basis of creative contributions in the field but *solely* on the basis of their loyalty to and being active campaigners of the RSS-BJP brigade with propagandist films celebrating the *Babri Masjid Demolition* or *Shapath Modi ki*.

It is a shame that an institute like FTII, which had such great personalities as Adoor Gopalakrishnan, Girish Karnad, Shyam Benegal, U.R. Ananthamurthy and Saeed Akhtar Mirza as Chairman in the past, is being foisted with such *Hindutva pracharaks*.

Few months back, Pahlaj Nihalni, who made promotional videos on Modi, was rewarded with the post of Film Censor Board censor board chief and the govt is also set to appoint Malayalam actor and Modi supporter Suresh Gopi as the chairman of NFDC !

Over the past year, we have been seeing continuous attempts by the Modi government to meddle with academic institutions. RSS ideologues and BJP supporters are being appointed as heads of important academic bodies. Curricula are being rewritten, functioning of schools, colleges and universities are being reworked to suit a communal-fascist narrative. A person who believes that the caste system and institutionalised hierarchies in Indian society had 'merits' has been appointed as the head of the ICHR; Dinanath Batra's communal and jingoist rants are becoming part of compulsory reading in schools; all dissenting voices are being threatened and banned!

This latest assault on FTII's long traditions of upholding progressive cinema and television has to be seen as a continuation of ongoing attacks on academic institutions. Clearly, the need of the hour is to forge united struggles and united resistance to all the ongoing assaults on our democratic spaces.

At stake is the integrity of the FTII, its progressive traditions, and need to defend a democratic ethos. In this struggle, JNUSU stands in complete solidarity.

JNUSU strongly supports FTII students' demands:

- Removal of Gajendra Singh as Chairperson
- Instituting a new mechanism to appoint the Chairman, wherein 51% of the Governing Council will be FTII alumni and the Governing Council in turn will elect the Chairman.

JNUSU

Do Not Remove Till 26.6.15

Students' Association
Film and Television Institute of India,
Law College Road,
Pune: 411004

Date – 13/6/2015

When the Finance Minister (who also happens to be the current I&B minister) announced that FTII will be made into an 'Institute of National Importance', Students hoped that concrete and substantial measures will be taken to grant more autonomy to the Institute and upgrade academic and physical infrastructure. The first step in that direction would have been to appoint a Chairman of highest artistic attitude, one whose values are in sync with the vision and ethos of the Institute. Instead, bypassing all academic and Institute requirements, the ministry has appointed Mr Gajendra Chauhan who lacks academic, administrative and artistic credentials in the field of Art and Film education. He has no significant contribution/ work to even qualify as a footnote or a passing reference in the history of Indian cinema and television.

Some of the eminent personalities who have been FTII chairman in the past includes Mrinal Sen, Adoor Gopalakrishnan , Shyam Benegal, U.R Anantha Murty, Saeed Akthar Mirza and many more. These people have been either Alumni of FTII or have had experience in serious Film practice or other Art forms. Their experience in their chosen field of work has brought in a vision to the functioning of FTII. This decision of the Ministry to appoint Mr. Chauhan is not only undesired but also brings the whole process of appointment into question.

FTII is a premier institute respected throughout the world for producing internationally reputed Film makers, Film Academicians and Independent Artists. We the students of FTII believe that such an appointment will not only undermine the relevance of the post but also set a wrong precedence for the future. We must never forget that FTII is a cultural hub that provides film education to students of different socioeconomic backgrounds from different parts of the country.

It is extremely sad that the government rather than enhancing the stature of many premiere institutes of the country has constantly tried to undermine the autonomy of these institutes by appointing partisan people with no merit. We see this decision in the light of continuing policies of the government to curb voices of all liberal and progressive art Institutions.

Unlike NFDC and CBFC where government has also meddled with the appointments, FTII is not going to take the bait. We strongly condemn the appointment of the new Chairman. We propose to the ministry to reconsider its appointment and also relook at the process of constituting the FTII society and its members. Until further clarity surfaces from the I&B Minsitry, we continue to standby our demands and mark our protest with a call for a strike.

We request all concerned citizens, artists, writers, performers, film makers, activists and alumnus of FTII to take notice and support our cause.

Harishankar Nachimuthu
President
Students' Association, FTII
ftiistudentsbody@gmail.com,
http://ftiistudentsbody.blogspot.com

cinematic Mickey Mouse. Here we shall add several other figures of the collective gaze, now resurrected in both avatars and – as the optical turned digital – into memes. Cinema has historically been a constituent presence in the amorphous social space also occupied by 'rumours, sermons, pamphlets, and manifestos, spread from person to person, from the pulpit, from the press, or by whatever means of communication were available'.[22] When digital modes of networking arrived, they revealed the capacity to recoup a history, and whenever necessary an entire vocabulary, of assembly – of analogue spaces and physical contact.

-22
Castells, *Networks of Outrage and Hope*, p. 15.

—

As early news of the stacking of FTII's Governing Council spread to other campuses, it was cast in a well-worn political language. The JNU Students Union's first announcement of support presented this as yet another 'shameless move ... to saffronize and downgrade institutions' by placing 'RSS ideologues and BJP supporters as heads of important academic bodies'. These positions were nothing but rewards for loyal party adherents, said JNUSU, seeing in them a deeper project in which 'curricula are being rewritten, functioning of schools, colleges and universities are being reworked to suit a communal-fascist narrative'.

A more complicated if equally fraught argument was the valorization of 'excellence'. The week after the announcement of the Governing Council, a Students' Association press release signed by Nachi as its president equated the 'premier' and 'autonomous' status of the place with the 'internationally reputed film academicians and artists' who had graduated from there. The issue of academic autonomy challenged by a 'Hindutva' agenda now began playing out on a rather less well-charted *moral* issue as it entered an art-house canon. The contrast was presented between the great and the good of Indian cinema – 'Mrinal Sen, Adoor Gopalakrishnan, Shyam Benegal, U.R. Ananthamurthy, Saeed Akhtar Mirza' (all former Chairmen) – pitted against an actor who had, the press release went on to say, 'made no significant work to even qualify as a footnote or a passing reference in the history of Indian cinema and television'.

—

This particular story soon abandoned its comfort zones. A stinging rebuke by the Ambedkarite platform Round Table India accused the 'liberal elites' of this country, sitting in their 'institutes of national importance', of being the very beneficiaries of the neoliberal order they claimed to attack. It is the 'actors, filmmakers, technicians produced by FTII ... [who] screen their films in multiplexes, endorse and advertise products of transnational corporations, dance, sing, host events funded by global capitalism, market, distribute and make a fortune out of the neoliberal infrastructure'.[23] Chauhan's disqualifying lowbrow status (JNUSU had even got his name wrong in its text, calling him 'Gajendra Singh' at one point) created strange bedfellows – several Bollywood names came out, without a hint of irony, on the side of elite high art, even as academics queried the archaic logic of contrasting the auteur against the B-movie sector, the porn film and the devotional. As campus elitism began getting mangled on right-wing television channels it clashed with a more nuanced political stand that the students were struggling, against considerable odds, to put together.

Two of them appear in the early minutes of Kshama Padalkar's intensely personal documentary, *The Strike and I* (2019). Ranjit Nair, then in his third year and a core committee member, is arguing with Satish Kumar, a first year cinematography student, who looks slightly shell-shocked. Later Satish would go on a one-person hunger strike protesting the laying off of 82 contractual workers on the campus. Ranjit gestures emphatically at the main gate, saying, 'You know what we are doing there ... problematizing the strike isn't helping us go anywhere if we stay with the same design.' A 'new language' is needed, he says, that 'will help us beyond the strike as well'. 'You, Satish, and I, Ranjit, need to find a way to define ourselves, and each to the other, independently of how they are doing it "out there".'

Much of the description cast the 'premier' exclusivity of the place in the language of taxpayer-subsidized privilege. Notwithstanding the nod to 'students of different socio-economic backgrounds' and the awareness of the diversity of students entering the place, the problematic slide of excellence into meritocracy – an issue of great salience in several of India's IITs, for example[24] – remained largely unresolved. 'We are being critical of each other, we

-23

Nidhin Shobhana, 'Merit Hona Mangta: An Essay on the FTII Strike', *Round Table India*, 24 July 2015.

-24

'The higher education debate in India is centred on two issues these days', writes P.V. Indiresan about the IITs: '(a) Is higher education a non-merit good deserving little or no subsidy as some finance experts make it out to be? That is, should higher education be a democratic right open to all, or should it be confined to a few? (b) If higher education is to be restricted to a few, should it be confined to those who are competent, or should it be the preserve of the politically privileged, or should it be purchasable by the rich?' P.V. Indiresan, 'W(h)ither IITs?', *Seminar*, no. 494: 'Unviable Universities: A Symposium on the Crisis in Higher Education', October 2000.

are not being critical of the design of the strike', says Ranjit, gesticulating every syllable with his hands.

Even as this rendition of the Institute went viral over multiple media outlets, it also reprised an older and tired identity crisis. Being a *film* institute, it has borne the burden of the well-known 'problem of the cinema' that has beset modern India, and it is one that every FTII student has had to negotiate in one way or another. Is this elite education or is it not? As students appeared increasingly unsure as to just what they were signing up for, a rhetorical question historically presumed to possess no plausible answer in India began to target a small number of very vulnerable young people. Why should the Indian state support its cinema, namely them?

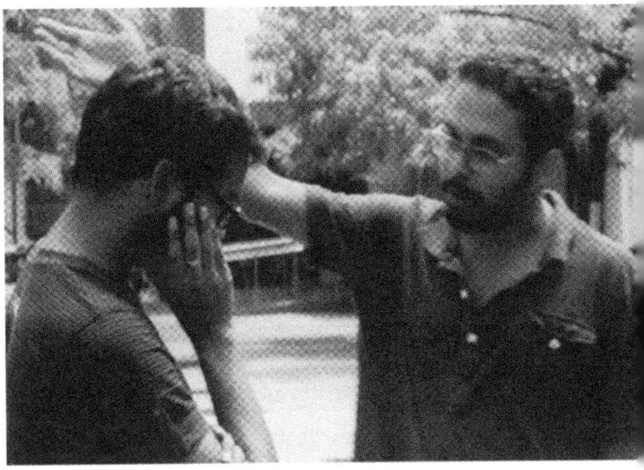

Satish Kumar and Ranjit Nair debating the design of the strike. From Kshama Padalkar's **The Strike and I** (2019).

The question, Ranjit Nair seems to be saying, has in all its naked exhaustion gotten baked into multiple bureaucratic, political and pedagogic variants of the 'what is cinema?'/'who are you?' ontology. Battles have taken place over just how it needed to be answered, between filmmakers, educationists, producers, financiers and censors, and one such was happening a few yards away.

—

Two weeks in, the invitation to negotiate finally arrived, and on 3 July, several students and ex-students filed into the offices of the Information and Broadcasting Minister Arun Jaitley and senior bureaucrats.

—

There are many descriptions of just what happened there. The saga of negotiations with the government didn't begin here and wouldn't end until the final meetings of October 2015. The numerous feints and moves were all somehow unexpectedly cinematic. To Vikas, thinking back, they resembled the complex negotiations of the filmmaking process itself: a series of actions and counter-actions, *agar aap yeh karenge toh wo woh karenge, agar wo woh karenge toh aapko yeh karne ke liye ready rehna padega* [if you do this, they will do that, if they do that, you have to be ready to respond].[25] Jaitley himself evoked a once-grand era of the cinema, and spoke of how that grandeur could be reintroduced. Vikas quotes Jaitley as making his barely concealed threats-cum-offers in profoundly cinematic language:

> *'Aaj kal toh kya filme banti hain? Hamare zamaane mein filme banti thi* [What kinds of films are being made today? The real cinema was from our times] – we need to change that culture. We need to do that makeover. I am the Finance Minister. You should make use of me. It's not where you guys will be. I have been there many times. You have all these old buildings. Make use of me. Let's build the infrastructure. Why do you worry about all those [people]? All we need is, you know, good buildings and good facilities.' The writing was on the wall that day – that we have to do this [strike] full-fledged, because this is the FTII, its history against these people.

Absent at that forty-five-minute South Block meeting was perhaps the key figure in the entire cinematic saga: its stalwart Minister of State Rajyavardhan Singh Rathore, the shadowy figure behind the Gajendra Chauhan cutout. Born in a Rajput military family, Rathore joined the army in 1990, fought in the Kargil War, participated in 'counter-terrorist' operations in Kashmir, all before doing what he is best known for: winning the Olympic Games silver medal for rifle shooting at Athens in 2004. His cinematic obsessions, and these were considerable, lay within a patrician militaristic imagination of national honour coloured into Bollywood sports spectacle. When his own sports biopic got made, as he was convinced it must, in the vein of *Mary Kom* and *Bhaag Milkha Bhaag*, he wanted Karan Johar to direct it and Ranveer Singh to play him.[26] Rathore had briefly entertained movie star ambitions of his own, and one possible, profoundly cinematic missing link in the saga was the popular rumour that soon after winning his Olympic medal, he had sought membership of the Cine and Television Actors' Association (CINTAA), when its president was – coincidentally, perhaps – yes, Gajendra Chauhan.

In any case, it soon became apparent that Chauhan was Rathore's concoction. Jaitley appeared embarrassed at this choice, more or less conceding that Chauhan was far from an ideal candidate. He hinted that this wasn't his idea, but then said there

-25

Conversation with Vikas Urs, 21 October 2021, Mumbai.

-26

'Rajyavardhan Singh Rathore Wants Karan Johar to Direct His Biopic', NDTV, PTI, 20 November 2018.

wasn't anything that could be done to change it; the only way forward was to consider it a minor issue, put it aside and keep eyes on the prize – a partnership to envision a very different institution, to exploit its vast potential for both excellence and profit generation. The through line was familiar, one close to what GraFTII too implicitly stood for. For all the much-touted figure of Rs 12 lakhs per student each year, Jaitley reiterated the government's commitment to revamping the place, to making both it and the Satyajit Ray Film and Television Institute into 'centre[s] of national importance'. A bandwagon was being rolled out, in short, and everyone was invited aboard.

The reasons for why they didn't respond to that carrot would prove fractious. Earlier, Jahnu Barua's rejection of his nomination to the FTII Governing Council had led to a Ministry communication that Barua considered a threat – one of the reasons for the agitated GraFTII meeting on the campus in the second week of the strike. Was political negotiation at all possible in a way that ensured the safety of both present and former students? Or was personal safety now inextricably welded to the survival of the Institute's vision? What flipped the entire issue was, more than anything practical, Jaitley's abrupt and chilling return to the coded, patronizing invitation-cum-threat with which that July meeting ended. Jaitley appeared to be deliberately evoking the historic cinephobia of state modernism, or, more precisely, modernism's shading into state developmentalism. Either you signed up to a new imagination, or (he said) 'in the wake of high costs involved, questions can always be raised about the relevance of funding such niche institutions instead of spending on primary education and health'.[27] He ended the meeting by requesting the delegation to 'reflect on' his advice.

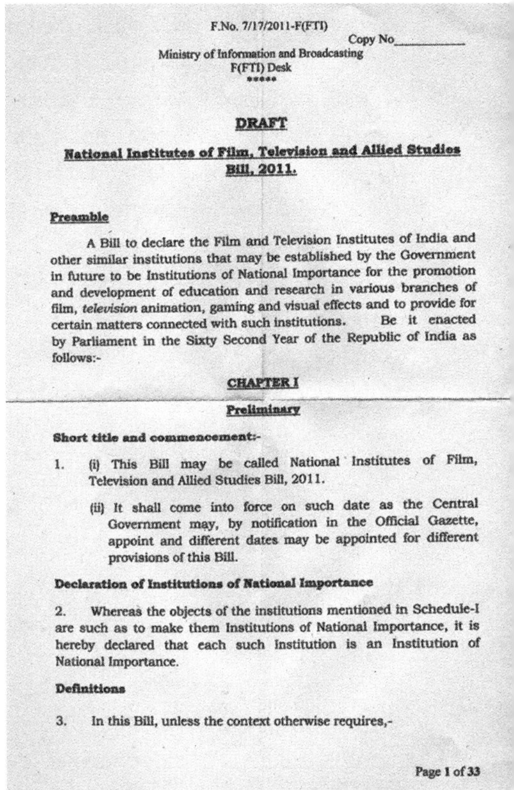
F.No. 7/17/2011-F(FTI)

Copy No.__________

Ministry of Information and Broadcasting
F(FTI) Desk
*****

DRAFT

National Institutes of Film, Television and Allied Studies Bill, 2011.

Preamble

A Bill to declare the Film and Television Institutes of India and other similar institutions that may be established by the Government in future to be Institutions of National Importance for the promotion and development of education and research in various branches of film, *television* animation, gaming and visual effects and to provide for certain matters connected with such institutions. Be it enacted by Parliament in the Sixty Second Year of the Republic of India as follows:-

CHAPTER I

Preliminary

Short title and commencement:-

1. (i) This Bill may be called National Institutes of Film, Television and Allied Studies Bill, 2011.

(ii) It shall come into force on such date as the Central Government may, by notification in the Official Gazette, appoint and different dates may be appointed for different provisions of this Bill.

Declaration of Institutions of National Importance

2. Whereas the objects of the institutions mentioned in Schedule-I are such as to make them Institutions of National Importance, it is hereby declared that each such institution is an Institution of National Importance.

Definitions

3. In this Bill, unless the context otherwise requires,-

Page 1 of 33

Draft National Institutes of Film, Television and Allied Studies Bill, 2011, converting the FTII and SRFTI into Institutes of National Importance. The Bill was eventually never passed.

—

For all its ability to produce a popular nationalism, Indian cinema has historically competed for relevance, in Jaitley's sermon, with water, health and education. State cinephobia, of the kind he

-27 'Government stays put with Gajendra Chauhan as FTII chairman', *India Today*, 5 July 2015.

appeared to be consciously evoking, has been evidenced in India across the ideological spectrum. It has reinvented itself with every transformation in the apparatus of governance. To the extent that the cinema has at all featured in governance plans, it is as something to be disciplined, contained. Despite its multiple successes, despite a significant domestic market, despite its auteurs, its cinematic avant-gardes and its diverse regional industries, the bureaucratic dream remains one of somehow cobbling together a 'good' cinema at once in line with governmental requirements and acceptable to the European art-house.

The fading of that dream has only intensified its identity crisis. Is the FTII an institution for the humanities or of technical training? Significantly, it has been both, and neither. The British colonial divide between the arts and the 'professions' was administratively translated into a division between the University Grants Commission (UGC) that manages its universities and the All-India Council for Technical Education (AICTE) which looks after 'vocational' courses. FTII, uniquely, falls under the Ministry of Information and Broadcasting. When this Ministry was formed it had mirrored the British Ministry of Information, which, when founded in 1939 to supervise its war propaganda machine, had been cloned from Goebbels' Ministry of Information. Although Britain wound up its own Ministry of Information in 1946, its state propaganda machine remained intact in India. The regulations that define much of the purpose of the I&B Ministry's institutions remain essentially those of a wartime state.

The question, then, of whether FTII's role is to service the film industry, produce technicians for its documentary sector and its public television, or make independent cinema, has wended its way through the political history of modern India. The Nehruvian and Indira Gandhi eras, as well as their neoliberal and Hindutva successors, have had their say on this question. They have mobilized multiple disciplines from the humanities to communication theory to try and answer it, and defined policy measures that have ranged from state propaganda to privatization. At each stage, they have encountered multiple languages of dissent.

—

How, now, in the days that followed in July, to make sense of all this? The intense discussions that occurred after the Jaitley meeting and in the marathon GBM in Pune were arguably among the most significant cinematic debates to have taken place in recent years in India. How to make sense of Jaitley, Rathore, Chauhan and their situation? The strike's demands were at one level inconsequential, for all they wanted was the replacement of a man who, everyone agreed, clearly didn't rate. What the response revealed was the state's way of thinking and the manner in which everyone, students present and former, were being manipulated to sign on to something at once minuscule and immeasurably large. Ex-students Fareeda Mehta and Paresh Kamdar, frequently on campus over the past decade, tried to share their own experiences. Neither would consider themselves in any way overtly political, but both apparently saw the need to define this obscenity that arose before them – the grotesque state power that lay behind a B-movie star.

> The entire idea of how [the] state controls you is not in ... big things. It's in the smaller meetings and smaller intimate discussions that actually decisions are made. The future of an institute is decided on these lines. And then the next strategy was it cannot be just an outreach. Now it has to be mounting a larger collective, bringing people on board from other walks of life and making this into a movement which is not limited to the Film Institute only.[28]

Through this history, it was the cinema that set up the apparatus of popular democracy. Spaces showing film have been a central part of the 'shops, public restaurants, hotels and palaces of public entertainment ... dedicated to the use of the general public' in Article 15 of the Constitution. Even as this public has been disciplined, lathi-charged and forced to behave, the fact has remained that, as K. Sivathamby famously argued, the 'cinema house was the first performance centre in which all Tamils sat under the same roof', possessed of a constitutionally endorsed equality of rights.[29] Such rights are not only those of entry. How (and to whom) films are shown, how audiences enter an auditorium and turn their gaze to the screen, has defined how films are written, shot, edited and composed.

Such a right of the public has, under state modernism, come into conflict with another equally fundamental right, that of Article 19,

-28

Conversation with Vikas Urs, 21 October 2021, Mumbai.

-29

Karthigesu Sivathamby, *The Tamil Film as a Medium of Political Communication*, Madras: New Century Book House, 1981, p. 18.

to speech. While Indian law well recognizes the filmmaker's authorial rights, less well known are the cinema's spectatorial rights, or the fact that the right to speech in public is basically derivative of the public's right to information.[30] Writers thus derive their right to publish from readers' *prior* right to be informed, and filmmakers exist because spectators have a right to see films. The pivotal question becomes less to do with making cinema – where the right may well be absolute – than the far more contentious and endangered right to *see* it.

The two rights, Articles 15 and 19, have different legacies and, in the Indian cinema, have pulled in different, even contradictory directions. Was a filmmaker's right to free speech the same as, say, that of a poet or painter? Or was this right in the cinema compromised by the presence of the spectator, to be curtailed by the public nature of its apparatus? Did the right of the spectator to enter the theatre also extend to a right to enter the film itself? And how to work out its impact on the rather different definition of the film-author's right to speech?

The conflict between the filmmaker's speech and the public's right to the cinema confounds an already vexed authorship question that has fought for its civil rights in multiple court judgments from the 1950s on. The landmark intervention is the K.A. Abbas Supreme Court judgment of 1970, followed by several in different High Courts. Both sets of rights find themselves beset by the anxiety-inducing history of *privilege* attributed by modernism to its artist–citizen–student, especially given that – at least in the time of celluloid – other less privileged makers and recipients found themselves excluded from the institutions of making, showing and teaching. Authorship – especially the kind that sought the canon as a site of self-protection – had to perform the delicate negotiation of balancing the risks and benefits of naming a visible auteur-subject as its maker, even as it dealt with the challenges of anonymous, un*authorized* practice of 'low' art.

In 2015, both autonomy and authorship found themselves entering dangerous new territory. Indian modernism in the cinema has, it is safe to say, derived from a British – as against a European or even American – legacy in characterizing a class-driven aesthetic legitimacy of 'high' art endorsed by institutionalized pedagogy, as

-30
Eric Barendt (in *Freedom of Speech*, Oxford: Oxford University Press, 2007, pp. 26–27) explores the consequences of an argument that recipients are the primary object of free speech concern, and that 'speakers have derivative rights, recognized only in order to protect the former's interests'.

against 'low', illegitimate and essentially *untrained* practice. 'High' has been a mode of enlightened making, teaching and appreciation, and has brought with it a privileged aesthetic apparatus bundled into the rights and privileges of the author-artist. Both authorship and autonomy would come to be exemplified by specific art forms – canonical texts on 35-millimetre celluloid, the three-act proscenium play, the literary novel, oil painting on canvas – that independent India inherited from its former colonial masters for its authorized self-representation.

Campus autonomy – defined in intellectual, administrative and now increasingly political terms – has, not uncontroversially, thus accompanied both elitism and meritocracy. Such elitism has adopted, negotiated, asserted, celebrated and sometimes radicalized the modernist canon, the aesthetic divisions of taste and the auteur who embodies it all.

Expanded Cinema and the University Campus

On 12 February 2016, JNUSU president Kanhaiya Kumar was arrested on the Jawaharlal Nehru University campus under Section 124A of the Indian Penal Code. Autonomy began to mean a great deal more when the university's teachers' and students' unions declared a space just outside its administrative block the 'Freedom Square'. The endeavour was launched in solidarity with several other campuses that too had seen their freedoms violated, specifically referring to 'not just JNU but HCU, FTII, Allahabad, Jadavpur and all the locations that were inflamed in early 2016'.[31]

G. Arunima draws attention to the extreme and high-visibility presence of cameras that proliferated on the JNU campus, all in one way or another featuring in the tropes of freedom. 'At least three kinds of camera forms ... CCTVs, photos and videos taken by security personnel or the administration, those taken by students, and finally a proposal that classrooms could have cameras to facilitate MOOC courses.'[32] As campuses began to find themselves 'awash with cameras and users', their proliferation 'democratized photography in the last decade in a manner that may have been unthinkable earlier'.

Hokkolorob itself had happened following the sustained work of hundreds of students – such as Arijit Chakraborty who did

-31

Janaki Nair, 'A teach-in for a JNU Spring', in *What the Nation Really Needs to Know*.

-32

G. Arunima, 'Cameras, campuses and the future of politics in an era of imaging technologies', *Contributions to Indian Sociology*, 54 (1), 2020, p. 16.

an entire video series that began with the *Mahamichhils* of 2014, and Abhirup Halder who dedicated his YouTube channel for the purpose[33] – who took it upon themselves to extend technologies of agitation into the areas of archiving, dissemination and public assembly. The voluntary work of these numerous students would produce what Arunima names a counter-archive, a 'resistance aesthetics'. The means of governance become 'enmeshed within cultural modes and histories of protests and prior histories of opposing institutional authority', says Arunima. 'Protests, speeches, marches, fasts, *dharnas* (sit-ins), and other forms of visual resistance, such as cartoons and posters, all of which are designed to counter administrative authority', find themselves accompanied by the daily production of an 'ethical mode of witnessing' that reveals a rather larger, more complex and potentially subversive gaze built into the 'objectivity of the mechanical eye'.[34]

As the summer of protest unfolded, the cinematic variant of the right to the public domain also took on multiple new forms. Campus freedom was centrally incarnated by the right to make and show film as a certain kind of synaesthetic cinema – or what, decades ago, Gene Youngblood had called a condition in which 'we can show both our experiences and emotions to one another ... see through each other's eyes, moving towards expanded vision and equally expanded consciousness'[35] – translated into new ways of making and showing films on campus. Attacks on this specific right took on transcendental significance when, on 3 February 2012, the ABVP forced Pune's Symbiosis University to cancel the screening of Sanjay Kak's *Jashn-e-Azadi: How We Celebrate Freedom*, and on 22 August 2013, when they attacked an FTII students' screening of Anand Patwardhan's *Jai Bhim Comrade* alongside performances by the Kabir Kala Manch at the National Film Archive of India's central auditorium. Two months after the FTII strike began, on 2 August 2015, a screening of Nakul Singh Sawhney's documentary, *Muzaffarnagar Baaqi Hai*, by the Kirori Mal College's Montage Film Society was attacked as 'anti-national' by the Delhi University Students' Union. Three weeks later, the Cinema of Resistance put out a public call for protest screenings of *Muzaffarnagar* and received over fifty responses, including several from campuses across the country. One day after the Kirori Mal episode, on 3 August,

-33

Arijit Chakraborty's YouTube channel, which includes *Hokkolorob* 1, 2, 11, 13, 14, 15

and Abhirup Halder's channel.

-34

G. Arunima, 'Cameras, campuses and the future of politics in an era of imaging technologies', p. 16.

-35

'Image-Exchange and the Post-Mass Audience Age', in Youngblood, *Expanded Cinema*, p. 130.

the Ambedkar Students Association of Hyderabad staged a protest titled 'Curbing Academic Space and Lynching Democracy', in solidarity with the FTII, Pondicherry University and Montage Film Society, led by a young student named Rohith Vemula.

As the dominant mood began viewing the campus as a nation in microcosm, rediscovering the democratic values that the larger nation had apparently abrogated, many also saw it as producing a form of intellectual if not territorial secession – *aazadi* in India, not from India, as Kanhaiya Kumar would later put it. Sedition was in the air. Talks at Freedom Square by several historians tried to discuss nationalism as it confronted new threats to the founding concepts of independence. The campus was returning, in a way the nation apparently could no longer do, to the era of 'debate, discussion and dissent, in the best spirit of the freedom of speech', 'demonstrating the importance of cordial, civil and respectful ways of listening, as part of our commitment to the right to be heard', writes Janaki Nair.[36]

-36
Janaki Nair, 'A teach-in for a JNU Spring', in *What the Nation Really Needs to Know*, p. xii.

On 17 January 2016, when Rohith Vemula committed suicide after writing a suicide note that became a national *cause célèbre* of outrage, the space in which the five students of Hyderabad Central University had camped after they were evicted from their hostel rooms found itself converted into a *velivada* (translated as a Dalit ghetto on the outskirts of a village). The same month as the first Freedom Square lectures but in contrast to JNU's emphasis on the values of elite civility, this *velivada* became another, rather more chaotic and spontaneous assertion of campus autonomy. It had few of the protocols or even respect for the academic canon being demonstrated by the JNU lectures. Its best representation remained an improvised assemblage of art, poetry and politics, alongside diverse kinds of radical voices and actions. As it took shape in its ShopCom area around a plaster-of-paris statue of Vemula, a students' filmmaking workshop that happened to be scheduled just then also took on new challenges. This workshop, later assembled into Ramachandra P.N.'s extraordinary *The Unbearable Being of Lightness* (2016), provides the pivot for numerous short films in which the campus imagines an outside, even as the world outside imagines the campus. Student-participants describe what they are seeing and read out what they have observed.

Eisenstein on the Streets

In 2015, then, the familiar 'what-is-cinema' question found itself framed in a new way. As the political limitations of state democracy began clashing with a growing if always elusive *popular* democracy, the aesthetic barriers that provided its modernist undergirding in the cinema too began to fall. As Eisenstein and Pudovkin and the rest of the masters, Tarkovsky, etc., arguably interchangeable with any of Europe's auteurs, found their names plastered on walls and chanted on the streets in processions asserting autonomy on the campus, they became unlikely inclusions into the pantheon that accompanied left or Dalit agitations. It was as though the cinema (and not just Indian cinema) had gone to war.

Viewing the FTII campus, or indeed the *velivada*, as a microcosm of the nation in the way the Freedom Square would wish us to, posed new frontiers for how the cinema would stage the

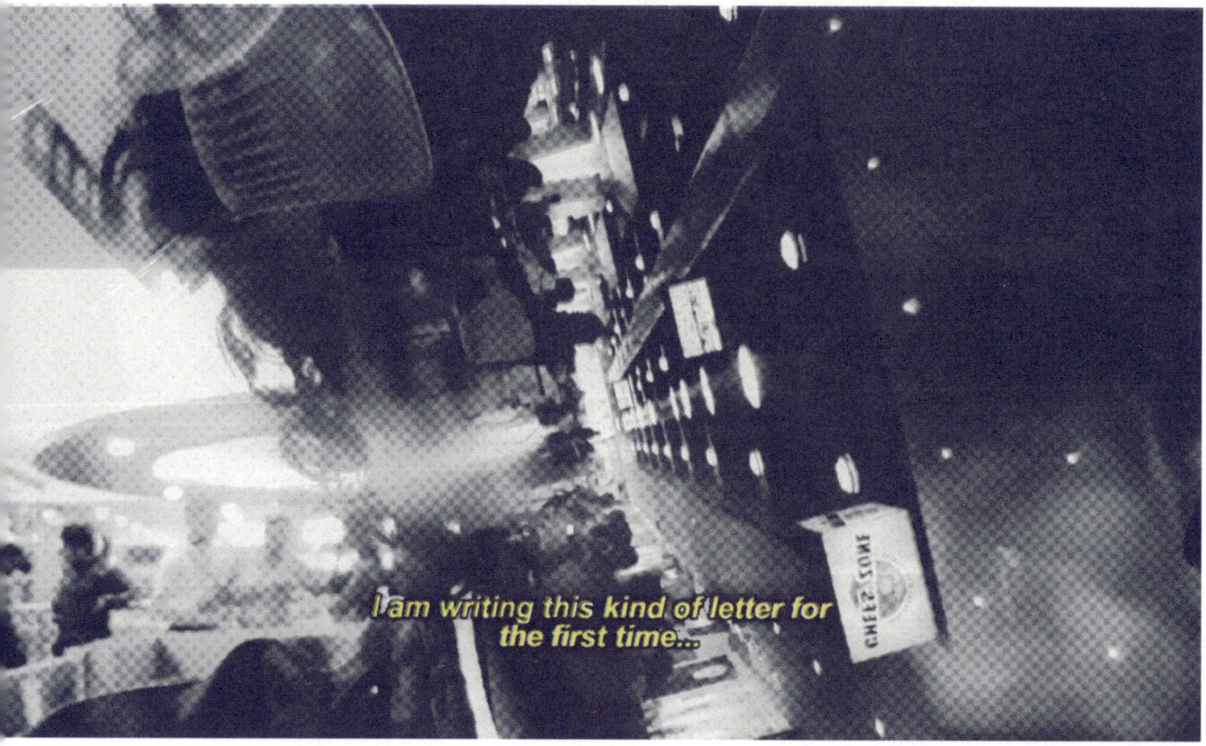

The suicide note. Student film projects at the Hyderabad Central University, in P.N. Ramachandra Rao's **The Unbearable Being of Lightness** (2016).

freedom debate on the campus. The FTII lacks the legitimacy of a university. Formally, it only offers a diploma that many consider not worth the paper, and it has been commonly viewed as no more than a space for 'technical training' with only a dubious and marginal academic presence on its campus – which brought special significance to the conscious effort of the 2015 strike to reach out and connect with universities, both in Pune itself and across the country.

The common perception in India that the very act of making a film – any film – could be political emerged in the earliest mythologicals of silent film, and remains so in the present when, as Monica Narula of the Raqs Media Collective once said, the sheer taking of a film camera into the street is to break the law. If Eisenstein and Pudovkin were joining this battle, it was to further escalate the cinema *itself* into a political *cause célèbre.* This was a stand that students had not necessarily thought through (although some of the GBMs were intense on this very question), but it is one that the Indian cinema logically presented on the campus at this particular moment in the long and crisis-ridden history of how both – cinema as well as campus – related to the nation.

CHAPTER 2

REINVENTING THE *REGISSEUR*

> Ritwik Ghatak was conducting a workshop with us and he began by asking us our names. 'Ashok Ahuja', 'Kundan Shah', 'Vinod Chopra', some of us replied. Ghatak heard us out and with each name he shook his head sadly.
>
> 'SERGEI MIKHAILOVICH EISENSTEIN. Shut your eyes and recite his name.'
>
> Not knowing what else to do we shut our eyes and recited the name.
>
> 'Doesn't it carry weight?' asked Ghatak. We opened our eyes and looked at each other. I think I now understood what he was getting at, so I raised my hand.
>
> 'What if I changed my name from Saeed Mirza to Saeed Akhtar Mirza?'
>
> Ritwik Ghatak smiled.
>
> 'That's it! SAEED AKHTAR MIRZA! Your name has weight now. Now you have the name of a film director.'
>
> – Saeed Akhtar Mirza
>
> (*Ammi: Letter to a Democratic Mother*, p. 120)

The conversation Mirza cites happened in all probability in 1974, which was also Ghatak's last visit to the FTII. In 1965 Ghatak had been employed as Vice Principal, but he left his full-time job after three months and did a part-time stint over the next two years.[1] He still went there occasionally and his interactions were legendary. When he was in residence he was the focus of everyone's attention, remembers Arun Khopkar of that particular visit.[2] He wasn't well, so nothing much could be planned in advance. The students were expected to be by him at all times, do as he wished, go with the flow.

The following January, EISENSTEIN – or at least the ambition to become one – found its authority directly challenged by the first major students' strike to take place at FTII. There had been a few agitations earlier in the late 1960s, and one in 1971, but this one was consequential. The 1975 protest was led by students of the acting course, who were agitating for more screen time to show their talent in student productions with a view to using these as showreels to

-1

Ghatak writes about this in *Chalachchitra Manush Ebong aro Kichu*, Kolkata: Deys Publishing, third edition, 2013, p. 291. Grateful acknowledgments to Sanghita Sen for the reference.

-2

Arun Khopkar vividly remembers the fortnight Ghatak spent: it was in 1974, and both Kumar Shahani and Mani Kaul came once a week to give classes, on Bazin and Eisenstein respectively. Khopkar recalls that Jagat Murari had brought from the USSR a complete set of Eisenstein's six volumes of writings in Russian, which he had given to the FTII library and which Khopkar may have been the only person ever to read through.

advance their careers in the film industry. The strike had a specific grievance, but it found itself pointing to a considerably larger problem – namely, the film director's ownership rights to his film. Even as direction students, assuming their directorial personae, were hiring fellow students to do cinematography, editing and sound, actors were being excluded from film education itself, and would indeed be evicted from the Institute entirely later that year.

In 1974 the campus was peopled by a gifted set of student batches. In addition to Kundan Shah and Vinod Chopra, the names Mirza mentions, Kamal Swaroop, Jahnu Barua, Ketan Mehta and Girish Kasaravalli would have been around, as perhaps were Naseeruddin Shah and Om Puri from the controversial acting batch. The discussions with Ghatak were animated. One of these, with Ravi Ojha and Judhajit Sarkar, was transcribed and published in the FTII's occasional in-house publication, *Film Miscellany*.[3] That conversation, Ghatak's last publicly recorded voice, gives us some sense of both his state of mind at the time and the flavour of the discussion that must have happened during that visit.

Ghatak is dismissive of the cinema's claims to be an art form or, indeed, to do anything more for society than 'recording change'. He speaks of Eisenstein and Tagore at some length, of Bangladesh and his still-unfinished epic, *Titash Ekti Nadir Naam*. Mainly, he speaks of his unhappiness, frustration and tiredness. He doesn't appear to carry much hope for young filmmakers. Calcutta is 'totally barren'. Although here and there, 'in Bombay, in Kerala, in Kashmir, even in Assam', you occasionally see 'young boys who are doing something', most are 'misguided'. There is theatre director Satyadev Dubey, to whom he is apparently close, but Ghatak doesn't think much of his plan to adapt Vijay Tendulkar's play *Shantata! Court Chalu Aahe*. Mani Kaul has a 'tilt in his brain ... always falling in love with words'. Kumar Shahani and John Abraham are the only students he appears, even as late as 1974, to still believe in.

That year, even as a bunch of enthusiastic and talented students sit at his feet, presumably hanging on to his every word, a crisis is heaving into sight on the horizon. He wouldn't live much longer, and now – even though he is here as visiting faculty and so should really be *teaching* the students something – what he wants to teach is no longer anything as simple as how to make films.

-3
Ravi Ojha and Judhajit Sarkar, 'An Interview with Ritwick Ghatak', *Film Miscellany*, Pune: Film and Television Institute of India, 1976, pp. 1–5.

After all, anybody can make films, for it is just a technical skill. The actual, infinitely more urgent problem lay elsewhere: it was how to *become filmmakers* – how to become Eisenstein, approximate to a responsibility, a vocation even.

The Film Director

The concept of a film director as defining a new era in artistic selfhood was not new. As far back as 1915, Dadasaheb Phalke had provided an astonishing moving image self-portrait of his newfound status in his documentary, *How Films are Made* – a Phalke persona that Kamal Swaroop would investigate through the 1990s and early 2000s. This egotism shaped the public images of both Pramathesh Barua and V. Shantaram in the 1940s, and a decade later, shaped Guru Dutt's tragic hero. Ever since V. Shantaram parked his Buick opposite what are now the administrative offices, filmmakers in this sense of the term have strutted up and down the main road of the campus. Satyajit Ray was an occasional visitor, and filmmakers across India have brought their films over to screen to students and to anxiously receive an opinion.

A few years before that last meeting between Ghatak and his students, however, the figure of the director underwent a transformation. In a variation of Walter Pater's proclamation that in their ultimate desire for abstraction 'all arts aspired to the condition of music', it seemed as though all arts were now aspiring to *film*, and, more importantly, all artists to the condition of *filmmaker*. Gulammohammed Sheikh says he returned from England in the late 1960s convinced that painting was dead and celluloid was the only future of art. It was a similar belief that led the painter Akbar Padamsee to set up his Vision Exchange Workshop in 1969, for multiple visual artists including Sheikh to try their hand at the Bolex that he had acquired, and for M.F. Husain and Tyeb Mehta to make Films Division-supported shorts.

But it was more than that. Recasting the idea of the artist into a new frontier identity also pushed that identity into politically uncharted territory. A central presence in the avant-garde across the twentieth century, the filmmaker was for Alexander Kluge somewhere between a 'highwire artist and a performing clown'; alone like Robinson Crusoe, esoteric like Adorno but with 'camouflage, mimicry'.[4] The filmmaker is the egotistical approximation of the apparatus of the cinema – a 'love affair of the [twentieth] century' – transformed into a *persona*.

As much as the fascination with film, it was this persona that attracted poets, painters, theatre directors and writers to try their hand at the next big thing. One such was the renowned Marathi poet, Dilip Chitre. After several initial experiments with celluloid, as with music, sound art, painting and journalism, Chitre made a full-length feature film in 1983 named *Godaam*, to mild acclaim.[5] His considerable reputation as perhaps Maharashtra's leading contemporary poet did not translate well into a 35-mm film that was largely self-financed and mostly shot by his son Akshaye (even though Govind Nihalani has DOP credit).

Godaam didn't get a commercial release and received only one major festival invitation, in 1984, to the Nantes Festival of Three Continents. At Nantes he got a small but appreciative audience, but he was overshadowed by the star Indian invitee that year, Raj Kapoor. Chitre himself appeared excited to be talking to Kapoor, and at Kapoor's press conference an animated discussion took place between the two, with Chitre describing how the *Aag* and *Barsaat* fire–water dialectic had been the topic of an early poem.

Later that evening in Nantes, musing on his own career, Chitre considered himself lucky that he had completed *Godaam*, lucky also that he could bring it here, where he was awarded a special jury prize. He admitted that there wasn't much more left for him to do, that the film had in all probability run its course. But then came the real regret: being a *regisseur* – Chitre used the French word, though he was speaking in Marathi – was, he realized, beyond him.

—

Regisseur is used across this monograph in the way Chitre meant it, as someone beyond a poet. He (and the category is historically male) is a particular sort of egotistical artist-subject cast in the majesty of the cinematic apparatus, and thus profoundly a product of celluloid. The *regisseur* may even have a typical representation familiar to readers of *American Cinematographer*, of a man with flowing hair and a beard standing under the sky with a viewfinder around his

-4

Timothy Corrigan, 'The Commerce of Auteurism: A Voice without Authority', *New German Critique*, no. 49: 'Special Issue on Alexander Kluge', Winter 1990, p. 52.

-5

The poet Dilip Purshottam Chitre's (1938–2009) filmmaking work – along with his painting, music and journalism – is comparatively unknown. He was a close friend and collaborator of Govind Nihalani, contributing to the films *Vijeta* (1982) and *Ardh Satya* (1983); he made experimental shorts (like *Dattu*, undated), and films on poets for Bharat Bhavan and the Sahitya Akademi. *Godaam*, his only feature-length work, was based on a Bhau Padhye story, which he produced, directed, scripted and composed music for with some financial support from NFDC.

neck and an Arriflex by his side, pointing into the distance as he sets up his shot. It was significant that it was Raj Kapoor's regal presence that had brought this thought on, but Chitre's musing also echoes Ghatak's advice to his students as Mirza further quotes him:

> All of you are going to be film directors. Do you know what that means? It means you are going to be in charge of great acts of creation. ... When your names appear on the titles people should feel that the film was made by a person of consequence.[6]

Such a director inherits, but also exceeds, the aura of the artist. In part the filmmaker shares with the artist the twin virtues of freedom – originality and autonomy – as almost nobody else could. Both concepts, of originality and autonomy, appeared in the early flush of Independence to be unprecedented in Indian history: and thus to allow the Progressive Artists Group to claim that little of significance had happened in modern Indian art before Amrita Sher-Gil, and for Satyajit Ray to contend in 1948 that 'there has yet been no Indian film which could be acclaimed on all counts'.[7]

Art's Safe Spaces

A difference, however, emerged between the filmmaker and other art practitioners that produced the modernist content of India's *homo nationalis*. Whereas Indian art practised its freedom in contained safe spaces, in small subsets of the public domain, these spaces appeared not to be available to the filmmaker. It was the very sophistication of art – in this regard like the humanities on campus – that, in making the comprehension of art inaccessible to the 'common man', also thereby protected this man's Article 15 rights from its excesses.

In 1954, the Esplanade Court of the Presidency Magistrate, deciding whether Akbar Padamsee's painting *The Lovers* was obscene within the meaning of Section 292 of the Indian Penal Code, judged that works of art were immune to the charge of obscenity because the 'place where they were exhibited' was such that the 'people who are normally likely to see such products of artistic talent' were the sort who 'would understand their intention'.[8] More than fifty years later Justice Sanjay Kishan Kaul, passing a judgment in the Delhi High Court in support of M.F. Husain's *Bharat Mata*, dismissed the complainants as 'not the types who would go to art galleries or have an interest in contemporary art, because if they did, they would

-6

Saeed Mirza, *Ammi: Letter to a Democratic Mother*, Chennai: Tranquebar Press, 2008, pp. 120–21.

-7

Satyajit Ray, 'What's Wrong with Indian Films' (1948), in *Our Films, Their Films*, Hyderabad: Orient Longman, 1976, p. 20.

-8

Court of the Presidency Magistrate, Esplanade, Bombay, *The State at the instance of S.H.J. Kanga v. Akbar Padamsee*, 1954 – following the accusation that Padamsee had exhibited two paintings at the Jehangir Art Gallery between 29 April and 1 May 1954, and charged with obscenity under Section 292 of the Indian Penal Code.

know that there are many other artists who embrace nudity as part of their contemporary art'.[9]

On the other hand, celluloid film has been a major presence in the twentieth-century public domain, viewed through this time with fear and trepidation for its capacity to inflict 'injurious effects' (an extensively used term in the 1928 Indian Cinematograph Committee Report) upon its publics, possessing an inherent *dangerousness*. It has defined the stature of the filmmaker as a kind of circus ringmaster keeping a wild beast in control. It has thereby also defined the filmmaker's social responsibilities. Through much of the twentieth century, before the mobs got at poets and painters, it was the filmmaker who was typically in the line of fire from the censor, the state, the police and the vandal. This visibility of the cinema also defined the *in*visible purpose of the Censor Board, specifically tasked with the responsibility of protecting the public from the filmmaker's cinematic excesses.

In 1969, the year that saw the birth of the New Indian Cinema, the G.D. Khosla Committee on Censorship reiterated several colonial fears about the dreaded social impact of the cinema. 'There is not the slightest doubt that the problem does exist', says the Report of the Committee, adding that for all the apprehensions about censorship, 'there is scarcely any demand in any quarter for the complete abolition of film censorship'.[10] The main problem was the impact of film, 'so vivid, so immediate and so ... complete' that 'not only are [the vast majority of film audience's] minds affected, but their conduct, their habits and behaviour towards other fellow-beings are ... influenced and shaped'.

The Fear of Cinema

Cinephobia. The term was first introduced into Indian film studies by Ravi Vasudevan to mean both a fear and hatred of the cinema, the opposite of cine*philia* or love for not just the films one may like, but the cinema itself. M.S.S. Pandian later usefully transformed it to something more specific. According to him, the elite, modernist, upper-caste fear of 'low' popular culture would further translate into an ideology of the state – an essential fear of something it could not control. His major example of state cinephobia was the Tamil Congress leader C. Rajagopalachari, who made multiple pronouncements

-9

Delhi High Court, *Maqbool Fida Husain vs Raj Kumar Pandey*, 2008.

-10

Report of the *Enquiry Committee on Film Censorship (G. D. Khosla, Chairman)*, 1969, Sec 8.10, p. 108; *Indian Culture* website, Ministry of Culture, Government of India.

about cinema, expressing the view (for instance) in 1939 that there is 'so much objectionable matter in the films prepared in India' that the objection that they are 'anti-Indian' 'pales into insignificance'.[11]

A rather deeper cinephobia is evidenced in Mahatma Gandhi's occasional and under-discussed pronouncements about film. In 1929, he considered the cinema to be central to a 'satanic' modernity into which everybody had sunk. We are, Gandhi warned, 'in the midst of a raging fire' of the 'cinema, the stage, the race course, the drinking booth and the opium den'.[12] In 1936, when Gandhi made the tactical argument that despite his avowed 'disapproval of cinemas, races, share market, gambling and the like', perhaps the time to confront the cinema was not now – since as a 'practical reformer' he needed to take into consideration 'what vices are ripe for being publicly dealt with',[13] – his views drew a protest. K.A. Abbas, in a famous rejoinder addressed directly to Gandhi, wondered how he could possibly have such opinions when, by his own admission, he had never seen a film. While some films did, Abbas admitted, 'exploit the baser passions of man to make money', they are also capable of bringing in a 'socially useful and morally uplifting element'. You could, for example, make documentaries, work with education, provide news. He listed a few Indian films that offered such content, typically saint films like *Sant Tukaram*, *Sant Tulsidas*, *Seeta* and *Vidyapati*, and reform socials like *Janma Bhoomi*, *Dharti Mata* and *Aadmi*.[14]

Abbas believed, sincerely it seems, that the usual moralist 'good cinema' argument would work, but he clearly hadn't understood Gandhi. The cinephobic was not only against bad films, but against the *cinema itself*. 'Sitting in a closed theatre,' Gandhi wrote in May 1947, 'one feels suffocated.' If he had his way, he would 'see to it that all the cinemas and theatres in India were converted into spinning halls and factories for handicrafts of all kinds'.[15] In December 1947 he went further and described the cinema as unsanitary, against which one needed to purify oneself.

> You should follow the rules of sanitation. Why do you need a cinema here? Instead of this, you can perform the various plays and stage dramas known to us. The cinema will only make you spend money. Then you will also learn to gamble and fall into other evil habits.[16]

The problem was certainly far more basic than anything that could be solved merely by making better films. The filmmaker-weaver's

-11

M.S.S. Pandian, 'Tamil Cultural Elites and Cinema: Outline of an Argument', *Economic and Political Weekly*, vol. 49, issue no. 46, 15 November 2014, p. 952.

-12

M.K. Gandhi, *Young India*, 28 March 1929, in *Collected Works of Mahatma Gandhi* (hereafter CWMG), vol. 45, pp. 216–17.

-13

M.K. Gandhi, *Harijan*, 14 October 1939, in CWMG, vol. 76, p. 378.

-14

Open letter by K.A. Abbas to M.K. Gandhi in *Filmindia* (October 1939), reprinted in Samik Bandyopadhyay, ed., *Indian Cinema: Contemporary Perceptions from the Thirties*, Jamshedpur: Celluloid Chapter, 1993.

-15

M.K. Gandhi, 'Talk with Socialists', May 1947, in CWMG, vol. 95, p. 150.

-16

M.K. Gandhi, 'Speech at a Prayer Meeting', 27 December 1947, in CWMG, vol. 98, p. 121.

job was to sanitize film, atone for its apparatus and cleanse the movie theatre.

—

Cinephobia entered into a new era of dangerous politics in 1969–70, when India transitioned into a popular democracy. An increasingly heterogeneous opposition, drawn for the first time since Independence from the peasantry, the lower castes and tribes, and other oppressed minorities, challenged (in Rajni Kothari's words) a 'small but powerful, educated, urban middle class controlling major economic, technological and financial institutions and in full command over the policy process and the decision-making framework'.[17] The cinema, an extreme form of unregulated and lumpenized popular culture capable of arousing the masses and throwing up a rabid leadership in who knew what uncontrollable form, had become an instrument of this opposition – unless, that is, it were somehow contained.

The Khosla Committee charged its *regisseur* with several new responsibilities. These included sanitizing the system with a fervour that at times recalled Gandhi. As an exemplary citizen, and human incarnate of the law of Article 19, the director's liberal freedoms would be zealously protected by the courts *on the condition* that the director also publicly demonstrated his use of such freedoms in a responsible way – as Govind Nihalani was commended for doing by Justice Sabhyasachi Mukharji when making *Tamas*, in which he successfully drew 'a lesson from our country's past history to ... rise above religious barriers and treat one another with kindness, sympathy and affection'. It is, says Mukharji, only possible 'for a motion picture to convey such a message ... [this is a filmmaking] achievement of great social value'.[18] This can only happen if the director literally leads by example: demonstrates how the 'reasonable restrictions' on free speech actually work, and how they can be translated into the aesthetic–technical practices of scriptwriting, shooting, editing and sound-mixing. Khosla outlines how this can be done through a comparison of two Hindi films, *Farz* and *Man ka Meet*, with Ingmar Bergman's *Wedding Swedish Style* and Michelangelo Antonioni's *Blow Up*. The Hindi films had strange

-17

Rajni Kothari, *State Against Democracy: In Search of Humane Governance*, Delhi: Ajanta Publications, 1988, pp. 273–74.

-18

Supreme Court of India, *Ramesh S/O Chotalal Dalal vs Union Of India & Ors* on 16 February 1988.

and incomprehensible sequences in which 'the heroine ... shakes her hips backwards and forwards and sideways ... no school or college girl would dance in this manner in front of a stranger, nor is such dancing at all resorted to by any of our young people ... [it] may almost be called the performance of a unilateral act of coitus'.[19] On the other hand, while Bergman and Antonioni also deal with sexual content, they do so in a sensitive way without any attempt to deprave and, on the way, even produce 'a slice of life'.

In 1970, this law of the cinema was made explicit in a major Supreme Court judgment, which defined a concept that Madhava Prasad has christened 'cinepolitics'.[20] At its most basic, it is a cinematic enactment of several conventions of popular democracy, played out as a narrative–spectatorial pact both inside a movie theatre – in the way films are made, in the multiple conventions of shooting, editing and sound used – and outside it, in the way stardom, or fan behaviour, expands into social and political realms.

A state-appointed *regisseur* – a *sarkari* Bergman, if you like – practising a state-endorsed cinematic realism now came to embody a 'secularized, contractual aspect' of film direction, says Prasad.[21] The director would work on behalf of a new kind of 'citizen–spectator' whose stern, interpretative authority would 'brook no challenge from the frame of representation'. The cinematic apparatus would also become the censor's apparatus. Censorship posed specific challenges to Realism, including how to confront it, how to skirt around it with multiple conventions, like cutaways and wink-and-nudge interpretations of seemingly legitimate content. Since the early 1980s (more precisely, following the amendment to the Certification Rules in 1983) these challenges came to define the filmmaker's skill. They also repurposed the censor into a film appreciation instructor, as the CBFC began giving extensive advice in its certification process on how filmmakers needed to remake their films, what bits of dialogue needed cutting, what acceptable substitutes to use, how sequences might be re-shot or re-edited.

Cinema and the Abbas Judgement

Thirty years after his open letter to Gandhi, K.A. Abbas re-entered the picture with another intervention. He was a member of the Khosla Committee and, dissatisfied with its debates, he made a short

-19

Report of Khosla Committee on Film Censorship, Section 8.40, p. 122.

-20

M. Madhava Prasad, *Cine Politics: Film Stars and Political Existence in South India*, Hyderabad: Orient Blackswan, 2014.

-21

M. Madhava Prasad, *Ideology of the Hindi Film: A Historical Construction*, Delhi: Oxford University Press, 1998, pp. 20–21.

film, *A Tale of Four Cities,* with the explicit purpose of challenging first the Committee and then the Censor Board itself. In a meeting of the Khosla Committee, the chairman of the Censor Board had denied that there was any political censorship, in a way that provoked Abbas deeply. 'They never had any social or political themes to which anyone might object. They only knew dancing, singing and hip-swinging. That provoked me to challenge the statement.'[22] And so he made this short film, screened it, and when, as expected, his brothel scene was objected to, filed a petition with the Supreme Court. In an extraordinary 'screenplay' about the events leading up to the trial – a story about a 'film sixteen minutes long' that was 'produced in the interests of Truth and Justice', but which became an 'eleven month-

22
K.A. Abbas, *I Am Not an Island: An Experiment in Autobiography*, Delhi: Vikas, 1977, p. 477.

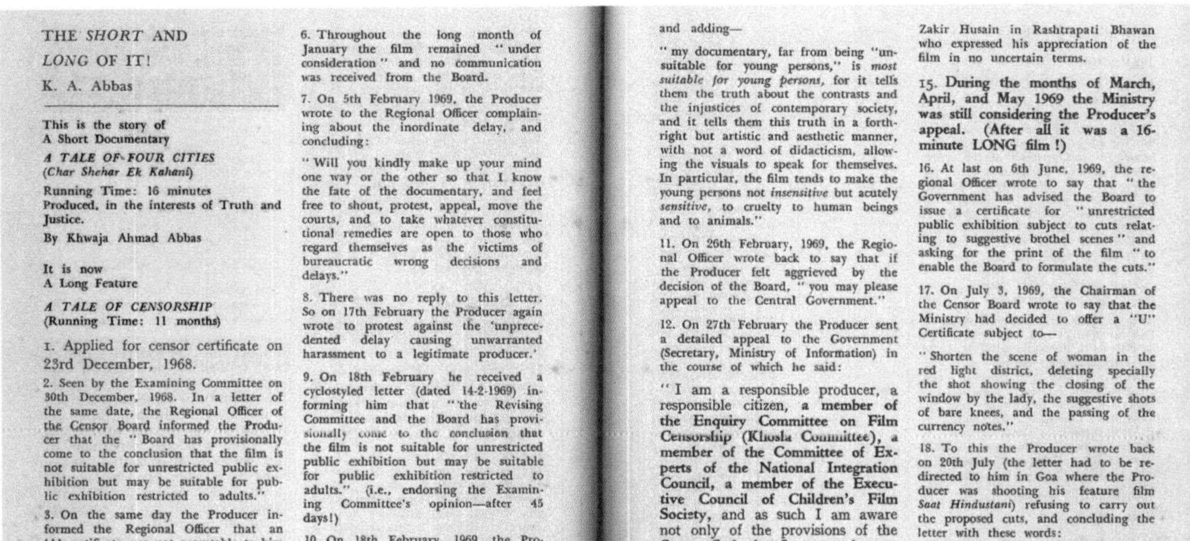

THE *SHORT* AND *LONG* OF IT!

K. A. Abbas

This is the story of A Short Documentary

***A TALE OF FOUR CITIES* (*Char Shehar Ek Kahani*)**

Running Time: 16 minutes

Produced, in the interests of Truth and Justice.

By Khwaja Ahmad Abbas

It is now A Long Feature

***A TALE OF CENSORSHIP* (Running Time: 11 months)**

1. Applied for censor certificate on 23rd December, 1968.

2. Seen by the Examining Committee on 30th December, 1968. In a letter of the same date, the Regional Officer of the Censor Board informed the Producer that the "Board has provisionally come to the conclusion that the film is not suitable for unrestricted public exhibition but may be suitable for public exhibition restricted to adults."

3. On the same day the Producer informed the Regional Officer that an 'A' certificate was not acceptable to him and so the film should be referred to the Revising Committee.

4. On the 31st December, 1968, the film was seen by the Revising Committee, and the screening was followed by a prolonged secret discussion. Afterwards the Producer was called and informed that the Revising Committee was referring the matter to the Government (i.e., the Ministry of Information) because the opinion of the members was divided—some were for outright banning it, some for awarding it an 'A' Certificate, and some for giving it a 'U' Certificate.

5. On 4th January, 1969, the Regional Officer informed the Producer that the film was "still under consideration."

110

6. Throughout the long month of January the film remained "under consideration" and no communication was received from the Board.

7. On 5th February 1969, the Producer wrote to the Regional Officer complaining about the inordinate delay, and concluding:

"Will you kindly make up your mind one way or the other so that I know the fate of the documentary, and feel free to shout, protest, appeal, move the courts, and to take whatever constitutional remedies are open to those who regard themselves as the victims of bureaucratic wrong decisions and delays."

8. There was no reply to this letter. So on 17th February the Producer again wrote to protest against the 'unprecedented delay causing unwarranted harassment to a legitimate producer.'

9. On 18th February he received a cyclostyled letter (dated 14-2-1969) informing him that "'the Revising Committee and the Board has provisionally come to the conclusion that the film is not suitable for unrestricted public exhibition but may be suitable for public exhibition restricted to adults." (i.e., endorsing the Examining Committee's opinion—after 45 days!)

10. On 18th February, 1969, the Producer wrote a lengthy letter in reply, quoting the relevant clauses which specifically define what would make a film "unsuitable for young persons":—

(i) anything which may strike terror in a young person, e.g., scenes depicting ghosts, brutality, mutilations, torture, cruelty, etc.;

(ii) anything tending to disrupt domestic harmony or the confidence of a child in his parents, e.g., scenes depicting parents quarreling violently, or one of them striking the other, or one or both of them behaving immorally;

(iii) anything tending to make a person of tender years insensitive to cruelty to other or to animals.

and adding—

"my documentary, far from being "unsuitable for young persons," is *most suitable for young persons,* for it tells them the truth about the contrasts and the injustices of contemporary society, and it tells them this truth in a forthright but artistic and aesthetic manner, with not a word of didacticism, allowing the visuals to speak for themselves. In particular, the film tends to make the young persons not *insensitive* but acutely *sensitive,* to cruelty to human beings and to animals."

11. On 26th February, 1969, the Regional Officer wrote back to say that if the Producer felt aggrieved by the decision of the Board, "you may please appeal to the Central Government."

12. On 27th February the Producer sent a detailed appeal to the Government (Secretary, Ministry of Information) in the course of which he said:

"I am a responsible producer, a responsible citizen, **a member of the Enquiry Committee on Film Censorship (Khosla Committee), a member of the Committee of Experts of the National Integration Council, a member of the Executive Council of Children's Film Society,** and as such I am aware not only of the provisions of the Censor Code, but I am acutely conscious of the film producers' social responsibility to people in general, and to children in particular, so that I am not likely to include anything in my films (least of all in a documentary) which may even remotely be injurious or detrimental to the interests and the character of the children of India."

13. On 12th March, the Under Secretary of the Ministry sent to the Producer a letter asking for a print of the film to be sent to Delhi "for preview by the Minister of Information."

14. On 9th April, 1969, the producer screened the documentary for President Zakir Husain in Rashtrapati Bhawan who expressed his appreciation of the film in no uncertain terms.

15. **During the months of March, April, and May 1969 the Ministry was still considering the Producer's appeal. (After all it was a 16-minute LONG film !)**

16. At last on 6th June, 1969, the regional Officer wrote to say that "the Government has advised the Board to issue a certificate for "unrestricted public exhibition subject to cuts relating to suggestive brothel scenes" and asking for the print of the film "to enable the Board to formulate the cuts."

17. On July 3, 1969, the Chairman of the Censor Board wrote to say that the Ministry had decided to offer a "U" Certificate subject to—

"Shorten the scene of woman in the red light district, deleting specially the shot showing the closing of the window by the lady, the suggestive shots of bare knees, and the passing of the currency notes."

18. To this the Producer wrote back on 20th July (the letter had to be re-directed to him in Goa where the Producer was shooting his feature film *Saat Hindustani*) refusing to carry out the proposed cuts, and concluding the letter with these words:

"I think once for all, the Courts and even the Supreme Court, will have to decide the issue, of whether a documentary of social protest can be banned or distorted under the cover of clauses which were originally intended to eliminate obscenity and pornography. That is where I propose to take the issue, besides the court of informed public opinion. This is not a threat. It is a promise." . . .

19. Writ Petition filed in Supreme Court, 19th Nov. '69.

20. Writ Petition Admitted by Supreme Court, 28th Nov. '69.

111

K.A. Abbas writes a blow-by-blow 'screenplay' of his encounter with the Censor Board. 'The Short and Long of It!', *Close-Up*, vol. 3, no. 5–6, 1970, pp. 110–11.

long feature' that could now be titled 'A Tale of Censorship' – Abbas recounts the campaign: from the time he first applied for a censor certificate for the film on 23 December 1968 to when he wrote a letter on 20 July 1969 refusing to carry out cuts, stating to the Court that,

> I think, once for all, the Supreme Court will have to decide the issue of whether a documentary of social protest can be banned or distorted under the cover of clauses which were originally intended to eliminate obscenity and pornography. That is where I propose to take the issue, besides the court of informed public opinion. This is not a threat. It is a promise.[23]

When the government relented and offered an unchanged version of the Universal certificate, Abbas further amended his petition to either be 'able to challenge pre-censorship itself as offensive to freedom of speech and expression, [or alternatively] ... to challenge the provisions of the [Indian Cinematography] Act and the rules, orders and directions under this Act, as vague and arbitrary'.[24] He did this, he said, because he 'wanted to put the censorship machinery in the docks'.

The judgment interpreted Abbas' petition with some gratitude as a filmmaker's noble effort to clear up once and for all the 'void for vagueness' doctrine that had beset the law and taken it 'to the verge of extinction' in all areas 'except in the ever-shrinking area of obscenity'. Justice Hidayatullah then followed up with an extended textual summary of what he thought *A Tale of Four Cities* was actually about. It was a graphic judicial embodiment of the legal gaze and (what Prasad calls) its 'interpretative authority'.

> [*A Tale of Four Cities*] is in black and white and is silent except for a song which the labourers sing while doing work and some background music and sounds for stage effect. The film, in motion sequences or still shots, shows contrasting scenes of palatial buildings, hotels and factories, evidence of the prosperity of a few, and shanties, huts and slums, evidence of poverty of the masses. These scenes alternate and in between are other scenes showing sweating labourers working to build the former and those showing the squalid private life of these labourers. ... Sometimes the inmates, becoming aware of the photographer, quickly withdraw themselves. Then we see one of the inmates shutting a window and afterwards we see the hands of a woman holding some currency notes and a male hand plucking away most of them leaving only a very few in the hands of the female. The suggestion in the first scene is that

-23

K.A. Abbas, 'The Short and Long of It!', *Close-Up*, vol. 3, no. 5–6, 1970, pp. 110–11.

-24

Supreme Court of India, *K.A. Abbas vs The Union Of India & Anr* on 24 September 1970, para 7.

a customer is being entertained behind closed shutters and in the next sequence that the amount received is being shared between the pimp and the prostitute, the former taking almost the whole of the money. The sequence continues and for the first time the woman who shut the window is again seen. She sits at the dressing table, combs her hair, glances at the two love-birds in a cage and looks around the room as if it were a cage. Then she goes behind a screen and emerges in other clothes and prepares for bed. She sleeps and dreams of her life before she took the present path.

There is nothing else in the film to be noticed either by us or by the public for which it is intended.[25]

There is no doubting to be permitted here, no ambiguity, no apophenic overinterpretation, no covert, wink-and-nudge, subversive content. While the legally enfranchised gaze of the citizen–spectator can admit to a diversity of reality, it cannot – when it becomes an act of citizenship – permit a diversification of perception, says Madhava Prasad. 'To admit that the eye's choice of objects from a field of perception could be arbitrary and unpredictable would be to jeopardize reality itself and would lead to anarchy.'[26] What you see is what you (should be able to) get.

What did Abbas get? Seen in one way, a lot. A Film Censorship Appellate Tribunal (or FCAT) was instituted of 'eminent persons' to exist independent of the government, a landmark in the history of film censorship in India, which was disbanded in April 2021 by the Modi-II regime. On the other hand, Chief Justice Hidayatullah reinstated both state cinephobia and the cleansing *regisseur*, and effectively claimed Abbas' support in his endeavour to do so. The judge thanked Abbas, reiterated his discomfort with censorship, but also parallelly the need for some kind of mechanism given the cinema's alarming ability to produce images 'more true to life than ... any other form of representative art'. What was required, Hidayatullah concluded, was that film be isolated for special treatment different from 'that of other forms of art and expression'. The problem of the cinema continued to lie in its unregulated excesses.

Who is a Filmmaker?-1: *Circa* 1975

In 1974, Anant Namjoshi, Minister of Education in Vasantdada Patil's Congress government in Maharashtra, wrote a curious short story in the *Illustrated Weekly of India*. Titled 'Should Students

-25

K.A. Abbas vs The Union Of India & Anr; emphasis mine.

-26

Prasad, *Ideology of the Hindi Film*, pp. 22–23.

Run Universities?',[27] it was written in theatrical style as a fictional conversation between the author and an anonymous young student. The student complains that they are 'nobodies' in an institution that, the author says, is 'run for you and for you alone, my young friends'. The student is not impressed: 'our syllabi are outdated and outmoded'. Namjoshi is building up to his big point: his proposed Maharashtra Universities Act, in which an elected Students Council would be formally recognized and given representation on every university's Senate.

A year later almost to the day, Namjoshi's party did the very opposite of that promise. It declared the Emergency. This is of course a controversial moment in Indian political history. The Emergency has been framed, for example by Rajni Kothari, as a combination of paramilitary forces and 'techno-managers' cracking down on the very people that Indira Gandhi had mobilized in a new era of mass politics.[28] The 1970s saw a 'steady and systematic destruction of institutions' as charismatic individuals taking on 'mythical qualities' found themselves 'bolstered ... by a powerful imagery of threats and dangers, of enemies that must be dealt with ... as anti-national and against national interest'. A central aspect of the uprisings that presaged the Emergency had been student militancy on and off the campus, the very students now widely characterized under the crackdown as 'lumpens' – hedonist males with no interest in education, art or anything that made for the good life.

The Navnirman movement in Gujarat in 1973–74, followed by the Bihar agitation led by the Chhatra Yuva Sangharsh Vahini in 1974, were the immediate political triggers for the declaration of the Emergency in 1975. During the Emergency, student action was quelled by a repressive state apparatus as students were forced underground, arrested, imprisoned, killed and abducted. Its repeal in 1977 saw the full-scale return of militancy. In 1978 the Students Anti Fee-Rise Action Committee (SAFAC), a Bombay-based coalition of the Vidhyarti Pradharthi Sanghathna (VPS), PROYOM and the All India Students Federation (AISF) led a stunningly successful operation in which they physically took over the Fort offices of Bombay University for a day, declared among themselves a Vice Chancellor and other office bearers, passed several executive orders, and then one by one melted into the crowd gathered outside,

-27

Anant Namjoshi, 'Should Students Run Universities?', *The Illustrated Weekly of India*, 16 June 1974.

-28

Rajni Kothari, 'Integration and Exclusion in Indian Politics', *Economic and Political Weekly*, vol. 23, no. 43, 1988, p. 2227.

even as the military was summoned to surround the campus.[29] Between 1979 and 1990, multiple issues – primarily around caste-based reservations and fee rises – saw students take over the frontline of political action, making for a long-term ancestor to the agitations in Delhi, Kolkata and Hyderabad over 2016–19.[30]

The late 1970s' student ferment across the nation was presumably unaware of – and even had they known, would have been largely unimpressed by – the small bit of action at the FTII in January 1975, when twenty-two acting course students complained that they weren't getting good roles in diploma films. A later FTII strike in 1977 attracted marginally more interest, in part because of its connection with Information and Broadcasting Minister Vidyacharan Shukla's complicated investments in the film industry that sought to, as reported in *Screen*, 'misuse ... censorship, the raw stock supply scheme and the machinery of film exports to bully and blackmail the industry into lending film ... as a medium of political propaganda'.[31] Mostly, however, FTII did not exist within the university imagination, and its internal grievances remained closed to the world, despite the occasional attention gathered by, for example, September 1984, when the entire student body *gherao*ed the Governing Council over a dispute around the right to change course electives and were hauled off *en masse* by the police.

To the acting students, the problem was straightforward. As Naseeruddin Shah recounts it, young student directors would 'cast anyone they liked, acting student or not', while several students of acting 'went through their two years without once facing a camera'. Meanwhile directors were making films 'with titles like (and I exaggerate a bit but only a bit) *Apocalypsis-cum-Genesis*, *And unto the Cosmic Void*, *Madhyasuryaya Mrigtrishna*, *Tribheeshan ka Teevra Maadhyam*'.[32] When Hrishikesh Mukherjee tried explaining 'in words of two syllables why in movies the director is so much more important than the actor', he was asked by students 'to cut the baby talk'.

> Without mincing words, but deleting the expletives that rise like bile every time I recall all this, we student actors thought there was something mighty rotten with this situation. It stank. Apart from the fact of student actors missing out on what should have been an assured part of their training not being perceived as an injustice, it just didn't seem to sit well with anyone that we actors were asking

-29

'Bombay University Occupied!, Story of a Student', *Asura*, 16 January 2015.

-30

Sanjiv Shah, who joined FTII in late 1977 (admissions had been delayed due to the 1977 strike, which was followed by yet another strike a month after he joined) and left in 1982, recalls that the 'apolitical nature of the student body as a whole' was especially notable, coming as he did from Ahmedabad, which had during the 1973 Navnirman movement seen both CEPT (Centre for Environment Planning and Technology) and NID (National Institute of Design) 'forbidding the students from engaging with the protesters'. Shah sees the difference between these and institutes that had started to 'impart education for professions that were not mainstream' and so 'were seen as esoteric, and which somewhere attracted the more privileged, and the larger organized political groups saw little gain in engaging with these institutes. And these institutes promoted, even revelled in, exclusion of the outside.' Email to the author dated 20 November 2021.

-31

'Shukla's Twenty Month Reign of Terror: Industry Speaks Out At Last', *Screen, 18* March 1977.

-32

Both this and the following quotation are from Nasreeuddin Shah, *And Then One Day: A Memoir*, Penguin Books, 2014, pp. 198, 227.

to be considered as essential participants in the making of the films, on par with the technicians.

Challenges to the 'Director System'

How do we look back, as we develop our project of reading the nation into the campus, on a weird strike like this one? There is, for one, graphic evidence of the *regisseur*-in-formation. The 'director system' of filmmaking was a European import borrowed from the theatre to replace an earlier 'cameraman system'. It survived in Hollywood only for a short period, before it was itself jettisoned by the industrial production line. In India after the War, and following the decline of the studio era, the director was more often the star-impresario, a Raj Kapoor or a V. Shantaram, fronting several murky financial systems that lay beneath. When the *regisseur* was adopted by the Indian state in the 1970s, it turned controversial. There was a tacit hierarchy at work, with the film director at the top of an 'above-the-line' list and acting, minus the star, somewhere at the bottom. Although actors led the way for recognition, they were followed by cinematographers who fought for the right to be upgraded to Directors of Photography and receive 'co-authorship' status,[33] scenarists who demanded copyright contracts and royalty for usage, and lyrics-writers and singers who too asserted intellectual property rights over their different contributions.[34] Actors received no such rights. By August 1975, a new two-year integrated course did away with the acting course entirely. It was effectively outsourced to the National School of Drama, with the FTII only offering six-month advanced courses for its final year students, which too were then done away with.

Many of the student films Naseeruddin Shah mocks reveal precisely this tension. One that is clearly referenced in his sarcastic list is Arun Khopkar's 1974 short fiction film, *Teevra Madhyam*, an exploration of the political role of art through the moral centre of a young classical singer (Smita Patil's first screen role) surrounded by student activists. Quotations include Caudwell on how 'Bernard Shaw became a mere entertainer for the bourgeoisie', and 'a revolutionary laughs only once, when he hears the last laugh'. In one scene, male student activists are preparing for an anti-fee-rise *morcha*.

One of them, played by Saeed Mirza, prints leaflets on a

-33

Scan to see Anil Mehta on the need for 'co-authorship' acknowledgment with cinematographers: 'A Conversation with Anil Mehta – On Cinematography and Influences, Part I'.

-34

See, in particular, battles by screenwriters and music composers that led in 2012 to significant amendments to the Copyright Act, 1957. Anjum Rajabali and the Progressive Writers Group (PWG) within the Film Writers Association fought for writers retaining their right over screenplays and lyrics, leading to an amendment to Section 18 of the Act, asserting that 'the author of the literary or musical work included in a cinematograph film shall not assign or waive the right to receive royalties to be shared on an equal basis with the assignee of copyright for the utilization of such work in any form other than for the communication to the public of the work along with the cinematograph film in a cinema hall'. Likewise, the movement of the Indian Performing Rights Society (IPRS) to amend the copyright law to address song remixes led to the amendment of Section 31-c (Statutory License for Cover versions).

cyclostyling machine. Another, played by Ketan Mehta, describes a scene he considers funny, in which a rich student willing to pay higher fees sees this problem as someone else's. Returning even to a film like this, we get to unearth a rather more complicated convergence: between politics playing out in the filmmakers' work and in the actions occurring on the campus – not least, we shall soon see, those of Saeed Mirza and Ketan Mehta.

We shall see this convergence manifested on campus (in Mehta's *Holi* and the 1977 strike) and off it, especially in the birth of film cooperatives (Yukt, later Odessa) that spilled over beyond the frame and thus also beyond orthodox institutional limitations. As politics converged with cinema, it split the *regisseur* apart. The conflict between the director's creative rights as against the cinema's capacity to accommodate the 'hordes' – the multitude walking in *morcha*s against the fee-rise now turned into normative film spectators – would enter a wider public domain. The multiple FTII strikes would become interesting punctuations in that astonishing, under-discussed convergence.

The Fear of Noise

In 1971 Satyajit Ray waded in with his own idea of what the refurbished Indian *regisseur* needed to bear in mind. Such a filmmaker had of course to be the bearer of free speech, and thus needed to keep alive his 'urge for self-expression, common to all artists'. However this urge had to be tempered by the equally pressing need to 'establish rapport with an audience'. For all the success of the film society movement, of which he was himself a founder and a key representative, Ray was sceptical of the governmental project to convert a 'perceptive minority' of the public into 'patrons of ... art theatres', or for the cinema to truly claim for itself the *niche* safe spaces that the other arts possessed. Even if such a possibility exists, Ray asserted, it still needed filmmakers to have a plan that would make their

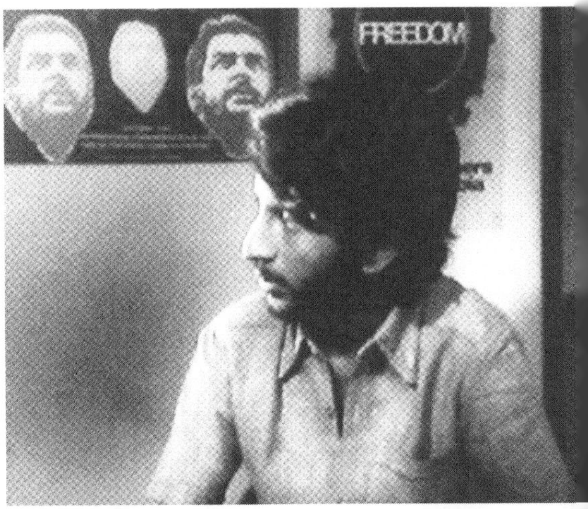

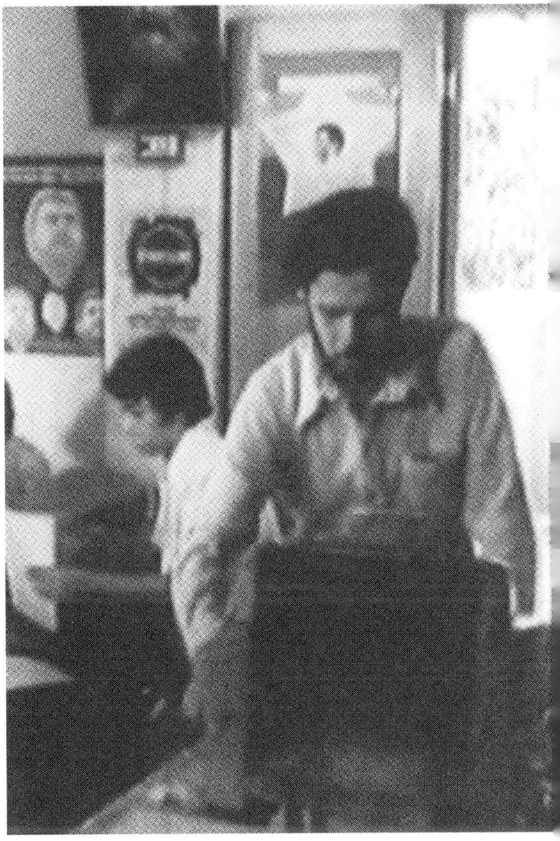

Above Ketan Mehta, **below** Saeed Akhtar Mirza – details from Arun Khopkar's diploma film, **Teevra Madhyam** (1974)

productions accountable, financially and otherwise, to the state.[35]

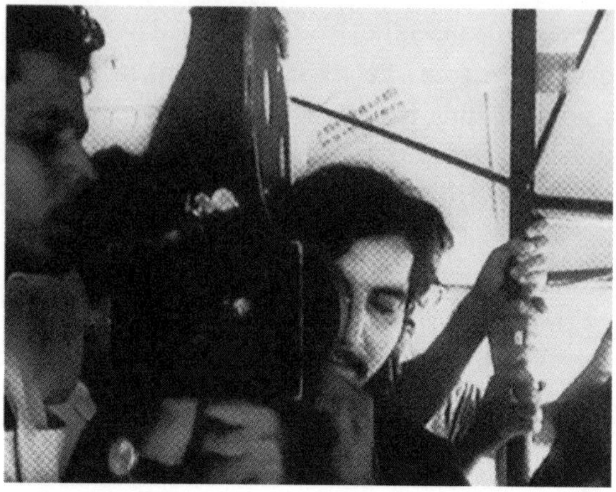

K.K. Mahajan with an Arri-2 in Mrinal Sen's **Interview** (1971).

Ray was speaking at a time of serious crisis for independent filmmakers. Specifically, the crisis was to do with the fact that many films made with government loans – including critically acclaimed ones – were getting no release to reach their audiences, were being frozen out of the distribution system, and had begun defaulting on their debt. The Film Finance Corporation was implementing draconian measures to recover its money. An FFC representative was quoted as saying that they would go after filmmakers in every way possible. 'We will not relent, we will follow. But if (the filmmaker) goes completely out of business and he has no assets to declare and there is nothing to his credit ... naturally, the amount has to be written off.'[36]

—

Of course, it was more complicated. The arrival of lightweight Arriflex cameras meant that for the first time filmmakers were freed up to displace script- and location-bound cinema with the introduction of *verité* noise: to bring into the frame what new media theorist Hito Steyerl would decades later call 'dirty data'.[37] An early example of such data came about in the late 1960s when Mrinal Sen, one of the pioneers of the New Cinema movement that the FFC was then supporting, began shooting political processions in Calcutta with, as he said, little clarity on how, if at all, he would use the footage. In the event, Sen used this footage across his Calcutta trilogy and in his *Bhuvan Shome*. By 1971 the numerous rallies that he had filmed had coalesced into a specific direction as they directly took on the Congress government of Chief Minister Siddharta Shankar Ray, gradually turning violent with attacks on statues of nationalist leaders and clashing directly with the police. In 1971 itself, the year that Sen references in his film, the colonial Bengal Suppression of Terrorist Outrages Act of 1936 was replaced by the Prevention of Violent Activities Bill, even as the violence turned systemic with

-35

All quotations are from Satyajit Ray's controversial essay, 'An Indian New Wave?', in *Our Films, Their Films*, pp. 81–99.

-36

'Committee on Public Undertakings (1975–76): 79th Report: Film Finance Corporation', Delhi: Lok Sabha Secretariat.

-37

Scan to see Hito Steyerl, 'A Sea of Data: Apophenia and Pattern (Mis-) Recognition', *e-flux*, issue 72, April 2016.

retaliatory police crackdowns killing over 4,000 young supporters of the Communist Party of India (Marxist–Leninist) (the official figure was 1,783).

In 1972, *Calcutta 71* received a limited commercial release at Chowringhee's Metro Cinema. Several of the documentary shots inserted into the film's finale suddenly found a whole new meaning as students came to screenings to spot their friends among the pictured crowds. 'Young boys ... would keep coming back', Sen said later. 'People with their family and their friends. They would watch [the film] over and over again, just for another glimpse of their friend.'[38] The scenes began providing unexpected evidence of people in the crowd who had later disappeared or been killed in police encounters. As the screenings became something of a regular political event for activists to meet nightly, police began mounting surveillance every time and everywhere that *Calcutta 71* was shown. New controversy followed as the footage got converted into diverse forms of textual

-38

Mrinal Sen, *Over the Years: An Interview with Samik Bandyopadhyay*, Kolkata: Seagull Books, 2003, p. 67.

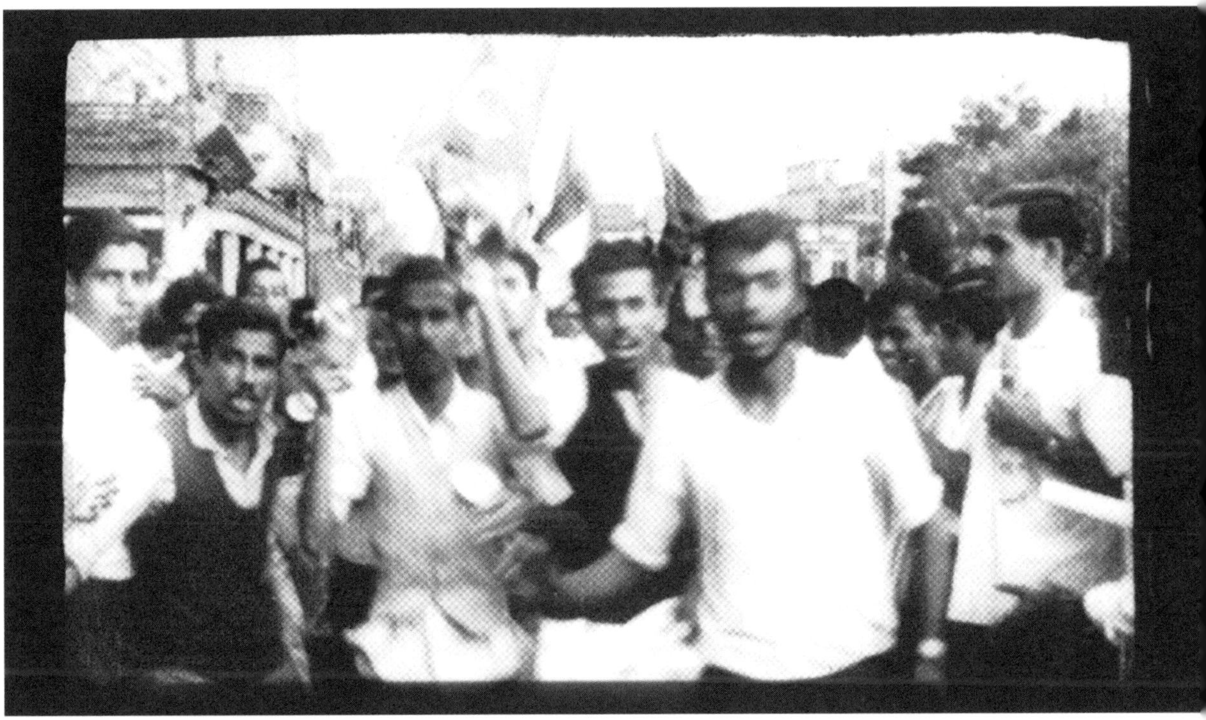

Documentary shots of protesters in Mrinal Sen's **Calcutta 71** (1972).

'noise' and spilled over into debates that may have had nothing to do with the film Sen believed he had made. Arguments took place: Sen first told students he had begun shooting *Calcutta 71* only in September 1971, but then admitted, as activists confronted him with faces on the screen whom they knew had disappeared well before then, that he may have also used street footage from as far back as 1969.

By 1971, cinephobia had taken on a yet further dimension, closer to what Steyerl has called 'apophenia', or the fear of 'perception of patterns within random data'. 'Pattern recognition resonates with the wider question of political recognition', she writes, for 'who is recognized on a political level and as what? As a subject? A person? A legitimate category of the population?'[39]

Ray's view on the filmmaker's responsibility – a responsibility that he was effectively accusing Sen of having abdicated – was driven by a clearly apophenic fear of rampant misinterpretation, precisely such as what the students were indulging in at the Metro screenings. This directorial abdication is to him evidenced in Sen's self-indulgent, 'modish narrative devices' in *Akash Kusum* and *Bhuvan Shome*.[40] Ray spoke of *Bhuvan Shome* as something that 'looks a bit like its French counterpart, but is essentially old-fashioned and Indian beneath its trendy habit'. If *Bhuvan Shome* was, at base, no more than a story of 'Big Bad Bureaucrat reformed by Rustic Belle', such a story could well be equally plausibly told in 'a simple but forceful language' shorn of unnecessary excess.

—

Earlier, in 1968, the FFC had expanded its operations to include distribution and export; by 1973 it was channelling all imported celluloid raw stock; and by 1974 (after the withdrawal of the MPEAA from the Indian market) it was importing foreign films for local distribution. At this time it began dangling a carrot of loans to 'modest but off-beat films of talented and promising people in the field', with the stick that these filmmakers use this chance to create 'an effective instrument for the promotion of national culture, education and healthy entertainment'.[41] In 1976, at the height of the Emergency, a year after the strike of the acting students and Ghatak's sage advice on how to have a name befitting a filmmaker, carrot-and-

-39

Steyerl, 'A Sea of Data'.

-40

Sakti Basu and Shuvendu Dasgupta, eds, *Film Polemics*, Kolkata: Cine Club of Calcutta, 1992, p. 38.

-41

Report of Committee on Public Undertakings (1975–76), pp. 3–4.

stick was further sharpened into a financial-cum-aesthetic strategy: where you could at once be an independent filmmaker *and* support a state project, make your own 'artistic' film *and* have a 'reasonable prospect of being commercially successful'. It would be a 'balanced view', and it would follow an art-house 'check list' including the 'following criteria ... for granting loans: 1. *Human interest* in the story; 2. *Indianness* in theme and approach; 3. *Characters* with whom the audience can identify; 4. *Dramatic content*'.[42] Much of this was extrapolated from the advice Ray gave to young filmmakers in 1971, including that they should always make films with a 'well worked-out scenario' revealing 'a modicum of craftsmanship';[43] not only aesthetic necessities but economically vital.

Being *regisseurs* and thus defenders of free speech, India's independent filmmakers were by default on the same side of the political fence. Opposing Emergency censorship was the easy part. The problem deepened and then led to, as one critic called it, 'schismatic warfare' between the independent filmmakers themselves, when it began implicating a larger, more elusive and infinitely more problematic state project around cinematic realism.[44] Iqbal Masud saw it as a divide between the cinema's 'radicals and its gradualists', 'root and branch' filmmakers conflicting with 'gradual change' filmmakers. For many, there was nothing reformist about 'gradual change'.

For all their avowed opposition to the Emergency, in freezing a film's overt content – in reproducing the chilling Hidayatullah diktat that the film means only *this* and *nothing else* – filmmakers found themselves effectively reproducing the functions of the censor. Justice Mukharji, speaking on *Tamas*, warned filmmakers that they needed to rise to the challenge of 'meeting the explosively expanding cinema menace'.[45] The menace had, he said, to be 'strictly policed': and you can read the dark hint that if the textuality police (a.k.a film directors) didn't supervise the narrative adequately, the actual police would step in.

Who is a Filmmaker?-2: Previewing 1997

Both canon and *regisseur* were in the balance when, on 14 December 1997, the FTII gathered to celebrate its 21st Convocation Day. It was a glittering occasion. Mahesh Bhatt, Chairman of the Governing Council, had invited a celebrity, Dilip Kumar, to hand out the

-42
Ibid., p. 16.

-43
Ray, 'An Indian New Wave?', pp. 98–99.

-44
Iqbal Masud, 'Fierce Little Bushwar in the Indian Film World', in 'Is There a New Cinema Movement?', *Cinema Vision India*, 1980, pp. 83–88.

-45
Supreme Court of India, *Ramesh S/O Chotalal Dalal vs Union Of India & Ors* on 16 February 1988.

Facing page and overleaf
Adoor Gopalakrishnan's April 1996 letter to the I&B Ministry, when he was Chair of the Governing Council of FTII, on the role of the filmmaker and modifications to the course on film direction.

student diplomas. But there was a problem, a raging crisis that had eaten up most of Bhatt's chairmanship tenure. The previous year, the Institute had yet again changed its entire academic structure. Known as the 2+1 system, it sought to reduce its camera and sound courses from three to two years, and make the much-vaunted direction stream into a kind of advanced one-year course available only to students who had first completed a 'technical' diploma in camera, editing or sound. Film direction, no longer art, would be a form of advanced technical training. There would also be new courses in art direction, production management and in acting.

Astonishingly, the idea was implemented under the tenure of Bhatt's predecessor – of all people, Adoor Gopalakrishnan. In what appears to have been a personal letter to the I&B Ministry with his residential address on top, Gopalakrishnan makes the flabbergasting argument that FTII's direction department, having produced 'hardly a dozen filmmakers of note', has 'historically' been its weakest. He then recommends that film direction itself needs a fundamental rethink. To him, the need of the hour is not to have more *regisseurs*, so to say, but to produce 'technician-turned-directors' who might find a 'berth in the industry'. Such technician-directors could always, if they really want to be independent, function as 'single-man units'.

Gopalakrishnan has since then tended to shrug off this moment, but it remains of significance – for this, truly, is where the saga began. It was the first time that the *regisseur*, viewed as an advanced technician, was formally dethroned. The issue would unfold over the next twenty years and span four major strikes. When it first arose, it appears to have caught everyone by surprise. Kavita Pai describes it as a bolt from the blue.[46] She still subscribes to the common assumption that had the old 1+2 system been maintained – given that it had worked until then and at least two strikes had fought to retain it – all might still have been well. Gopalakrishnan's intervention would prove to be the originary moment of an issue that would resurface in 1997 in Agashe's Conceptual Proposals, in 2000 in his Restructured Revised Syllabus, in 2010 with Hewitt, and then in 2016 with B.P. Singh's astonishing 'Vision Document' to convert FTII into a Digital Media University.

-46
Conversation with Kavita Pai on Zoom, 5 November 2020.

ADOOR GOPALAKRISHNAN
DARSANAM TRIVANDRUM 695 017 KERALA INDIA
TELEPHONE & FAX 0471-446567

Sri.Raghu Menon,
Joint Secretary,
Ministry of Information & Broadcasting,
Govt.of India, Shastri Bhavan,
New Delhi - 110 001.

Sub: FTII... Re-structuring of Courses...

Dear Sri.Raghu Menon,

It is learnt that the recent students' strike at the FTII Pune has been called off on the assurance that all their demands would be granted.
I have read in news papers that one of the concessions promised is the rescission of the re-structured courses and the resuscitation of the old.
One of the objections of the student leaders,as I understand, is that the duration of the courses had been reduced to two from three and this cuts into their free time to think, contemplate and evolve against commercialism and the 'polytechnic' culture.

As one of those chiefly responsible for the re-structuring of the old courses and the introduction of the new ones, I think I must explain things a bit:

It is universally agreed that in filmmaking, the director's is the most decisive role and everything else should be subservient to it.
Historically, the Direction Dept. has been the weakest in the Institute, since its inception in 1961. In the last three-and-a-half decades, it has produced hardly a dozen filmmakers of note (more than 200 have been trained for sure). And those who are gainfully employed in the profession do not make up for more than 25%, let alone the grade and quality of their work.
While technicians like editors,cameramen and sound engineers trained at the Institute have more or less been evenly absorbed into the body of national cinema, the Direction graduates of the FTII do not constitute even 10% of the young and new filmmakers who make their debut films every year.

Facts and figures like this prompted us to do some soul-

searching amongst the film fraternity and the alumni of the Institute. It cannot be denied that while creativity is a subjective matter, the quality of training is a major contributing factor.

It was clear to see that while in every other department, a student specialised in a technical branch, the Direction trainee was sort of a jack of all trades, mastering none.

Even at the time of admission, the Institute has no sure means to probe a candidate's 'directorial aptitude'. In most cases, as a fresher, the candidate is also not quite certain about his potential faculties. For most the concept of cinema as a medium of artistic expression evolves over a period of time as they undergo training and familiarise themselves with the best of world cinema.

So, the choice of specialisation in film direction should legitimately wait until the Institute as well as the student are certain that they are making the right and ripe decision.

This is the rationale behind stopping direct admission to the course in Direction.
It is now structured into a post-diploma course.
Only a candidate with a post-graduate degree or diploma in any branch of filmmaking is eligible for admission.
So, contrary to the propaganda/complaint that the course had been cut down to two years, the minimum time one needs to spend at the FTII to get a diploma in Direction has been increased to four years.

From the beginning, FTII has been running two-year courses in Editing and Screen-play Writing(with Elements of Direction). And then there was a one-year post-diploma course in Advanced Film Direction for those who pass the Screenplay Writing-cum-Elements of Direction.
In later years, owing to the increased apathy of the Direction students to the tedium of writing scripts, the two courses got merged into one and became a three-year course.

Under the revised system, the scope of the course has simply been widened; the inputs have been made more diverse and intense(the newly introduced courses, Production Management and Scenic Design are of two years duration. In fact the

Institute should consider the re-introduction of the two-year course in Screen-play writing too) as graduates and diploma holders in different disciplines could bring in new perceptions and a certain maturity of approach to film-making.
A technician-turned director will have a natural advantage over the others to start with. It should be comparatively easier for him to find a berth in the industry even if he is not assigned a directorial job right away. He should use this time to build his contacts and develop the skills further adapting and attuning himself to the new environment. On the other hand, those who wish to be independent and make non-feature films can bank on their technicl specialisation to function as single-man film units.

While proposing the new courses, we found that Cinematography and Sound Engineering were the only two courses which were of three years duration. Mr.Mehboob Khan, Dean proposed that these two courses could also be brought down to two years. This proposal was endorsed by the Head of the Cinematography Dept. Sri.Bhanu Murthy when he said that there was little to teach after the first two years. I remember ascertaining with the Heads of Cinamtography and Sound Depts if what they used to teach in three years could be taught in two years without leaving anything out in terms of theory and practice. As you know, the proposals as well as the details of the syllabi were gone over thoroughly by the Academic Council which had two student representatives and all the Heads of Depts on it.

It may also be noted that earlier the minimum qualification for admission to these two courses was a pass in the Pre-degree exam with physical sciences and Maths as subjects. Subsequently the basic qualification was raised to graduation for all the courses and the upper age limit was removed.

Limiting the duration of the courses to two years was done with the express idea that a student should be put through full-time work. The emphasis was clearly and unmistakably on a culture of hard work and not by any means on relaxation

...9

and lethargy.
In order not to lose anything that a student had access to in the three-year course, it was proposed that if need be, the daily working hours be increased by atleast two hours (instead of 10 am to 5 pm, it could be 9 am to 6 pm).

I must admit that saving of one year and the resulting economic relief to the middle class parents was also a major consideration(apart from the substantial saving for the exchequer). The case of many who leave lucrative jobs in pursuit of a career in cinema had to be taken into account too.

Over and above all these considerations, any person with a creative urge, per se, should be in a hurry and be impatient to learn the art and craft in the shortest possible time. The tendency on the part of some students, clearly a small, privileged and articulate minority, to laze around and gravitate in the campus under one excuse or the other does not indicate a healthy trend worthy of encouragement.

Thanking you for the attention.
Yours sincerely,

Adoor Gopalakrishnan Trivandrum 28-4-1996

That April the students demanded, and the administration agreed, that a review committee be set up with some well-known names, mostly of former students. Direction included Sriram Raghavan and Rajat Kapoor, editing had Paresh Kamdar and Reena Mohan, and sound, A.M. Padmanabhan and Vikram Joglekar. They would sit alongside student representatives and carefully think each stream through. Recognizing the urgency and the pressure, the review teams produced provisional recommendations. Many of these would become long-term ancestors, a decade later in 2011, to the *Vision FTII: The Next Fifty Years* Report of the Nair Committee.

—

In 1997, these recommendations were summarily rejected by the Governing Council. Bhatt had by then replaced Gopalakrishnan as Chairman. An indefinite hunger strike was declared as madness descended upon the campus. This was not the first time that the educational apparatus there had gone belly up. It had happened both in 1977, around the integrated course, and in 1984, when students demanded the right to change their streams of specialization. It was nevertheless the first time that such a drastic move to fundamentally reinvent the FTII was being attempted. The story would take two decades to unfold.

It is likely that Mahesh Bhatt himself had no strong views on the 2+1 structure. The 1996 student president Shammi Nanda says that Bhatt had been sympathetic to the appointment of the review committees, and we must believe Nanda.[47] What we do know is that the problem was still unresolved when the day of the convocation arrived. Inevitably, the students brought their protest there, and equally inevitably, caused a full-on debacle. They wore black bands when they went up to receive their diplomas at the hands of the famous chief guest, and even heckled when he spoke. Dilip Kumar was upset and sought to disown his involvement, asking students not to wash their dirty linen in public. The administration was even more upset, with the result that for the next decade no convocation would be organized at the FTII.

It was Mahesh Bhatt who went ballistic. The knock-down-drag-out fight that ensued was over who was a 'filmmaker'. Bhatt

-47 Shammi Nanda, 'Mournings and Celebrations from the FTII strike in 1997 and acknowledging Mahesh Bhatt's contribution to FTII as the Chairperson', *Courageous Communication*, 17 July 2015.

said that the students were 'cobblers', not artists, thus evoking (as his friend Pritish Nandy pointed out the following week) a caste hierarchy 'written ... into the script of modern Indian politics'.[48] Great filmmakers were not taught, Bhatt raged on, artistic talent could not be produced 'on an assembly line'. Indeed, the very idea of a film school was a waste of money, he said, warming up to his theme, given that 'subsidized education for good cinema' was a luxury in a nation 'where so much of the population does not even get drinking water'. He concluded his tirade by resigning his chairmanship.

Bhatt was invoking a familiar distinction between the elite art-house and the lowbrow, at the time in defence of the latter (even saying, as quoted by Nandy, that he didn't make good cinema, he made big bucks). He was, predictably, attacked with an equally modernist response invoking the celluloid auteur. For one, Bhatt's position that the art-house cinema was an indulgence in a poor country had a particular pedigree. His 'make films versus provide drinking water' line directly echoed Nargis Dutt's 1980 attack on Satyajit Ray in Parliament. For another, there was the attribution of cultural illegitimacy to the film industry, evidenced in the contempt shown to the chief guest of the day. The following week an editorial in the venerated *Economic and Political Weekly* asked if Bhatt's 'misfits' also included Ketan Mehta, Jahnu Barua, Girish Kasaravalli, Saeed Mirza and Kumar Shahani, and wondered what Indian cinema might have looked like without them. Was the 'real world', of which Bhatt said the students are ignorant, limited to 'commercial showbiz where only the crudest can survive'? Was this the only world that Bhatt was making his graduates fit to serve?[49]

Video Debuts

The somewhat tired reprisal of an old divide was especially out of sync with what was going on at the FTII – or indeed in the country – just then. In 1981, when Indira Gandhi returned to power and the Special Plan for Expansion of Television was announced, it was clear that the Indian state's love/hate affair with the cinema was all but over.[50] Video and television was where the action was, and it was helpful when the new Director – eminent theatre actor and well-known Hindi film bad guy Mohan Agashe – gave these developments an interpretation, a gloss, that had been until then

-48

Pritish Nandy, 'Sultan of Sham', *Rediff on the Net*, 22 December 1997.

-49

'Ousting Good Cinema', Editorial, *Economic and Political Weekly*, vol. 31, no. 4, 27 January 1996, p. 185.

-50

Speaking of that period, Sanjiv Shah reflects on changing attitudes to the idea of cinema. On the one hand, there was a 'strange mix of the mainstream Hindi Cinema, some sprinkling ... of the European New Wave and a lot of appreciation of the non-fiction work from Latin America and Europe'. On the other hand, relatively few filmmakers of the time ventured into directing features. 'Direction was not a specialized course, in any case, unless you did a post-diploma after your integrated course; and not many did.' He remembers the period 1977 to about 1980 as one signified by the rise of documentary film, paralleling the rise of video (starting with Umatic, and reasonably good VHS recorders), allowing 'filmmaking with a different purpose, provided the filmmaker was happy working on the fringes or in alternative spaces'. 'Several Media Centres were coming up [emphasizing] more community-based, direct engagement and offered platforms for such work.' 'The ISRO–DECU experiment was also an alternative ... which, for the first time, offered work opportunities outside of the film industry or the state-owned Films Division or Doordarshan. It was also fairly liberal in content and allowed some freedom to the filmmakers.' Email to author, 21 November 2021.

Facing page and overleaf
Syllabus Review Committee in the wake of the 1996-97 strikes: includes opening pages with the names of the Committee members, the Chronological Overview, and the Context framed by Agashe's 'Plans'.

1. CHRONOLOGICAL OVERVIEW

1.		Change from 3 yr. to 2 yr. course is a mess
2.	Apr 14 96	Students go on strike demanding 3 yr. course
3.	Apr 21 96	Syllabus Review Committee formed by AC
4.	Jul 18 96	Committee formulates Revised Syllabus
5.	Sep 18 96	AC meets Holds that the Revised Syllabus needs to be whetted by outside experts for infrastructure and scheduling Recommends zero semester Recommends that meantime Pre-96 syllabus for next batch (to be admitted in Aug 97).
6.	Oct 12 96	GC meets Rejects AC recommendations Holds that the inputs of Revised syllabus be incorporated in the 2 yr. structure
7.	Oct 23 96	Students go on indefinite hunger strike Demand implementation of AC recommendations
8.	Oct 30 96	Minister intervenes and upholds the implementation of the AC recommendations
9.	Nov 96	GC meets to uphold AC recommendations
10.	Dec 96	AC meets Decides to admit next batch from Aug 97 with pre-96 syllabus Constitutes the outside experts committee
11.	Nov 9 97	GC meets Dr. Agashe asks time to work out 'conceptual plans'
12.	Dec 17 97	AC meets Faculty asks for time on the Revised Syllabus Dr. Agashe tables 'conceptual plans' Issue of zero semester to be decided on 31 Dec.
13.	Dec 20 97	Students go on indefinite strike demanding implementation of the Revised Syllabus.

2. REVIEW COMMITTEE (Revised Syllabus Committee)

Camera:
Rajan Kothari
Anup Jotwani
Hari Nair
Prof. Naria - Nodal Committee member
Shammi Nanda - Faculty
- Student

Direction:
Sriram Raghavan
Rajat Kapoor - Nodal Committee member
Avinash Deshpande
Prof. Menon - Faculty
Surabhi Sharma. - Student

Editing:
Paresh Kamdar - Nodal Committee member
Reena Mohan
Nandini Bedi
Prof. Mathur - Faculty
Narayanan AV - Student

Sound:
A.M. Padmanabhan - Nodal Committee member
Vikram Joglekar
Bishwadeep Chatterjee
Prof. Satish Kumar - Faculty
Vinod Subramanian - Student

Outside Experts Committee

Direction: Govind Nihalani
Sound : S. Selvaraj
Editing : Afaque Hussain
Camera : Ashok Kumar

3. BACKGROUND TO THE ISSUE

GENESIS OF THE REVISED SYLLABUS

The course structure has been changed 7 times in the past 11 years. This is unheard of in any academic institution. The last such change was made in 1996 when the 3 yr. courses were slashed to two years during the tenure of John Shankaramangalam (The faculty of FTII had drafted this 2 yr. syllabus within a matter of 15 days).

Following a strike a review committee was set up by the AC consisting of experts in various fields (ex-students), a representative from the faculty and a representative from the students. This was done for each area of specialization. The committee worked over a period of 4 months and finalised a document which was the Revised Syllabus.

This was tabled at the following AC. The AC decided that it must be whetted by outside experts (not graduates of FTII) and in the meantime after a zero semester the next batch be admitted with the pre-96 syllabus (this batch was admitted in Aug 97).

In the following GC all the AC recommendations were rejected. Following a hunger strike the then minister of I & B, Mr. C M Ibrahim intervened and directed that the GC accept all AC recommendations. In the next AC a committee of outside experts was formed and to this date no further work has been done on the Revised Syllabus.

Consequently the students demanded that an AC meeting be convened at the earliest to implement the syllabus for the coming batch (Aug 98), the prospectus for which would have to be out by January 1998 at the latest. Moreover the term of this AC was due to expire in December 97. After much pressure the AC meeting was declared to be on the 17th of December 1997.

CONTENTS OF THE REVISED SYLLABUS

While drafting the syllabus the members kept in mind the following:

1. Components that had become obsolete were to be dropped.
2. Additional focus was put on visiting faculty and a workshop oriented structure.
3. New inputs were added keeping with the contemporary developments in the video and digital field.
4. Inputs which had over the years been diluted or deleted (even though the infrastructure then was much less as compared to now) were restored.

A week by week breakdown was worked out for all the years and all the specialisations, including the co-ordination of all the departments for inter-departmental excersises. The Revised Syllabus was also drafted bearing in mind the existing infrastructure of the institute.

GENESIS OF DR. AGASHE'S PLANS

On his assuming office Dr. Agashe spent a few months traveling to various film schools in the world:- FEMIS (France), Berlin Film School and a film school in Australia. Four months after his having assumed office, he came up with a host of tentative interlinked proposals which were called by him his 'conceptual proposals' which were to 'radically restructure academics and administration in FTII.'

CONTENTS OF DR. AGASHE'S PLANS

Some of the plans he proposed were:

Eighty students were to be admitted to the common integrated course, at the end of which 40 would be asked to leave with a certification that they were competent enough to be assistants in the industry. The other 40 would be allowed to continue specialising in a discipline decided by the faculty.

Short term courses would be introduced in all disciplines. This was based on the observation that any number of such courses with dubious credentials are running in the country, and that the institue had come into competition with such set-ups.

A specialisation in videography would be introduced.

To alleviate the financial pressures on the institue the students would shoot all excersises (till now shot on film), except their diploma films, on video.

The institute would also hike the fees to Rs. 3 lakhs per year for each student. Students would be admitted under different grades, seats being kept reserved for aspirants being sponsored by corporate houses. FTII would also produce 2 commercial feature films with outside directors on which it would be mandatory for every final year student to assist. All these plans were to be aimed at helping the institute generate revenue.

Dr. Agashe has also talked about digitisation (introduction of contemporary technology) the final aim being the merger of the film and television wings.

entirely missing. That November he presented a series of 'conceptual proposals' culled together after several months of study and travel, and after visiting film schools in France, Germany and Australia, and the CILECT Congress in Ebeltoft, Denmark.

After all this travel Agashe had finally gotten to the nub of the problem: the cinema was undergoing fundamental change. Its relationship with the state needed basic recalibration. Before the Institute could rethink what it taught, to whom and how, it needed to renegotiate its 'overdependence on the Ministry of Information and Broadcasting'. The first order of debate was whether FTII was an autonomous place, or just another 'Central Government Department'.

This renegotiation would take place on the founding proposition that the cinema was no longer filmmaking as it once had been but had morphed into an 'audio-visual industry'. The change was being powered by 'growing awareness and demand from Ministries and Corporate Sector for ... software requirement from multiple channels'. Agashe's 1997 proposals returned us to another of the great fantasies of state modernism, namely, belief in the ability to scrub clean a historical slate and start afresh. They also reprised the belief in what had come to be known, through the 1980s, as 'leapfrogging', or the ability to make historical leaps to the latest available technology and update an entire social infrastructure around that catalyst. In 1997, the cinema posed a large problem to the FTII; rather, two problems merged into one. One, technology demanded that the cinema needed fundamental redefinition; and two, this could only happen if an older bureaucratic state mechanism was replaced with something more market-driven. What brought the two together, however, was what lay beyond both: Bhatt's 'real world' of capital and industry.

—

To access *this* world, Agashe effectively planned – administratively, academically and technologically – to merge film with television. Next he planned to update his equipment, gradually, over time, replacing celluloid with video. And lastly, perhaps most significantly, he also planned to phase out the era of the *regisseur*. From now on, the institution would mainly house 'short term training and retraining courses for professionals who are already working in the industry'. And the fees would be commercial.

In November 1997, it finally became clear that Agashe had, in a disarmingly straightforward way, forged the path for privatization. Privatization, or state 'disinvestment' – an early version of what would turn a decade later into neoliberalism proper – had been inaugurated in India in 1991 by then Finance Minister Manmohan Singh, and was by the late 90s the single-point solution to all that was wrong with state institutions.[51] Directed mainly to services like water, electricity, telecommunications and transport, and to major PSUs in steel and energy, it was premised on disqualifying the ethical right of a state, now viewed as irretrievably riddled with inefficiency and corruption, from running these entities.

Such disqualification in the specific case of the cinema meant that Agashe had to exorcise the three evils that had beset the campus. Privatization now named them: *state*, *celluloid* and *regisseur*.

Agashe's proposals did nothing to assuage the misfits whose very existence on the campus became an obscene reminder of the mess of history that they now embodied. It would take the entire saga into a mythic rather than rational space, as it indeed did in Ketan Mehta's 1984 film *Holi*. In December 1997, footage shot by Ashish Avikunthak along with British filmmaker Benjamin Friedman, then an exchange student from Central Saint Martins, and edited with Shaina Anand, would become *Kavita Gherao*, a 'poem-blockade'.[52] It shows 'Kavita' (Kavita Pai playing herself) along with other students – 'Neeraj', 'Sudipto', 'Shammi' – confronting the Director and the administration, and eventually the police. 'Kavita' speaks in tight close-up: the camera is mostly on her face, occasionally on her hands making emphatic gestures, as she incarnates all that campus autonomy and the rights to free speech and inquiry might mean in the cinema – namely, the right to call oneself a filmmaker and to be educated like one, as against becoming industry-fodder. To her, the original purpose of the Institute was unambiguously to 'train technicians for the industry'. This role was flipped in 1971 by the G.D. Khosla Committee on the Film Institute, which sought to bring it further within the ambit of the New Cinema associated with the Indira Gandhi regime, which, in Kavita's telling, saw no reason

-51

Neeraj Sahay, who was a central figure in the 1997 agitations, recalls that the students 'were supported with active participation of trade unions, gate blockades, demands for rights of non-teaching, non-permanent staff, as a piece with the then environment of protesting privatization, etc. FTII students also marched with trade unions in their morchas etc.' Correspondence with author, 24 November 2021.

-52

Kavita Gherao was an assemblage of 16 mm footage which shows Hi-8 (interviews) and spliced-in sequences from film history. Key figures in the making of this version are credited briefly. There is an acknowledgment of 'the participation of Ashish Avikuntak, the Bombay Film Republic, the People's Film Department'. Anand's role is reduced to 'translation and subtitling'. Many thanks to Avikuntak and Shaina Anand for reconstructing the film. It was uploaded by the FTII Students' Association on Vimeo in 2013.

Facing page and overleaf
November 1997: Mohan Agashe's 'Conceptual Proposal' for 'restructuring and functionally reorienting' the FTII.

For G.C. Members of FTII, Pune - 9.11.1997.

Conceptual proposal for restructuring and functionally reorienting Film and Television Institute of India, Pune.

After having studied for initial period of six months the academic and administrative aspects of Film and Television Institute of India and having had some discussions with both the Deans as well as some ex-students and outside experts and having attended the CILECT Congress in Ebeltoft where issues like curriculum, training methodology and digitization were discussed at length, I submit the following for the consideration of Governing Council.

Inspite of several problems faced by the Institute and student unrest of last few years, the fact is that FTII still remains to be probably the only premier training Institute of its kind and the facilities available and offered for the training of the students are envious when compared to schools all over the world. Inspite of this, the last few years have witnessed a kind of plateau with occasional drops due to piling up of certain administrative and academic problems leading to chronicity. These are :

(1) Long standing administrative problems like grievances of academic staff regarding poor pay strucuture, pensionary benefits, disparity of grades etc.

(2) Lack of clarity as to whether to function as an Autonomous Body or as Central Government Department. This is reflected in the approach of administration where references are always made to Central Government rules.

(3) Non-resolution of issues like future of persons originally working for Prototype, status of Mess and Canteen employees, filling up of vacant posts etc.

(2) Taking into consideration the phenomenal growth of audio-visual industry, growing awareness and demands from Ministries and Corporate Sector for film and audio-visual material, growing software requirement from multiple channels make it mandatory that training in television & video is perceived as one of the specialities and newly admitted students have the possibility to pursue the same like other specialisations.

(3) Clearly identifying the lower end of equipment required for training as against the equipment required for production and accordingly restructuring the training exercises for the students and implementation of revised syllabus as approved by the Committee of Experts.

(4) Reviewing and reorienting the financial strategies in order to develop policies for generating income which would be able to take care of the Institute's recurrent expenditure atleast to the tune of 30 - 40 per cent of its total expenditure, thereby minimising the financial dependence on Information and Broadcasting Ministry.

(5) Redefining the functions of full time faculty as against the visiting faculty and promoting effective liaison with professionals of repute so that they can give the benefit of their expertise to the students.

(6) To initiate short term training and retraining courses on payment basis for professionals who are already working in the industry.

(7) Initiating computer-based Animation and Special Effect Department in the Institute.

(8) Redefining the student fee structure in the light of new economic policies adopted by the Government and the changes which have taken place in charging the fees to students of professional training Institutes like Engineering, Medicine etc., and the last but not the least

for the government to supply the industry with technicians when they ought really to be supporting the state with socially relevant low-budget cinema.

—

Whatever this history, it was all in the past; 'Kavita' no longer has any use for the canon. That history was of a time when we had lived 'under the illusion of the welfare state', but now 'all that's gone ... there is not even the pretence of promoting low budget cinema or promoting alternative cinema'. What has happened instead is the radical resurrection of yet another an old idea in the name of privatization. Film editors are once again being taught 'just to learn to cut and to wind film', and cameramen 'to be only camera operators'.

Friedman's film intercuts conversations with students, with shots of the campus on strike. These are further intercut with film clips from Soviet cinema and from lowbrow Hindi films ripped from VCDs. 'Neeraj' (cinematographer Neeraj Sahay) is crouched in a corridor, and makes for a tactical argument for recognizing that the student body should see itself as – and should behave like – a *minority*, and should work its tactics in a way as to take on the majoritarian establishment. 'Mohan Agashe', sideburns and all, is shown standing next to armed police, trying to be conciliatory to the striking students. 'You are standing there with a policeman next

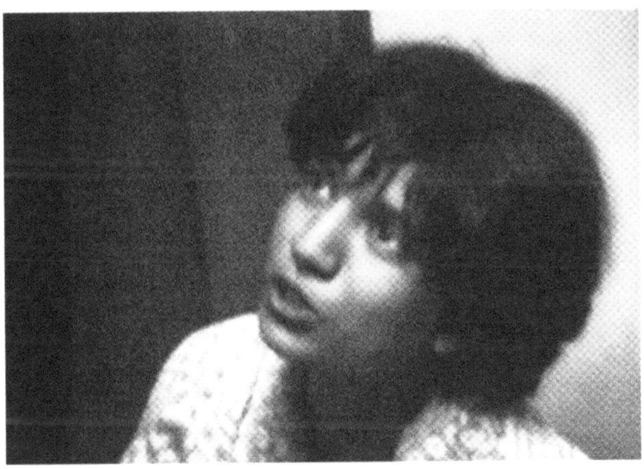

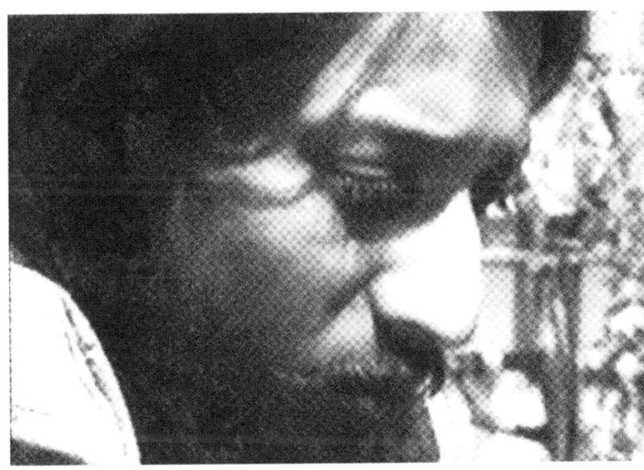

Left 'Kavita' (Kavita Pai) and **right** 'Neeraj' (Neeraj Sahay) in the film **Kavita Gherao** (1997).

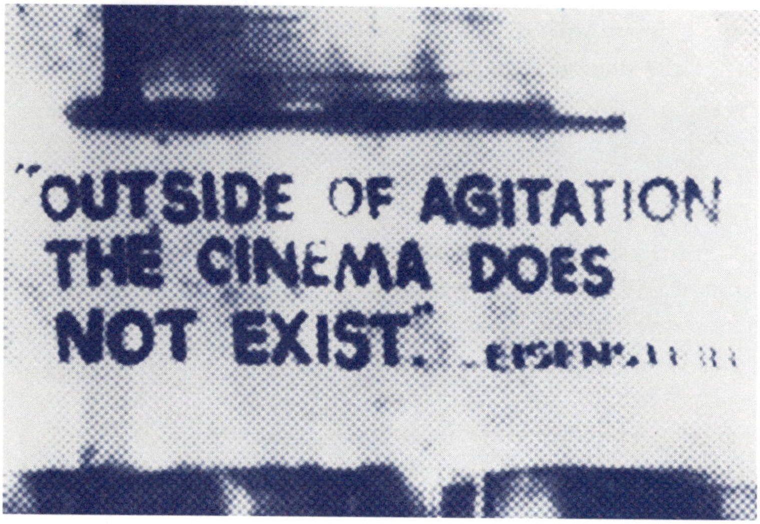

Quotation from Eisenstein's **Montage of Cine Attractions** on an FTII campus wall, taken from **Kavita Gherao** (1998).

to you, and you are saying this is not a threat?' asks one student as the film intercuts Agashe with images of his villainous screen roles.

The students are effectively trapped by S.K. Patil's ghost, between a state that says it is on the one hand for low-budget alternative cinema, but is on the other nakedly seeking to produce trained labour. What 'Kavita' wants, increasingly desperately as the film goes on, is a way by which aesthetics and theory do not conflict with technique – where, she says at one point, 'you cannot totally deny Eisenstein'. There is a prominent line on a campus wall that quotes Eisenstein's agit-prop line: 'Outside of agitation the cinema does not exist.'

CHAPTER 3

COLLECTIVE ACTS AND LUMPEN STUDENTS

The Importance of Cinema

Inside the Glass House of Mumbai's Press Club, on the afternoon of 15 November 2015, Kundan Shah stands in a row along with other filmmakers. This presciently named addition to the venerated media venue sees metaphorical stones thrown daily at press conferences, news briefings, political and PR announcements, launches, reports, allegations and exposés, all in the service of (its motto) 'champion[ing] Objectivity. Boldness. Perspective'. 'Institutions. What are they, if not champions of a certain set of values?' its statement of purpose asks.

On this day, belying the routine of soggy wafers, *samosa* and tea in paper cups, there is unusual tension at the Press Club, for a rather different set of institutional values are about to be challenged.

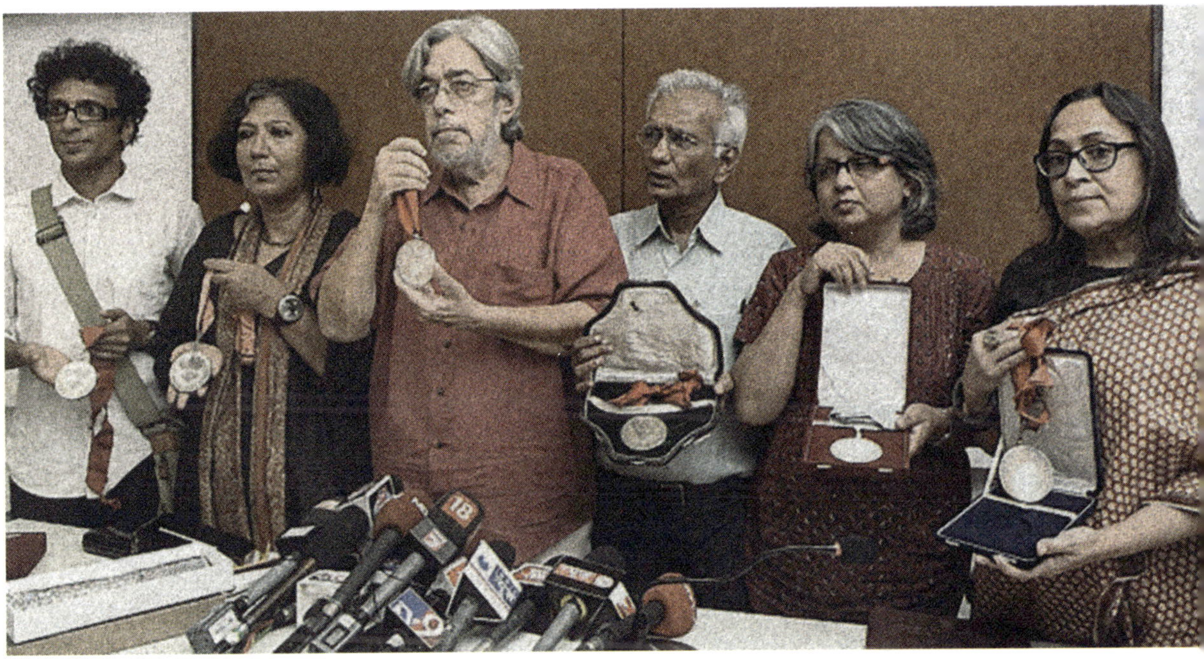

15 November 2015. From left: Satheesh P.M., Madhusree Dutta, Saeed Akhtar Mirza, Kundan Shah, Irene Dhar Malik and Bina Sarkar Elias, returning their National Film Awards.

Twenty-four filmmakers, young and old, have convened to surrender awards received by them from the Indian state for cinematic excellence, protesting its response to the students' strike of 2015. Some are well-known names, while many others – editors, writers, cinematographers, composers, sound designers – aren't.

They are taking a risk here. Their actions, intended to challenge the Indian state, could have unpredictable, even dangerous consequences for their lives and futures. Some part of their complicated positions had been reported, some had been debunked and caricatured. None of this could exhaust either the questions or the complex emotions being relentlessly attached to their action of holding out their medals that day.

A booklet is circulated.[1] Set to an animated graphic by Nalini Malani of a mutant gradually rising, standing up and mumbling before uttering the word 'freedom', it carries statements by the filmmakers who have gathered, letters and some additional texts. There are references to the killing of Govind Pansare and

-1

In Defence of Our Present records statements by 36 filmmakers surrendering their awards. Released on this occasion, the booklet was taken to the Goa IFFI protest later that month. The awards campaign was a major means of expanding and pluralizing the question of cinema outside the campus, after the strike ended on the campus on 28 October.

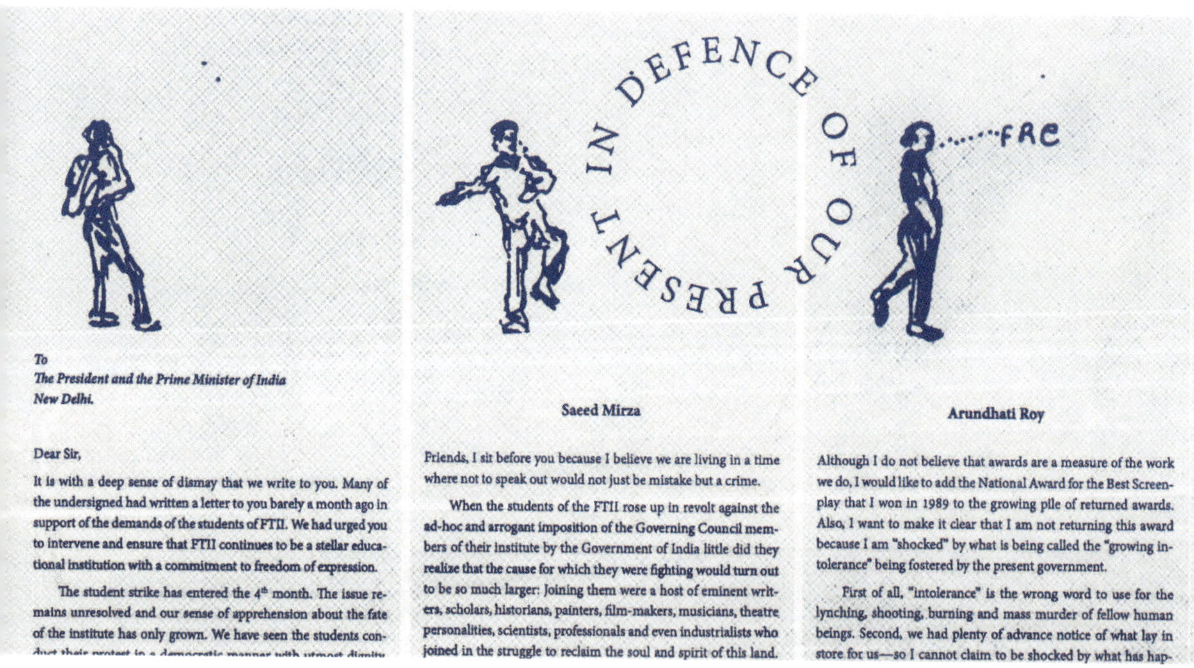

To
The President and the Prime Minister of India
New Delhi.

Dear Sir,

It is with a deep sense of dismay that we write to you. Many of the undersigned had written a letter to you barely a month ago in support of the demands of the students of FTII. We had urged you to intervene and ensure that FTII continues to be a stellar educational institution with a commitment to freedom of expression.

The student strike has entered the 4th month. The issue remains unresolved and our sense of apprehension about the fate of the institute has only grown. We have seen the students con-

Saeed Mirza

Friends, I sit before you because I believe we are living in a time where not to speak out would not just be mistake but a crime.

When the students of the FTII rose up in revolt against the ad-hoc and arrogant imposition of the Governing Council members of their institute by the Government of India little did they realize that the cause for which they were fighting would turn out to be so much larger: Joining them were a host of eminent writers, scholars, historians, painters, film-makers, musicians, theatre personalities, scientists, professionals and even industrialists who joined in the struggle to reclaim the soul and spirit of this land.

Arundhati Roy

Although I do not believe that awards are a measure of the work we do, I would like to add the National Award for the Best Screenplay that I won in 1989 to the growing pile of returned awards. Also, I want to make it clear that I am not returning this award because I am "shocked" by what is being called the "growing intolerance" being fostered by the present government.

First of all, "intolerance" is the wrong word to use for the lynching, shooting, burning and mass murder of fellow human beings. Second, we had plenty of advance notice of what lay in store for us—so I cannot claim to be shocked by what has hap-

October 2015: Details from **In Defence of Our Present: On Giving Up the National Awards**. Issued by Solidarity with FTII Students, coinciding with the students' return to the classroom. Images by Nalini Malani.

M.M. Kalburgi, and to the mob lynching of Akhlaq Khan. The booklet ends with an unexpected political parallel drawn by the writer Aspi Mistry, connecting the present moment with the most magical of cinematic actions – the spring of 1968 in Paris when filmmakers in numbers similar to those gathered here had taken on the French state to defend the Cinémathèque Française, and had also thereby fired 'the first shot ... across the bow of the Fifth Republic of France'.

> 'Are films more important than life?' asks Jean-Pierre Léaud (who plays the immature, spoiled and needy Alphonse) in *Day for Night*, François Truffaut's loving tribute to filmmaking. For Truffaut the answer was in the affirmative.

There is a larger point, Mistry suggests, to all this. Paresh Kamdar asserts, for example, that he is not returning his award (received for editing Nandan Kudhyadi's *Rasayatra*, 1994), he is *sacrificing* it. Most others struggle to put things in words. Some try hard to emphasize that this isn't only to do with the ruling government, or limited to the concerns of the 2015 strike. Saeed Mirza, by now the *éminence grise* of the movement, produces a small history lesson. He wants everyone to 'go a little further back in our country's history ... to the time when India became a Constitutional Republic'. He speaks of how the Congress party, for all its professed secularism, saw 'communal and caste riots ... in state after state under its watch'. He speaks of the Naxalite movement in Chhattisgarh, Orissa, Andhra Pradesh, southern Bihar and Jharkhand 'to which the poor and marginalized had rallied because they had nowhere else to turn', the insurrections in Manipur, Nagaland and Mizoram, the farmers' agitations in western Uttar Pradesh and Rajasthan demanding subsidies and economic relief, Assam, Punjab and Kashmir, before he turns to the Bharatiya Janata Party, a 'bit player with a communal agenda' that rose to national prominence over 'the destruction of a medieval mosque saying that it was built on the ruins of a sacred temple'. To him the need is to uncover, from somewhere deep within Indic history, a lost idea of political freedom that the cinema might have tapped had it been given a chance in modern India.

Others make more personal links with history. Ajay Raina, who had won the Rajat Kamal in 2005 for his documentary *Wapsi: The Returning*, recalls his own nationalist commitments when he had shot 'undercover, at grave risk and almost life-threatening circumstances', his film about the Partition. To him, the award had been a recognition by the state for precisely this complex nationalism, and so returning it is 'not an easy decision to make'. Sound designer Vivek Sachidanand, returning his audiography citation for his extraordinary soundtrack in Amit Dutta's experimental *Ksha Tra Gya* (2005), can no longer accept compliments for his abilities from a state that actively promoted the view that 'FTII has not produced any real talent in years', or that students were 'naxals and anti-nationals': it is time to 'make my voice heard and return the awards that the same Indian government has given me as an "FTII product"'.

A part of what was said that day was understood within an established language of dissent, framed within a debate on artistic autonomy, censorship and free speech. Several statements echoed the need expressed by artists since at least the Emergency to stay at arm's length from governmental recognition – such as, among others, by Marathi author Durga Bhagwat who had been jailed during the Emergency and refused, even after the Janata Party came to power, to accept the Jnanpith award.[2]

But then things went further. It became a deeply emotional negotiation with the *regisseur*–citizen. This is not, Kundan Shah too asserts, 'a protest against BJP only'. Over the years he and others had 'protested through our works': his films and even his television serials had been 'against the Congress government too'. *Police Station*, he reminds everyone, had been banned in 1985 with the remark 'Incendiary' by Doordarshan.

But this is different – this is personal. This 'appointment of an inappropriate person as the Chairman of FTII' is an affront. He had (with other co-signatories to the President and Prime Minister of India) watched with disappointment 'how the ruling party's leaders and supporters abused these filmmakers and belittled their gesture'. He would no longer tolerate seeing his 'fellow filmmakers mocked'. Respectfully therefore, as a 'concerned citizen of this country whose work has been recognized by the Government of India', recognizing the 'great honour' extended to him by the state, he was saying thank you/no thank you.

Shah spoke emotionally that day. The Indira Gandhi Award for Best Debut Film was still a new award when he had got it for *Jaane Bhi Do Yaaron* in 1983. His batchmate Ashok Ahuja had received

-2

Durga Bhagwat's position on artists' need to refuse all state patronage was perhaps the most extreme stand on this vexed topic in post-Independence India. Although Bhagwat first defined this position during the Emergency, in 1975 at the Marathi Sahitya Sammelan in Karad (after which she was jailed), she stayed with her position, first turning down the Padma Shri and then the Jnanpith award.

it the previous year for *Aadharshila* (1982), and Sudhir Mishra would get it a few years later for *Yeh Woh Manzil toh Nahin* (1987). It is, he says, the 'only National award I have ... and I feel very, very sad to part with it'. The problem however is this: 'There would've been no *Jaane Bhi Do Yaaron* if I had not studied at FTII.' This was a common refrain, but in Shah's case and with this film in particular, it came close to the truth. Many of the speeches suggested (to use a tired phrase) an idealism lost, but none pointed so clearly to what this film meant and just what was lost – the sheer 'anything-is-possible' sense of what it meant to *belong*, once upon a time, to the nation and then to the cinema, to make *that* film somehow and to see it up there, on the screen.

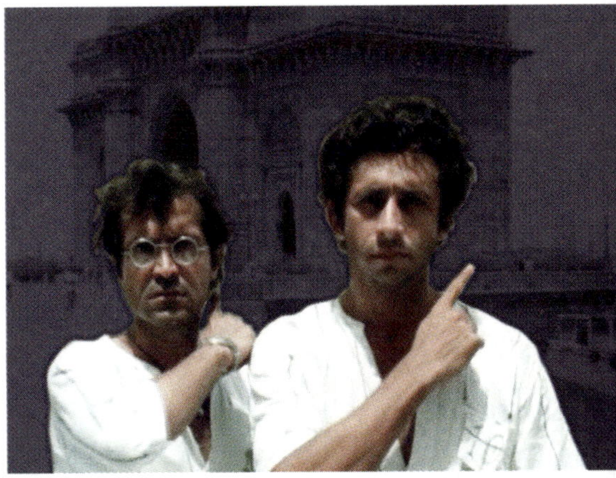

The throat-slitting gesture in Kundan Shah's **Jaane Bhi Do Yaaron** (1983).

And then Shah ended his speech by performing a gesture of running his finger across his throat. This was how *Jaane Bhi Do Yaaron* (*JBDY*) had ended, when Vinod Chopra and Sudhir Mishra, his two bumbling citizen-protagonists now turned criminals, slit their throats and hung their heads marked to the tune of '*Hum honge kaamyaab*' ('We shall overcome').

It was a small gesture. It was however as significant as any by an artist in the history of modern India: a tiny hand movement that, more graphically than anything else that afternoon, signalled that he – and the filmmakers gathered there – were effectively declaring that they had emotionally, perhaps intellectually, seceded from the Indian state.

The Return of the Prodigals

The oracles descend from the hill at the climactic moment of John Abraham's *Agraharathil Kazhuthai*. The year is 1977, and they sing of good times, for

> The prodigal will surely return to the house
> Good times are coming
> A prince will be born here.

Do not however be taken in, they go on, for the evil that has seeped into the *agraharam* is more than superficial: happiness is illusory for 'this village faces destruction', and its actions in seeking to exorcise itself will turn against it.

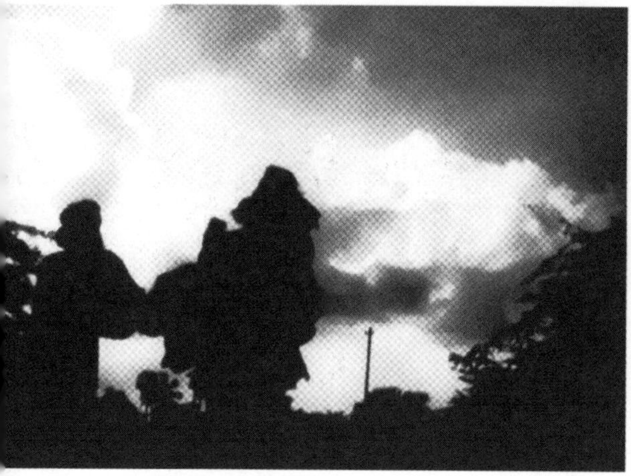

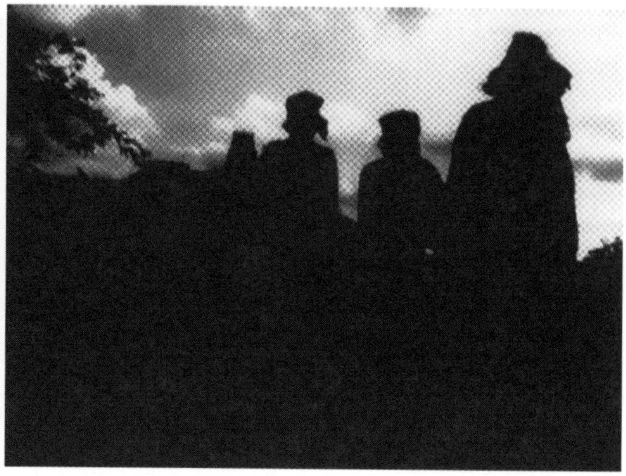

The oracles in John Abraham's **Agraharathil Kazhuthai** (1977)

The oracles are filmmakers: specifically, John Abraham and T.V. Chandran. They are also clairvoyants of a different sort. Chandran's extraordinary directorial career was still to take off, but he had been cast as the guerrilla leader in P.A. Backer's pathbreaking *Kabani Nadhi Chuvannappol* (1975) the previous year, while Abraham was well on the way to inheriting, as Kamal Swaroop too would, Ghatak's mantle as the director-prophet of his era. *Agraharathil Kazhuthai*'s making had itself been close to a miracle, made possible by multiple bit players. It had been financed by Abraham's sister Susan Joseph and then by the tiny Ashwini Film Society, and still later, when distribution in Tamil Nadu became impossible following an upper-caste backlash, by Kerala's CPI(M)-affiliated Janashakthi Films. The astonishing conditions of *Agraharathil Kazhuthai*'s survival merge with Abraham's dark forebodings of what the future held for India in 1977. The rot, the prophet-filmmakers appeared to say, had gone deep. The evil lay within and the fire that would burn down the village had to be celebrated in a pagan ritual.

You shall perform the dance of ecstasy
Fire is the flaming sun
Fire is the essence of light
May it (the village, the nation) burn
We feed it with melted butter
We feed it with flesh.

—

Three years later, and a year before Kundan Shah's debut, Ashok Ahuja's *Aadharshila* (1982) begins in black-and-white with a student film by a direction graduate named Ajay (played by Naseeruddin Shah). He is showing the film to his girlfriend Asha (Anita Kanwar) inside the hallowed FTII Main Theatre. (It will, we later understand, turn out to be Ahuja's own graduation film.) We are not shown how it ends, and are required to accept that it has shaded into the film that Ajay now wants to make. All of Ajay's imagined encounters with film – his fantasies, his incomplete and unrealized projects, commissioned works – are metamorphosed as actual sequences performed by a small group of struggling authors, actors and sundry wannabes. We thus get a curious little anthology of 1980s' prevalent film styles, some in the developmental state realism mode presaging the Emergency, others in the mainstream commercial idiom, yet others in the documentary format that was then coming into its own.

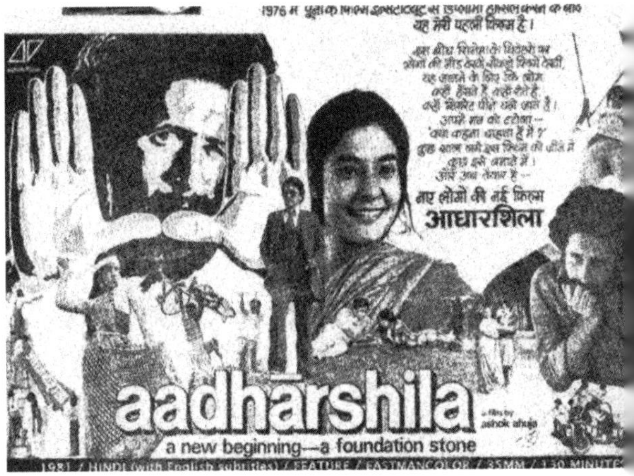

Aadharshila poster, with the director's statement: 'After 1976, when I received my Diploma at Pune's Film Institute, this is my first film. In between I saw the crowds of people in theatres, as I saw hundreds of films, to know better where people laugh, where they cry, when they get up to have a cigarette. My mind struggled with the question, "What do I want to say?" Some years went into living this film, some more into making it, and now it's ready – a new film for new people.'

As *Aadharshila* unfolds, it becomes virtually impossible to figure out just where this particular work leaves off, and where the several others that were made, planned or dreamed up by batchloads of fantasists, take over. This film-about-a-film-about-a film was the closest anyone got in those years to the muddled encoding of what being a filmmaker meant, as a recent graduate himself becomes the film he is, unbeknownst to him, actually making.

In the end, after a long and eventually fruitless effort to get a well-known author to give him film rights, Ajay realizes that *Aadharshila* – namely the film we are watching – is the one he ought to make, or may have indeed actually made unawares as he lived out his struggles. The final sequence is set outside an auditorium. Inside it his film has been released and as we hear the echoes of applause on the soundtrack, it is revealed as precisely the film we are seeing in the moment we are seeing it.

Unlike his colleagues Shah and Mirza, Ahuja chose not to go to the NFDC for financial support, opting instead to 'put [his] neck on the line', to make this into a 'test for oneself that [what] one believed in was what one was doing'. He also chose, with remarkable faith in posterity (especially given the litany of unmade films scarring his protagonist), to make it at his own cost in 35 mm instead of the blown-up 16 mm format in vogue.[3] He did this because he found the entire NFDC procedure – of 'giving them eight copies of your script with bank draft for so many rupees and certificate in triplicate and fill out an application form in triplicate'[4] – to be simply a way of thrusting humiliation in one's face.

-3

In the early 1980s Manmohan Shetty of Adlabs acquired a machine for blowing up 16 mm negatives directly on to 35 mm prints, thereby reducing the overall production budget of a film by almost a quarter. It was the format of choice for most independent filmmakers at the time.

-4

Conversation with Ashok Ahuja on Zoom, 9 November 2020.

Aadharshila's basic format – arising phoenix-like from the exercise Ahuja had made as a student, and the debris of ideas, failed projects and unrealized ambition that follow both within and outside the production – is that of a work that refuses to die. It survived the muck and the mire from its original idea as a student project to the digital remastered iteration that Ahuja has been able to put together, again with his own resources, which he now shows me in his house. As I sit and watch this most recent avatar, the film itself turns – like *Agraharathil Kazhuthai*, like Ajay's realized–unrealized ambitions, like the hundreds of films that were imagined, conceived, started and not finished, or finished and never shown, or shown if at all to a tiny festival audience before being consigned to celluloid decay – into a kind of evanescent, uncanny object defined primarily by the simple unarguable fact that it *exists*. All these films, made and unmade, are in one way or another a part of the 'new cinema' movement. Some were more directly affiliated with the 'national cinema' that the NFDC had sought to create. Most others were either self-produced, like Ahuja's labour of love, or financed by friends or family, such as Abraham's sister. Few sought any national role.

In their stubborn endurance, the surviving films became in 2015 a testimony, a warning even – of the horrors of their time that they captured, and the way they survived a technological holocaust – that fed Abraham's sermon on the mount that things were not about to go well.

What the Camera Saw

India was still under Emergency rule when Kundan Shah graduated. There weren't many opportunities for paid work. There was 'no television, the film industry ... we didn't want to join, we were very clear because you will be seventeenth ... that time Manmohan Desai had seventeen assistants. Somebody tried to put me there and I realized I would be the eighteenth assistant there.'[5] There was the odd documentary commission from Films Division 'if you were lucky'. Once you had decided that you weren't going to join the film industry, you knew things would get sticky.

So Shah and three of his batchmates – Ravi Ojha (the same Ojha who had interviewed Ghatak in *Film Miscellany*), Rajendra Shaw and Gopal Singh Golan – decided they would start a 'cinema commune'. The commune didn't have much of an idea of what it was going to look like or do. They settled in Hyderabad at the suggestion of their editing head, K. Ramachandra Rao, where – inspired by the 'conscientization' movement of Paulo Freire, Padmaja Shaw tells me – they began visiting slums and photographing living conditions, to 'create self-awareness in the communities on sanitation, education etc.'.[6] Occasionally they did commissioned government films on health and education; they documented the 1977 Andhra Pradesh cyclone; they made an advertising film for a soft drink named Nova Cola.

Shah was the first to leave. He returned to Bombay. Gopal Singh too soon left. Ojha and Shaw stuck it out for a bit longer before Ojha too returned to Bombay, where he would assist Shah and Mirza when they began *Nukkad*. Shaw stayed on, and in 1981 his fortunes turned as he transformed the old commune into the Centre for Development Communication, making visual aids with photographs, slide and tape presentations, and printed graphic material like flip charts and strip charts, for organizations and cooperatives working with farmers, weavers, mine workers and plantation workers.

In 1977, the Commune – or what was left of it, namely Ojha and Shaw – started a photo studio that they named Photofare. It was Shaw's idea, given his investment in still photography, that they might as well earn some money on the side doing commercial work. But it was to prove too much. And so it was that one night, when Ojha visited his old friend Shah in Bombay, he told him all about Photofare and how they were (or were not) managing.

Shah was married by then but his wife was away, so the two spent the night in his house talking. As the grimness of the struggle flooded their conversation, it became funnier and funnier. Shah was at that time trying to write a script of his own that remade a

-5

All quotes from Kundan Shah are from a long and extraordinary conversation included in *Jaane Bhi Do Yaaron*, Disc 2, Director's Perspective, NFDC/Cinemas of India, 2012.

-6

Email exchange with Padmaja Shaw, 5 and 9 September 2020.

celluloid master's canonical work, as was the approved style. It was Kurosawa's postwar tragicomic romance, *One Wonderful Sunday*. Shah had not seen Kurosawa's film but was nevertheless trying to relocate the bittersweet romance, set in Occupied Tokyo, of a young couple spending a day together trying to make thirty-five yen last as long as possible, in present-day Bombay. But he suddenly said to Ojha, 'I think I can see a film in this. I want to attempt a film on two photographers.' *JBDY* happened 'by very ... what you call chance kind of circumstance'.

—

It was more than a film. It became an extended filmmaker's hack. Its plot is very well known, partly because summarizing its 'story' usually leaves out everything of significance. It is about two photographers named Vinod Chopra and Sudhir Mishra. The actual Chopra was of course Shah's batchmate, and although his directorial career was well on its way with an Oscar nomination for a short film (*Encounter with Faces*, 1978) and a feature (*Sazaa-e-Maut*, 1981) financed in part by his then father-in-law, Chopra took upon himself the responsibility of being *JBDY*'s Production Controller. The actual Mishra, credited with co-scripting the film, was not officially an Institute student, but his brother Sudhanshu was, and he would begin his career as part of the team: assisting both Vinod Chopra and Saeed Mirza in their respective productions.

And so it was that Ravi Baswani and Naseeruddin Shah ended up playing Vinod Chopra and Sudhir Mishra playing Ravi Ojha and Rajendra Shaw. This relay extends not only to those in the film but to all those who actually made it and to their friends, as one contends with Shah's personal conviction that *JBDY* miraculously made itself. He insisted on crediting everyone who was involved with the film – Mishra has, for example, often disowned his script credit saying it was Shah's film in every way – which included multiple friends with no money and lots of time, for 'there was not much else to do' but dream up big ideas, write scripts, remake Antonioni and Kurosawa, hope that someone somewhere would put up the money.

Although the Cinema Commune was officially over, much of its informal sociality continued. Shah lived at the time in a tiny

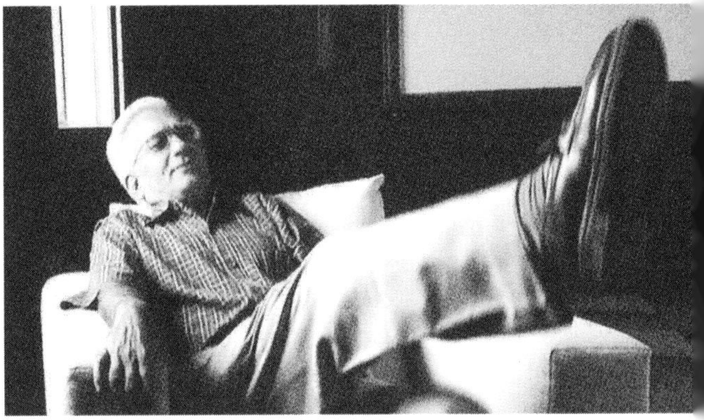

Kundan Shah describing Parker, the rationing officer. From **Jaane Bhi Do Yaaron,** Disc 2, Director's Perspective, NFDC/ Cinemas of India, 2012.

apartment in Byculla, where friends often stayed over, and where he was holed up with dialogue writers Ranjit Kapoor and Satish Kaushik as they hammered *JBDY* together. Every other day, when they felt they had written enough dialogue, Kapoor and Kaushik would play Vinod Chopra and Sudhir Mishra for the real Vinod Chopra who dropped by with Renu Saluja to hear what they had written. What they wrote about was themselves, each other, their friends, their unmade films – and literally what they saw around them. Shah was at the time the 'building secretary' of the cooperative housing society in which he lived, and when 'gutter water (began) dripping into the drinking water tank', he was tasked with the responsibility of doing something about it. Cement rationing was in force and he needed ten bags to get the tank repaired, so he went to a 'rationing officer ... I remember his name now also, his name was Parker, and he was sitting in front of me on his table and putting his feet like this, and his shoe staring at me,' Shah raises his feet in the air, 'you know, in my face, and he says, "So what, *yaar*, half of Bombay is drinking gutter water."' Both the extended references in the film to cement scarcity and the 'gutter' metaphor come from that. Everyone knew that 'the struggle was going to be grim'. 'There was a lot of anger, frustration, all things I was living through and what you are reading in papers, and you know, Antulay was Chief Minister at that time, and you were hearing that builders and some kind of ...'. Shah's voice trails off. 'May be true, may be not true, all those things came [into the film].'

To be able to make a film such as this, 'you have to come down to that level'. 'You can't make *JBDY* in a thirty crore budget, it can't take the weight.' 'It has to be done on that level. Because you are doing everything to fail. Because you can almost say, we had the freedom to go wrong, we had freedom without any responsibility.'

There was of course that juvenile 'anything-is-possible' idealism attached to controlling the celluloid apparatus: of being one of the big boys now. The very fact of striking a print, the arrival of a release positive, and its actual screening in a proper auditorium with proper equipment and good projection, was a career landmark. Completion was an end in itself. *JBDY*, and indeed the Yukt Film Cooperative's *Ghashiram Kotwal* (1976), Ketan Mehta's *Holi*, Ashok Ahuja's *Aadharshila*, Kamal Swaroop's *Om Dar-b-dar* (1988), Sanjiv Shah's *Hun Hunshi Hunshilal* (1992), all seemed at some stage of their making like they might remain incomplete. It was an underlying assumption with first-time filmmakers that when you got a chance to make your film you had to make the very most of it, for it was written in the stars that you would never get another.

Some filmmakers had long careers. Others never made a second film. None, however, outgrew their debuts. Having entered this space, like 'Vinod Chopra' and 'Sudhir Mishra', you had to follow the film as though with horrified fascination and see what the gruesome celluloid image had captured. Whatever it was, it opened up something otherwise inaccessible, a record developed in spite of and beyond the control of its makers: a cinema as though with a mind of its own, the one thing about it that Khosla and Hidayatullah most feared.

Our Films, My Film: Homosociality, Batch and Collective

In 1954 Ritwik Ghatak proposed a 'thesis' to the Communist Party of India. He asked that some forms – stage and drama, music and singing, ballet and dancing – be recognized as innately collective forms of artistic creativity. He proposed the starting of a 'Federation of Collective Arts'. It would be 'as heterogeneous as possible', and would be involved in both making and screening or staging art as an alternative to 'exhibition spaces ... controlled by big capital'.[7] It would 'create repertories and institutes to solve the issue of exhibition and training of artistes and craftspeople. He wanted to better understand who, or rather what, made such works happen. Its makers could be trade unions, professional groups, even amateur enthusiasts of a *mohalla* coming together once a year.' It would 'create repertories and institutes to solve the issue of exhibition and training of artistes and craftspeople'.[8]

Ghatak's Federation was never realized, but his collective concept has had a surprisingly long career in group projects assembled across ideological preoccupations to ask the very question that was at the back of his mind, namely, who makes a film? Ghatak himself was part of a loose group that bore some similarity to Shah's

-7

Sanghita Sen, 'Ghatak in the Shadows: Films that Struggled', in J. Fenwick, K. Foster and D. Eldridge, eds, *Shadow Cinema: The Historical and Production Contexts of Unmade Films*, New York: Bloomsbury Academic, 2021, p. 117.

-8

Ritwik Ghatak, *On the Cultural 'Front': A Thesis Submitted by Ritwik Kumar Ghatak to the Communist Party of India in 1954*, Kolkata: Ritwik Memorial Trust, 2000, pp. 42–43.

commune, in Calcutta and then in Bombay where three years after he wrote that proposal, an independent 'Film Group' made *Musafir* with Bimal Roy's support.

—

Since Ghatak's bold proposal of 1954 there have been at least three generations of film collectives, revealing a surprising consistency of preoccupations. There were the 16 mm collectives in the 1970s. Then there were the post-Emergency video collectives of the 1980s. And finally, there have been several media collectives formed mainly around digital practices in the early 2000s. Each era has been defined by the technology that enabled them.

In 2011 the Bhopal-based Ektara Collective echoed, across a historical ocean, both Ghatak and Shah, when they wrote in their founding document that 'working through a collective process ... means ... that everyone is invested in the whole idea even while they do what they are specifically doing or interested in doing'. There is a 'centralization of thought and decentralization of work', so that everyone is responsible for the process in its entirety even if not everyone makes every decision. 'Maybe not everyone will be interested in doing everything, but at least some will be and will shoulder the responsibility whether together or in turns. The others will add what they can.'[9]

Many loose principles of similar vintage prevailed in 1967, when John Abraham left the FTII and gravitated to Madras in search of opportunity. Abraham hung out with K.G. George and P.A. Backer in a place that locally came to be known as 'Poona House', while looking for the elusive producer to back his ideas.[10] When he finally found his producer, a film journalist pen-named Minnal who agreed to produce *Vidyarthikale Ithile Ithile*, Abraham assembled a team of campus batchmates. 'Our shooting unit entirely consisted of Film Institute graduates', says the film's cinematographer Ramachandra Babu. Babu was still a student but with some free time since the 1971 acting course strike was under way and the Institute was closed.[11] 'Director John, scriptwriter M. Azad, editor Ravi and sound recordist Devadas [who] was working in the Chitraleka Film Cooperative in Trivandrum and ... used to come and join us with

-9 Rinchin and Maheen, 'Collectivizing Cinema: The Story of Ektara', EktaraCollective.in, January 2017.

-10 V.K. Cherian, 'John Abraham and the Socio-Political Contexts of New Cinema in Kerala', *Sahapedia*, 8 June 2018.

-11 All quotes are from Ramachandra Babu's personal blogspot, entry made on 6 June 2013, updated August 2017.

the Nagra Recorder', since, at that time, 'sound recordists at Madras were reluctant to use a portable recorder'.

As they lived together, worked, ate, drank and got into various escapades, they also gradually turned into (from Babu's description) a loose and increasingly anarchist, essentially *male*, collective. In the process – inaugurating a mode that Abraham would later internalize with *Amma Ariyan* – events off- and on-screen began to merge.

The moment of repudiation arrived when the group, which had become increasingly alienated from *Vidyarthikale Ithile Ithile*, decided one day that they could no longer claim ownership of the film. And so they agreed to formally disown the film and, further, to insert their rejection into the film itself. They wrote a scene in which, says Babu, 'myself, the cameraman, editor Ravi, script writer Azad, and other technicians sit in a smoking den and express our dislike for the film'.

Abraham's dissenting scene was edited out by its producer from the version of the film that was eventually released, and so there is only one still photograph that exists of the scene. Ramachandra Babu identifies those in it as 'Ravi ... at extreme right and myself sitting on the left. The person lying in the lap of John is Kasturi Ramachandra Murthy [who was] my batchmate from the Film Institute and had worked as associate cinematographer. ... I am not very sure of the other two persons ... one of them may be Kuthiravattom Pappu.'

Thirty years on, cinematographer Saumyananda Sahi echoes Kundan Shah when he is asked if he had ever worked as an assistant on a film. He says no. This is because where he comes from there is an 'unwritten obligation' that students have to 'each assist on the projects of fellow students – within as well as across batches'. What is required is not 'halfhearted help, but trustworthy and fully committed teamwork', for the 'person carrying the tripod up the mountain is an integral part of the team ... because the sun never waits'.[12] This commitment is far more important to him than assisting someone in the industry.

'Narrative is fascist by its very nature'

A rather less anarchist, more macho and more articulated socialist vision brought together fourteen primarily male FTII students – comprising the majority of the second- and third-year batches – in

-12 'Soumyananda Sahi: in a chat with a cinematographer', *FTII People*, 4 November 2019.

Facing page
John Abraham's **Vidyarthikale Ithile Ithile** (1971). The filmmaker and his entire crew disown the film and stage their stoned-out repudiation inside the film itself.

Overleaf
Ghashiram Kotwal (1974) lists directors, actors, cinematographers, sound recordists and editors in single file as **tantradnya** (or **technicians**), erasing all professional designations.

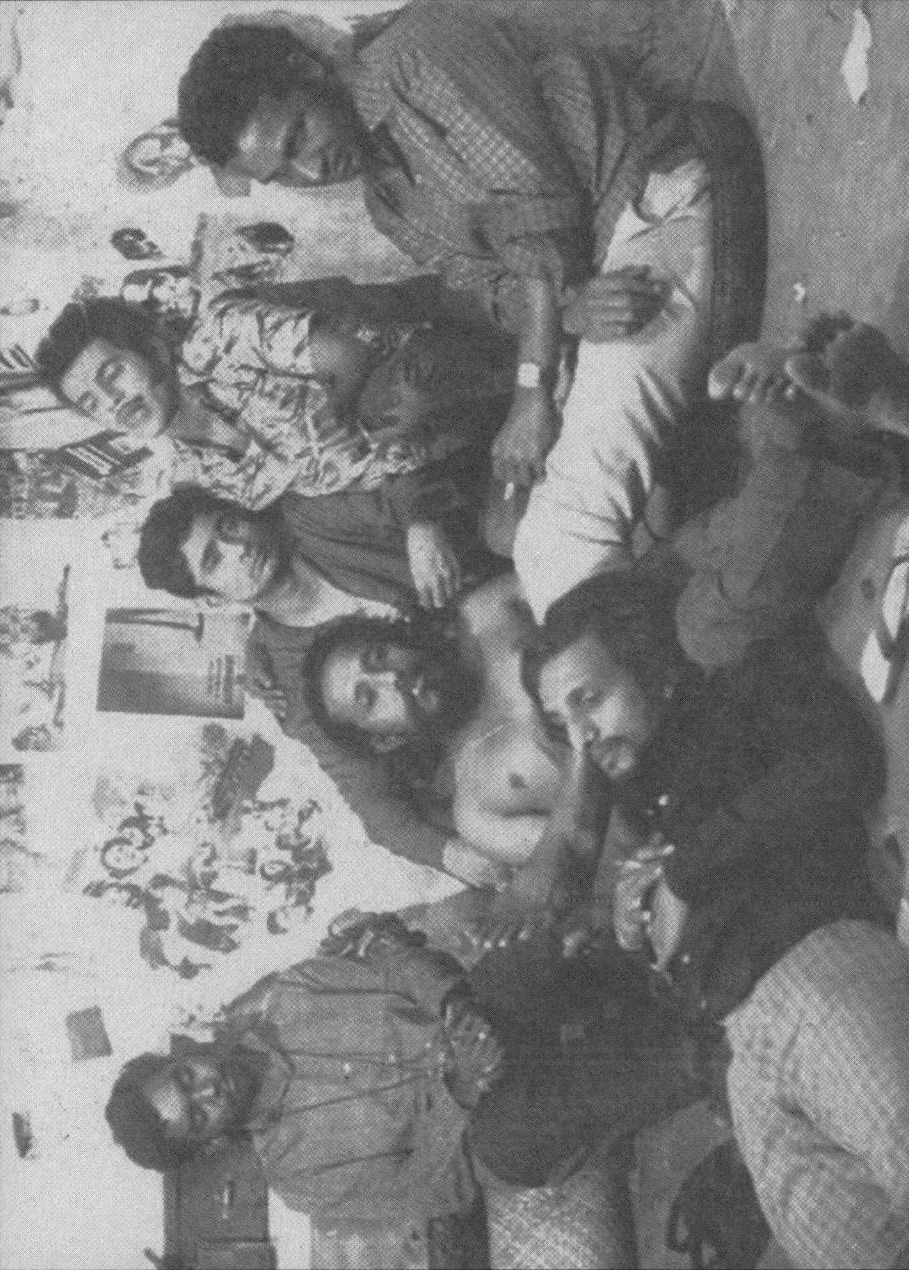

तंत्रज्ञ

अ. म. पद्मनाभन

अशोक त्यागी

अशोक शुक्ला

ओम पुरी

कमल स्वरूप

कमलेंद्र मंडल

कृष्णन् हरिहरन्

बिनोद प्रधान

मणी कौल

मनमोहन सिंह

विनय श्रीवास्तव

वीरेंद्र सैनी

रविंद्र गुप्ता

राजेश जोशी

सईद अख़्तर मिर्ज़ा

हितेंद्र घोष

1975 into another collective. If the original Nehruvian purpose of the cooperative had been economic, to mediate the more equitable relationship between state and market, the Yukt Film Cooperative claimed an economic imagination that was no less significant. Yukt's members spoke with some fervour of the conditions of the industry, the need to support its workers, the need for alternative distribution.

They now made a claim that they would transform the cinema's very relationship to the people with an 'epic' mode of filmmaking. This mode had a definite socialist genealogy informed by Eisenstein and the Soviets. But it also tried to recoup, from the same socialist approach, a proletarian storytelling tradition taken from medieval saint-poets such as Chokhamela – to whom an entire sequence in the film is dedicated – and the 'low' cultures of popular art. It would be an artisanal mode now in the people's hands, and it would redefine how films are made by redefining who they are truly for.

To realize what they considered the originary purpose of a collective, Yukt made a radical internationalist departure. To Eisenstein and Brecht, they added the lineage of the New York-based Film-Makers' Cooperative founded in 1962 by Jonas Mekas and Stan Brakhage. In all probability, the connection was made by Mani Kaul with the Vision Exchange Workshop (VIEW) of which he had been a key part.

There is a possible formal connection between VIEW's interest in ideas of randomness, chance and what Nancy Adajania calls the 'aleatory throw of the dice', which she traces to Akbar Padamsee's interest in John Cage, architect–musician Ianis Xenakis and Robert Rauschenberg.[13] An equally significant connection may have been with what Annette Michelson has called the 'artisanal mode' of filmmaking. Both Brakhage and Hollis Frampton worked directly on the material of celluloid, in their case, 16 mm positive picture stock without sound. They had made it into an art material, says Michelson, so as to reclaim control of the 'rationalized division of labour in industrial production'. The Film-Makers' Cooperative's 'modesty of means and the constriction of exhibition choices' had been converted to advantage to 'rethink the medium of film itself'.[14] VIEW's most explicit experiments in this 'artisanal' mode were Nalini Malani's short films on super-8 reversal stock, digital versions of which have become recently available, as well as her cameraless

-13

Nancy Adajania, 'Zigzag Afterlives: Film Experiments from the 1960s and 1970s in India', Camden Art Centre, November 2020.

-14

Annette Michelson, 'Frampton's Sieve', *October*, vol. 32, Cambridge, Mass.: The MIT Press, 1985, p. 153.

experiments working directly on celluloid material.[15]

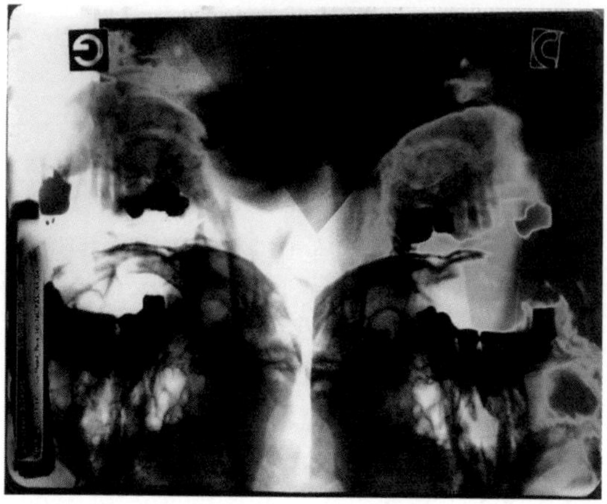

Damaged Survivors (1970, collage and photogram): montage by Nalini Malani built upon x-rays found in a local hospital.

Yukt's nod to the artisanal mode in *Ghashiram Kotwal* was to abolish the distinction between director, cinematographer and other technical credits. All those who worked on the film were alphabetically listed as technicians (*tantradnya*), and another thirty-six as artists (*kalakaar*). The only professional credits were to the original playwright, Vijay Tendulkar, the original music composer, Bhaskar Chandavarkar, and the costume designers, Nachiket and Jayoo Patwardhan. It is generally assumed however that Mani Kaul, K. Hariharan, Saeed Mirza and Kamal Swaroop took charge of different sections of it, and that there were yet other directors involved (like Nandan Kudhyadi), apart from two sound designers (A.M. Padmanabhan, Hitendra Ghosh) and three cinematographers (Virendra Saini, Binod Pradhan and Manmohan Singh).

In October 1979, Saeed Mirza outlined some of Yukt's experimental concerns at a small workshop-seminar. The topic of the seminar, convened by the journal *Social Scientist*, was 'Marxism and Aesthetics', and it was the first of many such held at artist Vivan Sundaram's house in Kasauli.[16] Mirza himself had just completed his first feature film, *Arvind Desai ki Ajeeb Dastaan*, Yukt's second and eventually final production. This seminar was dedicated to an ambitious internationalist aesthetic project for the arts. The idea, as playwright and academic G.P. Deshpande described it, was to discuss 'specific, concrete conditions and ... the context of practice' in India. Leading the way was dance practitioner Chandralekha with a manifesto-statement that returned to the pre-classical, even tribal, origins of 'national' dance forms such as Odissi and Bharata Natyam, to unveil a decade-long project that would revolutionize contemporary dance. Architect Deepak Kambuj proposed a turn to 'Commune-Architecture' that would make all of Indian society into a 'single office and a single factory, and a single field, with equality of labour and pay'. Geeta Kapur detoured into the Soviet Union and into Germany, into Brecht and Lukács, opening out what the

-15

In Nalini Malani's retrospective, *You Can't Keep Acid in a Paper Bag*, at the Kiran Nadar Museum of Art, New Delhi, 2014, she showed several of her early 1970s experiments, such as the films *Utopia* and *Dream Houses 1/2*, in 8 mm celluloid reversal stock, as well has her 'cameraless' collages and photograms.

-16

The proceedings of the seminar were published across two issues of *Social Scientist*: vol. 8, no. 89–90, December 1979–January 1980, and vol. 9, no. 98–99, September–October 1980.

realism–modernism dichotomy might mean to us. Kalpana Sahni returned to Mayakovsky and Meyerhold, to futurism, constructivism and suprematism.

Mirza seemed sufficiently inspired to not just add the cinema to that list, but indeed place it at its very top.[17] It was here that he produced his much-quoted 'basic rule', that

> a certain kind of cinema exists because a certain kind of state exists. If one wants to change the nature of the state, one needs to change the nature of the cinema.

He used constructivist imagery as he spoke, with wonder and animation, of a complex and all-consuming apparatus that included

> film stock, cameras, laboratories where chemicals, temperatures and densities; optics, wide-angle, telephoto, deep focus, fast and slow lenses; the science of acoustics, microphones, mixers ...

all of which would be used to make cinema that would exist in

> a dark auditorium. The curtain goes up. The image is on the screen. Colour, music, sound, the close-up magnifying a face 500 times, a gripping story, the audience identifying with the characters at the dream level, sharp cutting to underline the psychological or dramatic tension. Sound overlaps to jerk you upright. Every element used to destroy your sense of yourself as a viewer and convert you into an unthinking participant.

Mirza now opens up a 'vast new area' unfolding before the filmmaker. 'Technology is at the service of art', but unless you are careful, technology *can itself become the content*, can take on an '*independent existence to swamp the medium*, mesmerize audiences with its sheer technique, elevate itself to the realm of magic, and eventually lead nowhere' (emphasis mine).

Mirza then proclaims his conclusion – that the 'dramatic, narrative form of the cinema' appears to be 'fascist by its very nature'. To overcome this dramatic mode, filmmakers needed to redefine the cinema itself. They had to return to 'colour, sound, light and shade, grain depth, time and space alteration' as the *material* of the cinema. This material would now set up a challenge to the spoken word and the narrative style would allow the cinema to 'break free from the shackles of the story, plot or narrative and discover a reality which is inherent to the very nature of the medium itself'.

-17 Saeed Akhtar Mirza, 'Outlook for the Cinema', *Social Scientist*, vol. 8, no. 89–90, December 1979–January 1980, pp. 121–25.

By the mid-1970s, the collective – and its specific FTII batch-driven homosociality that Soumyananda Sahi insists is a serious and defensible way of making a film – had come up against its official state variant, the film *cooperative*. In 1965, Adoor Gopalakrishnan, Kulathoor Bhaskaran Nair and K.P. Kumaran founded Chitralekha, a cooperative, with a government loan of Rs 15 lakh. At the very time that Abraham was staging his ganja-soaked repudiation of *Vidyarthikale Ithile Ithile,* Chitralekha had grown to become a 'huge establishment' (writes V.K. Cherian), with a membership comprising the who's who of Trivandrum, a Laurie Baker-designed studio complex including a recording theatre, a processing laboratory and editing facilities, with plans for an artists' village.[18] Chitralekha managed to produce three feature films including Gopalakrishnan's acclaimed *Swayamvaram* and *Kodiyettam*, a commissioned film on family planning, and twenty-five documentaries. It also entered film distribution.

In a way that the student batches looking to work together appear not to have quite figured out, Chitralekha was a cooperative *as against* a collective, closer to a developmental intervention that several state governments had put in place for collective marketing in agriculture, housing, handicrafts and dairy. From the 1950s, cooperatives of small peasants, artisans and low-end producers had overcome the hold of moneylenders and middlemen in this way. Although there is little reference to *film* cooperatives in policy documents, by the mid-70s, several state governments were beginning to consider such organizations as an instrument to tackle a growing crisis around the cinema: that of black money.[19]

Major state support was given to Chitralekha by the Communist Party-led Kerala government of C. Achutha Menon, expanding over the decade to other cooperatives. P. Govinda Pillai, a CPI(M) ideologue, founded Janashakthi Films in 1977, initially in association with the Deshabhimani Study Circle and later as a formally registered society. Janashakthi began as a distribution outlet for several 'award-winning' films, including by Mrinal Sen, Ritwik Ghatak, B.V. Karanth, Girish Kasaravalli, P. Lankesh, Shyam Benegal and others, which it screened in noon shows at Ernakulam's Kavitha theatre and in festivals at Shenoys theatre. It distributed *Agraharathil Kazhuthai* and produced Abraham's next, the acclaimed *Cheriyachente Kroora Krithyangal*.

-18

V.K. Cherian, *India's Film Society Movement: The Journey and Its Impact,* New Delhi: Sage, 2017, p. 134.

-19

A report published by the National Institute of Public Finance and Policy (NIPFP) estimated that in the early 1980s, 'black' income stood at an astonishing 18–21 per cent of the country's overall GDP, and that – after 'real estate transactions and large scale manufacturing' – its third largest source was the film industry. The main reason for this was the stranglehold over film distribution by a small oligopoly of distributors and exhibitors. Shankar N. Acharya, *Aspects of the Black Economy in India*, New Delhi: NIPFP, 1986, p. 299.

In July 1979, a seminar took place at FTII titled 'Problems and Prospects of Film Cooperatives', organized by the National Cooperative Union of India. By then India had thirty-nine registered film cooperatives across eight states, led by Assam and Maharashtra with twelve each, and Orissa with eight. There was considerable confusion as to what the term meant, and how its official meaning might separate a cooperative from a collective masquerading as one.

Ketan Mehta, who set up the Sanchar Film Cooperative which made *Bhavni Bhavai* with an NFDC loan, outlined several large ideas that seemed to straddle both worlds: in an essay he wrote jointly with A.M. Padmanabhan, he evokes some of Yukt's fantasies when he speaks of 'a network of independent film production, distribution and exhibition ... 16 mm circuit in rural areas ... complete film facility complexes ... a Federation of Film Cooperatives'.[20]

-20 Ketan Mehta and A.M. Padmanabhan, 'Getting Together', 'Is there a New Cinema Movement?', *Cinema-Vision India*, 1980, pp. 70–71.

The contentious problem remained the role of the film director. Many spoke at the 1979 workshop of how everyone wanted to make films but nobody was especially interested in the responsibilities of marketing and distribution. In the end, *Ghashiram Kotwal*'s elimination of individual directorial credit didn't have many takers. Mani Kaul himself concluded after the *Ghashiram* experience that 'a director's job cannot be shared', and indeed Yukt's next film, Saeed Mirza's *Arvind Desai ki Ajeeb Dastaan*, returned to the single author format, as did both *JBDY* and *Om Dar-b-dar*, as well as other films made in later collectives such as Odessa's *Amma Ariyan*.

Nevertheless, it is not difficult to conceive of all these films as being in some way within the artisanal mode, as possessing the same collective energy that Kundan Shah tried to credit to *JBDY* and that *Ghashiram Kotwal*'s list of *tantradnya* sought to formalize. They are all to some degree *about* those who are *in* them. Each has an expansive understanding of who 'made' the film. These are films that were either actually made on the campus (*Holi*), or accessing its resources (*Ghashiram Kotwal*), or centrally about the place (*Aadharshila*) or simply made in its spirit (*Om Dar-b-dar* and *Hun Hunshi Hunshilal*).

All of them transform the relationship between what's in and what's around the frame, bring their makers' offscreen worlds into their frames even as they go into the street, the bazaar and the village, asserting all the while the existence of their makers, their makers' friends and friends' friends, the campus merging into other spaces they knew and could inhabit.

Facing page
Ketan Mehta and A.M. Padmanabhan on film cooperatives, specifically on Sanchar, founded in 1979. 'Is there a New Cinema Movement?', **Cinema-Vision India**, vol. 1, no. 3, 1980.

Overleaf
The 1977 strike featured on the front page of **Screen**, 20 May 1977.

The 1977 Strike: The Urban Lumpen and Street Theatre

On 16 December 1977, the anarchist threat appeared to finally make good. It was as though the cinema had spilled out of the frame when students of the FTII *gherao*ed its Director, Jagat Murari. *Gherao*s had happened before – in 1975 the Secretary of the I&B Ministry, Jamal Kidwai, had been accosted by acting course students. This one was oddly definitive. The specific problem was with the integrated course, which the Institute wanted to shrink in length. By December the agitation had gone on for some six months.

This was the first of a series of post-acting course actions concerning issues that would plague the FTII for the next two decades: the academic syllabus, disciplinary specialization, the quality of teaching, access to the NFAI's holdings, the role of visiting faculty. It was also the first of an increasingly familiar set of battles over the very purpose of the place. What it would be remembered for, however, was less the issues and more the incidents of this particular day when the rabble finally entered its elite environs. The day, which included a major physical confrontation with Class III and Class IV employees, saw students (said a Director's note)

> indulg[ing] in gross misconduct ... smoking cigarettes and *bidi*s and shout[ing] 'resign, resign'. ... Deepak Duggal, Anil Zankar and Jill Misquitta sat on the window to the left of my table and kept on smoking and throwing smoke on me. ... Occasionally they broke into songs – *Sarfaroshi ki tamanna ab hamare dil mein hai* – also often they burst into sustained loud laughter and made insulting remarks – *Bade besharam hai: hame sharam aati hai* [Such a shameless director, we feel shame], twice Director, what will he do now?[21]

The *gherao* framed an entirely new way by which to define the obscene object that was the lumpenized FTII student. A 'senior student' was quoted in the Satish Candra Inquiry Committee describing the 'whoring, drinking and drug taking' while 'call girls and girlfriends including a girl hostelier ... are sometimes found in boys' rooms late at night'. The Teachers' Association, which had supported the students over the integrated course, would go on its own strike in November 1977. 'Provoked by the continuous

21
Memorandum of the Students' Association, Shri Satish Candra Committee, *Report of the Committee Appointed to Enquire into the Working of the Film and Television Institute of India*, New Delhi: Ministry of Information and Broadcasting, 1978, Section 3.48.

"Co-operation has failed, but Co-operation must succeed"

— All-India Rural Credit Survey, The General Report, 1955

For the very first time in July 1979, representatives of the film co-operatives in the country converged at the Film & TV Institute of India. The occasion: A seminar on 'Problems & Prospects of Film Co-operatives' organised by the National Co operative Union of India, the Vaikunth Mehta National Institute of Co-operative Management and the FTII.

The main advantage of a co-operative is that the liability is on an abstract body and no member is personally liable. There are today 39 co-operatives in 8 states, with Assam and Maharashtra having the largest number: 12 each. Next in order is Orissa with 8, West Bengal 3, (2 are reportedly defunct) and one each in Gujarat, Karnataka, Kerala and Rajasthan.

Shama Zaidi, one of the founder-members of the Navya Film Co-operative, started in Bangalore, 1978 said Navya hadn't made any contribution or served any purpose thus far. Navya, a co-operative like MUKT of Bombay, was constituted to form a parallel distribution network. But the competition from the commercial cinema was tremendous. Even film co-operatives like YUKT which went into production have been defeated — mainly due to the attitude of the FFC and the members' own disinterest. FFC is suspicious of film co-operatives. A loan is given to a commercial producer rather than a co-operative comprising art filmmakers.

Mani Kaul — of YUKT — felt that in a co-operative sharing the artistic responsibility created ego problems, "A director's job cannot be shared." Classification of responsibility on the technical side, he felt was absolutely necessary. Again beyond making films, the members were not interested in distribution or in building up audiences through the film-society movement.

K. Hariharan, also of YUKT, said when they approached the Registrar of Co-operative Societies in 1976, they were told 'the co-operative movement is not meant for films but primarily for agricultural products.'

"I feel the only co-operative functioning to some extent, says Shama, is Chitralekha in Kerala, an all-purpose co-operative formed in 1966 by Adoor Gopalakrishnan from FTII and his colleagues. It went about systematically creating audiences for better films by starting numerous film societies, publishing literature on films and holding seminars and festivals. This movement was supported by the Press. Now there are about 200 film societies in Kerala."

Those in the field are unanimous in quoting the Chitralekha experience as an example of what can be done. They struggled along with an occasional documentary or two, till they made *Swayamvaram* (directed by Adoor) with FFC aid, which won national awards (1973) and thereafter, overwhelming audience response. Before it gained national recognition, however, no distributor was willing to take it on, and Chitralekha entered the distribution field as well.

For the co-operative movement to succeed, it is felt, the State Governments and the NFDC must take real interest — strictly speaking, with their mutual co-operation. The West Bengal Government, for instance, is trying to set up a distribution co-operative. The National Co-operative Union of India has promised co-operative loans to make films to be shown in their own institutions like the Anand Milk Co-operative in Gujarat. (Incidentally, Shyam Benegal's *Manthan* was financed by 500,000 farmers of the Gujarat Co-operative Milk Marketing Federation Ltd.) Such loans, however, will have to come through a National Federation of Film Co-operatives, but such a body is yet to be established.

GETTING TOGETHER

by Ketan Mehta & A. M. Padmanabhan

CONSIDER that there is a consensus of opinion that the Indian film industry by and large restricts itself to producing trash; that Cinema is now a major force in shaping our culture and establishing its values and norms. The situation is, to say the least, dangerous. Allowing our cultural resources to be so grossly misused must stop. Expecting a change in the content of the films without a change in their modes and methods of production is naive. Hence a co- operative film sector, which is morally-responsible, socially-conscious and beneficial to both the audience and producer.

•

When the Indian film industry was in its infancy in pre- World War II days, it attracted many able and talented people. These entrepreneurs got together, built up studios like Prabhat, New Theatres, etc. All the staff and artists were salaried employees of the studio and the mode of operation was more or less co-operative. Films could be made with low budgets, the business was profitable and made available surpluses which could be re- invested for the development of facilities and production of more films. With the onset of war, increased money supply and the emergence of black market and black money things began to change.

•

"When Henry Wallace, then a presidential candidate recklessly proclaimed this to be the century of the common man, he was as wide off the mark as only an ambitious politician can be. This is still and will be to its bitter end, the century of the middle-man.

— Peter Ustinov ('Dear Me')

The profiteering and speculative interests soon recognised the capacity of the film industry to absorb black money, and turned it into a high- budget, extremely- speculative industry with middle- man piled on middle- man, each intent on grabbing the largest share of the cake.

This is how a new generation of filmmakers faces the film industry where

— all the means of production, distribution and exhibition are controlled by the commercial, speculative interests.

— relations of production are extremely exploitative.

— concern for quality is non-existent.

The scenario is grim. For a new generation of filmmakers all eager to start a newer wave, the options are few: surrender, sell-out, separate — or co-operate, and so, getting together.

The resistance to new entrants is highlighted by the case of *Shatranj Ke Khilari* where the release of the film was blocked by some distributors. If the vested interests can do this to a man of Satyajit Ray's stature, what they could do to other entrants is not hard to imagine.

•

We were all graduates from the Film & TV Institute of India. We were all technically trained filmmakers wanting to make films. We got together and formed the Sanchar Film Co-operative Society on Jan. 1, 1979 at Ahmedabad. It was a decision to try and find an alternative way of functioning.

Various film co-operative societies were already functioning in the country with varying degrees of success.

The Chitralekha Film Co-operative, started in Kerala in 1966, has come a long way after facing difficult times in the beginning. It had already produced two feature films, some documentaries and had successfully established itself with its own sound studios, and further plans of expansion.

On the other hand, YUKT, promoted by FTII graduates, after starting off well by making two feature films within a short span was facing litigation as both the films were unable to find distribution outlets.

We started off with a lot of enthusiasm, determination, know- how, but no funds. We soon found out the weather was rough, the going tough. We were learning, 'No bank gives you a loan unless you can establish that you do not really need it.'

We discovered that it was easier canvassing work as individuals rather than as a co-operative — Films Division and other Government agencies accepted our individual qualifications and credentials, but as a group our identity was dubious.

Even the (then) FFC demanded individual guarantees for the loan (for a script found worthy) in preference to the collective guarantee of the group. So that much for co-operation.

Sanchar had to establish its credentials and the only way to do that was by doing work. So we went ahead, took the loan from FFC and started on our first project A feature film in Gujarati, *Bhavni Bhavai*.

•

In July, 1979 the National Co- operative Union of India organised a seminar on the Problems and Prospects of Film Co-operatives. As the title itself suggests, the problems were greater than the prospects.

It was heartening to know that as many as 37 film co-operatives were already functioning in India. It was disheartening to find out that their impact as an alternative force was negligible.

The Government's policy towards the film industry was indefinite, its stand towards the role of film co-operatives was, to say the least, ambiguous — further compounded by red-tapism and bureaucratic hurdles.

The management of the co- operative was itself a formidable problem. When there are many pebbles in a pot, they rattle. There were hardly any precedents to guide us. So progress was through trial and error. Absence of any infra-structure or support-activities for the film co-operatives was yet another survival hazard. So was direct and cut- throat competition/ confrontation by the already established dream-merchants.

If the problems were grim, our dreams were brighter. We were dreaming of a network of film production, distribution and exhibition co-operatives to take care of the entire process of filmmaking. We were dreaming of an independent 16 mm cinema circuit in rural areas with the help of the already established co-operative mechanism and viewers' co-operatives.

We were planning for complete film facility complexes in the co-operative sector. We were planning to co- operate on the National level and form a Federation of film co-operatives.

The stage is set, the lights are out, we wait for the curtain to rise.

•

"If you are still living, never say never.
What is certain, isn't certain.
Things will not stay as they are — and
Never Becomes Before The Day Is Out."

— Bertolt Brecht ■

Regd. No. M 7727

SCREEN

Largest Certified Net Sales Among All Film Weeklies in India

Vol. XXVI: No. 35 MADRAS: FRIDAY MAY 20, 1977 PRICE 75 PAISE PAGES 28

INTRODUCING NEWCOMER

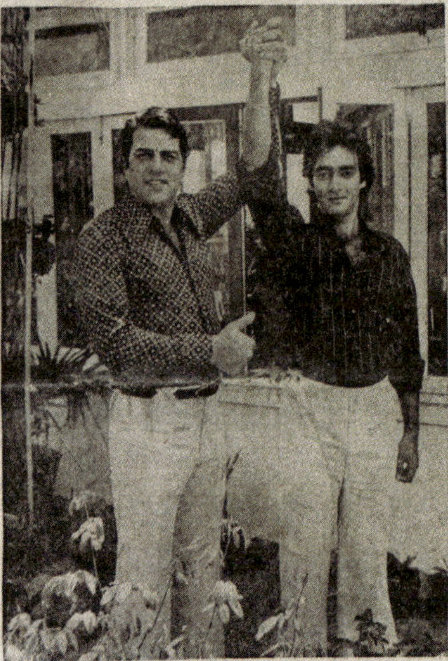

DHARMENDRA [illegible] introduces to "Screen" readers a young colleague, Dhruv, who makes his debut in a romantic role opposite Shabana Azmi in Arjun Hingorani's "Khel Khilari Ka" which also introduces two other talents, Shakti and Phandek, who are also diploma holders of the Film and Television Institute of India. Dharmendra, who heads the cast of "Khel Khilari Ka," himself made his debut many years ago with Arjun Hingorani's "Dil Bhi Tera Hum Bhi Tere."

TURMOIL AGAIN AT FILM-TV INSTITUTE

Students want integrated course retained

From Prakash Kardaley

POONA.

THE first and second year students of the integrated course of the Film and Television Institute of India, introduced in 1975, went on an indefinite strike last week to protest against the Institute's decision to do away with the integrated course from the coming academic session. The stalemate was continuing at the time of going to press.

These students are not apparently affected directly by this proposed change. They will continue to be in the integrated course, while those to be admitted this year would enrol themselves for different courses like acting, film direction, editing, photography and so on, as it used to be till 1975.

But their grievance is that they are the unfortunate victims of the Institute's experimentation with the pattern of studies there. Theirs will be the only two batches belonging to the integrated course.

And they are afraid that their prospects in the industry would be [illegible] affected as they would be [illegible] as those having undergone a "rejected" course.

The integrated course, introduced in 1975, following the recommendations of the Khosla Committee, comprises common studies on all disciplines for the first two years and specialisation according to one's aptitude and performance in the third year.

For the Institute, history has not repeated but has been reversed. It was a similar [illegible] strike by direction students who were irked by the non-co-operative behaviour of acting students three years ago which had triggered off a chain of events culminating in the introduction of the integrated course.

Now the students of this course had gone on strike to prevent the resumption of the old pattern.

"NO GLAMOUR" CRY

"We don't want glamour," their slogan says. [illegible]

[illegible]

SHUKLA'S HANDS

But the General Council, which [illegible]

[illegible]

"REMOVE MURARI"

They have also held Mr. Jagat Murari, Director of the Institute, responsible for this [illegible]

[illegible]

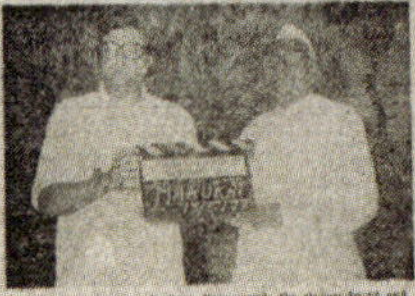

[illegible]

New disc firm's debut

CALCUTTA.

[illegible]

Ram launches political film

MR. JAGJIVAN RAM, [illegible]

[illegible]

Amol in "Kafan"

From Our Special Correspondent

CALCUTTA.

AMOL Palekar has been added to the cast of the Hindi version of Mrinal Sen's Hindi-Telugu bilingual in colour, "Kafan," based on the famous Premchand story of the same name. [illegible] in the Telugu version, will also appear in the Hindi version. Another member of the featured cast in the Telugu version is [illegible]

Mrinal is in Hyderabad, near where his month-long outdoor shooting programme will commence on May 23. Thereafter he will return to Calcutta to commence indoor shooting here. The film is scheduled to be completed in July.

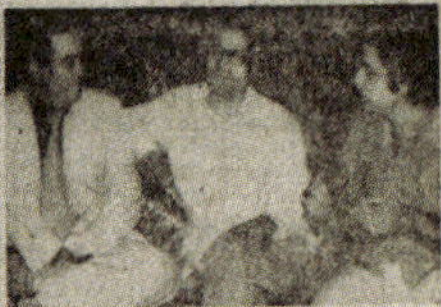

[illegible]

Mane to direct Shantaram film

[illegible]

COMPLETED

[illegible]

UTTAM IN CAST

[illegible]

New import policy: Kodak home use ban revived

[illegible]

NEW POLICY

[illegible]

(Continued on Page 4)

Court names panel

From Our Own Correspondent

NEW DELHI.

[illegible]

COMPLETE

[illegible]

IMPEC option modified

THE option given to the Indian Motion Pictures Export Corporation [illegible]

[illegible]

OPENS TODAY

[illegible]

Reviews

[illegible]

ragging of the first year students and abusive behaviour towards a warden and a teacher,' they 'sent a representation to the Director stating that it had become impossible for them to function with self-respect and dignity because of total absence of discipline among the students, as revealed in drunken behaviour, rowdyism and the use of offensive language against the teachers.' The teachers 'recommended rustication of three students and issue of warning to six others'.

1977 was also the year the Emergency was lifted. Its withdrawal brought in a new era of mass politics that contrasted sharply with the classic modes of organization idealized by official narratives of the freedom struggle. This was a 'lumpen' youth, one representing a 'revolt from the bottom and lower middle tiers of society, as also from the politicized elements of the middle classes'.[22] In 1979 the Janata government set up the Mandal Commission, inaugurating a decade of pitched battles over caste, often between the Scheduled Castes (SC) and a new economically powerful entity collectively named Other Backward Class (OBC). Rajni Kothari identifies a 'deadlock' here, a 'peculiar state of stagnation and exhaustion arising precisely out of so much action from so many opposing segments and sites that we have to evaluate the actual condition in which the mass of the people are placed'. 'Such conditioning perpetuates ... mass behaviour – from continuing drudgery to systemic exploitation.'

At the FTII itself, the problem turned into a single insistent question: What did the place teach that was worth studying? There was nothing that went beyond hands-on apprenticeship, as the Academic Council acknowledged in February 1975 when it said that 'in terms of ... knowledge of the whole medium of film, there is almost no difference between ... a photographer in the industry [who] starts off as a light-boy and a student who starts raw and after three years becomes a photographer'.[23] Specialization was, in direct conflict with the 'collective' mode, making 'inter-occupational mobility impossible', as 'direction and acting students ... have been left out on a limb when unemployed in their own special field'. By 1977 most people, including former FTII Directors Girish Karnad and N.V.K. Murthy,

-22

Rajni Kothari, 'Masses, Classes and the State', *Economic and Political Weekly*, vol. XXL, no. 5, 1 February 1986, p. 213.

-23

Cited by the Satish Candra Committee Report, Section 2.6.

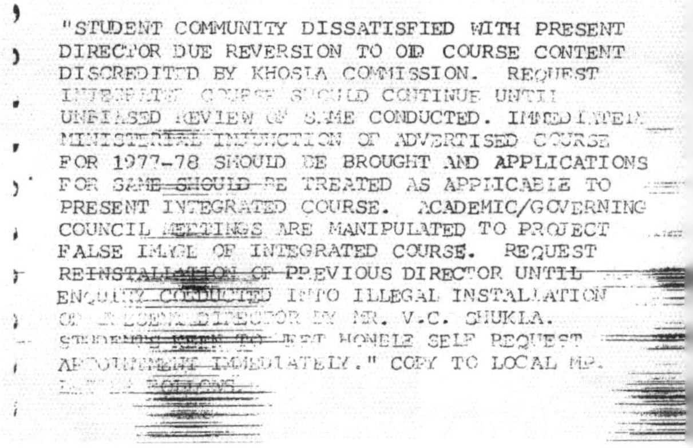
"STUDENT COMMUNITY DISSATISFIED WITH PRESENT DIRECTOR DUE REVERSION TO OLD COURSE CONTENT DISCREDITED BY KHOSLA COMMISSION. REQUEST INTEGRATED COURSE SHOULD CONTINUE UNTIL UNBIASED REVIEW OF SAME CONDUCTED. IMMEDIATE MINISTERIAL INJUNCTION OF ADVERTISED COURSE FOR 1977-78 SHOULD BE BROUGHT AND APPLICATIONS FOR SAME SHOULD BE TREATED AS APPLICABLE TO PRESENT INTEGRATED COURSE. ACADEMIC/GOVERNING COUNCIL MEETINGS ARE MANIPULATED TO PROJECT FALSE IMAGE OF INTEGRATED COURSE. REQUEST REINSTALLATION OF PREVIOUS DIRECTOR UNTIL ENQUIRY CONDUCTED INTO ILLEGAL INSTALLATION OF [illegible] DIRECTOR BY MR. V.C. SHUKLA. [illegible] HONBLE SELF REQUEST APPOINTMENT IMMEDIATELY." COPY TO LOCAL MP.

Telegram sent by the Students' Association to the I&B Ministry, 28 April 1977 (from the Satish Candra Committee Report).

and the best-known faculty member then on campus, Satish Bahadur (who was also secretary of the Teachers' Association), were in agreement with the students over the two-year integrated course. The main obstacle was Murari, adamant in his decision to bring it down to one year, and also to limit students' flexibility in choosing their later areas of specialization.

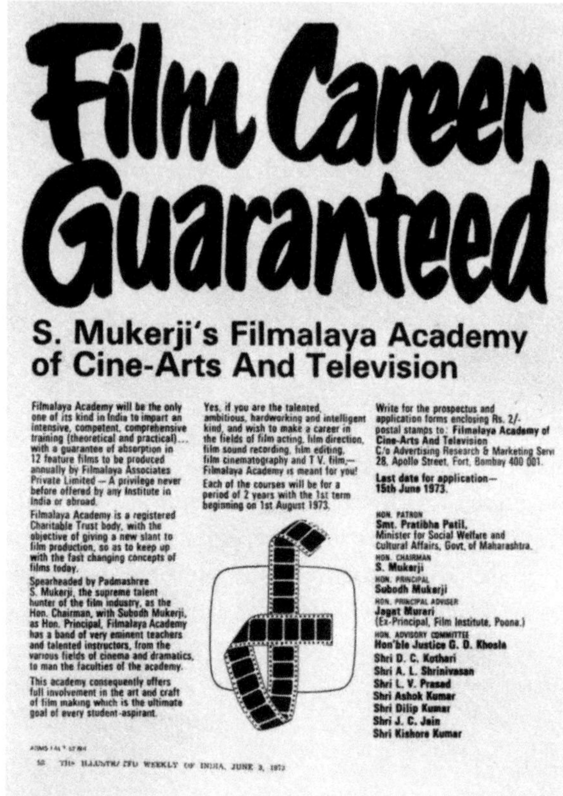

1973: the Filmalaya Studio, Mumbai, advertises an industry-friendly copycat film school, with Jagat Murari as honorary principal advisor **Illustrated Weekly of India**, 3 June 1973. Three years later, in 1976, Roshan Taneja, a professor of acting at FTII since its inception, walked out to start his own influential School of Acting in Mumbai, training generations of movie stars.

Although the Satish Candra Committee, like the Khosla Committee, was sympathetic to the students, what ultimately broke the deal was the lumpen. The Committee insisted on finding a motivated intentionality behind the crisis. Although it admitted that 'the students have suffered' and while it found 'their bitterness' understandable, the 'general academic mess' and 'total production collapse' could not be explained without recognizing 'definite vested interests' out to use these excuses as an 'effective argument against the Integrated Course and the present batch of students'. Departing from its general tone of neutrality, it began finger-wagging. 'In India,' it said, the 'so-called intellectual is far too removed from the grim realities of everyday existence as faced by millions of our countrymen.'

The Committee then accused the *students* of elitism, of setting up a 'barrier' separating the intellectual from the everyday. This barrier can 'be removed only if the student learns to work with his hands, to rely on his own efforts and to grapple with all the problems attendant in filmmaking at the basic, practical, realistic level'. Film, the Committee moralized, is a 'medium of such great financial hazards, and demands technical accomplishment of such a high order, that it has no place for lazy, slipshod, undisciplined and self-indulgent attitudes on the part of either the staff or the students'. 'Any assumption of a superior or elitist attitude to the craft ... should be scrupulously discountenanced.'

In many ways the representation of the time was shaped by *Holi*. Made as the outcome of a student workshop, *Holi* was a thinly disguised rendition of the events of December 1977. Shot primarily on the campus – and at its three most crucial locations, the boys' hostel, the Main Theatre and the student canteen – it tells of a day in an undergraduate arts college on which students wake up, many from a drunken stupor, to discover that their scheduled festival holiday has been cancelled due to a visit of the college founder. They further discover that their examinations have been postponed. They vandalize the campus and disrupt the founder's speech. There is an ongoing Class III employees' strike taking place outside the main gate. When the college principal (played by Om Puri, a clear reference to Murari) forces an upper-caste first-year student to reveal the names of the ringleaders, the student is ragged and tortured in a night-long Holi celebration that ends with the student's suicide. The next day, the entire student body is arrested and booked in a police station (as actually happened at FTII that very year, 1984).

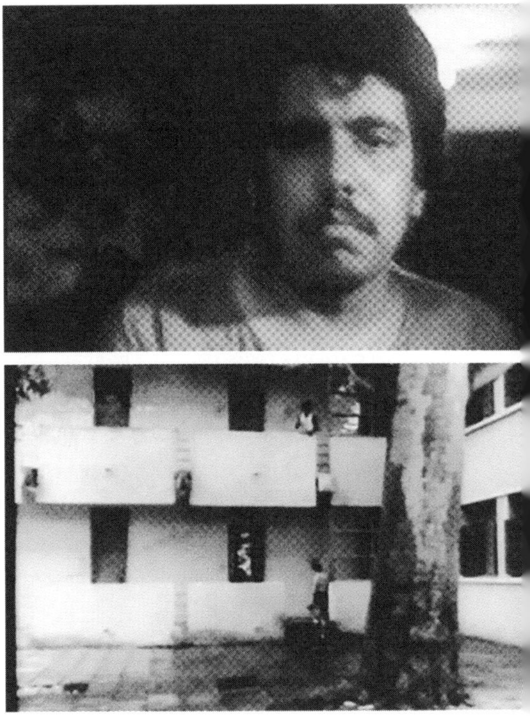

Ketan Mehta's **Holi** (1984), based on the 1977 strike. **Above:** the police interrogation; **below:** the boys' hostel.

Long Shot: Street, Theatre, Public Order

Holi was Mehta's second feature film after the much acclaimed *Bhavni Bhavai*, a folk tale on caste oppression, in part contextualized by the riots in Ahmedabad in 1980–81 around medical college admissions. *Bhavni Bhavai*, like *Ghashiram Kotwal*, was in the allegorical 'folk' mode favoured at the time both in theatre and film. It was made at a time when medical students in Ahmedabad, arguing for merit on campus to be the sole criterion for admission, led a major caste conflagration in which they were supported by government employees, professionals and landowning agricultural castes – an elite coalition dedicated to defining higher education as a walled academic garden of entrenched interests into which SC, ST and other lower castes were not permitted, on the ground that they did not possess the competence to do so.[24]

Placing *Holi* within the charged Mandal era, on the other hand, requires yet another connection to be made. *Holi* had a remarkable shooting strategy, a *plan-séquence* structure of extreme-long takes on

-24 See 'Ketan Mehta on Bhavni Bhavai', *Journal of Arts & Ideas*, no. 5, October–December 1983.

a perpetually moving hand-held camera mounted on a SteadiCam. Such continuous movement effectively displaced any moral centre that could hold the film together, or any ethical point of view from where to see it. There was no individual protagonist, but rather a collective body playing that role. As with *Aadharshila* and *Jaane Bhi Do Yaaron*, *Holi* too abolished the distinction between an inside and an outside – its cast, its makers and its audience as though blurred into a single overlapping entity.

As the filmmaker turned protester or, yet more dangerously, began inviting protesters into his frame, the film *regisseur* of the Abbas–Hidayatullah era, the former exemplar of responsible free speech, took a new turn as free speech itself increasingly came to be defined alongside the concept of *public order*. Public order had been absent in the original formulation of Article 19(2), and was added only later under the First Amendment Act, 1951. When it came in as the defining principle for restraint on free speech, it also brought in new legal challenges, such as how to understand the link between speech and order – and how to name the conditions under which speech caused any serious threat to public order.

Five years after *Holi*, the Supreme Court pronounced on the issue. It was not enough for speech to be merely incendiary. It had to have sufficient proximity to action to prove that it directly incited that action – was the 'spark in a powder keg'. If these conditions were met, preventive detention measures would come into play, as they increasingly did in this very time as Gautam Bhatia has shown.[25]

By the time Saeed Mirza made his first film, the epic classicism of the proletariat in *Ghashiram Kotwal* had been replaced by the need to take to the street, to repudiate the safe spaces of the art-house and bring the discredited 'lumpen' to the screen. Mirza says it took him four films and three different protagonists before he could finally come to the character that mattered the most to him – namely, Salim Langda. He also made *Salim Langde Pe Mat Ro* (1989) in the wake of the Bachchan era, at a time when the figure from the street had come to be incarnated by the extreme naturalism of Nana Patekar (*Ankush* and *Maficha Sakshidar*, both 1986) in stories that attributed to the tragic heroism of the lumpen, the moral authority of a nationalist freedom fighter fighting a second freedom struggle (*Krantiveer*, 1994).

Facing page
Mashup of Odessa Movies' pamphlet raising funds for **Amma Ariyan** (1984). A contribution of Rs 100 came for a share in the film's ownership.

Overleaf
'Activities Report' by Odessa Movies in the areas of Production, Distribution, Exhibition and Studies/Research. It simulates what a film cooperative might present to its donors/shareholders.

25 See Gautam Bhatia, 'Free Speech and Public Order', Centre for Internet and Society, 17 February 2016.

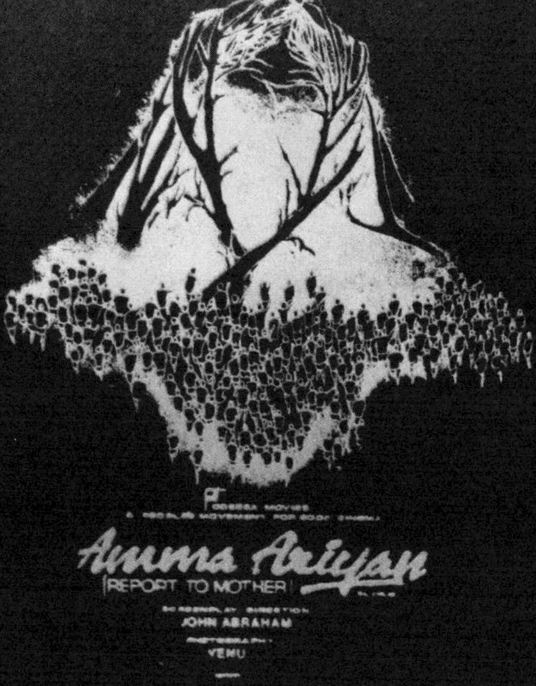

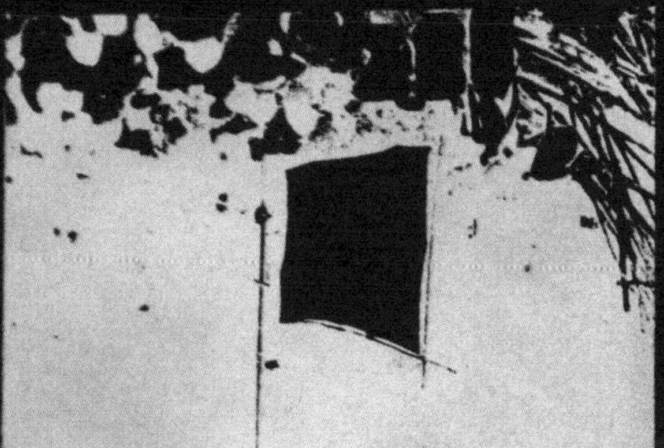

This film is the result of the efforts of thousands of people. The money came from the people in contributions of Rs.2 and Rs.10 and shares of Rs.100. All for creating a new socio-cine sensibility and culture.

odessa movies

odessa – A Movement of the People for Good Cinema

Sensible Cinema Meaningful Cinema and Purposeful Cinema

Activities In Cinema

ODESSA was formed in 1984 with a four fold programme in the medium of Cinema. The programme includes Production, Distribution, Exhibition and Studies and Research.

The ODESSA Activists with the actual participation of the people, have done much along these line of the programme, fulfilling the objectives set in each line during the last five years. The experience in cultivating the feeling of togetherness in purposeful activities, among the people, in encouraging indeed.

The Achievements in Five Years'

* Produced a Malayalam feature film **AMMA ARIYAN** (Report to Mother), directed by late John Abraham who lives still as the guiding spirit of ODESSA.
* The film was created on the strength of the participation of thousands of people with their contribution of Rs.25.10 100 etc.
* **AMMA ARIYAN** was honoured with the Special Jury Award for excellence in direction, in 1987, at the national level.
* This film has been exhibited in the International Festivals in London Berlin. Ankara, Paris, San Senastian etc.
* ODESSA Activists have screened this film in more than 1500 places, in the rural and urban India. We have developed 50 regular screening centres where regular discussions also take place.
* The purposeful and positive efforts of hundreds of people can reach out to thousands evoking a spirit of togetherness and creative adventure. This is not just a possibility but a daily experience shared by many. Thus ODESSA is essentially a Peoples Movement.

Exhibition/Distribution

* ODESSA screens and distributes selected good films in various languages and of various countries, in 16mm and Viedo, for creating a new cine sensibility among the people.
* ODESSA screening centres are spread over urban and rural people covering the tribal areas, coastal areas and slums. It covers educational and socio-cultural institutions and organisation's, hospitals and jails.
* ODESSA Activists carry projectors and films to far flung centres and screen them on roadsides and vacant lots. The shows, usually sponsored by local organisations or groups, are free to the public.
* ODESSA, at present, has ever 1000 screening centres in and out of Kerala.

In 1984, the proximate link between speech and action brought two autonomous aesthetic practices together. One, the ensemble performance, linked to the street or at least to street theatre. Two, a distilling of speech into the 'long take', usually a single shot over the duration of a 35 mm reel. Through the previous decade, the choreographed ten-minute *plan-séquence* had become a sign of cinematic virtuosity, the coming of age of a filmmaker. All the 'authorial' works of the time typically stamped their pedigree with at least one such virtuoso 'signature' shot – the complex crane sequence at the end of *Hun Hunshi Hunshilal*, the circular 360-degree pan in *Ghashiram Kotwal*, the semi-circular swivelling shot in *JBDY*.

Now, the long take *plan-séquence* took on a deeper meaning. It forged – unexpectedly – a link with the energies of several street theatre experiments taking place in India just then. *Holi* itself was made following a workshop on acting conducted in part by the doyen of street theatre of the time, Badal Sircar. In 1984, the same year as *Holi*, Odessa too marked its launch with the street play *Nayakali* in Fort Kochi, with Joy Mathew drawing explicit connections between both street and campus theatre and the political spectacle.[26] Sudhir Mishra credits his desire to enter film to the influence of Badal Sircar. Mishra had a theatre group in Delhi, the Workshop Theatre, where Sircar held workshops, and they had done two or three plays. It was all 'very idealistic': there was 'no notion of director': the seven to eight people who formed this group said 'there would be no director and so we will all, sort of, play the director'. 'In a sense, all those individuals tried to create something of their own', but the 'process was a way of opening up your head'.

-26 'Interview with Joy Mathew' by Jayan Shivapuram, *Bhashaposhini*, vol. 38, no. 8, August 2014, pp. 6–22; translated by Jenson Joseph.

What Really Happened at Antonioni Park

The pivotal moment in *Jaane Bhi Do Yaaron* is a curiously blank one – a 'nothing' moment in which the plot seems to be going nowhere. The protagonists appear to have no motivation left to take the story forward. There is only so much you can do with slapstick, Shah seems to be saying. The film deflates before you. Vinod Chopra and Sudhir Mishra stroll aimlessly in a park, and Sudhir finds a torn newspaper with an advertisement for a photography contest. They decide to enter the contest. Vinod, looking around for a nice picture, idly photographs a performing monkey holding up a mirror. When he develops that image in his dark room, he discovers that the camera – and the reflection in the monkey's mirror – may have captured something more than he had realized.

Jenson Joseph's detailed annotation of *Amma Ariyan* too records all that Abraham's camera captured. The story is told using multiple artists, activists and comrades appearing as themselves in Purushan's (Joy Mathew) journey to identify and reconstruct the life of a corpse.[27] Part of the film is documentary: a sequence at the Iringal quarry in Kozhikode recalls the plight of the worker Karuppusamy, whom we see at the beginning of this sequence talking to the camera and later to the group. He has lost his legs in an accident, and his appeal for help has been ignored by both the quarry owners and the trade unions affiliated to mainstream political parties.

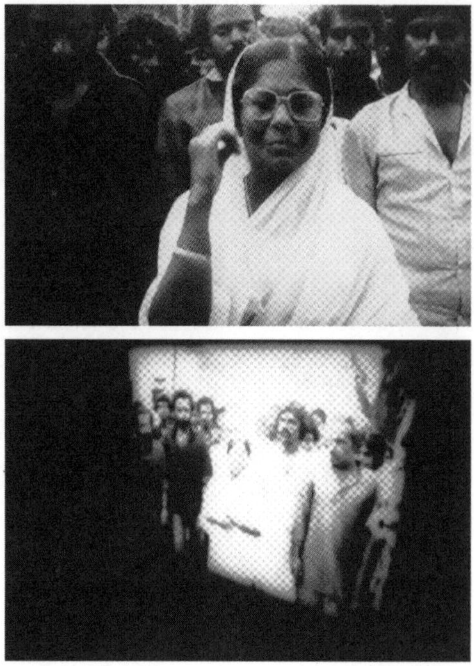

The film-within-a-film in John Abraham's **Amma Ariyan** (1984). The mother watches the film that we have seen.

Facing page
The crime scene in **Jaane Bhi Do Yaaron** (1983).

Overleaf
Collage of the corpse of the Municipal Commissioner (Satish Shah) in his funeral casket as it passes posters of New Indian Cinema films.

Other parts are elaborate reconstructions, such as a 'people's trial' conducted by the Janakeeya Samskarika Vedi (People's Cultural Forum) of medical staff outside the Government Medical College in Calicut. This space, says Joseph, has a political history, having been the location for several such trials of corrupt public officials all over Kerala: in this case, of a doctor known for taking bribes who was publicly 'tried' for his crimes. In the film, the protest leader Dr Rajan plays himself as he comes with Purushan to the mortuary to try and identify the dead body.

Celluloid enters *Jaane Bhi Do Yaaron* as though itself a character in the plot – as the film develops a mind of its own. As the duo develop and enlarge their print, they slowly glean from it the realization that the camera has recorded a murder: Tarneja's killing of the Municipal Commissioner, D'Mello.

What the viewer also sees is an explicit, overstated 'in'-joke/citation from Antonioni's *Blow-Up*. That night the two return to the park – known, in case the viewers haven't got it yet, as 'Antonioni Park' – where they discover further evidence of the crime. A bit later they actually stumble upon the corpse of the Municipal Commissioner, which, inside a maroon casket, takes on

-27
See Jenson Joseph's detailed annotation of *Amma Ariyan* at indiancine.ma.

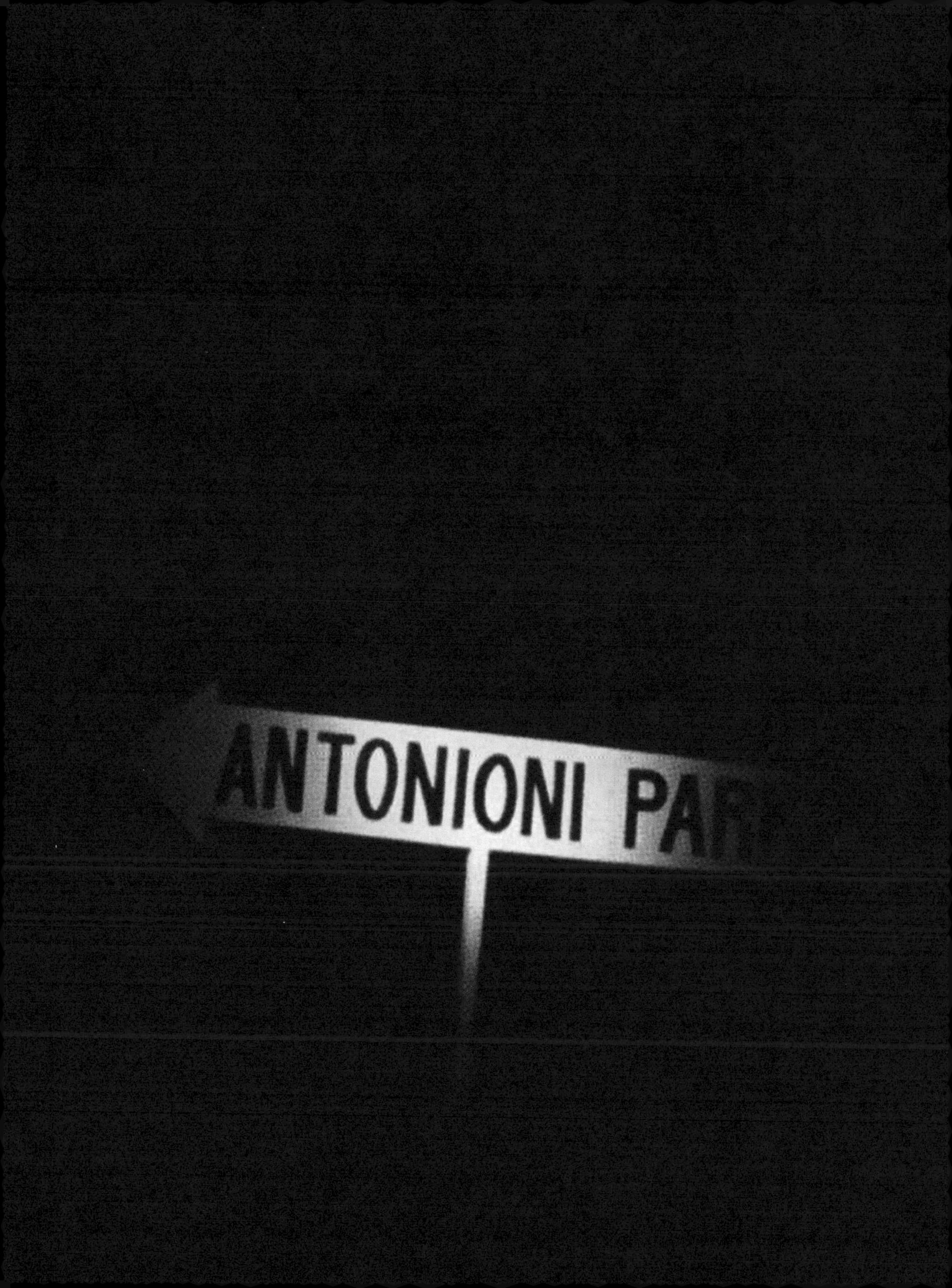
ANTONIONI PAR

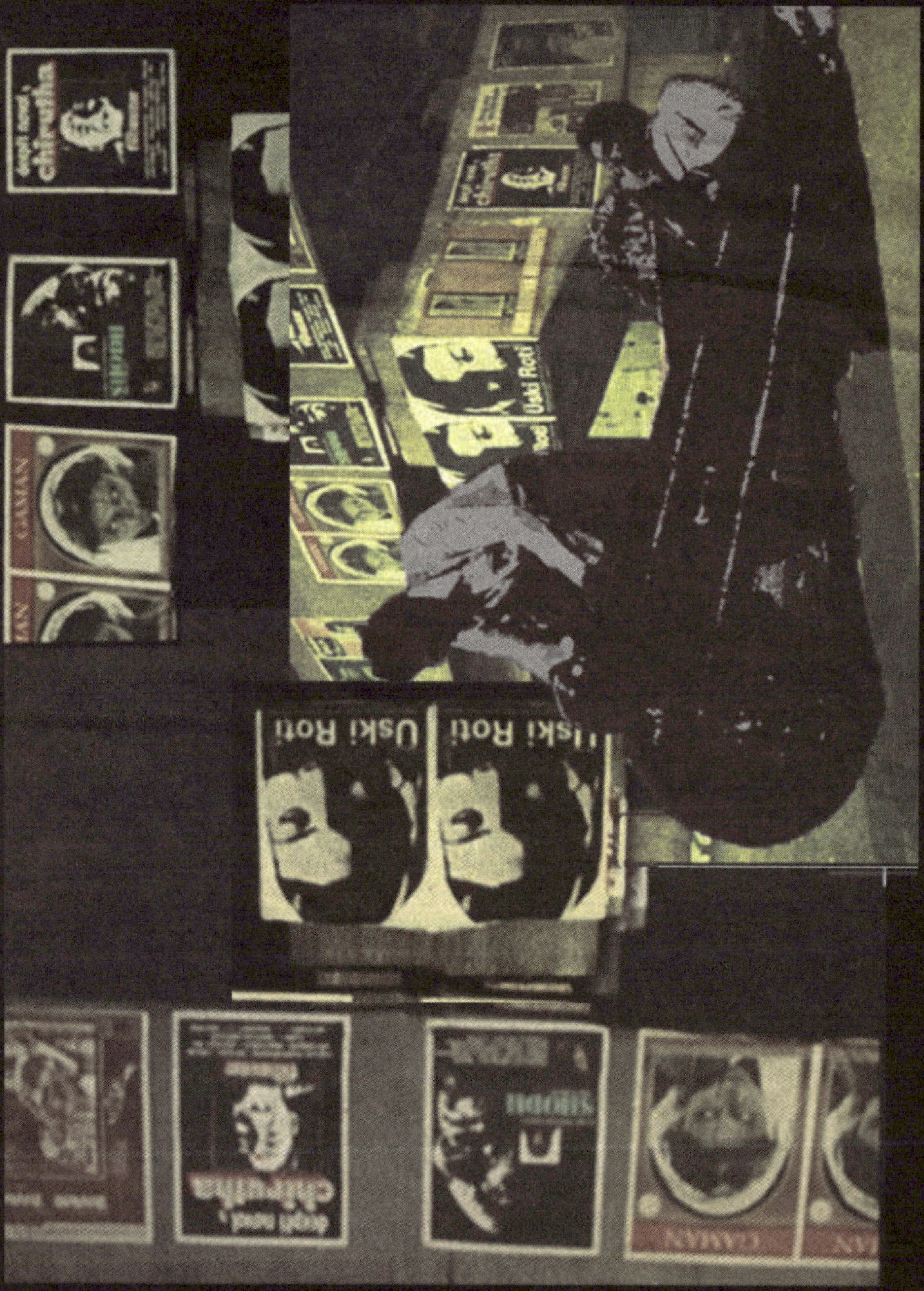
Uski Roti
Uski Roti
GAMAN

a life of *its* own as it gets wheels and winds through Byculla at night as multiple embedded signs come to the fore.

The corpse goes past movie posters of Mani Kaul's *Uski Roti* and Kumar Shahani's *Maya Darpan*, Tanvir Ahmed's *Chirutha*, Satyajit Ray's *Pratidwandi*, Rabindra Dharmaraj's *Chakra* and Mrinal Sen's *Calcutta 71*. The all-seeing camera was matched against a political cover-up, horror coming together with comedy into an extreme cinema to produce an instant cinematic snapshot of the Bombay, and indeed the India, of that time.

Even as everybody becomes obsessed with tracking down what the camera has seen, the film spins out of control. That search, in its manic persistence, takes over the story, eats up the film and overwhelms its maker. It comprises in-references that involve the camera, the telephone, the radio and the tape recorder, secret passwords such as 'Albert Pinto ko Gussa Kyon Aata Hai' for passing on dirt, and shadowy figures in trench coats eavesdropping and on the phone, pretend-journalists from America with a recording device and, on one elaborate occasion, a ticking bomb.

Jaane Bhi Do Yaaron, contrary to its opening frame that holds a fraction too long as it declares that 'all characters and situations are fictional', describes a profoundly non-fictional moment in history – that of politician A.R. Antulay's controversial reign as Maharashtra Chief Minister, during which he was found guilty of extortion by the Bombay High Court for forcing real estate developers to make political donations in exchange for illegal cement supply that was then under rationing. The two real estate developers in the film, Tarneja and Ahuja, directly reference Mumbai's then-largest property developer, Raheja. Shobha, the ruthless femme fatale and editor of the tabloid newspaper *Khabardar*, is clearly author and editor Shobha De, then in charge of the burgeoning sector of gossip journalism dominated by the publisher and movie producer Nari Hira – although the tabloid itself may be more directly the newspaper *Current*, started by D.F. Karaka and later run by Ayub Syed. Municipal Commissioner D'Mello echoes City Police Commissioner Julio Ribeiro, and the collapse of the flyover over which the developers scuffle is the actual collapse of Byculla bridge in 1982.

Both *Jaane Bhi Do Yaaron* and *Amma Ariyan* went beyond their makers. It was as though their films swallowed them. Abraham never made another and indeed died soon after, swallowed by the very fire of collective ambition he had predicted in *Agraharathil Kazhuthai*. Shah always referred to his film strangely, jumbling the words together into something that sounded a bit like *janiybdoyroo*. He of course made several commercial hits, like *Kabhi Haan Kabhi Naa* (1994), *Kya Kehna* (2000) and the landmark *Nukkad* (1986–87). And yet this film remained as though the only film he had ever made or would ever make. Shah spoke insistently of it, as Abraham too might have said of his own, as a failed film. It seemed important to him that it be viewed and judged as such. For only when 'you see *Jaane Bhi Do Yaaron* as a failure' can you also see that 'it has got ... everything why this film should fail, because the attempt is so ... so *this thing* ... you know' (emphatic throwaway gesture).

This, then, was the film the Indian state awarded him for – the award he later, as the circle completed, returned.

Who is a Filmmaker?–3

Filmmakers stood in a row, medals in hand. They had taken different routes to arrive here. Differences of scale and vastness, epic form and budget, had brought them along different paths to what appeared to be the same destination. They were all there to repudiate the two-faced authority the state had vested in their *regisseur*ial being. Whichever the route they had taken to get here, they had brought with them an essential cinematic text – whether as authored work, or as authorless or multi-author meme – that too had remade itself. Texts ceaselessly developed new value in the increasingly devious ways in which they were circulated, got retold, and, virus-like, grew and changed, even as they repurposed other texts on the way. None of the films mentioned had a mass audience in mind, and none reached a mass audience. All did, over the years, reach a public that may well be many times more than that of the average mass audience – a fugitive cult public, a popular, entirely unexplored distribution strategy in the New Cinema.

Mirza described *Ghashiram Kotwal* as a 'relevant failure'.[28] He felt its inability to realize its lofty ambitions had been instructive to the cause. To him, the problem was the film's impossibly low budget: 'If its budget could match its conception, the film might have achieved much more', Mirza said. This budget issue was

-28
'A relevant failure is, perhaps, more important than a minor success. In this context, a film which can be considered as a relevant failure is ... *Ghashiram Kotwal*.' Mirza, 'Outlook for the Cinema', p. 122.

contentious. The more popular view was the opposite, to *emphasize* low budgets and therefore the 'freedom to fail'. VIEW itself comprised, says Padamsee, 'a cinema projector, three 16 mm movie cameras and editing equipment'. To make *Duvidha*, Padamsee had given Mani Kaul 'Rs 60,000 worth of film stock, a camera and editing facilities, and told him he'd have to make a film with a tailor ratio of 1:1'.[29] (Kaul would later make 1:1 a virtue in his theory of randomness and never retaking a shot.) If one film reproduced the entire creative and technical team as its makers, a second folded one protagonist-maker inside another. Both had similar results.

It is easy enough to acknowledge the near-cult status of several films – K.P. Kumaran's *Atithi* (1975), Mani Kaul's *Satah Se Utatha Admi* (1980), Paresh Kamdar's *Tunnu ki Tina* (1997), to add to the already-mentioned *Om Dar-b-dar* and *Hun Hunshi Hunshilal* – that would have died, but for an afterlife that involved people passing prints around in informal screenings in informal spaces, on pirate networks in video, and then of course with peer-to-peer digital sharing. Such cult status was by definition unmonetizable. It was, for many years, the only way to get past the dual stranglehold of state support that was often the kiss of death given the impossibility of a commercial release, and censorship. The only solution left was to make a film that made itself: a film that nobody could control. The film director's work reduced to a poster beneath the flyover in the background as the manic corpse wended its way.

-29
Meenakshi Shedde, 'Art in the River of Life', in Bhanumati Padamsee and Annapurna Garimella (eds.), *Akbar Padamsee: Work in Language*, Mumbai: Marg Publications, 2010, p. 311.

CHAPTER 4

CELLULOID SPECTRES

As 1997 ended in stalemate, Mohan Agashe's acts of exorcism began to make another kind of sense. He froze all new admissions until the place could find a definition for why it existed, why it even needed to exist. As three zero semesters went by and after one court case of mandamus filed by students, Agashe finally returned the campus to business with a new batch in February 2000, with a 'Restructured Revised Syllabus'. The plan was named '1+1+1' and it was to admit eighty students to a basic integrated course. The end of the course would see between a third and a half of the batch weeded out, and the following year would see only twelve admissions each in direction, sound, editing and cinematography. A culling after the second year would reduce the number further, so that eventually, at the end of the final year, only eight students would complete each course. Each year would be viewed as a stand-alone programme, as against an integrated one. There would thus be an expanded intake but also a very high number of rejections.

All this was because, Jabeen Merchant concluded, after the December 1997 debacle, Agashe's 'medical man's mind' reasoned out that 'striking was like a virus' that was being 'transmitted from one batch to the next'. 'The way to eliminate it was through quarantine', to 'freeze new admissions until every last student had graduated and left the campus for good'.[1] In an extended slow-motion death by a thousand cuts, students were required, late in their courses, to rely on seat availability and to compete furiously with each other to qualify for the next year of their chosen specialization. By this time the authorities – and, it appears, some members of the faculty – had become convinced that breaking up the batches and forcing them to compete with each other was the only way to break the routine of strikes associated with 'batch mentality'. Along with this, in an effort to sync the FTII into the mainstream film industry, a bouquet of short courses in film production, art direction and acting was to be on offer for high fees. Most ambitiously, a small number of feature-length commercial films would be made on campus, that

Facing page
Gurvinder Singh, Rajula Shah and Anupam Srinivasan's lead essay in *Economic and Political Weekly* (18 November 2000) during the 1+1+1 strike, projected over a 2000 strike poster.

-1 Jabeen Merchant, 'FTII's biggest blessing is also its biggest tragedy – the government', *Scroll*, 27 June 2015.

Unmaking of Film Institute

The recent changes in the syllabus and course content of the Film and Television Institute of India will shift the focus of education from the aesthetics of film-making to operational matters and are directed at stifling experimentation. Is it any wonder that its students, who come to the institute for a comprehensive understanding of the mediums, are discontented?

GURVINDER SINGH, RAJULA SHAH, ANUPAM SRINIVASAN

The recent drastic and arbitrary changes in the syllabus and course structure of India's premier film training institute, the Film and Television Institute of India (FTII), are diluting the cause it stood for. At stake are its ethos and the very aims and objectives with which it was set up. The changes are so fundamental that they are no longer peripheral to the constitution of the institute, but hit at the right to free expression and individual thinking. The institute has become a target of the larger design of privatisation and globalisation (Americanisation?) and is today being viewed by decision-making authorities an industry for generating profits rather than a centre of learning. If the changes are not immediately halted and the tide reversed, the country will lose forever the only training ground for people committed to meaningful and socially relevant cinema.

Set up in 1961 with the aim of promoting good alternative cinema and setting new standards in film-making both aesthetically and technically, the institute has provided free space for thinking and learning to generations of would be film-makers. It has provided the film industry with highly professional, focused and specialised people in various aspects of film-making. Along with the National Film Archives of India (NFAI), the Films Division and the National Film Development Corporation (NFDC), FTII has been one of the pillars for promoting a plurality of voices via the medium of cinema. It has been unique in the world amongst all film schools, providing ample scope for experimentation and exploration. The government supported education has provided aspiring film-makers from all strata of society and the remotest parts of the country access to hands on experience on world class equipment and exposure to the best of world cinema. The excellent collection of films at the National Film Archives has acted as a rich resource for learning. The two institutes have together been a formidable base for nurturing talent.

Today, unfortunately, all these organisations are in a state of decay and are disowning their own voices. Their achievements stand questioned not on any grounds of excellence or competence but on commercial considerations. The latest proposals of I and B ministry aim at dissolving its bodies, namely, the NFDC, FD, FTII and NFAI. Only the censor board is being spared the axe! Should the state wash its hands off them because it fails to see their profits in terms of intellect, artistic endeavour and cultural renaissance? Should these institutes be wiped out simply because they could not become money-making machines? In the chain of FTII and NFDC, the third important link, that of establishing an exhibition network for these films by setting up small theatres was completely ignored. Thus, can these organisations now be blamed for their lack of commercial success if the film policy is a case of a half implemented plan? FTII's case is all the more pertinent as it stands at the root of other audio-visual organisations, providing them with succour in terms of a learned and proficiently trained manpower. Cutting off this root destroys the very raison d'etre of these institutions.

This change in thinking and the shrinking of aims has not been an overnight process but a gradual engagement of decision-makers over the recent years. FTII has seen arbitrary course changes: dilution of syllabus; experimentation with the course structure by compressing it in shorter time; opening new courses without any requisite resource or preparation; a stagnant in-house faculty; many important faculty positions lying vacant; falling standards of teaching; poor maintenance of costly professional equipment acquired over the years; a complete shift from aesthetics of film-making to operational matters.

Students who come to FTII are inclined towards a comprehensive and complete understanding of the medium, and any attempt to curtail that is bound to generate discontent. Thus, there has been a history of student protest at every stage of dilution and decay. This has been used and vociferously highlighted by authorities to vilify the agitating students without going into the causes of these discontents. So much so that the recent changes stem from a desire to have a control over students rather than any considerations for academic and professional excellence. Should that be the framework for designing the syllabus of an institute of FTII's repute?

In 1996, a new syllabus called the 'Revised Syllabus' was prepared by a committee comprising of outside experts, practising professionals, faculty and the students. It was a much needed improvement on the then existing syllabus. It provided for increased inputs from visiting professionals and was flexible and interactive in nature. After hanging in suspension for three years, it was unceremoniously shelved.

A new course has been implemented with the new batch that started in February this year after three zero semesters during which no admissions were done on the pretext of working out the logistics of implementing a new syllabus. The present course has nothing in common with the 'Revised Syllabus' but is called the 'Restructured Revised Syllabus'. Some of its highlights:

- Three individual course of one year duration each replacing the integrated three year diploma.
- Elimination of students at each yearly stage.
- Doubling the intake of students from the earlier 40 to 80 without increasing the budget or resources, thus reducing the resources available to each students by half.
- A fee hike ten times higher with provision for further increase at regular intervals.
- Students do not decide on the area of their specialisation. It depends on the availability of seats in the second year and on the teachers' recommendation.
- Disciplinary measures in the garb of assessment; marks for attendance; professional behaviour(!), and application (with no clear definition).
- Drastic reduction in film theory, history and appreciation.
- A clause called 'Recognised Prior Learning' that allows people direct entry

would both teach students how to exist in the industry and bring in money to the Institute.

On 29 August 2000, six months after they were admitted, the newly sanitized batch were back at work with their own action.

Cinema's Heraclitean Paradoxes

Like most students of the batch of 2000, Manoj Lobo remembers the events of those months well. Recently, however, Manoj took this memory a step further and unearthed an ancient set of three CDs that contained around twelve hours of unedited footage of that strike. Camcorders had only just become ubiquitous, and this footage had been mostly shot by his batchmate Satya Rai Nagpaul, now known for his cinematography – for example, in Gurvinder Singh's *Chauthi Koot* (2015).[2]

This footage produces an utterly extra-ordinary and previously unknown document of its time. Nagpaul has shot it as though discovering the freedom of a new *verité* era of lightweight digital equipment and extended-duration shooting. He hangs on and on and on, with obvious cinephiliac pleasure, to conversations, meetings, arguments, night-before and day-after discussions at public showdowns – and to encounters with several figures of authority. We see, over minutes on end, the Governing Council Chairman Vinod Khanna's entire visit to the campus in granular detail. There is Governing Council member Bobby Bedi in his white turban and round glasses talking for over an hour as students mill around him, some sitting on tables and others standing around in what looks like the canteen space. Old hand Neeraj Sahay makes a brief appearance. Abhijit Majumdar, who was then leading the Students' Association, Amala Popuri, Rajesh Shera, Chetana Kaul and multiple others produce a more substantial presence as they encounter Khanna in the Classroom Theatre. Agashe, rakishly decked up in a Nepali cap, silently registers wonder and amazement at what he is hearing. There is a long *thali* lunch during which Khanna, eating with the students (Agashe is noticeably absent), concedes to all that they have asked for. There is the Delhi campaign as the students sit on a lawn, presumably somewhere on the Delhi University campus, and debate their strategy, followed by an extended press conference at the Press Club, at which Anil Mehta,

-2

Nagpaul is also known for his work as a trans activist and for the group Sampoorna, which he founded in 1998.

Shikha Aleya, 'Interview: Satya Rai Nagpaul', *Plainspeak*, 2 April 2018.

Piyush Mishra and Rajat Kapoor speak alongside Majumdar. There are two confrontations with Agashe himself, in his office. In one of them, when an irate Agashe forbids shooting, the camera dips down, so all we see is an unnamed protester's backside, even as the sound stubbornly rolls on.

A prominent presence through this footage is the slight, bespectacled form of Ganga Mukhi – standing aggressively in front of Bobby Bedi, confronting Mohan Agashe, sitting next to Vinod Khanna when he meets the students. Ganga, who has recently joined the FTII's Direction and Screenplay faculty, is somewhat startled when she learns about this footage. Her militant presence in the film doesn't square with her own rather more sedate memory of the strike, in which respect had been shown to authority and debate for the right cause had won the day for the good guys.

Ganga grew up in the suburb of Kalyan in Mumbai, in a Sindhi family of Partition migrants. She studied and later taught at Ulhasnagar's Chandibai College, where she belonged to a small but vibrant intellectual and creative community energized as much by debates in the arts as by cinephiliac energy. She was a common attendee at Amrit Gangar's legendary film society, Screen Unit. There was a valorization of cinema as a cause to be nurtured and protected that she had discovered on the campus, in seniors like Gurvinder Singh and Rajula Shah, and colleagues like Amit Dutta and Satya Rai Nagpaul – and she remains clear that this was the cause that she brought to the strike. She remembers her role modestly, but she does admit to the confrontations with Bedi, which happened mainly because she says she didn't know who he was (had she known he was the producer of *Bandit Queen*, she might have been more respectful), with Agashe himself, and with Arun Jaitley – the same Minister who featured in July 2015 – who she recalls as having been extremely rude. Jaitley, having first made the delegation wait, then abruptly said that the 'meeting was over' for there was 'nothing to discuss'. Ganga did find

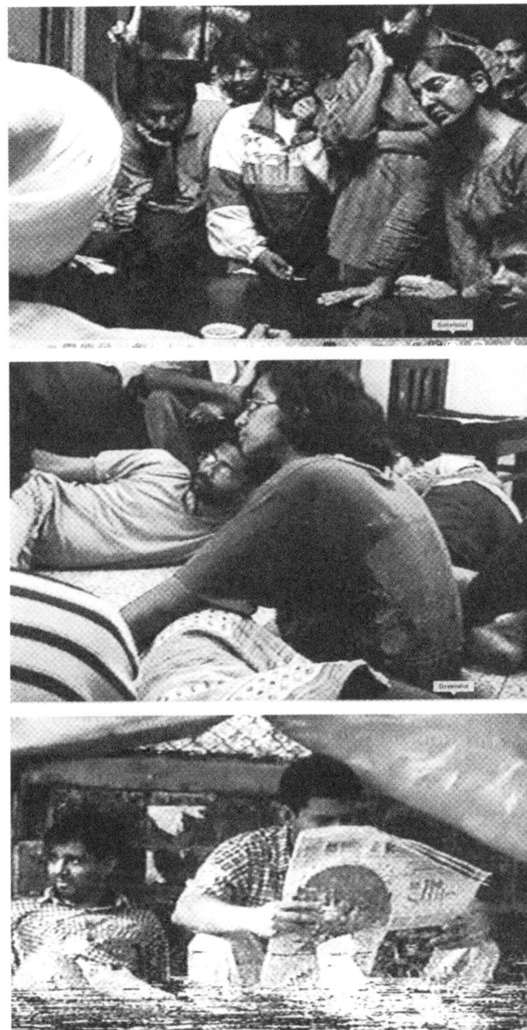

Documentary footage of the 2000 strike. Top to bottom: Ganga Mukhi confronts Bobby Bedi; Amala Popuri, Abhijit Majumdar and others the night before the press conference in Delhi; Amit Dutta.

'some courage to tell him ... "Sir, the meeting hasn't even begun."'[3]

Apart from the cause of cinema, what she remembers the strike for is the way her batch fought for both its own integrity and that of future students. Although she had officially joined for one year as per the 1+1+1 formula, like everyone else she expected to stay longer, and was appalled by the competitive rivalry for seats and the petty manipulations that went with it. It militated against what her entire batch felt was a collectivity intrinsic to filmmaking. Nagpaul's footage reveals the singleminded effort of the authorities – as Bobby Bedi tries, for instance, to solve the specific problem before this particular batch with 'industry' support – to somehow maintain the 'structure' while isolating the admitted students by promising them 'special case' admissions.

There is a curious contrast between Nagpaul's images, grainy and pixellated with sound in camera often muffled, and the frenzied desire that engulfed the campus in September 2000 to purge it of its spectres. As with all wipe-the-slate-clean fantasies, the effort unleashed a blowback far worse – and infinitely more complex – than anything it thought it was solving. Dead pasts, as we see in Manoj's old CDs, would prove yet again to be hard to bury.

Speaking in 1984 at JNU's celebrated Centre for Historical Studies, Kumar Shahani named a 'Heraclitean paradox' that appeared to him as intrinsic to the filmmaking process.[4] He had once sat next to Ghatak as the two watched Lumiere's train entering a station, looked on with 'palpitating hearts', and then smiled 'as if to reaffirm our faith in the magic that could be wrought from these mute, banal, mechanically reproduced images'. It occurred to Shahani that unlike the historian who apprehends the 'very substance of that flux that the world is made of' with methods like 'nam[ing] epochs and events, to grasp what lies underneath them', the filmmaker can at best only 'seize shadows and reflections' in the hope of joining the historian's effort 'to understand, and hopefully to change, the world'.

Shahani had been modest. By 2000, the 'shadows and reflections' of the moving image had become central to a major historical crossroads. As India stood dramatically at the threshold

-3

Conversation with Ganga Mukhi on Zoom, 25 July 2021.

-4

Kumar Shahani, 'Film as a Contemporary Art', in *Kumar Shahani: The Shock of Desire and other essays*, edited and introduced by Ashish Rajadhyaksha, New Delhi: Tulika Books, 2015, p. 204.

of digital technology, nothing separated us from the debris of the twentieth century more decisively than the sudden demise of celluloid. Privatization – or the rolling back of the state as a neoconservative panacea for all of society's problems – was at its height, and the 2008 financial crisis that saw the state apparatus reincarnated in a radically new neoliberal avatar, not yet a reality. The messy transition of celluloid into digital was directly parallelling the political transition then underway, from neocon to neolib. The distinction is not always made, but it can be relatively easily characterized as: *one*, under neoconservatism, an anti-statist, market-dominated governance; and *two*, under neoliberalism, an interventionist state–corporate policy combining tax benefits and corporate subsidies alongside targeted delivery of state benefits.

The corresponding shift in the basic definition of the public domain would be directly reflected in the cinema. If celluloid had been the incarnation of Article 15 in the way films were both made and shown, digital's privatization of film viewing – in the home and the multiplex – signalled the demise of *that* public in all its constitutional significance. It also thus signalled the replacement of democratic multitudes with a sanitized, privatized, credit card-bearing citizen-viewer dwelling in shiny new spaces of domesticated consumption.

India entered an era that was not only post-cinema but would soon become post-television, as it sought a utopian digital universe that was cleaner, more neutral, freer, more *autonomous*: 'untouched', writes IT czar Nandan Nilekani, 'by the legacies of the sarkar raj'.[5] Agashe's exorcist imagination was thus at one with the larger national phantasy around digitization – typically characterized as an Augean stables cleansing of the old state.

-5

Nandan Nilekani, *Imagining India: Ideas for the New Century*, New Delhi: Penguin, 2008, p. 365.

The Sarkar Raj, the Celluloid Virus and the Archive

Through much of the twentieth century, an unassailable conviction in the cinema's ability to capture modern history in its moving entirety has shaped the filmmaker's destiny, even as it shaped the great Prabhat Road institutions' endeavour to make, teach and archive cinema. Like paper and built form, celluloid's engagement with history was two-tiered: it was susceptible to the ravages of the very history it sought to capture, both materially and textually. All of these forms have faced the existential anxiety of being inherently doomed, by the modernist paradox, to be consumed by their ambition. *Unlike* paper fragments and the built form, condemned to ruin and classically represented *as* magnificent ruins, celluloid had no available vocabulary to describe its plight. Communications theory had committed it to indestructibility: committed it to being a means, not an end; a medium, never material.

When film found itself threatened with extinction, it was uniquely unprepared for the revelation that this was not merely an end, but *the end*: or to grasp why it was being swallowed by the history it had sought to so diligently capture – how celluloid, of all things, came to such a pass.

This was, in an inevitable paradox, not the end of the story. Celluloid *didn't* die, it went underground. Digitization, far from killing off ghosts of the dead past, gave the 'shadows and reflections' of history an entirely new lease of subterranean life. Its obduracy remained a roadblock to the dream of pristine virtualization being promised by neoliberal digital restorers everywhere.

Celluloid film begins, at this point, to bear resemblance to the life sciences, in which, says historian Carolyn Steedman, 'the task was also to think about the past-think pastness – about the imperishability of matter, through all the stages of growth and decay, to the point of recognition that ... nothing goes away'.[6]

Steedman would have taken literally, and with some seriousness, Agashe's medical desire to fumigate and rid the Institute of virus. 'We're talking epidemiology here, not metaphor: meningitis due to or as a complication of anthrax; Real Archive Fever, or Archive Fever Proper, a new entry for the medical dictionaries.'

Agashe's desire to cleanse is echoed not only in the suddenness of celluloid's extinction, but also in the ferocity with which it has been sought to be stamped out through the neoliberal double whammy of political and corporate forces coming together. It is equally inevitable that cinema has resisted – survived, leaked through – producing, in Steedman's words, a

> double nothingness in the writing of history and in the analysis of it: it is about something that never did happen in the way it comes to be represented (the happening exists in the telling or the text), and it is made out of materials that are not there, in an archive or anywhere else. There is actually nothing there: only absence, what once was: dust.

Facing page
Strike poster, June 2015. Ritwik Ghatak as the wraith-in-chief spooking the campus has remained an FTII legend.

Overleaf
Discarded Steenbecks outside the Film Laboratory, signalling a specific end of celluloid film. (Images: Sandeep Chatterjee)

-6

Carolyn Steedman, 'Something She Called a Fever: Michelet, Derrida, and Dust', *The American Historical Review*, vol. 106, no. 4, 2001, p. 1179.

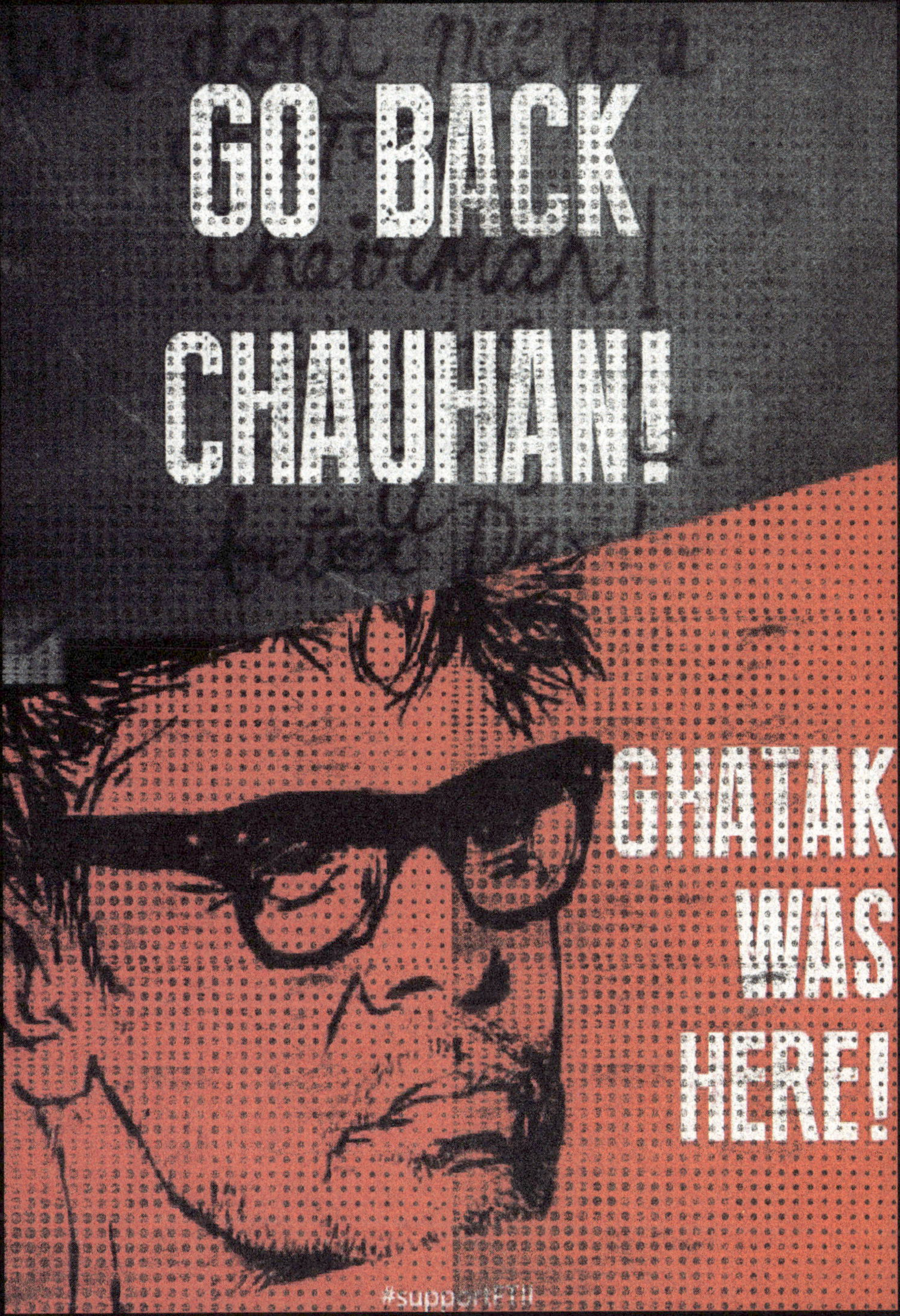
GO BACK
CHAUHAN!
GHATAK
WAS
HERE!

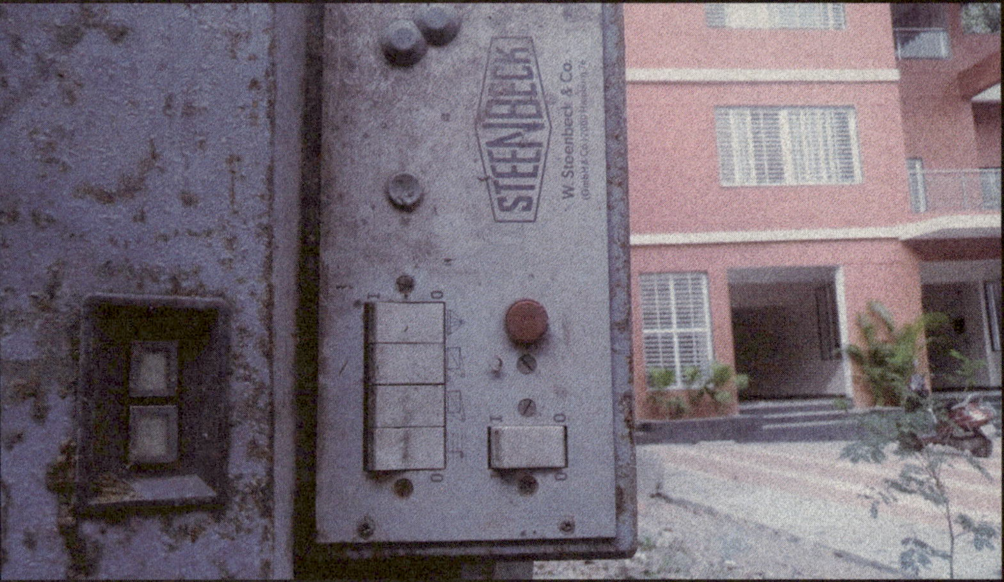
STEENBECK
W. Steenbeck & Co.

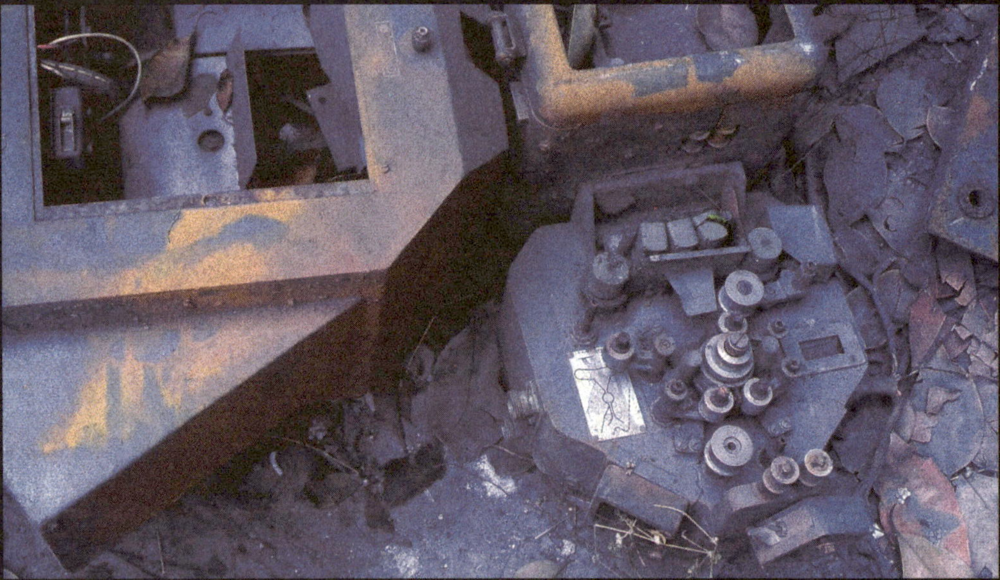

In 2015 it was this very artefact that threatened, in its obscenity, to derail the Ministry of Information and Broadcasting, whose existence has been inextricably welded to the *medium* as a key instrument of state propaganda. Although the I&B Ministry had by 1981 effectively jettisoned film in favour of television,[7] and was in 2000 all set to further jettison television in favour of the digital,[8] the *idea of cinema* – in its expanded definition, as inclusive of all forms of the moving image – was still sufficient to at least rattle the I&B Minister in his fateful encounter with the strike representatives in July 2015, forcing him to acknowledge the crisis and to propound a role, however disconcerting, for film schools in the Ministry's plans for its own future.

The Archives of Evil

In January 1999, Information and Broadcasting Minister Pramod Mahajan visited the FTII. Largely empty with zero admissions in force as Agashe was in the midst of his deep cleansing, it looked to Mahajan, presciently perhaps, akin to 'the debris of the Second World War'.[9] In 2002, the same year as Agashe's miserable reign ended, the Geetha Krishnan Committee formally recommended that his Ministry 'divest itself of this institution'.[10] It asked for 'an Association or Agency' to be found, or created, that may take it over with a careful assessment of what the asset is worth and thus 'safeguard government investments'. Rumours abounded: management consultants McKinsey were doing an evaluation of its value, went one. Both Reliance Media and Subhash Ghai had expressed interest in buying it, went another.

Coming at the fag end of a near-century of negligence, the *archive du mal* that stands for the horrors of the past may well possess a barely concealed intentionality. The speed of the demise of celluloid in India has been such that it often appears to have been actively pushed into ruin, even as its wealth has been plundered by the recycling agents of a new digital economy: for content by digital marketing and piracy, for material by the sheds in Dharavi reducing celluloid to its silver and plastic components.

The problems posed to the institutional housing of film, especially in a place like India, are large. They may, as Sudhir Mahadevan shows, well be more than what conventional institutions

-7

See P.C. Joshi, *An Indian Personality for Television: Report of the Working Group on Software on Doordarshan*, New Delhi: Ministry of Information and Broadcasting, Government of India, 1985, for this change.

-8

'The Information Technology Act, 2000', *Government of India Gazette*.

-9

Maharashtra Herald, 19-01-1999, quoted in G.B. Singh, *Critical Study of Academic Management of Post-graduate Diploma Courses Conducted at Film and Television Institute of India*, Pune: Savitribai Phule Pune University, 2009.

-10

Officially, the Expenditure Reforms Commission (ERC) set up by the Ministry of Finance in 2000 to begin the process of systematic downsizing of the government.

are qualified to handle.[11] Mahadevan separates out the conventional 'archive of the cinema-as-celluloid' from what he sees as the considerably wider informal archives dedicated to 'remembering ... the history of the cinema'. Such a separation is graphically on display in the split campus cloven into two halves – the ineffable magic of cinema on its right, and television, together with the mundane rationalities of an emotionless, amnesiac state bureaucracy on the left – reinforcing the spectral, transgressive character of film inside an institution supposedly dedicated to teaching it.

To your right as you enter are a series of sheds that provided the earliest housing of the National Film Archive of India. The existence on campus of the 'masterpieces' of cinema would become a two-edged sword. Unmatched access to world cinema was always countered by the sobering fact that less than 5 per cent of the films made in the world's most cinematically populous country existed in its vaults. Unlike print, film has never been a national priority. India has had no legal deposit requirement for film. More to the point, the role of the NFAI was never meant to conserve all films made in India. It would have to be ten times larger to even think of doing that.

There may have been yet other, more mysterious reasons related to uncontrolled celluloid remembering. Some years after it was set up, the NFAI moved into a 'heritage' bungalow. This bungalow was once owned by a local grandee named M.R. Jayakar, jurist, educationist and the first Vice Chancellor of Pune University. Jayakar was also a prominent cinephobe. In 1928, the Indian Cinematograph Committee circulated a questionnaire among multiple colonial elites about what it called the 'injurious effects' of the cinema. When Jayakar received this questionnaire, he simply sent back a terse paragraph saying that 'from what little' he has seen of the cinema industry, it appeared only to have 'taught Indians a number of vices ... new forms of burglary and immorality ... which the Indian mind could not have conceived without difficulty'. He had, he continued, 'very strong notions in this matter' and would have done something about this had he been on this Committee.[12] Now, as the cinema-hating Mr Jayakar's bungalow turned into India's national celluloid archives, there is good reason to imagine, like the medieval Forbek in Alain Resnais' *Life is a Bed of Roses*, Jayakar's immortal soul howling in pain as he encounters the ghosts

-11

Sudhir Mahadevan, 'The Abundant Ephemeral: The Protocols of Popular Film Historiography in India', in *A Very Old Machine: The Many Origins of the Cinema in India*, New York: SUNY Press, 2015, p. 166.

-12

Indian Cinematograph Committee Report, 1928–29, Vol. 4 (Evidence), p. 56.

of Devdas and Giulietta Masina stalking the corridors of his house.[13]

After another hundred yards, you turn right just before the old CRT. Another visitation takes place. A ramshackle set of rooms house what may be the only functional 35 mm black-and-white celluloid laboratory on any film school campus on earth. As the twenty-first century wears on, the lab has become increasingly dysfunctional. It continues to exist and is occasionally used, despite its demise being predicted since at least 2009. In 2018, giant Steenbeck editing machines lay in the open on one side, along with other discarded celluloid equipment.

Even as the process of conservation on digital platforms (which meant a simple automated 'as-is' transfer) could have been properly underway, a growing market emerges for restored As-They-Once-Were copies. Scrubbed-clean versions flood the restoration market, almost always of what Paolo Cherchi Usai darkly names the Absolute Masterpiece^{R} (Restoration^{TM} No. 456 ©), directed some time during the 1920s by an Undisputed Genius of Cinema. All these masterpieces lie in stark contrast to low-end 'housing shelters' made for 'millions of reels (of) anything', 'untreated supplicants' seeking a home in growing 'intermedial' databases committed to a belief that is as old as the cinema itself. Namely, that within the industrial production lines of celluloid, amid the multiple artefacts of picture and sound negatives, dupe negatives, internegatives, master and release positives, there was rarely a practical entity that might be described as a cinematic original.[14]

When the 'magic' generated by the chemical reaction between light and photosensitive material is converted into digital information, the 'inanimate images of the filmstrip not only come alive in projection, but ... ghostly images of the now-dead [are] resurrected into the appearance of life', says Laura Mulvey, discovering both ghosts and the uncanny in the sheer banality of the celluloid image when that image finds itself threatened with extinction. In that resurrection lie what Mulvey, quoting Freud, calls 'residues of archaic fears and superstitions', the belief that the 'spirits of the dead are able to visit the living' in a natural world 'itself inhabited and animated by the presence of spirits'.[15]

In 2008, the International Federation of Film Archives (FIAF) redefined celluloid. It was no longer to be seen as an evanescent

-13

Ref. a particularly ghostly moment in Shivendra Singh Dungarpur's film, *A Celluloid Man* (2012), in which P.K. Nair is seeing Fellini's *La Strada* alone in Jayakar's bungalow.

-14

Paolo Cherchi Usai, *The Death of Cinema: History, Cultural Memory and the Digital Dark Age*, London: British Film Institute, 2001, pp. 114, 117.

-15

Laura Mulvey, 'Uncertainty: Natural Magic and the Art of Deception', in *Death 24 x a Second: Stillness and the Moving Image*, London: Reaktion Books, 2006, p. 40.

carrier of information but rather as an 'artefact', like sculpture or any plastic art. It was now a *physical* 'human-eye-readable' entity, and it had to be treated 'like other museum or historic objects'.[16]

Three years after the FIAF manifesto, Shumona Goel and Shai Heredia shot a 35 mm homage to this museum object.[17] They shot their film inside the abandoned factory of the camera manufacturer National Instruments in Jadavpur. There is half-eaten food. Personal belongings are scattered about. The slow pans take in a place that seemed to have closed as though at an apocalyptic instant. On the soundtrack, as though looking down upon the colossal wreck that used to be cinema – Look on my Works, ye Mighty, and despair! – is the voice of Kamal Swaroop in contemplation.

—

In 1984, Mani Kaul brought in Kamal Swaroop, archivist of evil par excellence, to conceive and write his essay-film, *Mati Manas*. Ostensibly on the theme of pottery, they redefined its subject into the semiotically elusive material of clay (its English title is *Mind of Clay*, but it might also be translated as 'clay man'). Clay is of course fragile, fugitive and entirely impermanent, but it casts some of the oldest figurations of history. Its survival must therefore be complexly viewed – it survives as much through narratives of its conscious use as through the actual material. The former survival can, the filmmakers thought, be integrated into the recording devices of film, which had some of the same qualities. Relevant to such integration was a theory of historical consciousness that the filmmakers cobbled together from an eclectic mix of sources. Among those commonly mentioned were Anandavardhana's ninth-century text *Dhvanyaloka*, Abhinavagupta's eleventh-century works, and Marx's fifth thesis on Feuerbach.

Swaroop had an unusual job to do. He had to tap into this state of consciousness. It may have borne some link to what Frederic Jameson once named a 'political unconscious' that 'exists nowhere in empirical form, and therefore must be re-constructed ... in much the same way that the master-fantasies of the individual unconscious are reconstructed through the fragmentary and symptomatic texts of dreams, values, behaviour, verbal free-association, and the like'.[18]

-16

70th Anniversary Film Manifesto of the International Federation of Film Archives (FIAF).

-17

Shumona Goel and Shai Heredia, *I Am Micro* (2011), film-essay on the defunct factory of National Instruments Ltd (NIL) which once produced the National 35, the only 35 mm still camera ever manufactured in India.

-18

Frederic Jameson, 'Progress versus Utopia; Or, Can We Imagine the Future?' *Science Fiction Studies*, vol. 9, no. 2, 1982, p. 148.

Swaroop went off on a journey across central and southern India, armed with a tiny Kodak Instamatic and a notebook, to find stories and identify people who might make such a connection between the everyday and the master-fantasies that define the Indian landmass. He duly returned with a fund of stories and locations, some of which Mani Kaul chose for his film, but it remained unclear how many he actually found during his travels, how many he already knew, and how many were stream-of-consciousness records of his own dreams and hallucinations. What he produced was almost certainly an amalgam of all three, sometimes recorded on tape and amateur film, that coalesced into (what Kaul and Swaroop asserted was) a civilizational consciousness. Its survival was genealogical rather than historical. Its specificities were all parts of a larger whole. While any single shot or sequence could capture a part, the whole – stretched across a film that has to be seen only in its entirety – was only to be signified, contemplated.

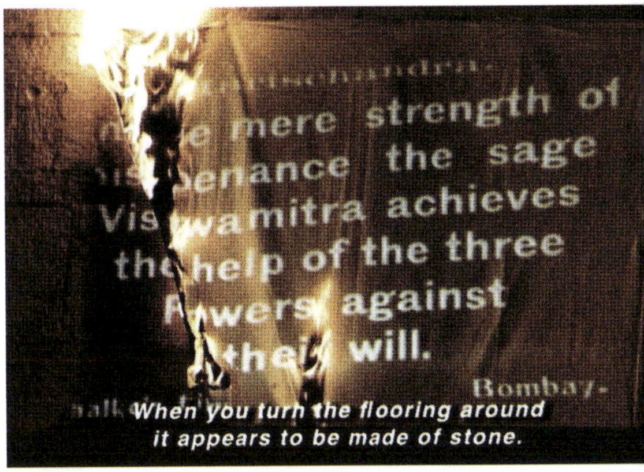

The screen catches fire: video projection of the famous text in Dadasaheb Phalke's **Raja Harishchandra** (1913), in Kamal Swaroop's inquiry into Phalke's origins, **Tracing Phalke** (2016).

Such an inscription on the shot would in time survive celluloid itself, and would produce its own archival logic for the death and rebirth of film. One cannot know whether Kaul and Swaroop saw cinema (by which I literally mean 35 mm celluloid) as almost clay-like in its transience. However, as they shot *Mati Manas* – travelling in a bus over forty-five days across central India, from Rajasthan through to Orissa and then into the deep south, in temperatures that were in the upper forties; when all stock, both exposed and unexposed, was stored by anxious crew in ice-cooled containers covered with Styrofoam – it would not have been strange for them to think that they were themselves working in a medium as fugitive as the clay figurines and mud pots they were filming.

Four years later Swaroop made his own debut film, *Om Dar-b-Dar*. By now it was entirely clear that celluloid film had become a fugitive art medium. He expanded his explorations of the unconscious into a story of a young boy whose cognitive ability, as he came of age, was linked to multiple myths and phantasies explored underwater, in the science laboratory and in outer space, derived as much from dreams as from the street and from cheap thrillers.

Swaroop's encounter with celluloid turned out, as had been foretold, to be messy. The entirety of his first schedule, shot on a 16 mm Aaton camera rented, as it happened, from Anand Patwardhan, was scrapped when the camera malfunctioned. A magical two-and-a-half-hour rough cut of the film was screened just once: by Mani Kaul late one evening for Ulrich Gregor of the Berlin Film Festival as he was on his way to the airport, at A.M. Padmanabhan's Aradhana Sound Studio in Andheri (where Kumar Shahani was then doing his sound on *Khayal Gatha*). It proved so compelling that several young filmmakers who saw that cut, Anup Singh and Paresh Kamdar among them, proclaimed it unprecedented in the cinema. When the first screening of the under-90-minute final cut (edited by Priya Krishnaswamy) took place at the NFDC, Singh was deeply distraught, convinced that the film had been ruined.

Om Dar-b-dar was screened thereafter only occasionally as celluloid. Its considerable current reputation is therefore primarily based on its spectral afterlife on video and bootleg digital versions, where the film seems to gain rather than lose, indeed appears to have recovered much of the stature of the elusive version screened at Aradhana Studio in 1988.

The obduracy of celluloid as matter with a mind of its own, refusing to die, extended to its makers. If Ghatak had become indistinguishable from his fictional Other in *Jukti Takko aar Gappo* and from its various memes on student posters, Swaroop too had by this time increasingly merged into his protagonist Om (both in *Om Dar-b-dar* and in multiple unmade sequels, *Om and the Satellite City* and *Miss Palmolive*) as the One Who Survived Celluloid.

—

By the early 1990s Kumar Shahani too was no longer speaking of evanescent 'shadows and reflections'. Film was not 'transparent celluloid' but opaque matter 'sculpted with light ... from the chiselling of granite and other rock', he said of Ghatak's *Titash Ekti Nadir Naam*.[19] The reimagination of film as material similar to 'granite and rock' was to directly impact the idea of the

-19 Kumar Shahani, 'The Passion of a Resurrected Spring', in *Kumar Shahani: The Shock of Desire and other essays*, p. 222.

regisseur; the filmmaker became a sculptor-in-time and eventually, something that most closely resembled the *hacker*. By the early 2000s, the 'medium' was best viewed as more like a spirit-channeller, enabling conversations with the dead. Celluloid's transience, first as evanescent material and then as *symptom* – both in its death and then, even more terrifyingly, its rebirth on ever-expanding bootleg digital platforms – was literally haunting the cinema, and it would soon haunt the campus.

A few months after the Geeta Krishnan Committee's recommendations, a second year student named Amit Dutta stood outside the administrative offices just past the Main Theatre. The date was 8 January 2003. On that wintry morning, he saw a small wisp of smoke from the NFAI's nitrate vault opposite the Wisdom Tree grow steadily larger. As he looked on, an entire air-conditioning vent came apart from the building and, as though flying in slow motion, took direct aim at him. Before long the entire campus was covered with a layer of silver. It felt, says Dutta, like a benediction. The *havan* would see a single, centralized haunted house replaced by numerous decentralized ghosts, as a considerably vaster film archive was reborn in the pirate bylanes of the digital highway.

The Lizard on the Canteen Wall

Years later Kislay thinks back on what may have been a central contradiction of the 2015 strike. *Was cinema a means to an end, or was it an end in itself?* Many elite students grew up, he says, with 'this obsession with celluloid, big screens', wanting to practise the kind of cinema that expected people to 'go and sit in a big auditorium and watch'.[20] On the one hand, there was 'this whole idea of this cinema, the medium, bigger than life [which] takes a secondary place ... there is a specificity of this particular medium'. As its specificity is fetishized, as you start 'going gaga over the technique', film grammar is replaced by what he calls 'subjective emotion', a desire to emulate – or again, in Kislay's words, 'copy–paste' the learnings of the celluloid masters. Your film had to approximate to Godard's *Weekend*, that 10-minute 'smooth track shot', to say, 'do something like this ... Oh! that film is very good because the 10-minute long shot is there.' Or, 'hold on to a shot for 15 minutes and say – see what time is doing', your own emotional reaction replaces any understanding you need

20
Conversation with Kislay, 19 September 2018, New Delhi.

to have of 'how the film was made, what happened, the concern of the filmmaker'.

Kislay began to feel that the cinema had become like an oracle, a self-fulfilling prophecy. All you knew was what you made of the film, you had nothing external to that understanding, nothing that tested it. 'Then again you have something else which is going on' – he struggles to use the word *democracy* for it – the 'digital medium on YouTube and other things'.

Kislay was part of a new media generation when he joined Delhi University's Kirori Mal College in 2006. He had grown up in Allahabad in a political family – his parents were communist ideologues associated with the New Socialist Initiative, his mother was with the Stree Mukti Sanghatan – and when he joined college, he had definite ambitions to become an economist. He nevertheless found himself gravitating, as was the trend at the time, to its legendary theatre group, The Players, where (under Keval Arora's tutelage) he discovered Brecht and did among other things a 25-minute street play version of *The Threepenny Opera* with two ladders and a rope.

The Players was by then a familiar space for future filmmakers. In 2000 Nakul Singh Sawhney joined the English Honours programme, and Prateek Vats (in 2002) and Shubham (in 2003) entered as Commerce students – but to all of them theatre, more precisely *street* theatre, was where the action was. Winters in Delhi in that decade abounded in art exhibitions, biennales, festivals and conferences. The Osian-Cinefan film festival, launched in 1999, was at its peak, initially run by Aruna Vasudev and then by Mani Kaul. Film scholar Kaushik Bhaumik who was programming for it remembers it as a time when he was given virtually a free hand to show whatever he liked and invite whoever he wanted. In 2000 Sarai was launched, with edgy programming on media, urban life and the public domain, at a time when such issues were hardly on the horizon in India.

—

Much of the buzz was around *tactical media*. This was a new term referring to a mediatized adaptation of synaesthetic cinema, specifically to deal with post-celluloid platforms. Introduced in

May 1997 with the inauguration of the Tactical Media Network of which Sarai would later be a part, David Garcia and Geert Lovink described it as a 'quick and dirty aesthetic', 'a *vérité* for the 90s', 'never perfect, always in becoming, performative and pragmatic', requiring 'confidence [that it can] survive intact as it travels from interface to interface'.[21] Its lightweight mobility has since then come to be a central feature in protest art as it moves 'from strategy to tactics', rendering 'the phenomenon of resistance fleeting, ephemeral, and subject to continual morphing' – to 'perform an intervention' which could be the gaining of sudden access to a space, a server or a URL, and then 'just as suddenly to disperse'.

By the late 1990s, street theatre's tactical manoeuvrability would be defined by another development on Delhi's university campuses. In 1997, the ABVP (Akhil Bharatiya Vidyarthi Parishad) for the first time swept the Delhi University Students Union (DUSU) elections. By the early 2000s, said the Lyngdoh Committee (appointed in 2006 by the Ministry of Human Resource Development to provide guidelines for student elections), student politics had turned into 'feeder devices for political candidates', since 'norms prescribed by the Election Commission ... did not apply to students'.[22] Lyngdoh quoted a 1983 UGC report on how, for some decades, campus agitations had performed disruptive actions like 'breaking open offices or hostels or some other provocation' that were 'designed to attract counter-measures'. 'In a situation when the leadership of a young group of a few hundred agitators can be grabbed on seemingly "democratic" or "humane" grounds, the temptation to give a political backing becomes irresistible.'

By the early 2000s, disruption had become rampant with what Nandini Sundar calls the 'heckler's veto', when 'national security rhetoric [was] invoked with the mere threat of disruption', and 'national-chauvinist passions as well as 'hurt sentiments [became] a common ground for restrictions on academic freedom'.[23] Sundar quotes the Supreme Court (in *S. Rangarajan Etc vs P. Jagjivan Ram* on 30 March 1989), that 'potential threats to law and order predicated on the protests of unreasonable or hypersensitive people could not be a reason to ban a film, and that the administration must provide security'. However, 'bans on books only got more frequent', extended to other bans on diverse kinds of university

-21

David Garcia and Geert Lovink, 'The ABC of Tactical Media', 10 January 2008.

-22

J.M. Lyngdoh Committee Recommendations on Student Body and Union Elections, 2005.

-23

Nandini Sundar, 'Academic Freedom and Indian Universities', *Economic and Political Weekly*, vol. LIII, no. 24, 16 June 2018, p. 52.

events. 'Scholars had their seminars disrupted' and academics started getting 'disinvited by university authorities or had their talks cancelled at the last minute for fear of potential disruption'. It had become increasingly common to 'avoid the opprobrium invited by the frequent use of the heckler's veto' by portraying 'essentially one-sided attacks on academic freedom as examples of "clashes" between student groups, thus requiring the administration to clamp down in the name of neutrality'.

In 1997, when Keval Arora returned to take charge of The Players, he saw theatre across Delhi campuses undergoing 'radical transformation cloaked in the garb of old'.[24] Campus policing with severe restrictions on access to rehearsal spaces on campus after office hours made theatre increasingly more difficult to practise. Such displays of authority over space were equated, in Keval's mind, with another form of authority specific to theatre: that of the text and the playwright's original intentions – so 'how actors wore *sari*s in the 1960s when doing *Baaki Itihas* was more important than how they might interpret the relevance of whatever play they were doing'.

In 1998, The Players did a *nukkad natak*, *Yeh Kahani Kiski Hai*, addressing sex trafficking. In 2000, they did one of their best-known street plays, *Khade Hain Lathi Taane*, directly targeting the Atal Behari Vajpayee government's saffronization of education. Keval has been wary of the more militant approaches that emerged in some street theatre, approaches that risked retaliation and violence. They were as problematic as they were admirable: 'If we end up offending places which shut us down, then how do we get to do the show? How do you reach out to an audience if you can't evade the censor?' He emphasized the need to establish textual ownership over the play so that whatever text students chose, however famous, it had to be modified and transformed in a way that allowed them to 'own' it, and thus to repurpose it. Textual discipline linked directly to the challenges of campus discipline, given that rehearsing plays into the night also meant taking on strictures on public behaviour.

> If you recognize that conflict is the ... bread and butter of speech and storytelling, then how do you abandon any possibilities even of contestation when you deal with authority in your own college? *Tum sarkar badalne ke liye baat karoge, tum capitalism ke khilaaf baat karoge* [you want to change the state, you want to challenge

-24
Conversation with Keval Arora on Zoom, 22 February 2021.

> capitalism] and then you wet your pants when your teacher comes and tells you, *idhar kya kar rahe ho?* [what are you doing here?]

While theatre led the way, other disciplines soon followed it into the street. In Bangalore, Naveen Padmanabha did a five-year course between 2001 and 2006 in art history and sculpture at the well-known art school Chitrakala Parishat, before he came to FTII. There he was taught by Suresh Jayaram, the art historian now better known for his efforts to rediscover his art history on the streets of the city, and to show it in his informal and edgy art space, 1Shanthiroad.

—

Across the arts, the interrogative relationship with the text was, says Keval, connected as much to authority as to authorial copyright. Such a transformation of the arts was 'part of the whole movement to allow photocopying', part of a new era in campus learning. In 1998 a photocopying service had been instituted in the Delhi School of Economics to produce course packs, causing a long and now legendary case of the *Chancellor, Masters and Scholars of the University of Oxford and Others v. Rameshwari Photocopy Services*, otherwise known as the Delhi Photocopying Case.[25] Keval gives an example of how their project to adapt *Sakharam Binder* into a story involving 'fuck-buddy' relationships became a way for students to bring their own experiences to bear on the play's references to sex and power.

When The Players did *Khade Hain Laathi Taane*, the ABVP was already 'flexing its muscles ... the saffronization of school textbooks had begun'. They had not yet begun disrupting plays or beating up actors, but they would heckle, 'they would murmur in the crowd, letting other people know that there is a disaffection with the way the play is working'. And so, in what could be considered an early instance of tactical media (though they didn't call it that), the performers produced a 'list of all the kinds of comments made on the play', for which they made plans B, C and D so that 'the scene will take a different shape depending on the kind of disruption you get'.

It reached a stage where, on one occasion, 'when ABVP guys had come in, a lot of people thought that we had planted them in the audience. Because it just worked so seamlessly, the comment coming

-25
Delhi High Court, *The Chancellor, Masters & Scholars of University Of Oxford & Ors vs Rameshwari Photocopy Services & ors*, 2016 – in which several major publishers together sued a photocopying shop within the Delhi School of Economics, which had been authorized to create course packs by photocopying and binding selected pages at a cost of 50 paisa per page. The case became a *cause célèbre*.

from there and an actor turning around and saying, "*ye kab tak chalega – ye log beech beech mein bolte jayenge, aur aap darshakgan banke reh jaoge*" [how long will this continue – these people will speak in between, and you spectators will remain silent], how will you become an actor?'

—

'Do you have a network?'

As the first decade of the new century unfolded, the new public sphere revealed itself as more gameable. It had become increasingly amenable to non-egalitarian and, not putting too fine a point on it, more *totalitarian* usage than older analogue panopticons had ever been. The filmmaker's struggle, with that of the performance artist as the art historian, was how to negotiate democracy's transition into the evolving digital public domain.

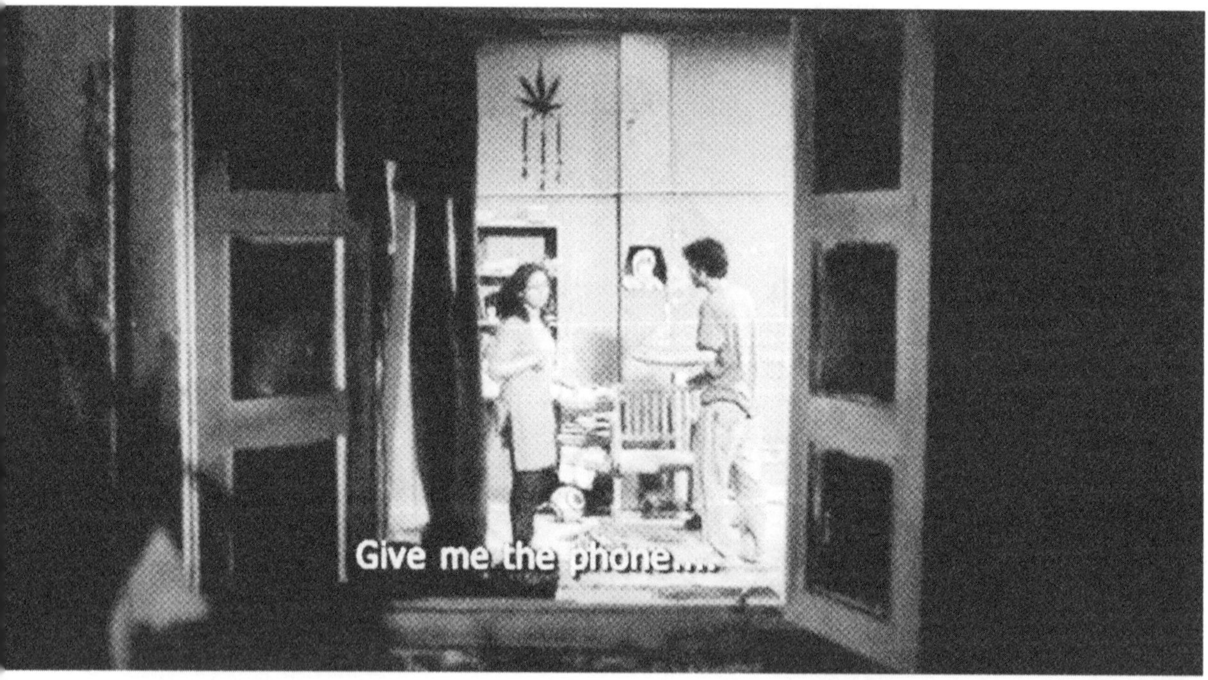

'Do you have a network?' Detail from Prateek Vats' iconic **Kal 15 August Dukaan Band Rahegi** (2008).

In 2006 – and you can even put a date to it, 31 August, the day Orkut launched its multilingual Indian iteration – social media was born in India. Orkut pioneered a revolution that jumped, over the next four years, to 83 million internet users overall, 60 per cent of whom were on one or other social media platform.[26] Orkut itself would have a short shelf life, replaced on the frontlines by 2008 with Facebook. A major struggle would be launched in 2006 over the idea of a visible public subject as the shadowy meme-author was confronted by a major state initiative launched by the Department of Information Technology, better known as the Aadhaar biometric, giving every single Indian resident a digital visibility. Its initial 2006 form, targeting BPL (below poverty line) families, would expand in 2008 into 'identification of *each and every person uniquely* at the national level'.[27]

Some years later, on 2 August 2015, when the screening of Nakul Singh Sawhney's documentary *Muzaffarnagar Baaqi Hai* in his alma mater was disrupted by the ABVP, Keval recalls the incident as curiously connected to the vulnerabilities of the proscenium form.

> So the proscenium space actually, if you ask me, renders a certain kind of theatre very vulnerable to disruption, *khaas karke* the two people who come in and say, *yeh natak bandh karo* [shut this play], are promising to break the damaged furniture in the auditorium. Half the time the disruption happens because you're trying to protect the space. When *Muzaffarnagar* was disrupted at Kirori Mal, our first thought was for the equipment – Nakul was there, but miraculously these guys didn't recognize Nakul. And we just bundled him into a corner and said, *tu bolna mat* [you keep quiet], and Nakul, thank God, was unhurt and also documented some of the things that happened at that point. But nobody, people were told, nobody use his name, nobody recognized that the filmmaker is with us, and they came in threatening to tear down the projection screen and to smash the projector.

Through the early 2000s, street theatre became popular across Delhi University's many colleges. Among the popular initiatives were the Nishant Natya Manch run at Satyavati College by the political scientist Shamsul Islam, and Arvind Gaur's Asmita Theatre. Much of this energy came from its flexibility. 'When someone threatens to destroy property, then the property owner begins to call the

-26
OSC Media Aid, Open Source Centre, 21 December 2010.

-27
Expert Committee on Metadata and Data Standards, 'Personal Identification Codification', Draft V, 8 August 2008.

shots, and colleges and gallery owners and whoever else will always say, we have to look after our *saamaan* [belongings], we believe in your theatre but *kya karein* [what to do].' On the 'street' you were no longer restricted to the vulnerabilities of equipment and infrastructure: you were logistically 'maintenance-free', for doing a play 'did not require renting a space; you create [a space] on your own'. You did not even have a script, you worked with the energy and vibrancy of the participants for everything, and 'it was very, very infectious'. While much of the *nukkad natak* was on 'soft topics', there were 'hard core' political plays that directly took on its opposition and risked violence.

Years later Prateek would set his second year dialogue exercise, *Kal 15 August Dukaan Band Rahegi*, in this vacant and suspenseful moment in Delhi's student history. It is an evening inside a tiny students' paying guest apartment hostel on the eve of India's Independence Day. A small group of students prepare for a play in the midst of campus elections. Props need to be made, dialogue and casting needs working out, even as slogans need to be thought up for an independent candidate. Alcohol too needs to be acquired in advance, for the next day is officially 'dry'. Two men bearing some kind of authority arrive at the door – it is not clear whether they are the police or simply goons, for they never produce any official identification – seeking to terrorize the students. A bottle of rum falls over to the street, the goons return and abduct one of the students, perhaps because he has a Muslim name ('Kabir'). Another tries to make a phone call, and the film ends with the enigmatic line, 'Do you have a network?'

The Hacker's Arrival

In 2000, the Information Technology Act was the first to give a name to this inchoate Other: the hacker. The IT Act spent much time discussing how to digitally reproduce the ideals of citizenship. Virtual identities were still being invented in what was even now quaintly described as 'cyberspace', often as blurry alter-egos commonly described as 'cyborgs' (ambiguously human and ambiguously gendered mutant figures on the edges of legality). Inevitably, the IT Act also individuated its chosen good/bad guy against whom it was mobilizing the might of the state, or whom it might now hire in the digital war against the faceless 'cyber-hacker'. Such a hacker, declared an Enemy of the People and the target of its notorious Section 66, was anyone who caused 'wrongful loss or damage to the public' or altered information in a computer that might 'diminish its value or utility'.[28]

As the very survival of numerous Indian 'residents' came to depend on their possession of a digital existence, these residents were further segregated by the extent of citizenship rights – often repackaged as 'benefits' – for which they had to qualify. Privacy-entitled 'citizens' were separated out from multiple elusive and unidentifiable categories of illegals. In 2003, the Rules on Registration of Citizens and Issue of National Identity Cards defined, for the first time, a 'Local Register of Indian Citizens' in which 'individuals whose Citizenship is doubtful' would be weeded out.[29] From now on identity meant, first and foremost, isolating the outsider, and so, in 2004, the Citizenship Amendment Act declared *descent* rather than *birth* as providing the right of citizenship. That same year, the Unlawful Activities Prevention Act was also amended, and would find several famous targets in some of the country's best known political dissidents: the PUCL's Binayak Sen, Maoist leader Kobad Ghandy, activists from the Bhima Koregaon agitation, Assamese peasant activist Akhil Gogoi, Telugu poet and activist Varavara Rao, and students arrested during Delhi's anti-CAA agitations. The two amendments, the CAA and the UAPA, though separate, came to be increasingly read together as they fused *migrants*, *terrorists*, *displaced peasantry* and *political dissidents* into society's new dangerous classes.

Over the next two decades, as data production turned into surveillance, it also produced the official imprimatur of the faceless Other. As art, whether partial text, picture or sound, came to be first translated into and then originally produced on digital platforms, the negotiation between analogue and digital would prove tricky and sometimes dangerous. It became a negotiation between visibility and invisibility, the surface and the subterranean. It would receive a distinct edge in the transformation of the public (analogue) artist–filmmaker into an anonymous (digital) producer–perpetuator of information. Such a transformation would take on board new digital publics which it discovered as hardwired into a hierarchy of retail

-28

Section 66 of the IT Act: Hacking with computer system: 'Whoever with the intent to cause or knowing that he is likely to cause wrongful loss or damage to the public or any person destroys or deletes or alters any information residing in a computer resource or diminishes its value or utility or affects it injuriously by any means, commits hack.'

-29

Citizenship (Registration of Citizens and Issue of National Identity Cards) Rules, 2003.

points, and thus far less egalitarian than their analogue predecessors. It would also discover multiple ways of circulating post-original and post-authorial moving images. It would above all be an era of the transformation of the hypervisible *regisseur* into the invisible hacker.

To *be a filmmaker* in Ghatak's sense came to be defined by an ability to handle the horrors of celluloid: like his fictional Neelkanth, to hold its poison. The idea of filmmaker as hacker is curiously underdeveloped in theory in India. In its practice, hacking comes on the heels of the collage, the readymade and the copy, its primary actions defined by quotation, splicing, sampling and remixing. It is a foundational repudiation of originality: both in the identity of the maker and in the object made. Hackers do not write original code and filmmaker-hackers do not make original films. Both enter spaces where others have been. Both work with materials others have previously handled. They thus typically *re*write, translate, modify. Hito Steyerl tries to describe the concept with the idea of 'dirty data': something gathered in the process of shooting, meaningless bits of matter that are now attributed meaning – or the capacity to extract

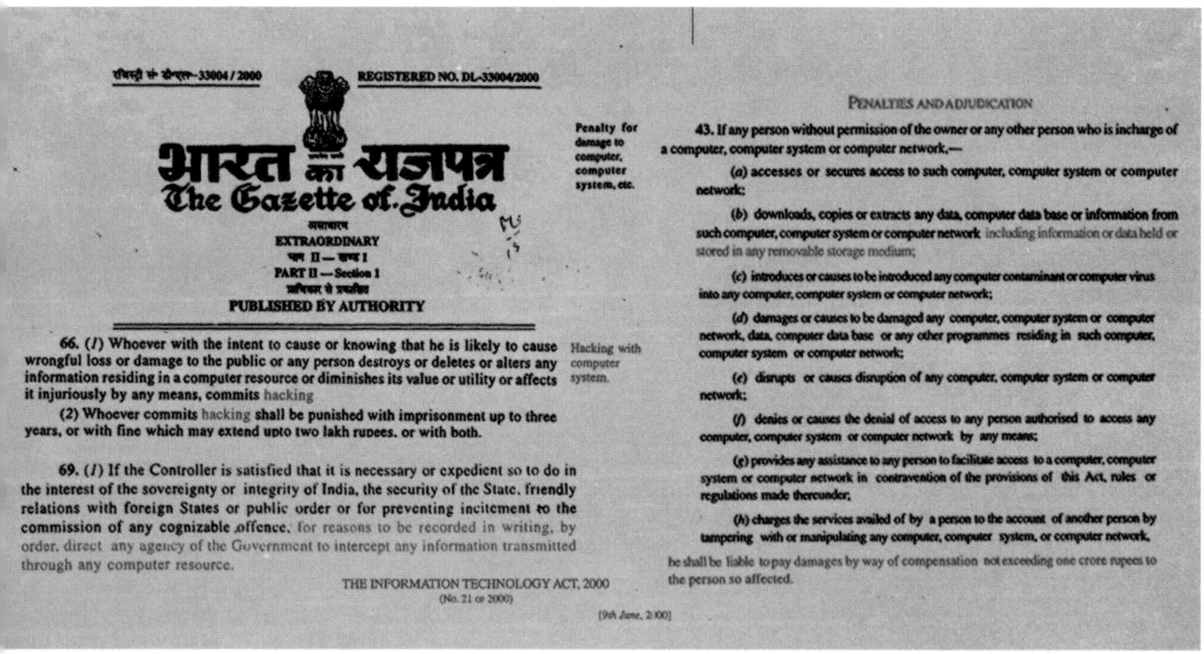

रजिस्ट्री सं डीएल-33004/2000 REGISTERED NO. DL-33004/2000

भारत का राजपत्र
The Gazette of India

असाधारण
EXTRAORDINARY
भाग II — खण्ड 1
PART II — Section 1
प्राधिकार से प्रकाशित
PUBLISHED BY AUTHORITY

66. (*1*) Whoever with the intent to cause or knowing that he is likely to cause wrongful loss or damage to the public or any person destroys or deletes or alters any information residing in a computer resource or diminishes its value or utility or affects it injuriously by any means, commits hacking

(2) Whoever commits hacking shall be punished with imprisonment up to three years, or with fine which may extend upto two lakh rupees, or with both.

Hacking with computer system.

69. (*1*) If the Controller is satisfied that it is necessary or expedient so to do in the interest of the sovereignty or integrity of India, the security of the State, friendly relations with foreign States or public order or for preventing incitement to the commission of any cognizable offence, for reasons to be recorded in writing, by order, direct any agency of the Government to intercept any information transmitted through any computer resource.

THE INFORMATION TECHNOLOGY ACT, 2000
(No. 21 of 2000)

[9th *June*, 2000]

PENALTIES AND ADJUDICATION

Penalty for damage to computer, computer system, etc.

43. If any person without permission of the owner or any other person who is incharge of a computer, computer system or computer network,—

(*a*) accesses or secures access to such computer, computer system or computer network;

(*b*) downloads, copies or extracts any data, computer data base or information from such computer, computer system or computer network including information or data held or stored in any removable storage medium;

(*c*) introduces or causes to be introduced any computer contaminant or computer virus into any computer, computer system or computer network;

(*d*) damages or causes to be damaged any computer, computer system or computer network, data, computer data base or any other programmes residing in such computer, computer system or computer network;

(*e*) disrupts or causes disruption of any computer, computer system or computer network;

(*f*) denies or causes the denial of access to any person authorised to access any computer, computer system or computer network by any means;

(*g*) provides any assistance to any person to facilitate access to a computer, computer system or computer network in contravention of the provisions of this Act, rules or regulations made thereunder;

(*h*) charges the services availed of by a person to the account of another person by tampering with or manipulating any computer, computer system, or computer network,

he shall be liable to pay damages by way of compensation not exceeding one crore rupees to the person so affected.

The first official construction of the 'hacker': The Information Technology Act, 2000, mash-up with Sections 43, 66-A and 69.

meaning that may well both pre-exist and lie beyond the filmmaker's intervention.[30]

-30

Hito Steyerl, 'A Sea of Data: Apophenia and Pattern (Mis-) Recognition', *e-flux*, issue 72, April 2016.

-31

Gurvinder Singh, Rajula Shah, Anupam Srinivasan, 'Unmaking of Film Institute', *Economic and Political Weekly*, 18 November 2000, pp. 4092–93.

The Hacker's Unconscious

In 2000, as a second wave of strikes broke out against Agashe's revised syllabus, Gurvinder Singh and Rajula Shah wrote a joint note (which the *Economic and Political Weekly* uniquely chose to publish in its front political section), where they described a change 'so fundamental' that it went beyond the FTII. It 'hit at the right to free expression and individual thinking'.[31] Singh and Shah saw the development politically, as a 'larger design of privatization and globalization' that would lead to the place being viewed as a means for 'generating profits rather than a centre of learning'. The change they foresaw took place by stealth and saw multiple little skirmishes break out on the campus that built up over the decade, exploding into the Great War over celluloid in 2010 during the Hewitt scandal.

By the mid-2000s, as the problems Singh and Shah feared gradually came true, the material of celluloid became something of a *cause célèbre*. Its physical fragility leaked into pedagogic practices. Syllabi became harder to complete, exercises took longer, and unexpected problems arose including a profound lack of clarity about just *whose* problems they were.

These developments defined several of the basic characteristics of hacker cinema, it seemed. *One*, its volatile and often contentious relationship with whatever it worked on or, more likely, *worked over*. In contrast to the era of the high-modern *regisseur* when it was assumed that filmmakers had the absolute right to modify and transform matter received from multiple places – literary texts, performative idioms, whatever – the processes of both modification and transformation became increasingly more aggressive. An early example here was probably Mani Kaul's hacking of Muktibodh's literature in *Satah Se Utatha Admi*, controversial for several Marxist admirers of the original author.

Two, its repurposing of the material of cinema – celluloid, in this instance – in the awareness of its essentially transient and fugitive nature: most starkly evident in its tensions with video and digital platforms. These tensions were especially evidenced by, and may have even been the defining feature of, the *prayoga* practitioners, in Amrit Gangar's well known use of the term.[32] The hacker's return to cinematic materiality also appeared, paradoxically, to have the added benefit of producing a rough-and-ready archival resolution of celluloid's material transience.

For, *three*, it also led to a morphing of the filmmaker from a modernist-originalist into something else: into a recycler of material. A non- or perhaps post-original cinema both relied on precedent 'dirty data' as well as created its own dirt for future hackers to work on. Cinema, especially documentary cinema – but really all films working with found materials – came to be part of a larger production chain, taking from previous material and itself becoming available to others for future use. As filmmaking and film viewing increasingly fused into a single identity – as viewers also began watching with their hands, so to say – what was once 'reception' theory now entered a new-generation maker culture that inched closer to gaming and memes.

Pedagogy became more a rite of initiation than a technical learning: it included secret knowledges, workarounds and tricks handed down from batch to batch as the 'seniors', more than institutional teachers, guided the freshers, including in controversial practices like *satsangs* (a benign term for ragging). Mani Kaul marvels at the FTII's resilience in Gurvinder Singh's loving tribute to the place in a short that he simply named *An Untitled Film* (2008), believing it to be the ghost of Ghatak stalking the corridors. To many students, it is also the invisible workforce on the campus – the casual labour whose interests became a key flashpoint in both 2011 and 2015.

This workforce included several people who either themselves once belonged to or were descended from the old Prabhat Studio era, as we see in Aman Wadhan's mesmerizing 2011 student dialogue project *Prabhat Nagari 1*, shot mainly in the main studio. Their existence on campus merged into the popular belief that if you worked late in the sound studio, you could sometimes hear the orchestras of Keshavrao Bhole tuning up, or even the horse-hooves of Master Krishnarao riding up the main road. Sanjay Leela Bhansali, editing student in 1985 before he was rusticated,[33] remains convinced that the ghost of *Devdas* lives atop the Wisdom Tree and 'comes down and makes you see things'.[34]

-32

Prayoga: Amrit Gangar's preferred term for experimental film, first introduced at the Experimenta in 2005. Scan to see Shai Heredia in conversation with Gangar, *experimenta.in*.

-33

Priya Gupta, 'I was thrown out of the Film Institute: Sanjay Leela Bhansali', *Times of India*, 25 November 2013.

-34

Anupama Chopra, 'FTII celebrates 40 years of existence with film festival', *India Today*, 1 December 2003.

Vikas Urs reflects some of Steedman's 'double nothingness' when he describes the experience of shooting on the campus: how to shoot anything, *that* tree, *that* wall, differently from the thousand other shots in which that precise tree and wall have previously appeared in someone else's film. It is partly the fact that the amount of shooting that has been done, and is done daily, has seeped into every inch, revealed every crack, of that over-filmed and visually drained campus. The feeling that whatever you do it's all been done before, further merges into the uncanny of the Great Masters looking over your shoulder at every moment as you look through your viewfinder and set up your shot.

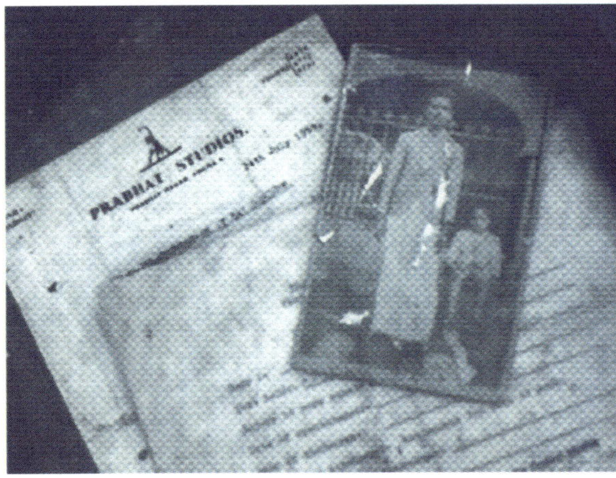

Ghostly presences proliferate: figures both alive and dead from the former Prabhat Studios on the campus, in Aman Wadhan's **Prabhat Nagari–1** (2011).

To Vikas, it is in the playback or 'song picturization' exercise that the problem becomes most acute: when students often pick up famous film songs or other pieces of filmed sound and reset them to an entirely new visual setting. He speaks of the Holi celebrations in which students, in the middle of the often drunken phantasmagoria, watch a giant loop of song-playback exercises (once, legend has it, they watched 'censor cuts' loaned by P.K. Nair from the National Film Archive) only to look for, and to celebrate, a truly new twist that a young filmmaker may have brought to the overly familiar resources in the overly familiar space.[35] Living on campus has an incessant sense of the uncanny, defining the misbehaviour, *badtameezi*, escapades and violations, merging the formality of classroom instruction with informal debates into the night.

—

Authorial insecurities began to take strange shapes. By 2006, unusual genres began appearing in student films, such as horror, to take one instance in sound designer Anish John's student short *Hostel*. This short is apparently very popular on YouTube, where it is also known for being Rajkummar Rao's first ever screen appearance. Shot and also effectively set on the campus (disguised in the fiction as a medical college), it has a young female student being 'ragged' when she is locked into her room with the chopped hand of a corpse.

35 Conversation with Vikas Urs, 11 December 2018, Goa.

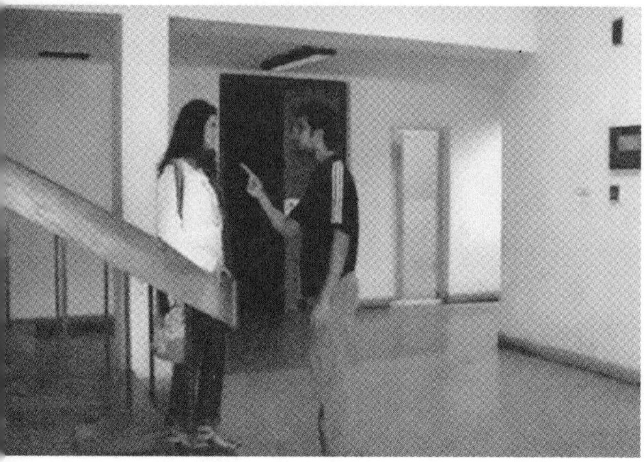

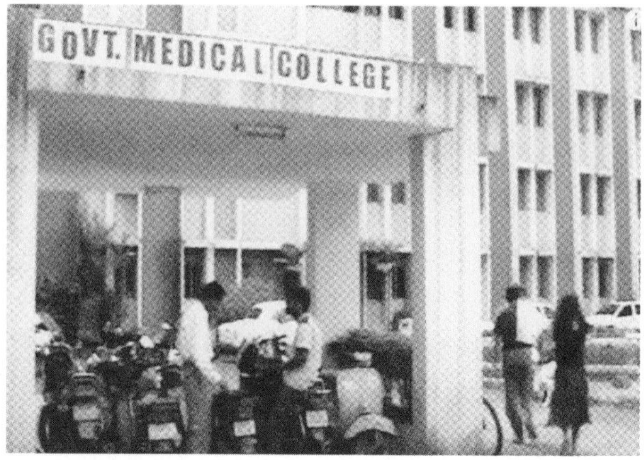

The spooking turns to horror in Anish John's diploma film, **Hostel** (2006), as the campus is dressed up to look like a medical college.

When the bullies open the door, the girl has turned into a cannibal, eating the hand. The explicit locations on the campus – the familiar student hostel and the main administrative building corridor – echo *Holi*, allowing us to also read into the metaphor of being locked up with a corpse and then devouring it. It is a direct reference to the cannibalism to which students make common reference, the push and pull of the 'medium', and the academic and technological exorcism of celluloid.

In 2006, another student diploma production, Indraneel Kaul's short fiction film *In Thin Air*, revealed a new twenty-first century imagination of the strike-torn campus. A student is struggling with a script. The problem he has, however, is that he is writing it in a world that has turned upside down and in which everyone is walking backwards. The campus is itself a militarized zone full of heavily armed troops behind bunkers. A senior documentary filmmaker now enters the CRT to advise students on their projects and finds himself stumbling into various innocuous screenplay ideas that the students outline one by one, all of which turn out to be, in odd ways, about the campus agitation going on outside, even as that agitation descends into a semi-permanent pitched battle.

Two different film projects now merge. The senior filmmaker has his own covert reasons to be there. The first is to figure out the situation by tracing it to a long-ago former student of the 1972 batch named Vyas Khanna who still haunts the campus. The second is a screenplay idea on the only man left who seems to be able to still walk forwards, the canteen *chaiwala*. This man leads the documentarist

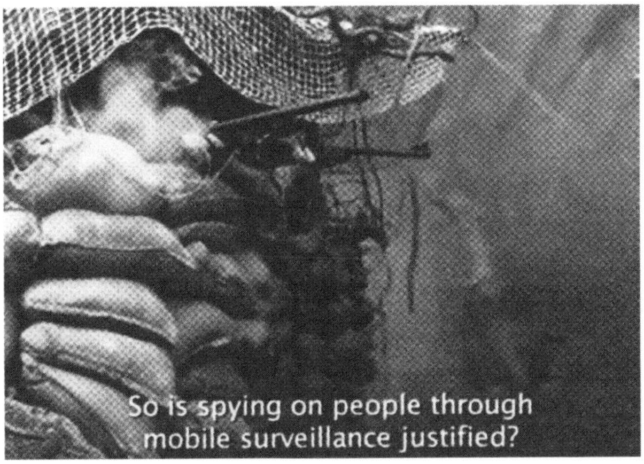

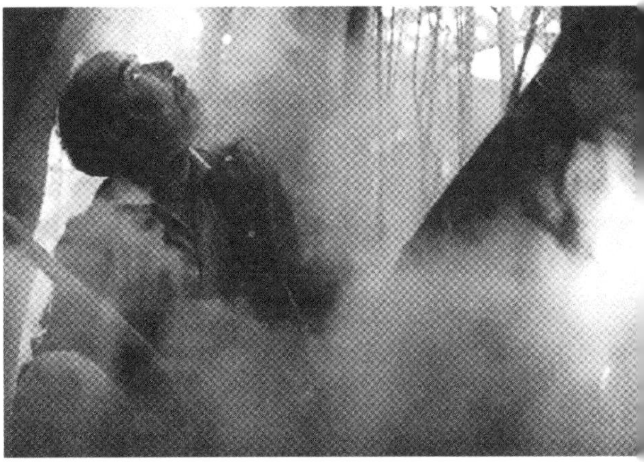

The campus as a war zone: students make films in the midst of gunfire in Indraneel Kaul's **In Thin Air** (2006).

to armed guerrillas who are hiding out on treetops. Their leader named Chipkoo turns out to be the 1972 strike leader, living on as an immobile lizard on the canteen wall (on which another student, it happens, wants to make his film).

We move into the present. The filmmaker realizes that his search for a figure from the past has actually revealed a very contemporary struggle, as we hear a voice shout 'going for take ... silence'. A shot is being taken, but right in the middle of it an accident happens on the set. A member of the faculty insists however that they shoot on, for the studio will not be available for a month. This leads to full-scale military war as gunfire is exchanged between the entrenched troops and students holding placards asking for creative freedom, even as the faculty member bemoans lack of funding and threatens the campus with closure.

'Imagination ... [as] a photographic emulsion'

On the campus, as students found it more difficult to realize whatever it was that they were trying to do, their struggles brought new meaning to the old 1977 Satish Candra Committee dictum that the student 'work with his hands ... grapple with all the problems attendant in filmmaking at the basic, practical, realistic level'.

To Amit Dutta, it became a question of how to convert a technological crisis into a *material* challenge. In 2000, when Sony PD-100 camcorders first arrived on the campus, Dutta says they treated video like a 'kind of 16 mm'.[36] He asserts his indebtedness to the Bauhaus and to Stan Brakhage, neither of whom was

-36
Conversation with Amit Dutta on WhatsApp, 23 December 2020.

part of any campus curriculum. At the same time – and he saw no contradiction here – he also became increasingly interested in filmmaking as a kind of *craft* practice, indeed to even ascribe to it a tribal origin. In his first year at the FTII, he borrowed one of its PD-150 devices to make a film on Warli art for the Anthropology Department of Pune University. His later work would include the art of the Gond community, and the artist Jangarh Singh Shyam.[37]

When Dutta joined Agashe's post-sanitization batch, he had had little exposure to art other than a familial relationship with the poet Abid Munavari, and some familiarity with Urdu, Persian and Dogri. In 2003, for his student diploma, he returned the craft question to some of the oldest practices of filmmaking in India: the special effects of Phalke and Baburao Painter. He began to make optical special effects by working directly on celluloid material. For this he used a campus heirloom: a Panavision Mitchell BNC camera, apparently inherited from Prabhat Studios. The Mitchell was enormous, mounted on a stand that required four people to lift, and looked, he said, almost like a *palki* (palanquin). It had been previously used for in-camera optical effects by Cinematography Professor R.M. Rao in the 1980s for advertising films.[38] Dutta now turned, for his student film *Ksha Tra Gya*, to the legendary Hindi filmmaker Babubhai Mistry, maker of several of India's best-known mythologicals and stunt films, and to Mistry's optical special effects work. As he wrote in the screenplay of a proposed film on Mistry, Dutta was fascinated with how Mistry achieved

> extraordinary actions of gods and goddesses (appearing/disappearing effect, multiplying heads, arrows suddenly stopping in the sky) or the making of mobile icons (in continuation of Dadasaheb Phalke). Mistry designed double roles, flying cars, natural cataclysms, optical effects for song picturizations and invented surprising scenarios mixing the story of gods and humans.[39]

'Indispensable to the world of Mistry', says Dutta's screenplay, was the Mitchell. 'This camera has been the continuation of Mistry's eye, the extension of his body.'

> What is so special about the Mitchell camera that was so appealing to the Indian trick photographers? Is there a secret inside this camera that has never been discovered? Re-manipulating a Mitchell camera is a way to question cinema as a whole, meditating upon the

-37

Dutta has been fascinated with Jangarh Singh Shyam, a 39-year-old Pardhan-Gond artist from Patangarh village in Madhya Pradesh, who took his own life inside a museum in Japan. Dutta has written a book on him, *Invisible Webs: An Art Historical Inquiry into the Life And Death of Jangarh Singh Shyam*, Shimla: Indian Institute of Advanced Study, 2018.

-38

Interview with R.M. Rao, C.K. Muraleedharan and Raqs Media Collective, in *The History and Practice of Cinematography in India*, November 1996.

-39

From the documentary film proposal, 'The Fabulous World of Babubhai Mistry', by Amit Dutta and Emmanuel Grimaud. The film was never made. I am grateful to Dutta for sharing the proposal statement.

mystery of the cinematic device, because Mistry's imagination and photographic emulsion are deeply intertwined, forming a unique chemical operation.

The trick here was to repeatedly re-expose footage on the Mitchell. You could do this by either covering different parts – a moving image equivalent of 'dodging', used when developing still photographs – or you could superimpose effects. Such in-camera special effects were of practical significance, says Dutta, since they lessened the filmmaker's dependence on the laboratory, which was often poor, and commercial labs rarely processed their films with clean liquid.

But then they began speaking to a different history. It was why young cinematographers, for example, preferred Fuji colour stock to Kodak, the industry standard. Fuji had, Dutta says, a 'saturated, dreamlike, unworldly' quality. He tried this technique again in his better known *Kramasha* (2007), and has since then made special effects something of a signature technique, especially in the merging of live action with animation (*Nainsukh*, 2010; *Chitrashala*, 2015).

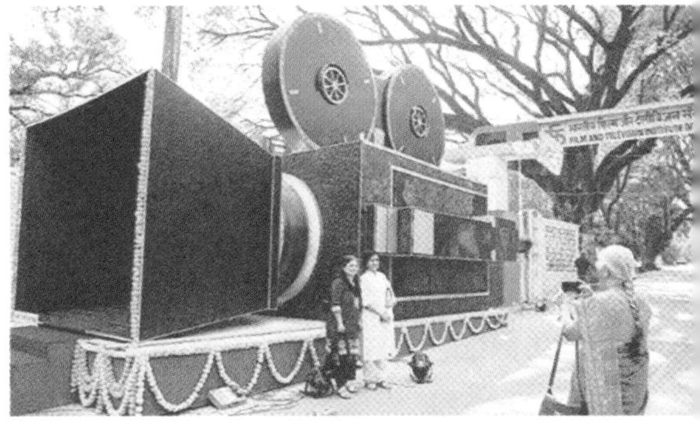

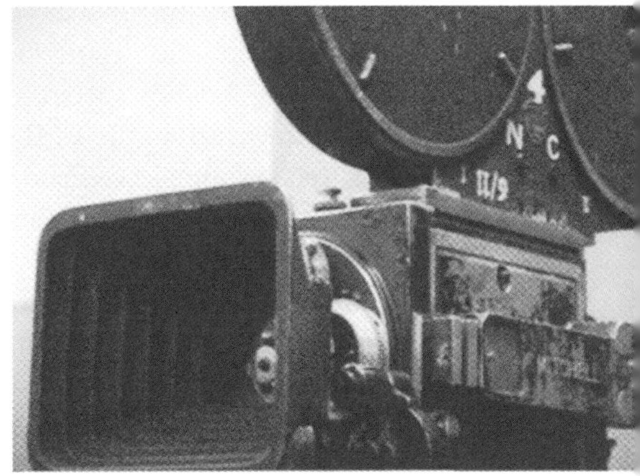

The Mitchell and the Trick Photographer. Above: The Mitchell heirloom reconstructed outside the campus main gate, to see the **Prabhat to FTII** exhibition created by Ashutosh Kavishwar of the Art Direction and Production Design Department in March 2000. **Below:** The original Mitchell in Rais Siddiqui's **A Day's Feel in the FTII** (2010) (detail).

—

To Dutta, Mistry possessed a condition of consciousness that was a 'unique chemical operation', an 'imagination' intertwined with 'photographic emulsion'. The same year as *In Thin Air* produced its Chipkoo the lizard, the invisible student haunting the campus became an entirely new and far more complex, shadowy and elusive public author – as meme, troll, data shadow ['Kamal Swaroop'].

In 2011 Naveen made a student film, *Open Café V 2.5*, in which Kamal Swaroop, who describes himself inside the film as a self-confessed vagrant walking up and down streets, sits in an Irani café, and in a poignant moment, reads together with an equally lonely fellow customer a passage from Edgar Allen Poe's *The Raven*. By then Swaroop had become an iconic figure on the FTII campus. Embodying the chaos of celluloid, its trial by fire, he had virtually assumed the status of a Neelkantha figure, direct successor to Ghatak himself: a man who had swallowed the deadly poison of the celluloid era and lived to tell the tale.

Along the way, Swaroop completed something of a hacker's classic: a reconstruction of the life and career of Indian cinema's self-proclaimed founder, Dadasaheb Phalke. This included an entire cycle of films, including *Phalke's Children* (1994), *Rangbhoomi* (2013), *Tracing Phalke* (2016) and *Samudra Manthan* (2019), and one astonishing scrap book. In *Tracing Phalke*, Swaroop and several of his students from the FTII – well-known names including cinematographer Saumyananda Sahi, filmmakers Hansa Thapliyal, Renu Sawant and Amit Dutta – set out to visit every city Phalke had lived in, to uncover what his cinema might mean to digital practitioners today.

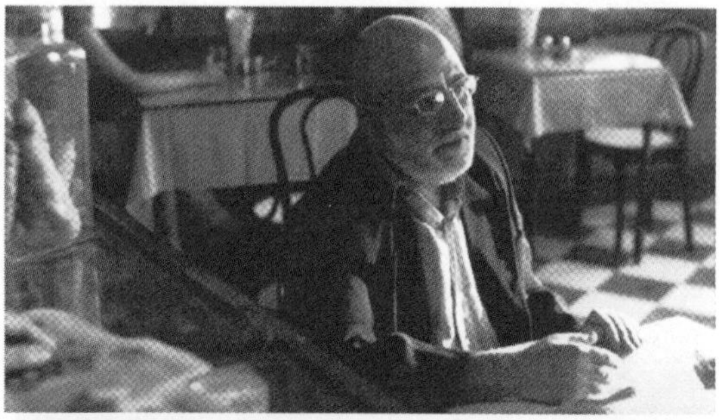

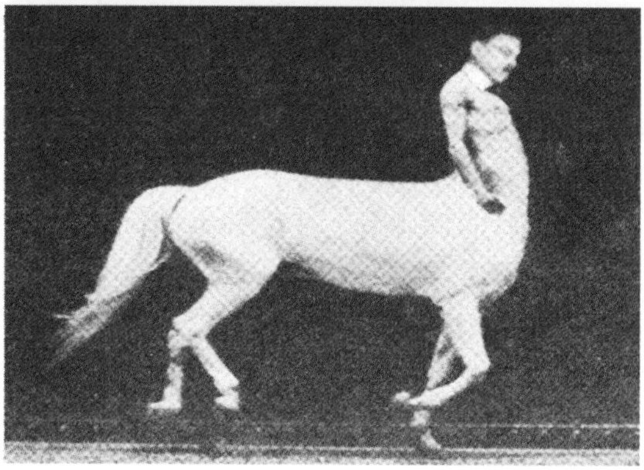

Kamal Swaroop as wraith. Above: Alone in the Irani café, in Naveen Padmanabha's **Open Café V 2.5** (2011). **Below:** Dadasaheb Phalke grafted atop a George Melies centaur, in Kamal Swaroop's **Tracing Phalke** (2016).

They encounter mounds of data, especially in Benaras, and then set about reading diverse patterns and meanings into these. They move from magic to photography, from tribal cultures to the elite courtly practices of Baroda and Travancore, and from Muybridge – whose experiment with horses becomes a leitmotif – and Méliès to the Shiva temple of Trymbakeshwar.

Both Mistry and (we may now presume) Phalke became, for Dutta and Swaroop respectively, 'makers' whose consciousness was defined by the dirty data they had received, processed and produced. Phalke and Mistry are, as they were now being processed, no longer auteurs but early versions of a long history of the celluloid medium turning into a *medium*. We may now see in Mistry's 'imagination ... [as] a photographic emulsion', a graphic example of Hito Steyerl's upgrading of Walter Benjamin's optical unconscious into the 'unconscious of computational image divination'. Steyerl uses the term 'inceptionism'. It is borrowed apparently from Google researchers as a kind of 'deep dreaming' – untrammelled overinterpretation randomly using presets and stereotypes regardless of whether they 'apply' or not, with intriguing results in which 'even a relatively simple neural network can be used to over-interpret an image'.[40] The material consciousness of the cinema coalesced multiple states of what Mani Kaul would name *samakramikata* in multiple locations.[41]

The Camera and the Tsunami

Across the early 2000s a small number of filmmakers began to arrive on the FTII campus – almost all of them ex-students. From 2006 you start seeing their names in the 'acknowledged-with-gratitude' lists in the end-credits of student films. Naveen's *Open Café V 2.5* thanks Kamal Swaroop, Kumar Shahani and R.V. Ramani, and his film *Glass* thanks Shahani, Ramani, Swaroop, Fareeda Mehta and Amitabh Chakraborty. These names, both of in-house faculty (such as Arghya Basu) and visiting faculty (such as editor Paresh Kamdar, cinematographers Piyush Shah, Rajeev Ravi and Anil Mehta, sound designer Resul Pookutty) become visible roughly from 2006, and remain prominent presences across a decade of external workshops in direction, editing, camera and sound, mostly conducted by ex-students helping out with the technological morass into which the place had begun to descend. All of these names later find themselves implicated, in one way or another, in the 2015 strike. A few are accused of instigation and would feature in an informal institutional blacklist of those banned from official invitation to the campus.

Several of these names are well known in the film industry. Others have niche art-house reputations. All can however be defined by a key characteristic. They saw the demise of celluloid, and the equally horrifying mounds of digital content that their apparatus of picture and sound could now generate – and lived to tell the tale. They thus knew something about the *subjective experience* of navigating the transition. Like the protagonist in Tarkovsky's *The Stalker*, like the malevolent Harprasad in Ghatak's *Subarnarekha*, they became as though tour-guides hand-holding – with varying degrees of success – a confused institution, a faculty out of its depth and students struggling to survive, through a bombed-out digital landscape, a tricky and often treacherous 'zone' of post-celluloid technology.

Perhaps the most graphic metaphor for the filmmaker's struggle with the horrors of dirty data was provided by Ramani's interpretation of his encounter with the 2004 tsunami, and the out-

-40

Steyerl, 'A Sea of Data'.

-41

When you make a film, Kaul argues, you shoot in a 'fully conscious state', you edit in a condition that is closer to dream-work because of 'how we join time, how we connect spaces, cutting in a way that severs the time–space link that was established while shooting'. In contrast, the film-viewing experience coalesces these differential states into 'one knot'. The mind, having no 'location' other than its awareness that it exists, is 'defined by the simultaneity, *samakramikata*, of these different stages'. *Uncloven Space: Mani Kaul in Conversation with Udayan Vajpeyi* (translation of *Abhed Akaash* by Gurvinder Singh).

of-body experience he shared with his beloved PD-100. Ramani began his career with celluloid – his famous debut work, *Saa* (1991), is made on 16 mm – but since then took to video and so became a one-person film unit, perhaps the most independent of India's independent filmmakers.

He was in Nagercoil when the deadly wave hit. The camera became an extension of his body as he hung on to it for dear life, with each trying to save the other from going under – 'Drowning and being dragged half a kilometre over a rough surface, crashing through coconut groves, trees, bushes, ditches, rocks, walls ... I kept repeating only two things to myself: hold your breath, and don't let go of the camera.'[42] When he got up, 'slowly, dazed, and reeling with disbelief', he discovered that his 'camera still remained firm in the palm of my right hand, broken ... there were dead bodies scattered all around me'. He wrote from Nagercoil of his friends, dead or injured, and finally of his camera, 'broken, clogged with water and sand. I don't know if it can be repaired or if the footage can be salvaged. The images, hitherto unseen ... would be heart-rending. But no more so than my memories.'

When *My Camera and the Tsunami* was eventually completed in 2011 (it took Ramani that long to work out what had happened), both camera and wave came together to become an elegy for the life, the family and the multiple ongoing interests filmed over the years: stuff lying, like mildewed photo albums and scrawled writing pads, across hard disks waiting to be used, or, equally likely, never used. A technological crisis turns existential as nature merges into an informational tsunami that his lightweight camera, his all-seeing 'third eye', appears relentlessly able to produce. It was in this time, between 2006 and 2015, that Ramani conducted his direction and editing, and very occasional cinematography, workshops, struggling once again to teach them to 'be filmmakers' at a time when there was technically no more film but simply data: piles of evanescent debris.

Fareeda Mehta's sole feature-length film, the acclaimed *Kali Salwar* (2002), was still a new work when she began doing workshops at FTII in 2006, the same year as Ramani. She was a regular on the campus for the next decade, working with direction, scriptwriting and sound. In this time she came (Prateek says) 'many times, for months, for all batches, different streams, direction, camera ... [to

-42 R.V. Ramani, 'Waves of Wrath', *Sarai Reader 06: Turbulence*, Delhi: The Sarai Programme, CSDS, 2006, pp. 97–98.

conduct] probably the most intense workshops' they had ever had.[43] Vikas speaks of her workshops as merging dreamwork with *haiku* poetry, and an effort to get students to 'move away from politics and into poetics', to introduce a consciousness of subjectivity on the campus at a critical moment in its history.[44]

Ramani is modest. He took students on field visits to Rajasthan, Kerala and deep Maharashtra (Ralegan Siddhi), trying mainly to get them to 'think independently', to 'try and find deeper expression'.[45] His workshops have been entirely on video – the possibility of celluloid 'never really came up' – and he focuses in his teachings on handheld cameras and on keeping things simple.

Mehta too is reticent about what she did there. She describes her effort as an attempt to 'discourage *uchalo*ing', and asks me if I know that famous 'FTII word'.[46]

-43

Conversation with Prateek Vats, 14 December 2018, Mumbai.

-44

Conversation with Vikas Urs, 11 December 2018, Goa.

-45

Conversation with R.V. Ramani on Zoom, 3 January 2021.

-46

WhatsApp message to author from Fareeda Mehta, 10 September 2020. Like all colloquialisms, the word is not easily translatable. Meaning to 'throw', 'toss' or 'bounce', it can mean overdoing things, producing shortcuts, claiming more than is achieved or overstating your case.

CHAPTER 5

FREEDOM AND DREAD

In 2004, the Oriya filmmaker Sushant Mishra (known for his landmark *Indradhanura Chhai*, 1993) inaugurated a new kind of film festival in the coastal town of Puri. Launched together with fellow FTII alumnus Gurpal Singh, they named it the BYOFF or 'Bring Your Own Film Festival'.

In 1990, the MIFF (Mumbai International Film Festival) was launched, dedicated to documentaries and short films. It ended the dominance of the only international film festival India had had until then, the IFFI, officially one of only fifteen competitive festivals recognized by the FIAPF (International Federation of Film Producers Associations). In 1996–97 annual film festivals began in Kolkata and Trivandrum, creating a format that has now expanded to several cities. All of these are government-run.

BYOFF defined its identity in contrast to all of these: it did not, for one, select the films it showed; it offered no awards; it made no promise of 'quality'. Anyone could roll up and screen their creations if they fulfilled a few basic criteria and paid a small entry fee. BYOFF has run purely on cinephiliac energy – and has been able to generate plenty of that in spectacular screenings over the years, such as the first-ever 2013 projection of Q's legendary 2010 film *Gandu* over a residential apartment block used as a screen.

In the same year that BYOFF began, MIFF too saw a major act of filmmaker resistance. As Anand Patwardhan recounts it, MIFF was aware that several films had been made on the deadly riots that had recently taken place in Gujarat, and that many entries would be 'on the carnage in Gujarat exposing the ruling party's complicity [that would] embarrass it on an international stage'.[1] And so MIFF amended its entry procedures, requiring all Indian films to show a censor certificate even though foreign films remained exempt (film festivals have historically been exempt from censorship requirements).

In response, some 275 filmmakers took their films and crossed the street. They found another venue in front of MIFF, where they

Facing page
Proposed plan for a major extension of the FTII campus conceived by the 'Group of Experts Convened by the Governing Council', informally known as the Nair Committee, 2011. The space across the Hanuman Tekdi hillock would be accessed through an underpass, with lakes, amphitheatres, studios named after Ritwik Ghatak, K.K. Mahajan and S.B. Thakar. Sketch by Nachiket and Jayoo Patwardhan.

-1 Anand Patwardhan, 'Films for Freedom', *Frontline*, 27 February 2004.

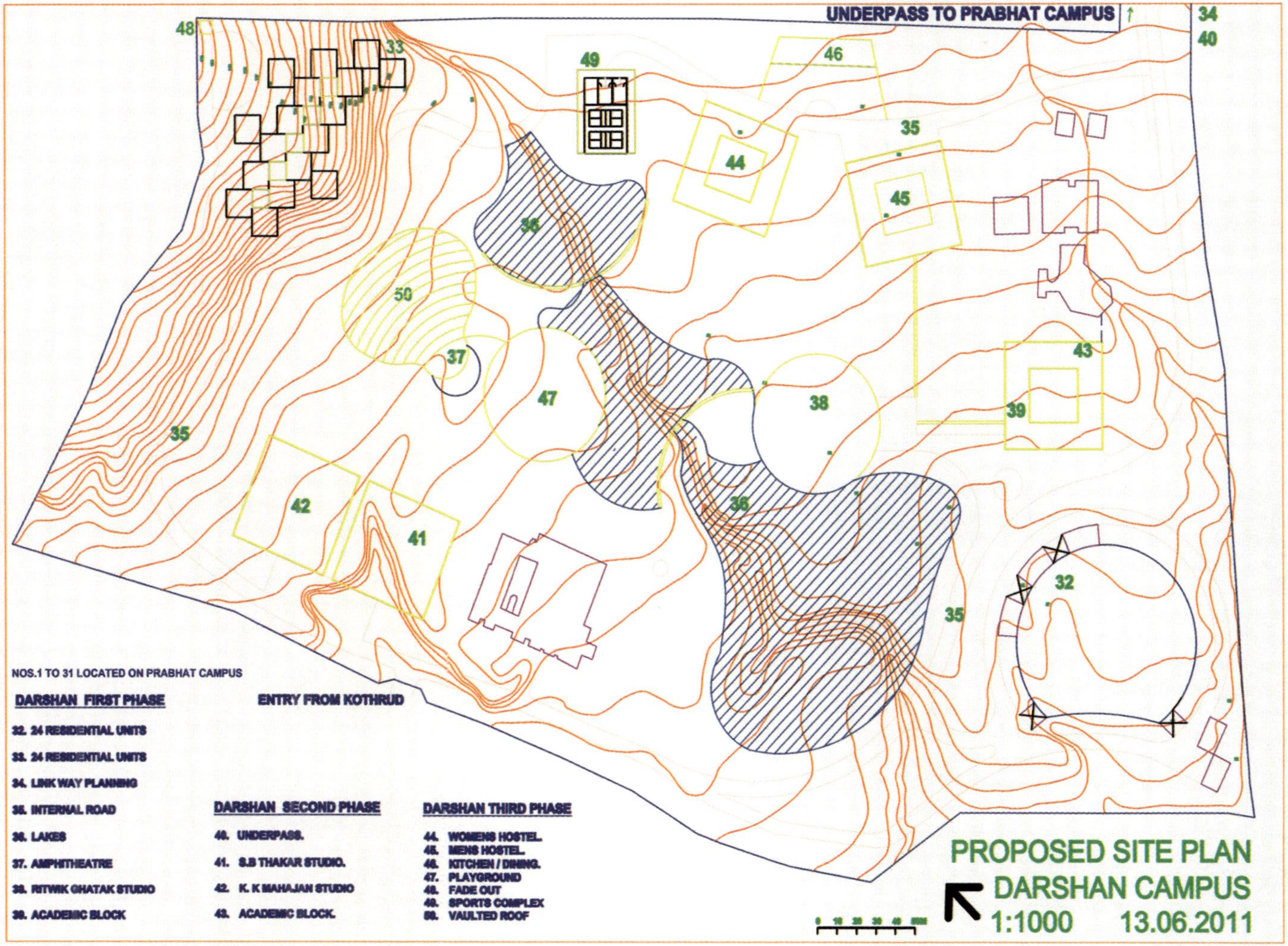
UNDERPASS TO PRABHAT CAMPUS
ENTRY FROM KOTHRUD
NOS.1 TO 31 LOCATED ON PRABHAT CAMPUS
DARSHAN FIRST PHASE
32. 24 RESIDENTIAL UNITS
33. 24 RESIDENTIAL UNITS
34. LINK WAY PLANNING
35. INTERNAL ROAD
36. LAKES
37. AMPHITHEATRE
38. RITWIK GHATAK STUDIO
39. ACADEMIC BLOCK
DARSHAN SECOND PHASE
40. UNDERPASS.
41. S.B THAKAR STUDIO.
42. K. K MAHAJAN STUDIO
43. ACADEMIC BLOCK.
DARSHAN THIRD PHASE
44. WOMENS HOSTEL.
45. MENS HOSTEL.
46. KITCHEN / DINING.
47. PLAYGROUND
48. FADE OUT
49. SPORTS COMPLEX
50. VAULTED ROOF
PROPOSED SITE PLAN
DARSHAN CAMPUS
1:1000 13.06.2011

set up a counter-festival which they named Vikalp, and with it, a Campaign Against Censorship. Patwardhan writes:

> The Bhupesh Gupta Bhavan houses the printing press of the Communist Party of India. Their solidarity was unconditional, and their hall came free. Acoustic problems were overcome by thick curtains on windows and mattresses on the floor. Volunteers poured in from all over and the buzz was electric. Despite word-of-mouth publicity we had packed houses every day. VIKALP opened with an excerpt from Sadaat Hasan Manto's *Safed Jhoot*, an indictment of censorship and hypocrisy, performed by Jamil Khan, directed by Naseeruddin Shah. From this high we never came down. For 6 days rapt audiences saw and debated over 50 films and participated in panel discussions on censorship featuring Arundhati Roy, Nikhil Wagle and many others.[2]

-2
Anand Patwardhan, 'MIFF 2004 and its VIKALP', 10 February 2004, patwardhan.com

Both BYOFF and Vikalp were possible because new lightweight video equipment and easily available software for shooting, recording, editing and projection had by then allowed films to be made and shown independently of celluloid labs, and without censor certificates. Censorship in 2004 was still celluloid-bound, sedition laws hadn't yet kicked in, whereas filmmaking was at the cusp of major change.

Two halves of the story would now merge. On one side was documentary film, physically released from its projection limitations, moved from the safe spaces of the movie theatre, the lab and the festival – historically the containment zones of celluloid – to discover multiple platforms, locations and venues, private and public, on the street as well as in secret underground locations. And on the other, tactical media, using new numerous devices and analytics for tracking, surveillance and covert action.

—

In September 2010, Ramani found himself double-booked. He was scheduled to do a workshop with the FTII's second year direction batch, but he was also invited by BYOFF to an interesting experiment they were trying in Rajasthan, a fundraising-cum-filmmaking project supported by a motor sport and tour guides' association, linked to an invitation to travel through the state, generate geo-miles, to make films – and he didn't want to refuse that.

It occurred to Ramani that the best of both worlds might be achieved by combining the two. He persuaded FTII to let him move his workshop to Rajasthan. Their only contribution would be bus fare to the students and four PD-100s. BYOFF and Ramani's hosts would pay for the students' hospitality. Ramani made a road movie named *Padharo Mharey Desh* [Welcome to My Country], shot over nearly 2,000 kilometres of travel, and many students shot footage, some of which they completed while others remained exercises.

In the middle of the heat, the travel and the shooting, one of the students, Naveen Padmanabha, received an email. He had just been elected general secretary of the FTII Students' Association, and received an interim draft document submitted by Hewitt Associates, the consultancy company for outsourcing the management of human capital. That May, Hewitt had been commissioned by the Ministry of Information and Broadcasting to outline a vision and an operational roadmap for the FTII. Now they were submitting a Draft Project Report, a first cut of their plan for its upgradation to 'international standards'.

The Report appeared as though it was written in 'another universe'. As Naveen read it in the middle of the BYOFF experiment, the Hewitt DPR seemed at least twice removed from any reality he knew. It bore no relation either to the campus or to the film student. More importantly, perhaps, it bore no connection to the cinema as he was experiencing it at that moment; sitting under the cloudless Rajasthan flatlands, he felt the gap with particular intensity.

The Other Universe

Years later, in August 2015, when the strike reached its crescendo, Professor of Music and Acting Dean of Film Kedarnath Awati wrote a formal letter to the Ministry of Information and Broadcasting.[3] The letter was written in support of the students, mainly to throw light on a major crisis they faced. He was making a larger point. The problem of 2015, Awati stressed, was not new. It had been brewing since 2000, with the way the forced year-by-year elimination (that the brutal 1+1+1 system had envisaged) had been withdrawn. The problem was that the FTII had maintained the year-ending projects envisaged by the revised syllabus, 'without realizing that the original justification was no longer valid and the number of students in the

-3
Letter from Kedarnath Awati, dated 25 August 2015, shared with the author via email on 16 April 2021.

final year were 50% more than originally planned for'. The faculty knew 'from that time itself [2001] that the schedule was going to go haywire'. In 2008, 'even before the new students had arrived on campus, the faculty was pretty much certain that there was no way that the incoming batch of students could possibly complete their work within the three years laid down'.

By 2008, when the new batch – the very batch that would be the prime cause of the August 2015 *gherao* of the Director and the midnight entry of the police – was admitted against all faculty advice, the FTII was seriously overpopulated. Multiple batches found themselves working with scarce equipment and studio space; there was an acute shortage of hostel accommodation; and there were major fee hikes.[4] Numerous ad-hoc short-term 'self-financing' courses dominated the campus. The perennially provisional curriculum was impossible to complete in the allotted time. And to top it all, everybody was dealing with digital equipment that radically departed from anything the FTII had previously known.

Samarth Dixit, who was then the Students' Association president, Naveen and other student representatives spent time with the Hewitt staff trying hard to explain all this. They never felt they were getting through. Initially this was attributed to the inexperience of the Hewitt team. Prateek remembers his first meeting well: 'two people ... we couldn't believe they were some two 25–26-year-olds [entering] a film school for the first time ever, I am assuming, and saying this all needs to be done to a 60-year-old institute'.[5] Naveen too remembers them as young people, 'our age only', not familiar with, and in the end not very interested in, either the FTII or any campus-specific issues.[6]

The initial idea was to slow things down somehow, 'give them a pile of paperwork to read, *ke padh ke aao yeh sab, phir baat karna* [read all this and then come]. But it soon appeared that they already had a mandate. Prateek ticks off the items of that mandate from memory: *one*, to hike fees; *two*, to have three-month short-term courses 'and to build a lot of things on campus in name of infrastructure or hostel, classroom, this and that'; and *three* – the real carrot – the '27 acres of land just behind the campus'. They had 'massive designs of restructuring that land into a gaming and animation school to be run as a public–private partnership (or

-4

Chetna Kaul writes: 'In 2000, when I joined the institute, Mr Mohan Agashe was the Director and he had increased the fees from Rs 5000 to Rs 22500 in one academic year. If our only batch had not called for the successful strike he was about to raise it to Rupees One lakh. If that would have happened, after the Kashmiri Pandit exodus of 1990 with both of them working my parents could still not have afforded to pay my fee at the film school in spite of my clearing the entrance.' 'Government Spokesperson Sanjay Kaul clueless about the running of FTII', *Hillele*, 15 July 2015.

-5

Conversation with Prateek Vats, 14 December 2008, Mumbai.

-6

Conversation with Naveen Padmanabha, 4 October 2018, Bangalore.

PPP) between Reliance Entertainment and FTII'. 'If I remember correctly, about 55 crores was being given to FTII to upgrade itself, of which 45 crores was going to this new gaming and animation school ... it was [basically a] land deal.'

The reaction was swift. Students still had academic representation at the time and were able to get the Governing Council to appoint a 'consultative workshop of experts' to gather and review the Hewitt Report. A team of thirty-eight experts was assembled, comprising mostly ex-students including a few who had been involved in previous agitations, current student representatives and in-house faculty. They met over two days on 29 and 30 September 2010.

It was a contentious meeting, complicated and emotionally draining, of which there are multiple descriptions, elaborate official minutes and even a short documentary.[7] The problem wasn't Hewitt. Indeed, in the first couple of hours of the meeting the Hewitt Report 'was debated and discussed in detail and found to be inappropriate', and set aside 'on account of [its] flawed premises'.[8] That was the easy part. The main problem was how to read the Hewitt Report against its grain, to decipher from it the true intentions of the powers that be, to figure out how they may be challenged and a credible alternative vision put together that stood any hope in hell of being realized.

Taking Charge

In the end, the short shrift given to the disastrous Hewitt DPR was disproportionate to the visibility the strike would later bring to the name of the venerable management company. It was, after all, the second time within a decade that students had directly challenged the Ministry of Information and Broadcasting. The crisis was larger than Hewitt. The FTII had lost its way. It was overrun with batches facing technological, pedagogic and logistical problems, and extreme demoralization. If anyone could do something about it, it had to be the 'experts' who had gathered in that room. They needed to roll up their sleeves and make their own DPR – if necessary, do their own visioning and costing, and produce their own alternative report. And so the meeting agreed to use the 'remaining time for the scheduled workshop ... to prepare a vision statement and to suggest a strategy to implement this vision'. Chandita Mukherjee took over leadership for the day. She divided everyone into smaller groups

-7

Interviews on 29/30 Sept. 2010 (during the meeting), student video made during the Hewitt agitation.

-8

Group of Experts appointed by the Governing Council of the FTII (Chair: P.K. Nair), *Vision FTII: The next 50 years, Detailed Project Report for presentation to the Governing Council of the FTII*, Pune: Film and Television Institute of India, 2011; hereafter Nair Report, 2011. This quote is from Appendix #1 (Minutes of the first meeting of 29 September 2010).

to discuss different aspects of the problem – vision statement, infrastructure, curriculum, courses, use of campus space, budgets – and together, they put together the beginnings of a plan.[9]

Thus was born the 'Nair Committee' (officially the 'Group of Experts convened by the Governing Council'), called that because P.K. Nair, venerable founder of the NFAI and once himself an employee of the FTII, happened to be the seniormost person in that room and also, everyone felt, the most qualified to lead this initiative.[10] Nair later said that it was Kumar Shahani and Saeed Mirza who persuaded him to accede to chair a committee that would seek to do what Hewitt so manifestly could not. Twelve people were named as a Group of Experts – among them Nair himself, Shama Zaidi, Kundan Shah, Nachiket Patwardhan, Shaji N. Karun, Chandita Mukherjee, Jabeen Merchant, Hansa Thapliyal and Kavita Pai. There would be one representative each from the staff and students' associations.

As the Nair Committee defined itself, it came as close as we have seen in the Indian cinema to a blank slate, a license to reconceive the FTII bottom–up: to rethink every leaf of every tree and every stone that made the place, as though to say, 'imagine what we could do if we actually ran the place'. It was a utopian moment when, on 11 November, U.R. Ananthamurthy, Chairman of the Governing Council, arrived and confronted the anxious students. 'In 1999 it was McKinsey, in 2000 it was the fee increase, in 2003–2005 it is self-financed short-term courses, and in 2010 it is the Hewitt Report', Prateek said to Ananthamurthy. 'We keep saying we are against privatization but we do everything that is to do with privatization and disinvestment. What do you have to say about that, Sir?' 'I have the same doubts', Ananthamurthy gravely replied, and then obliquely added: 'We should not have been under this [Information and Broadcasting] Ministry.' He too offered his complete backing to the Nair Committee.[11]

By this time one half of the road appeared clear. The first order of business was to bury Hewitt. This was duly done on 15 November when the Group of Experts met with a representative

-9

Based on a conversation with Naveen Padmanabha, 4 October 2018, Bangalore.

-10

There was argument and anxiety about whether the Nair Committee would be awarded statutory status. Prateek Vats writes that the authorities were 'shying away from granting official status to the Nair Committee'. 'The struggle is an ongoing one, given that even after the tremendous support that we have received, there is no assurance that transparent processes to bring in better quality education relevant to students of diverse backgrounds will be accepted': Prateek Vats, 'FTII Agitation', shared with the author via email on 16 December 2018.

-11

Conversations taken from *Part 2: FTII Students Agitation Nov. 16*, student documentary on the Hewitt strike.

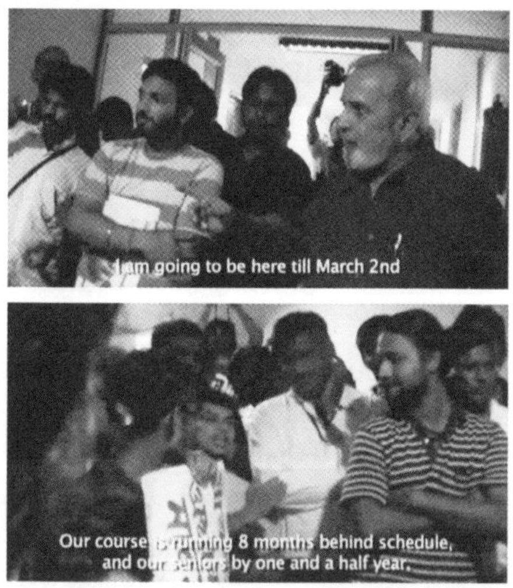

November 2010: students confront Chairman U.R. Ananthamurthy. Taken from the documentary **Part 2: FTII Student Agitation Nov. 16** (2010).

named Siddharth Nagpal. Multiple questions were asked and clarifications requested. Few answers were forthcoming. Nair, to take only one example, asked why the Report made no reference 'to the present state of affairs: delays and piling up of backlogs in respect of academic projects, resulting in the stretching of a three-year programme to four and even five years in individual cases?'[12] When told that this was 'not in the mandate', a furious Nair retorted, 'if you're asked to draw up a plan for the second and third floor of a building, do you need a mandate to find out whether the first and ground floors are intact?' It was painfully obvious that 're-writing sections [of the Hewitt Report was] not going to solve the problem'. The entire Report needed to be binned, 'set aside on account of its flawed vision, superficial so-called research, and inadequate understanding of the subject and its context'. What to replace it with, however, proved to be a far more difficult question.

-12

'Meeting on Detailed Project Report held on Monday, 8 November 2010 at Conference Hall, FTII, Pune', Nair Report, 2011, p. 174.

-13

Ibid., p. 180.

A 'Day-for-Night Effect, Almost'

Reading both Hewitt and Nair side by side, the stark difference is striking; these were, as Naveen felt that day in Rajasthan, two irreconcilable universes. The two universes also became, in 2010, two ways to think the post-celluloid digital nation. Seen one way (the way the Nair Committee saw it), Hewitt 'reduce[d] education at FTII to the level of a technical polytechnic'. The FTII 'is not a PSU which can be evaluated on the basis of profit & loss balance sheets', it said, 'nor is it a government office which can be arbitrarily shrunk or expanded. It is an educational institution which is a national treasure, having made a huge, unquantifiable contribution to the culture of India.'[13] Seen this way, the original sin of the present crisis – the 1997 decision to modify courses (from 1+2 to 2+1+advanced) that Adoor Gopalakrishnan had then endorsed – was, and has historically remained, an inexplicable anomaly. Many still speak of their bafflement as to where it came from. Once 1997 happened, however, many foresaw the sequel errors – of 2000 (the 1+1+1 plan), 2003–04 when the self-financing courses arrived and the fee hikes followed, and 2010.

A minimal shift of the kaleidoscope reveals another way of looking at the picture. By this alternative logic, we see a clear and indeed startling *continuity* from Agashe to Hewitt, and from Hewitt to B.P. Singh's 2016 'Vision Document' of a Digital Media University. Such a view is also in sync with an influential 'report' published in 2000 (the same year as the Information Technology Act), on new policy frameworks in higher education. Co-authored by Mukesh Ambani and Kumaramangalam Birla, it placed major emphasis on vocational education, distance learning and privatization.[14] Six years after Birla–Ambani, the old question of whether FTII was for the arts, the humanities or technical training would be updated to a new one around digitization.

In 2006, the year digitization took formal hold as an instrument for governance, a brief pause button was hit – both for the nation and for its cinema. India stood on the threshold of mass digitization. The old Information and Broadcasting Ministry was renovating itself in the information age and the FTII had to follow, if it had to survive. The utopian moment in which you could glimpse the new potential of post-national digital freedom was barely masked by its dystopian opposite, the *fear* of what the new held.

Sandeep Chatterjee, who moved here in 2009 from Kolkata's Satyajit Ray Film and Television Institute (SRFTI) to become Professor of Direction, vividly recalls the 'new'.[15] Not too long ago, he says, coming to the FTII would be a revelation for students. Everyone remembers their first encounter both with film equipment and then with world cinema at the NFAI. This was no longer the case. Students now already knew, or believed they knew, world cinema, and they all possessed some amateur experience of shooting, editing and recording. There was little evidence of the sheer novelty of filmmaking. Which meant, he says, that new demands were being made in class. 'Why should I go and sit in class, what am I getting from it?', 'Why should I even be here?', 'What is this education all about?' – 'Is it just about learning technique or it is a doorway to the film industry?' 'Are we training technicians to work in government departments? Or is there a larger purpose ... in the arena of a kind of a postgraduate higher learning place where a kind of questioning can happen around aesthetics?' – questions that were often hard to answer.

-14

Kumaramangalam Birla and Mukesh Ambani, 'A Policy Framework for Reforms in Education', report submitted to the Prime Minister's Council for Trade and Industry, 2000.

-15

Conversation with Sandeep Chatterjee on Zoom, 20 June 2021.

It was this moment of pause that also saw the FTII confront, for the first time, the yet larger question of whether it was at all sustainable as an institution. The problem of course was precisely *not* that it was merely a badly run place – it has always been that – nor that more efficient management might magically solve its scheduling problems. Prateek recalls that for all the expansions to the moving image, in the early 2000s, the career choices for a film student were still the Indian Institute of Mass Communications (IIMC), the Mass Communication Research Centre (MCRC)–Jamia Millia Islamia and the FTII (or SRFTI) – the 'usual stuff' – or you 'entered the field', which meant moving to Mumbai. In 2006, the year Prateek joined, the year Orkut began and also the year the National E-Governance Plan took shape, a fourth option became available to young wannabe filmmakers with the formal launch of Whistling Woods International by FTII alumnus Subhash Ghai. In a short decade Whistling Woods became the epitome of all that Hewitt would later propound: a wealthier, more hip, more efficient, technology-rich, new media-friendly, post-statist avatar of the formerly rule-bound *sarkari* institution. Others followed. 'It is no coincidence that Ekta Kapoor is drawing up plans to start a rival school the very year FTII celebrates its golden jubilee', *Business Standard* reported, wondering if yet another 'street-smart entrepreneur' had once again 'identified a state-run institute as a soft target'.[16] Now, if the problem went deeper, and if at least some of it was to find a way that did not turn it into another Whistling Woods, then Hewitt needed to be challenged with a *foundationally* alternative vision that went beyond tinkering.

It was entirely unclear as to whether there was one. There was no obvious way in 2006 and all the way up to the events of 2010 that the perception of the FTII as a 'national treasure' albeit inefficient, 'a huge, unquantifiable contribution to the culture of India', could translate into any obvious *policy* road map, let alone a credible alternative to something like Whistling Woods. Was the training that FTII has given a more elusive *affect*, a 'structure of feeling' as Raymond Williams called it,[17] or a *pratha* to use Vikas Urs' term? Having disposed off Hewitt, could Nair truly do better? Could the combination of 'unrealistic scheduling, clashing demands on infrastructure and equipment, compounded by lack of preparedness

-16

Aabhas Sharma, 'Is FTII losing the plot?', *Business Standard*, 20 January 2013

-17

Remarkably, one of Williams' most cited concepts actually emerges from the cinema. He sees the cinema as able to incarnate the 'totality' of all that makes art. Such a totality includes numerous 'separable parts', including the 'remains [of] some elements for which there is no external counterpart'. Such elements are what he names 'the structure of feeling of a period, and it is only realizable through experience of the work of art itself, as a whole'. Raymond Williams and Michael Orrom, *Preface to Film* (1954), reprinted in Scott MacKenzie (ed.), *Film Manifestos and Global Cinema Cultures*, Berkeley: University of California Press, 2014, p. 611.

of students and lack of guidance by faculty', be explained in any more complex manner that simple managerial inefficiency?

Nair and the Campus-Nation

The answer was only dimly perceived as having the vestiges of a political argument. It was in the end the campus-*nation* as against campus-*corporation*. And with it the basic fact that a student at the FTII, like a citizen of this country, had rights, could belong – and could *dissent*. As the Nair Committee set to work with a will, it almost appeared at times to be setting out a campus Bill of Rights. Every small decision was seen as having major consequences. Unlike Hewitt, nobody was paid for their labour. It was as though this voluntarism freed them up, for the imagined freedom was – as a song famously has it – 'just another word for nothing left to lose'. Some believe that Kundan Shah's heart trouble was exacerbated by the effort he put into this exercise as he and the eleven other 'experts' produced a document for the ages, an astonishing vision, from architecture to accounts, of text, visuals and charts, for the campus and thence for the Indian cinema itself.

From late colonialism and even more so after Independence, Indian cinema, by the very nature of its existence in the public domain, has stood for possibilities that *include* but do not *exhaust* the cinematic genre that we have come to name as 'political'. Films have of course been made over the years with explicit political intent, including by members of the FTII pantheon. Some have seen startling aesthetic success, while others have participated in significant political transformation, producing new techniques that have both supported and protested against statist and populist governmentality. By 2006, however, it was clear that the 'political' question was, across the spectrum, on the threshold of a new and perhaps unprecedented next step. And further, that step was linked, in ways yet not entirely clear, to (a) the nation, (b) institutionalization and (c) digitization.

Over all these years, the FTII had somehow survived as a bad-to-middling film school producing, in spite of itself, the great names of cinema with a national–modern workflow – that in Prateek's words '*aise hi hota hai kaam* [this is how it has always been]', you got the raw stock, did your lighting in this way, '*ek tarah se shooting ka grammar hua, uska processing hoga, rush print aayega, phir uspe ek tarah se sound hoga, then re-recording* [one kind of shooting grammar, then the processing, the rush print, the sound and re-recording]'[18] – without being forced to confront the change that was in the air. How, now, to confront *that* stasis?

Both the urgent interim document that the Nair Committee first put together, providing a forensic analysis of the academic and infrastructural crisis it was facing,[19] and the main *Vision FTII: the Next Fifty Years*, deserve to be read symptomatically as documents of their time, within a list of post-Independence documents on the troubled relationship of the Indian state with its cinema and with the arts. The Nair Committee needs to be placed in the wake of the 1951 Patil, the 1968 Khosla and 1979 Shivarama Karanth Film Study Group on film, and the 1990 P.N. Haksar Committee Report on India's Arts Akademis.

Indeed, in its light, the discarded Hewitt Report too merits a second look for where it comes from, written at a time when the Indian cinema – or at least its Bollywoodized variant – was making its digital peace with the revolution in the 'creative' economy outlined the following year by the KPMG/FICCI Report, *Digital Dawn: The Metamorphosis Begins*.[20]

And both need to be viewed, in hindsight, with Agashe's 'Conceptual Proposals' of 1997, to figure out what the fight in 2010 was about, what was achieved and what may have proven a bridge too far.

Freedom and Dread

We need to hang on to this uncertainty – to the two paths – for a bit as we consider the entirely unfamiliar protocol of filmmaking encountered by Prateek, who joined the FTII in 2006, by Naveen in 2007, Ajayan in 2008, Kislay in 2009 and Vikas in 2011: a befuddling best-of-times/worst-of-times mix of administrative control and laissez-faire.[21] Left largely to fend for themselves, their batches appeared to have the run of the place. Students were increasingly free to take decisions, including academic ones. More and more of the scheduling of overcrowded studios, sharing of scarce equipment and messy collaborative exercises were being left to the students to solve as best as they could.

It was a strangely liberated moment, Prateek recalls, as students

-18

Conversation with Prateek Vats, 14 December 2008, Mumbai.

-19

Ref. 'Interim Report of the Group of Experts Towards Preparing a Detailed Project Report for the Revitalization of FTII', Pune, 25 January 2011. Jabeen Merchant recalls that Mr Nair had insisted on this Interim Report, saying that 'we cannot start any work until we first address this'. Kundan Shah did several exercises with students 'mapping out schedules (for student exercises), how much time you need and what can be done parallel to what ... they made this huge chart, a physical chart [with] boxes and timetables'. Verbatim conversation with Jabeen Merchant, 17 September 2021.

-20

Digital Dawn: the Metamorphosis Begins, Mumbai: KPMG, 2012.

-21

Jabeen Merchant in fact dates many symptoms of the rot from as far back as the mid-1990s, an entire decade before they became publicly visible. Conversation with Jabeen Merchant, 17 September 2021.

actually began to feel they *owned* the campus, 'both in a good and bad sense'. Between 2004 and 2005, in an extraordinary burst of creativity, a staggering seventeen diploma films were made in one year, including Amit Dutta's *Ksha Tra Gya*, Umesh Kulkarni's *Girni* and Ashoke Viswanathan's *Usha*. As the FTII approached its golden jubilee, it became 'like the Commonwealth Games, new construction, new grass, new tiles, this, that. They were going berserk.'

But the freedom was laced with dread, a schizophrenic experience reproduced by the experience of enormous spending taking place alongside an equally paranoid, overweening desire to cut costs. It was as though the three-year batches, in the freedom they had apparently won after the hard-fought battle of 2000, were being surrounded by a change happening on the edges – as though from an *In Thin Air* scene – by the circling wagons of new short-term, high-fee, 'self-financing' courses that had been added since 2003 (in acting, art direction, screenplay, animation and computer graphics), dominating the already stretched resources.

The Interim Report of the Nair Committee refers to the weird sense of campus freedom. The Institute had been so reduced as to be seen by many as no more than a 'production facility which provides a basic package, and each client adds items of his or her preference to it'. One example it quotes had a student 'hiring and bringing in outside lights and a crane into the campus for a Dialogue film shooting, and subsequently sending the negative to Hyderabad for processing and digital intermediate work at her own expense'. It adds that 'in the absence of monitoring, students seeking perfection carry on with post-production work on their projects far beyond the allotted time. Limits are not enforced by faculty, there is unhealthy competition for extra facilities, and exercises further down the line are kept waiting, adding to the backlog.'[22]

This was in part a creative consequence of the transformation in the technology – of doing new things that were clearly possible, of exploring the medium. It also elevated student exercises into full-blown projects that bore no relation to why they had been originally put in place. In his August 2015 letter Awati too refers to the dialogue exercise. Once a 'harmless old ... exercise' originally conceived in the 1980s on 16 mm using sync sound, to be assessed with edited picture but original sound, by 2002 it had been elevated

-22

This has been contentious. Kedarnath Awati writes about the preparations made for the impending digitization of the filmmaking process: 'Pro Tools and Final Cut Pro were installed on several computers all over campus and the facilities kept open for students of all years in the hope that they would make use of the facilities to familiarize themselves with the software. The students did not do so ... we found that as the 2006 and 2007 batch students came to last part of their exercises and projects – the sound post-production, we found out that they were often taking twice the number of shifts allotted. Experts from outside were got in to conduct special workshops, and also to advise on how many shifts for post-production could be regarded as a reasonable number.' Letter from Awati, 25 August 2015.

to a 'show reel', and by 2004 into a full-scale 35 mm film with married prints. By 2011 it had moved to the DCP output. On the way, the original purpose – an assessment of the student's ability to work with sync sound – had been entirely lost. The new purpose of the exercise was to make a near diploma-level project, a 'product' that could be shown to the world.

The elevation of exercises into full-on public projects had several knock-on consequences. The faculty, as the Interim Report of the Nair Committee too points out, got downgraded into becoming facilitators. Awati adds another aspect not really addressed by Nair. The position of the faculty, he asserts, had become untenable. They had been systematically downgraded, existing mostly on contracts. Meanwhile the Director, typically appointed from the civil services, was parallelly elevated to 'enormous power [even as] no one else at the FTII has any power at all'. The Director has a 'primary allegiance to the Ministry and only a secondary one to the institution'.

—

Behind this strange autonomy, the fantasy of rule by market, was a clearly visible silhouette, the ghost of our old *regisseur*. The 'problem' of campus pedagogy, however defined, was in the end that of the filmmaker, not of the lab, or the classroom or the archive. Students were being thrown – and sometimes asked to be thrown – into the deep end because that was how real filmmakers did it.

There was yet another change – the very nature of our citizen–filmmakers. Even as their art-house avatar became inflated, the authority that had once flowed from the awe-inspiring lenses of the Mitchell or Arriflex had been replaced by lightweight palmtop cameras that symptomatically transformed the filmmaker into a combination of eavesdropper, hacker and archivist. Twenty-first-century filmmakers were often defined, like other digital avatars, by their *in*visibility.

Jugaad Exports and Amateur Film

The Nair Committee embraced this radical–utopian fantasy. It spoke of a new era in which 'image-making has become unbelievably democratized', when 'boundaries between amateur and professional quality images are blurring', when 'even a child can point a camcorder at a subject and make a film', when activists are making 'documentaries, video art and personal films'.[23] Filmmaking had become ever closer to data processing, to be done by individuals in the privacy of their homes or cafes, on laptops using easily hacked software and portable disks, as against an editing suite or indeed a film classroom. 'Independent filmmakers', said Nair, are able to 'work without any other crew, shooting, editing and producing complete films which bear the stamp of one individual creator'.

In hindsight, however, Prateek thinks they should have known as far back as 2007 that the 'shit was going to hit the fan'.[24] This fantasy freedom was never going to end well: 'You end up running the Institute for them, and that was not a good thing.' The 2006 and 2007 batch students found themselves, Awati writes, 'taking twice the number of shifts allotted' for post-production, requiring 'experts from outside [to be] got in to conduct special workshops, and also to advise on how many shifts for post-production could be regarded as a reasonable number'.

Prateek wonders whether, when the students dragged things on across 2009 and into 2010, they had not eventually done more harm than good.[25] As the new era also dawned on Ghatak's admonition to become filmmakers as against merely learning how to make films, the 2008 and 2009 batches felt the ground shift beneath their feet. The same dialogue exercise Awati mentions, on being moved to 35 mm using sync sound inside the studio, saw another crisis when picture was edited on Steenbeck but sound – which by then had gone digital – was done on ProTools through *jugaad* (makeshift) exports on to personal devices. Frame mismatches inevitably followed, quality suffered, and a chain of further problems was set off in the post-production process. To Naveen, this 'methodology was already kind of breaking; it was not good for the film school'.[26]

'How Would It Work?'

As the year went on, ideological divides emerged that once defined, veered off to take on multiple meanings. The divide split apart the direction, editing, cinematography and sound departments. It also separated students from their faculties. 'Either [the] sound department had to come back to analogue design [or] editing

-23

Nair Report, 2011, p. 56.

-24

'And problem *wahi ho jata hai*, you end up running the Institute for them, and that was not a good thing. We sort of dragged it until 2010, 2011, and maybe did more harm in the long run than good. A lot of people decided for the three days *ke khud se karna hai, ya ek dusre se karte hai, ya* senior junior *se karte hai* (learn by yourself in three days, or teach each other, or learn from your seniors).' Verbatim conversation with Prateek Vats, 14 December 2018, Mumbai.

-25

The letter signed by Samarth Dixit (president) and Naveen Padmanabha (general secretary) of the Students' Association to the Minister of Information and Broadcasting on 31 October 2009 reiterates the impending crisis: 'The Institute is not equipped to handle the students currently on the campus. After nine months of continuous dialogue, debate and discussions with the administration to look into the issues that were discussed, they are still willing to bring in students who will, like the current batches, not receive the quality of education that the Institute offers on paper.' Appendix 9, Nair Report, 2011.

-26

For Vikas there was an inexorable logic to the fact that, 'if you have to manage your shoots, you also have to manage the infrastructure that is dependent on these shoots, and that infrastructure is managed by the administration.' It also 'leads up to the fact that the Students' Association remained the singular entity [that could handle] this *gadha mazdoori* [donkey work]'. This logic took new shape after 2000 with a 'new generation of students coming in who are not invested in the space emotionally'. Conversation with Vikas Urs, 21 October 2021, Mumbai.

people had to give up their Steenbeck', says Naveen. It was a key moment when 'the [real] learning was happening'.[27] His batch met, convinced everybody the way had to be forward, not back – that the sound department needed to learn 5.1 mixing, that 'you can't ask them to come back for the old school effect'. Having agreed, there was nobody to teach how 5.1 mixing worked. You either sat around for six months 'hoping they will tell you how to pan one [bit of] sound or you could spend three days learning it yourself'.

A larger technological breakdown thus rapidly took multiple forms of bureaucratic breakdown. The first year usually held together, as there was some sync between teaching, screenings and exercises, but from the second year onwards the system began to unravel. Links with the NFAI withered away, permissions to organize night screenings at the CRT – which had been a routine affair – were denied. The digital archiving of student work turned chaotic – '*Digital ka kya matlab hai, sirf* DVD copy *bana dena*? [Does digitization merely mean making a DVD copy?] How are you storing original content? How are you making an archive out of the films? What is NFAI doing? And are FTII and NFAI on the same page about this?'[28] Disciplinary divisions spilled over into departmental divides as collaborative exercises – in which different disciplines are separately graded for the same exercise – became harder and harder to pull off. Cinematography students wanted to know why they needed three years to complete a course they could do in two. Sound had moved almost entirely to digital; editing was equally wedded to the Steenbeck and to non-linear systems. When dialogue films moved from black-and-white – for which there was an in-house laboratory – to colour, it necessarily meant getting a laboratory in Mumbai to process and to grade. This meant waiting, because only one or two prints needed to be struck and commercial labs weren't willing to prioritize the students' work. There were additional fears that celluloid would become entirely unavailable in the market.

As more and more parts of the workflow moved to digital, it became unpredictable, and then unschedulable. Students started getting penalized for doing things that 'were a direct offshoot of the technology'. In order to maintain the older curricular workflow, celluloid was mimicked to strange extremes: memory cards

-27

Conversation with Naveen Padmanabha, 4 October 2018, Bangalore.

-28

The following section is based entirely on the conversation with Prateek Vats, 14 December 2018, Mumbai.

pretended to be raw stock, and only a specified amount of rush-footage was permitted. 'Day-to-day chaos' arose 'in every detail'.

Exacerbating the issue was the perennial solutionist fantasy that off-the-shelf solutions existed 'elsewhere'. On an exchange programme, students had visited an Arriflex factory in Germany and seen how Steenbecks might be seamlessly integrated into a digital workflow. If the FTII indeed saw value in teaching how to work on celluloid, how to do negative-cutting, and if it had seen its way to allocating some exercises on film and some on digital, a possible transition might still have been achieved.

The problem was mainly how to acknowledge, within bureaucratic language, that there was a problem at all. To recognize its existence meant first to penalize someone, and then to find someone else who could fix it. Neither appeared possible. One consequence of what seemed to be a strange refusal to recognize something as simple as the existence of a Steenbeck that could provide a synced digital audio output, was the pro-privatization view that faculty with permanent jobs, out of their depth and rapidly losing respect, were – exceptions always excepted – part of the very remains of history that needed fumigation.

'Why Are You Here?'

The same inflamed November – as it would turn out, the very day the Hewitt strike began – a wide-eyed newbie named Vikas Urs arrived on the campus for his admission interview and orientation. As the interviews took place inside the Preview Theatre of the TV wing, surreal sounds of slogans and drums percolated into the room. They made for a contradictory experience: a mystical, sometimes tension-filled engagement, at once welcoming and forbidding.

Vikas had experienced this push–pull effect earlier. The previous year he had enrolled for a ten-day videography course at the FTII. It had been an expensive course, costing a 'good fifteen or twenty thousand rupees', taught by a Cinematography Assistant Professor committed to a television aesthetic, and he wasn't sure it had been worth it. What he did retain, however, were memories of the hostel, seeing a couple of films on campus, and being heckled in the canteen by a direction student named Ganesh Gaikwad for taking such an 'expensive' course and for 'blowing up his father's money'. It was a ritual of initiation; if Vikas could afford a short course like this, he must be rich.[29]

Wandering during that same visit into the Main Theatre where a student film was being screened, he thought more about 'the whole *mahaul* [ambience]'.

> It was one of their graduating films; it was screened, and what the pratha [conventional practice] is nobody knows. We just walked in and that happened to be there that day. And that really intrigued me. Finally, whatever the space is and whatever the teaching is, if this is what people are doing then there must be something more to the place. Maybe I have missed out on it. Perhaps I could have spoken to a few more people. Okay, fine, and then I just left it there.

The mystique was again in place when Vikas went to Bangalore's National College to take his admission examinations, surprised by how few people had turned up for them. He answered the general knowledge questions, the twenty 'objective' questions (of which one was to identify the director of *Mother India* and another the city where the National Library was housed) and the 'subjective writing' section. He thought he stood a chance. And so it proved to be. He was selected, invited for an interview, and arrived that November with a bagful of still images on glossy paper and a small video he had made 'for a friend of mine'. He showed these to his interviewers and they appeared to like what they saw.

Then the faint sounds from outside began merging with the proceedings in the room. Interviewing the candidates for admission was Cinematography Professor R.M. Rao. It was a familiar name – Vikas remembered the man who had shot the *Mile Sur Mera Tumhara* videos that he had grown up watching on Doordarshan, and he was impressed.

As the orientation went on, however, Vikas kept being asked in various ways if he *really* wanted to come to FTII after what he was seeing and hearing outside. 'They never spelt it out ... but they sensed that you could make out what is happening. They really were in one way trying to discourage you from coming in. There was a lot of "You don't know what you are signing up for. You have to spend a long time here. How will you sustain yourself?"'

> It was already brought up directly in our orientation and interviews too, that you will really have to slog it out now. How one person would take it is their choice, but this was spelt out. So, I don't think

29 The following section is based entirely on the conversation with Vikas Urs, 12 December 2018, Porvorim, Goa.

> … anybody from the administration or the faculty shied away from it. It was a given. So, you had to decide whether you wanted to sign up for it or not. I mean I never had to answer it *per se* so directly, but I said – yes, I am very much aware of what's happening and I am very much willing to be part of the larger canvas that is here and that's the learning.

Now the whispered 'come/don't come' message had to be faced. In that same orientation, sitting more distantly, was another young applicant, Koel Sen. Koel too was fascinated by what was going on outside. When the candidates were asked, as part of the induction process, to make a short film on something around them, she made one on the Hewitt strikers. She was quizzed on that by Kedarnath Awati.[30]

The orientation itself happened by day. By night another, rather different orientation took place. As the out-of-town students returned to their hostel rooms, they often found 'the seniors … line[d] up and … asking … "Okay, you, where are you from and do you know what is happening?"'

The 2010 batch was the largest ever in FTII's history, with 90 students. Mandal-II rules had kicked in and OBC admissions had significantly increased the intake. The number would now be added to an already chaotic campus, which had multiple batches of students left over from as far back as 2005. Even as the orientation went on, on another floor of the same building the senior students on strike were being assured by the Director, Pankaj Raag, standing next to Ananthamurthy, that 'until the infrastructure issues are solved, there will be no classes held for the next batch'.[31]

Vikas was on his way back to Mysore when a senior, a friend, called to tell him his application had gone through. Bipin Naria, Head of Cinematography, had liked his work, and so he was in. He should 'get ready for the ragging'. That was quick, Vikas thought. The official announcement soon followed, and he was even more pleased that he had received a scholarship. He had – and it is astonishing how many students said they had done this – applied for admission without telling his parents, had forged his father's signature, and this announcement was helpful. Things were going well.

Then the wait began, across that winter and through the following summer. Multiple calls and multiple replies around the

-30
Conversation with Koel Sen on Zoom, 23 June 2021.

-31
Part 2: FTII Students Agitation Nov. 16, student documentary, 2010.

theme of: 'No, we don't have any information yet, we'll let you know, why are you worried?' By July, eight months after the batch had been admitted, 'everybody had kind of realized that this [was] perhaps getting too much out of control and … started even doubting … whether this [was] true. Maybe they would really not take anyone in.'

It was yet again the informal network – Naveen, in fact, via their mutual friend Mahavir – who told Vikas what was going on. The reason for the delay was the construction of a new hostel, following the minimum demand of the Hewitt protest that at least this part of the infrastructure be in place before new admissions could take place. The new batch would, he was told, most probably assemble in August 2011.

Rites of Initiation

In 2010, the National Cinematography Award was won for the first time by a film shot on a digital camera. It went to Madhu Ambat for the Malayalam film *Adaminte Makan Abu*. Ambat had used the Arriflex D-21, the first high-definition digital camera to set itself up in explicit imitation of/competition to 35 mm celluloid. 3-D was on the horizon, and students knew of Werner Herzog's *Cave of Forgotten Dreams* made that very year, and Wim Wenders' *Pina*. Vikas mentions these films as the new frontier, the digital future. Somewhere that future included the allure of the truly independent individual filmmaker, one such as Ramani, carving for himself an existence entirely outside of the capitalist infrastructure. Ramani remembers that when he was a student even the Arri wasn't macho enough, only the Mitchell truly defined who you were.[32] There was the enduring attraction of celluloid. And then, somewhere deep inside all this, there was the filmmaker's right to dissent. The binaries of celluloid–digital had split into multiple further splits: between day and night even.

There was the day schedule – the heavy curriculum, the classroom sessions in the CRT, the exercises and the screenings. You were 'kind of completely bombarded with the space and its history and its paraphernalia' that had been 'gathered over time … you have to deal with that'. There were the evening screenings both in the CRT (usually digital) and the Main Theatre (35 mm), which Vikas says he never missed.

-32
R.V. Ramani, comment during his 'Explore Filmmaking with R.V. Ramani' course 3, 7 February 2021.

And then there was the informality of the night, on which there was particularly high premium at that moment in FTII's history: the *satsangs*, a night-time ritual called that since 'ragging' is officially banned. The Maharashtra Prohibition of Ragging Act of 1999 describes it as a 'display of disorderly conduct ... likely to cause physical or psychological harm or raise apprehension or fear or shame or embarrassment to a student through ... teasing, abusing, threatening or playing practical jokes on, or causing hurt to, such student or ... asking a student to do any act or perform something which such student will not, in the ordinary course, willingly, do.'[33]

I am speaking to Vikas and Prabhati (Gharat) in Goa.[34] They go back a long way, to before they joined the FTII. They disagree as we speak, as many students did in 2011 when the senior batches had imposed new *satsang* rules. Both the previous 2009 and following 2012 batches had boycotted them. Prabhati considered them frankly humiliating. You 'had to go, we would be, like, dragged out of the room, dozing off there and then 10 o'clock there is a class in the morning, you are dozing off there also.'

Vikas accepts that the initiation rites could occasionally be distressingly tribal, potentially sexist. They were nevertheless a key part of the rituals of admission and the traditions that kept the place alive. For all their problems, they were an important part of the initiation process, the 'senior–junior' relationship that played a role in keeping the pedagogy in the place functional. This also was where batch identity originated. New batches were expected to maintain 'screening diaries', so you couldn't 'doze off'. Inside the *satsang*, you were sometimes asked to 'randomly read out your screening diary ... and if you had not written, you had to come back with a written diary the next night'. There would be a freshers' party where you had to show your portfolio at the CRT. Vikas says the seniors were 'happy to see what all we had done before coming here, and everybody want[ed] to get to know everybody'. To Prabhati, on the other hand, it had an 'ugly power dynamic'.

> People took it the way they wanted to take it, but there were times where you were made to feel like you don't belong to this place or ... you have to prove that you belong to this place. And I was just like, I am here to make films. I am not here to prove to somebody who came here two years before me whether I belong to this place or not.

-33 The Maharashtra Prohibition of Ragging Act, 1999.

-34 Conversation with Vikas Urs and Prabhati Gharat, 12 December 2018, Goa.

She doesn't think she would have done this to someone who came just a year after her. 'I am sorry. I'll let my work speak for itself.'

Vikas struggles to make his point. There comes a moment, he concedes, when 'they [try] to break you'. He admits that the power dynamic was sometimes unacceptable. It was however intrinsic to a rite of filmmaking itself. And when it worked, it often led to 'breaking the rigidities that you are carrying, or the baggages that you perhaps have built about yourself, the self-worth'.

> You were kind of grappling with too many things; too many things which deal with the place and its essence which is being ... passed on to you in the hope that you will take it forward. And you soaked in [that essence]. Basically, you became like a sponge and you soaked in everything that you could. And the fun was in that soaking in.

Although several did participate, many found it intrusive. Actors, Vikas recalls, had the hardest time, because they were considered the 'dumbest' – in a remarkable rewind of the strikes of the 1970s – and the lowest in the filmmaking hierarchy. An 'internal hierarchy' was thus reinstated: 'An actor is an actor, you are a mere actor, and since you had to act for the rest of your lives you may as well do it now.' Vikas contends that some of the actors did 'shed their baggage' and were the 'first to let themselves loose, because their body and their being is what is going to make them actors', while others did not.

As Vikas began getting involved with the larger issues of the campus – figuring out the 'functioning of the batch, understanding what happens where, who is administration, who is faculty, who is the support staff, who are you in the middle of all of this' – he also began figuring out what his role there might be.

> So, it's that macro again that is determining your own learning there, because you are now a new entrant. You have to deal with it; to negotiate with the fact that you are part of that bigger group and its dynamics. How you are to manage your own sessions and exercises in the process. There is nobody who is going to deal with it. You have to deal with it. All that the admin is doing is just making dates and putting up schedules. They don't want to deal with all of that. Though they are saying they will support, but they are really not. And the workflow is film.

Batch Behaviour and Digital Freedoms

And then there was the collective: the batch itself, the student body, and the campus. Soon enough Vikas forged a more direct connection between the abstract handing over of the ritual baton and the concrete question of celluloid. It was a specific little action that alerted him to the protocol, and it was also his first consequential intervention into the campus. This was a second-year camera practical exam at which he wanted to see his 16 mm rushes projected, for two reasons: one, he wanted to see them on the screen; two, the projection was part of a shot he had conceived, of someone watching his film. The projector in the Main Theatre was dead, and he was anyway flatly told he had only one rush print and that was meant for editing. If it got damaged in the projection, that would be the end of his exercise. Vikas nevertheless persisted, and got the projector repaired.

Getting that projector back to work was an intervention into a space where he could now say to his ragging seniors – '*Itni baat kar rahe ho film, film, film*, but they couldn't even get this projector repaired.' 'So then you realize that these guys have already exhausted their fight. They are at the fag end. ... Now you are the new energy. You have to take that forward. So, my first understanding of "fight" for whatever it is worth, started with this little thing. I made it happen for my entire batch. And perhaps the next few batches, at least until the projector stay[ed] up and running. Your actions inside the campus are not as limited to you only, but they are largely reflecting on the space in itself.'

Naveen extends the question. By 2010, there were various kinds of 'departmental hatred' simmering, in large measure through tensions brewing around a single collaborative exercise being used for different disciplinary assessments. 'How to balance all the courses in that one integrated exercise? The direction student writes it, and directs it, but he [has to write it so as] to get in all the art directors, sound people, cinematographers, to show their work.'[35] On occasion external editing assessments 'blasted' the direction students for 'not writing scripts that gave editors or art direction students [a chance] to show their talent'. A dialogue exercise would become the final diploma film of the two-year art direction course, for which new sets were often built and painted, leading to a three-day shoot taking ten days with enhanced lighting requirements.

-35
Conversation with Naveen Padmanabha, 4 October 2018, Bangalore.

By 2010, the Nair Committee noted a consensus among students that 'the only meaningful learning activity at FTII is embedded in the coordinated student exercises'.[36] In part this arose from a more basic question: Was filmmaking at all any longer a collective process? Or was the filmmaker's ability to 'work without any other crew, shooting, editing and producing complete films which bear the stamp of one individual creator', as the Nair Committee had it, to be the future of the cinema?

Vikas gives another example that featured celluloid more centrally: the 'long take' or *plan-séquence*, which would be assessed for both cinematography and sound. It was to be one single take shot on 35 mm, conventionally processed in a single print and screened to invited examiners in the main theatre. The FTII now began separating out camera assessments – for which they made a soundless 'picture print, only for assessing camera students' – from sound assessments which were done on a 'low-resolution digital copy' that was 'projected in the old sound studio'. 'This defeated the very purpose of doing the first collaborative exercise where you are doing this separate assessment.' The students asked for a single assessment and proposed a compromise: to replace celluloid assessments with an HD telecine of negatives followed by a 'digitized assessment of our married sound and picture on the digital format'. They lost the celluloid, but gained the possibility of being assessed together.

In 2011, the Red Digital Cinema company – manufacturers of the Red One camera, widely seen then as having revolutionized digital cinematography – sponsored a second year workshop, to be led by the well-known cinematographer (and FTII alumnus) Binod Pradhan. The purpose of the sponsorship was evident: they were trying to sell their camera, which was then in competition with Arriflex's Alexa. The choice between the two cameras was itself of significance: while the Red was futuristic, marketed as a next-generation camera, the Alexa had a more pronouncedly retrospective look and a stronger claim to continue celluloid's legacy.

Pradhan's Red workshop was formally boycotted by the entire cinematography batch.[37] The reasons aren't entirely clear, but they appear to have been led by an adherence to celluloid: more precisely, to black-and-white, and yet more specifically, as a gesture of solidarity to the showpiece on-campus black-and-white

-36

'Interim Report' of the Nair Committee, 2011, section 5.10.3.

-37

Based on reconstructions with Naveen Padmanabha, 4 October 2018, Bangalore, and Vikas Urs, 12 December 2018, Goa.

processing lab that had been on its last legs since 2007. It had that year gone unused for six months with no chemical supply even as student productions remained stuck – in part because of a budget crunch, but mostly because of the growing belief that Kodak stock would soon go out of the market. This changed briefly in 2010 when the lab got a small grant as a part of the golden jubilee celebrations, but it was only a brief respite, for since 2016 it has become almost entirely dead with the new, post-2015 strike batches having no contact whatsoever with celluloid. Speaking to the Nair Committee, K. Ayyathurai, the laboratory manager, attributed its dilapidated state to the 'lack of co-operation on the part of the FTII management towards proposals to upgrade the laboratory, inspite of repeated proposals and sanction of funds', and the repeated decision to send all colour film to Mumbai-based labs for processing and printing despite the extra expense, while 'refus[ing] to upgrade facilities on campus'.[38]

There was a more substantial sequel. Around 2012, when the decision on acquiring a new camera came up, Vikas and the students recommended the Alexa, made by a 'time-tested' company with a long celluloid history. Their advice was heeded, in part perhaps because it coincided with the faculty recommendation.

However, when the camera arrived in its packing, nobody had the confidence to unpack it and switch it on. Access to it was forbidden and it stayed in its box even as the department reversed its pedagogic process, stayed with the known 35 mm black-and-white on-campus lab, until finally they were persuaded to invite the cinematographer Piyush Shah to do a comprehensive workshop with this new device. When he came, says Vikas, the 'entire camera department participated: students, faculty, everyone'. Distinctions between teacher and student vanished. Piyush Shah had himself never made a full-length film yet on the Alexa, and although the students were ahead of the faculty on the broad digital curve, it was evident that everyone was in this together, equally ignorant, and therefore together against something new. 'He never saw us as students learning. He saw us as equals in the learning curve.'

-38
K. Ayyathurai, cited in Nair Report, 2011, p. 193.

'Digital brought in a flatness to the whole hierarchy.' To Vikas it was the combination of collective ignorance, student involvement and the equality wrought by the digital ecosystem that brought in an element of egalitarianism, as 'interactions with everyone became more fluid'. 'I could walk into [former Cinematography Professor K.G.] Soman's room any time, I could walk into [Virendra] Saini's room any time, I could walk into D.J. [Narain]'s room any time, yell at him.'

It all *seemed* free, but who knew what freedom meant and how long it would last. As formal education collapsed, students often went away for extended periods and even took on professional assignments outside; attendance was no longer monitored and 'work schedules [were] often revised or projects put on hold to wait for crew members to return from their outside jobs' (says the Interim Nair Committee Report). 'Film screenings, reading, participation in discussions and other activities' were 'relegated to second place', and even when 'visiting filmmakers came, or when special workshops and seminars were held, attendance was sparse'. On the other hand, in the still rosy digital–utopian future that beckoned, there lay a non-hierarchical world of technological democracy, open source platforms producing free content and round-the-clock online pedagogy.

For all the crises, the Hewitt era was a good time on the campus. The agitation spilled over into the fiftieth anniversary, into new funding, into the International Student Film Festival in 2010 that saw twenty-eight film schools worldwide take part[39] – and, for all its creaking infrastructure, the extra-large number of students brought in a good new energy. Students possessed hard disks, shared films that a scarce few years earlier would have required miles of celluloid vaults, and they were seeing more films than ever, reading more than ever.

'It was like everybody was trying to dominate the discourse with their own vision of what this place should be or could be', says Vikas. 'We were all fledglings in that time. We [were] all influenced yet we also want[ed] to make our point because all of us [were] exposed.' To Vikas it was a central part of the initiation, a lesson in how to 'actively participate' in whatever it was that the place offered.

> You have left everything to come here, you might as well completely indulge in the good, the bad and the ugly of this space. If you fight, fight. Fight with a lot of passion. You want to do it, I will do it. You want to come, you come. You don't want to come, you don't

-39
This was the First International Student Film Festival, held over five days in September 2010. Coordinated by then-faculty member Gayatri Chatterjee, it saw day-long screenings of student works from several famous film schools across Europe, the USA, Australia, China and Africa, symposia with participating faculty from Kolkata, Mumbai and Chennai.

> come. But I will do what I feel like doing. So yes, there is a sense of entitlement that perhaps you immediately feel, but that entitlement I wouldn't say is misplaced. It's an entitlement of a person who is also willing to participate in the active nature of the space.

It was an issue that Vikas had 'with most of [his] batchmates', that he would take directly into the 2015 strike.

> That you want entitlement, but you don't want to participate. You don't want to deal with the dirt, you only want the best part of it. You only want things that suffice for you, so you are not really dealing with what is going to suffice for everyone. What is it? So, there is nothing that suffices for everyone. Everyone only talks of the self. You need to engage yourself; you need to carry the other.

An Idea Never To Be Realized

'What is cinema, what is art, what is life?', *Vision FTII: the Next Fifty Years* asks at one point.[40] Has the very idea of a film school been rendered passé by digital technology? Given the common view that 'everyone can make films and can learn on their own as self-learning resources and low-cost technologies are easily available', many people these days 'question the value of running film schools'. Such a view, Nair says, misses the issue. The question had to be framed wider. 'Can creativity be taught? How does an institute train a creative artist of the future?'

The issue may well have been closer to the one Fareeda Mehta would ask at a particularly emotional GBM a week after the disastrous July 2015 meeting with Information and Broadcasting Minister Arun Jaitley. Mehta joined the students and advised them to, as Samrat Chakraborty quotes it,

> forget strategy and all that. Just each one speak about what he or she holds dear about this institute. Why this issue bothers them and how it affects them. There were over 80 people in that GBM. Everyone spoke. People we've never heard speak in a public forum spoke. There were issues of language. People were falling short of words. But everyone came forward and spoke. This happened for 14 hours and everyone stayed put and listened.[41]

In 2011 a regime change saw Saeed Mirza take over as Chair of the Governing Council and D.J. Narain as Director – ushering in perhaps the most student-friendly era in recent memory. But it was a brokered peace: a way of keeping things quiet by more or less

-40
Nair Report, 2011, p. 30.

-41
Samrat Chakrabarty, 'Going Hungry under the Wisdom Tree', *The Hindu*, 27 October 2015.

giving students whatever they wanted, staying with the simple one-point strategy of keeping the place going and avoiding more strikes, postponing the inevitable breakdown.

It was a moment, then, of suspense: a temporary truce, as the FTII found itself at a crossroads – two ways forward, one defined by Hewitt and the other by Nair. Of the two, Hewitt was more easily comprehensible, and also more repudiable: market-driven, creative economy-informed, envisioning the FTII as an 'International Centre of Excellence', as 'training professionals through a balanced pedagogy' while nevertheless developing 'qualified and socially sensitive filmmakers and television professionals', written at a time when such management-speak perhaps still carried a vestige of believability.

It is the Nair Committee Report, the infinitely more elaborate labour of love, that is harder to interpret. This is not only because its long-term vision-and-mission exercise took place at a moment in history when planning of any sort, even in the short term, was perilous – let alone for the 'next fifty years'. It is mainly because of how it took a national model of ambiguous survival – a mysterious thriving inspite of itself – and sought to convert that into what looked like and quacked like an operational plan of some kind.[42]

At the time the Nair Report was first conceived, a scant decade ago, celluloid's demise wasn't by any means a given. Indeed, there was a well-entrenched school of thought that the way to go was to define the FTII around its most unique feature, its 35 mm black-and-white lab – and to make it not just another common or garden film school, but a globally unique institution dedicated to celluloid training and archiving. The Nair Committee, however, places firm faith in digital – and perhaps there was no real choice. It views digital as capable of reviving the utopian vision of the cinema itself, 'the initial days of cinema, where mosaics were being made from diverse artistic traditions to tell stories of contemporary relevance'. 'Digital technology is capable of breaking the stranglehold of heavy capital investment in film making and can enable artistic collaborations between different disciplines and across geographies.'

It also places its faith in the possibilities of a partnership between the various stakeholders, namely students, alumni, staff, faculty and administration. 'If the Governing Council can find a way of making

-42

Thinking back, Jabeen Merchant tries to reconstruct what they thought they were doing with this massive endeavour. 'There are things you've been thinking about, and now [it seemed we could all] put it down and thrash it out, discuss it. If we can at least have it on record, something like we have always told ourselves, something we have always known – that the FTII administration structure is out-dated and old and no longer works, that we need a different kind of administration – that alone would help. They seemed to be practical ideas, not fantasy.' There was, she admits, a degree of fantasy when they discovered this 'forest area ... the other side of the hill that apparently belongs to FTII', and Nachiket Patwardhan dreamed up an idea to 'construct a tunnel under the mountains so that people can go from one campus to the other'. But this was also because they were repeatedly being told that 'FTII has these resources, that the Ministry is willing to spend crores of rupees [if only they were presented with] a good solid plan'. The first draft, co-authored by Chandita Mukherjee and Shama Zaidi, was 'much more poetic and beautiful', but it did not have financial figures. Mr Nair insisted that 'it had to be like a DPR, otherwise they will not accept it'. 'I have been part of government departments, I understand how it works, and they will just reject it unless we put in figures.' Verbatim conversation with Jabeen Merchant, 17 September 2021.

these five segments of the FTII community work together effectively, all the decades of tension and despair could dissolve, and a way forward found.' Such a collaborative structure would transform the campus into a verdant zone of fertile creativity. It would be based on a solid foundation course and a series of centres (a Knowledge Centre and a Moving Image and Sound Research Centre) coming together to 'provide a ... rich, varied and bountiful ambience so that students can discover the art, science and potential of cinema'. All students, regardless of their specialization, would be 'encouraged to develop an easy, personal relationship with the digital camera and basic post-production processes'. There would always be 'space for any student to requisition low-end cameras and other equipment from a common store, to have access to an editing system and make short films or undertake projects to further her own understanding of cinema'.[43]

-43
Nair Report, 2011, p. 56.

All of these freedoms would grow amid creative efflorescence that showed respect for heritage, amid discreet and tasteful architecture. The Knowledge Centre would be named after Satish Bahadur, there would be an S.B. Thakar Studio and a K.K. Mahajan Studio. The most ambitious was the Ritwik Ghatak Studio, to be of the same size as the gigantic Studio No. 1 on Prabhat campus, at the edge of a lake on the Darshan campus, with an open plan, a fixed roof and catwalks but collapsible walls that could be opened to be dressed and used as the situation requires, fitted with state-of-the-art facilities, all to be made commercially available to generate income. There were multiple other plans, architected and costed, for each of its three campuses – the main Prabhat campus, the campus across the road and the as-yet undeveloped space across the hill.

—

Perhaps the only problem was a disarmingly simple one – the faith it placed in what we might call the 'good state'. It noted the existence of 'movements with the power to change regimes emerging from video clips flashed over social networks by ordinary people'.

Nevertheless, given that 'creativity ... needs guidance', it also needs 'institutions which give scope for learning in a group of peers'. 'The state has an important role to play in encouraging the proliferation of such spaces.' What, however, if creativity in 2010 – especially as the move to digital gradually coalesced – came to be targeted in opposition to the state? What if a founding purpose of the filmmaker was to remain *elusive* to the state, and maybe even, who knows, seek to destabilize it?

What, then, of a report that may be suggesting such an unnameable thought? One that may need to be read against the grain, in a way similar to what one of its architects, Kundan Shah, had once said of his debut film: that it was an idea in which 'you are doing everything to fail'? Might the Nair Committee be viewed as an exercise, in the astonishing, breath-taking ambitiousness of its canvas, a tragic utopian poetics of what might have been? As producing the ultimate unreachable star, the filmmaker's unrealizable dream? As the passionate assertion, in Fareeda Mehta's words, of the right to belong?

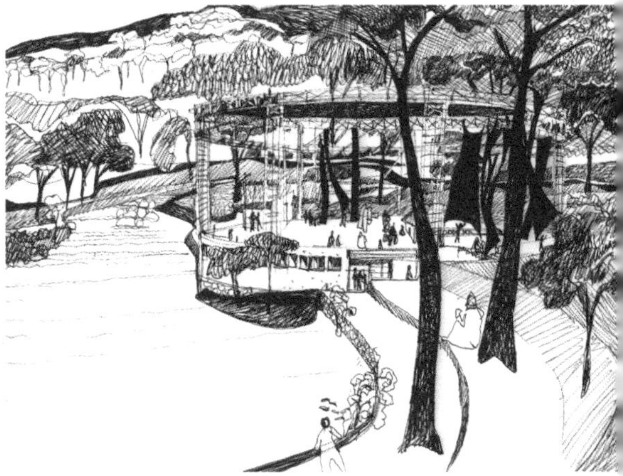

Artist's sketch of the fantasy, state-of-the-art, open-plan Ritwik Ghatak Studio on the imagined extension of the FTII campus. Nair Report, 2011.

CHAPTER 6

THE MACABRE SPECTACLE

Pune, August 2013

On 20 August 2013, Narendra Dabholkar was shot dead in Pune while on his morning walk. Dabholkar was a well-known figure in the city. A medical doctor, he had spent much of the previous decade leading a popular movement committed to scientific rationalism. In this time, he had campaigned in the Maharashtra state legislature for an anti-superstition bill, viewed – in its overt critique of pro-Hindutva 'godmen' – as targeting the pro-Hindutva right. He had, as a result, received multiple threats to his life and mostly chosen to ignore them.

Two days later, the student body of the FTII organized a screening of Anand Patwardhan's *Jai Bhim Comrade*. It was a memorial for Dabholkar. They also invited Deepak Dengle, Jyoti Jagtap and Rupali Jadhav of the Pune-based theatre group Kabir Kala Manch, which had featured centrally in Patwardhan's film and would be appearing in public for the first time since May 2011, when Dengle was arrested under the revised Unlawful Activities

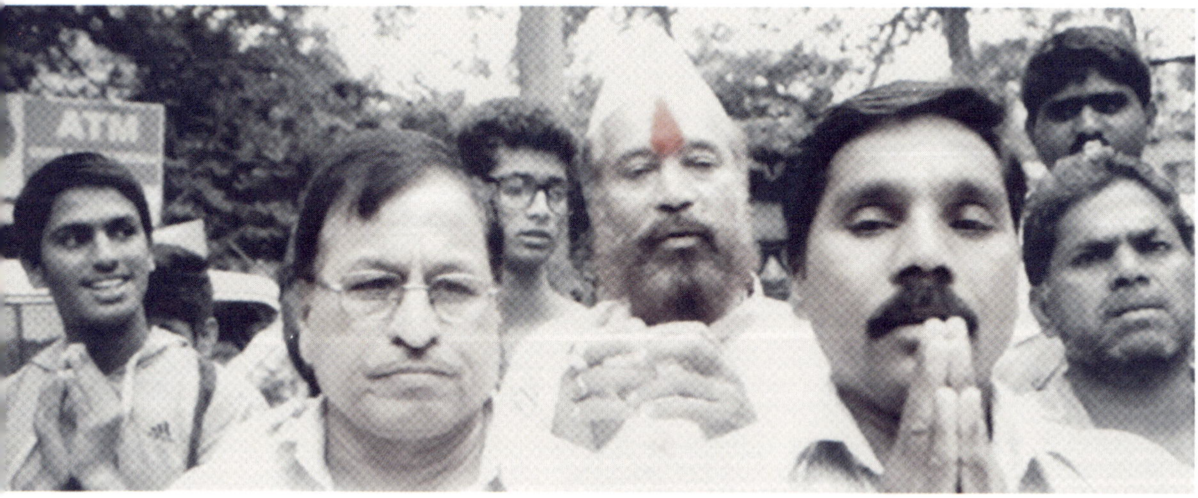

Patit Pavan Sanghatana, a Pune-based political organization with an aggressively brahmin-dominated Hindutva ideology, stages an event outside the FTII gates on 21 July 2015. Detail from Kshama Padalkar's **The Strike and I** (2019).

Prevention Act (UAPA). The idea for the event came from Ajayan Adat and Kislay who held the idealistic – and at the time still largely innocent – belief in the need for FTII to be more connected to the city. They partnered with Yugpath, a youth organization involved in networking among rural volunteer groups, and scheduled their event at the National Film Archive of India's main theatre.

The screening went well. It was a full house. Kabir Kala Manch was a depleted group given that three of their members were still in jail. Jyoti Jagtap began the evening by saying, in Marathi, 'We are not trained musicians from the Gwalior *gharana*, or the Jaipur or Agra *gharana*s. We are working class youth from the *basti*, factory and farm-labour *gharana*s. We won't be able to deliver the perfect note or play the perfect instrument, but if you listen to our words, I am confident that what we have to say will be of interest.' They then sang four songs. The first, dedicated to Dabholkar, had the opening line, '*Amhi Devhara Bajula Saarlay* [We have set aside our gods]'; the second was an anti-nuclear song on Jaitapur; then 'Sau', an ode to Savitribai Phule; and finally, the defiant 'Kabir wants to break his shackles to dance and sing. Let him dance and sing.'[1]

It was when everyone was leaving that a few of the organizers who had stayed behind to wind up noticed a group of around twelve men in the NFAI compound. These men accosted the students and asked them to explain how they had invited people associated with 'anti-national activities'. As the situation grew tense, said Ajayan, Kislay, Samvatha and Shaaz in their public statement, they withdrew to the Law College Road – intuitively perhaps, Kislay thinks, to move the possible confrontation away from the vulnerabilities of the Film Archive – and so it was on the street that the attack actually occurred.[2] Slogans like '*Bharat Maata ki Jai*', '*Vande Mataram*' and 'Down down Naxals' were heard, and orange flags were taken out. The immediate thought on everyone's mind was Dabholkar.

A year earlier, in February 2012, Pune's Symbiosis College of Arts and Commerce scheduled a national symposium. They called it *Voices from Kashmir*. With funding from the University Grants Commission, Symbiosis invited several well-known names, like the journalist Dileep Padgaonkar who had led a team of national 'peace interlocutors' to negotiate between the Congress party-led UPA government and the local leadership in Kashmir, theatre director

-1 Anand Patwardhan, 'A Personal Account of the Attack on Kabir Kala Manch at the FTII in Punyanagari (The Virtuous City)', dbsjeyraj.com, 23 August 2013.

-2 'FTII Students' Statement Against ABVP's Attack on Kabir Kala Manch', *indiaresists.com*, s.d.

M.K. Raina and filmmaker Iffat Fatima (who was to show her film *Where Have You Hidden My New Moon Crescent*). On the opening day, they wanted to screen Sanjay Kak's well-known documentary, *Jashn-e-Azadi: How We Celebrate Freedom*.

But four days earlier, the College Principal Hrishikesh Soman received a phone call from a man named Shailendra Dalvi who said he was the Pune unit secretary of the ABVP. Dalvi asked Soman to cancel the screening of *Jashn-e-Azadi*. A letter followed from a Deputy Commissioner of the Police Special Branch named Makarand Ranade, advising the Principal that 'the film is controversial'.[3] Soman hastened to fall in line. The plan to show *Jashn-e-Azadi* had been an accident and a mistake, he announced. Although they couldn't now back out of the invitation to Sanjay Kak, he promised to lay down a condition that Kak would avoid all reference to politics when he spoke, and he promised not to screen Kak's film. The ABVP leadership remained unsatisfied and Dalvi asked that the entire event be indefinitely postponed. Once more Soman agreed.

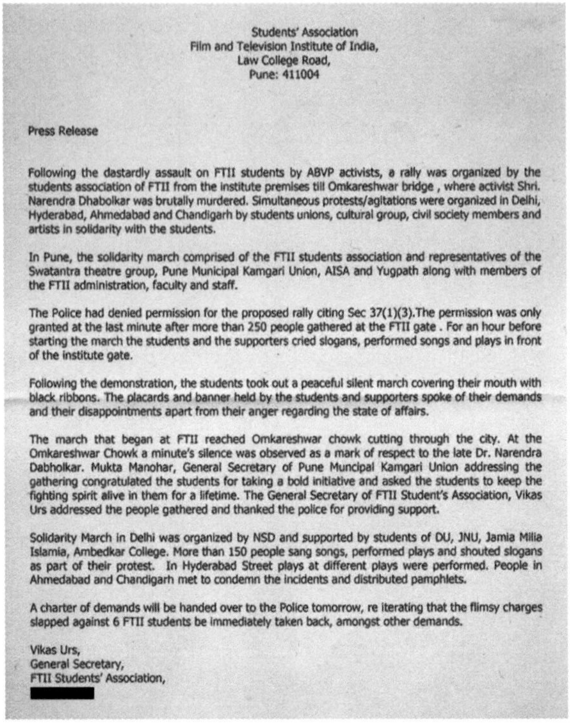
Students' Association
Film and Television Institute of India,
Law College Road,
Pune: 411004

Press Release

Following the dastardly assault on FTII students by ABVP activists, a rally was organized by the students association of FTII from the institute premises till Omkareshwar bridge , where activist Shri. Narendra Dhabolkar was brutally murdered. Simultaneous protests/agitations were organized in Delhi, Hyderabad, Ahmedabad and Chandigarh by students unions, cultural group, civil society members and artists in solidarity with the students.

In Pune, the solidarity march comprised of the FTII students association and representatives of the Swatantra theatre group, Pune Municipal Kamgari Union, AISA and Yugpath along with members of the FTII administration, faculty and staff.

The Police had denied permission for the proposed rally citing Sec 37(1)(3).The permission was only granted at the last minute after more than 250 people gathered at the FTII gate . For an hour before starting the march the students and the supporters cried slogans, performed songs and plays in front of the institute gate.

Following the demonstration, the students took out a peaceful silent march covering their mouth with black ribbons. The placards and banner held by the students and supporters spoke of their demands and their disappointments apart from their anger regarding the state of affairs.

The march that began at FTII reached Omkareshwar chowk cutting through the city. At the Omkareshwar Chowk a minute's silence was observed as a mark of respect to the late Dr. Narendra Dabholkar. Mukta Manohar, General Secretary of Pune Muncipal Kamgari Union addressing the gathering congratulated the students for taking a bold initiative and asked the students to keep the fighting spirit alive in them for a lifetime. The General Secretary of FTII Student's Association, Vikas Urs addressed the people gathered and thanked the police for providing support.

Solidarity March in Delhi was organized by NSD and supported by students of DU, JNU, Jamia Milia Islamia, Ambedkar College. More than 150 people sang songs, performed plays and shouted slogans as part of their protest. In Hyderabad Street plays at different plays were performed. People in Ahmedabad and Chandigarh met to condemn the incidents and distributed pamphlets.

A charter of demands will be handed over to the Police tomorrow, re iterating that the flimsy charges slapped against 6 FTII students be immediately taken back, amongst other demands.

Vikas Urs,
General Secretary,
FTII Students' Association,

Students' Association press release after the attack.

The horrific public assassination of Dabholkar sent seismic waves through Pune. The city has historically had a long and internally fractious tradition of right-wing politics, separate from (and sometimes antagonistic to) that of Mumbai. It included complicated brahmin and OBC adherences platformed on the enduring relevance of Shivaji, the Peshwai and Bal Gangadhar Tilak. While the original force after Independence was that of the Rashtriya Swayamsevak Sangh (RSS), splinter groups have emerged over the years that reflect its history around caste and colonialism. Such splintering also made the political atmosphere of Pune more in line with what was happening across the Konkan, Marathwada and Vidarbha. Some groups, born of the RSS itself, were part of a grand design: such as the ABVP (to mobilize students), the

-3 Amruta Byatnal, 'Police too didn't want film screened', *The Hindu*, 30 January 2012.

Vanavasi Kalyan Ashram (tribals) and the Bharatiya Mazdoor Sangh (industrial labour).[4] Others, like the Patit Pavan Sanghatana and Sambhaji Brigade, had a more eccentric history.

Patit Pavan, one of the city's most visible cultural fronts, came closest to a uniquely Pune tradition of militant brahminism tracking back to the Peshwai.[5] It has *shakha*s in thirty colleges and multiple *mandal*s, a major concentration in the Deccan Gymkhana area adjacent to the FTII, and has been the city's pre-eminent organizer of both the Ganesh and Janmashtami festivals.[6] Rivalling them have been their major antagonist, the Sambhaji Brigade, a front of the Maratha Seva Sangh dedicated to the interests of the economically powerful, often anti-brahmin, Maratha OBC community. Both are, for all their differences with the Sangh Parivar, modelled on the same principles, and both have a record of disruption. Among many, Patit Pavan's attack on Vijay Tendulkar's play *Ghashiram Kotwal* in 1980 and the Sambhaji Brigade's vandalization of the venerated Bhandarkar Oriental Research Institute in 2004 are well known.

After the Babri Masjid demolition and 1993, further splinter groups emerged with newly radicalized factions explicitly declaring terrorist intent. One such, the Sanatan Sanstha, preaching 'a mix of pseudoscience, spirituality and religious mysticism',[7] was held responsible for the killing of Dabholkar and thus bringing terrorism to the doorstep of Pune's traditional middle classes. It also directly challenged the protective dominance of established Sangh Parivar organizations and their hold over Hindu majoritarianism in the city. While Maharastra had known Hindu terror since 2006, when bomb blasts took place in Nanded and Malegaon (involving Sadhvi Pragya Singh and Shrikant Purohit), this time around it wasn't far away, in another city. This was happening at home.

This, then, was the Pune into which the students descended in their effort to engage with the city, starting off a long chain of incidents both on the campus and in the city. It was the ABVP itself, not one of the splinter groups, that arrived at the doorstep of the NFAI that day. As Ajayan, Kislay, Shriram (Raja) and other students found themselves facing the sticks, they heard their attackers 'shout "*ABVP Zindabad*, and *Naxalwadi Bhag Jao*"' says Ajayan. 'They were carrying ABVP flags.'[8] Four students were hurt and were treated at the nearby Joshi Hospital. Two ABVP supporters also

-4

Sujata Patel, 'Seva, Sanghatanas and Gurus: Service and the Making of the Hindu Nation', in Gurpreet Mahajan and Surinder S. Jodhka, eds, *Religion, Communities and Development: Changing Contours of Politics and Policy in India*, New Delhi: Routledge, 2010, p. 111.

-5

This is a history explored in *22 June 1897* (1979), Nachiket and Jayoo Patwardhan's best known film.

-6

Patel, 'Seva, Sanghatanas and Gurus', pp. 114–15.

-7

Sanghamitra Prabal, 'Sanatan Sanstha and its Hindutva Designs', *Economic and Political Weekly*, vol. LIII, no. 41, 13 October 2018, p. 18.

-8

'ABVP activists "beat up" students of FTII for inviting KKM artistes', *Indian Express*, 22 August 2013.

claimed to have been hurt. Each side made police complaints against the other.

A day later, the FTII Students' Association organized a public procession. There were around 250 people there from the campus, including students, faculty and staff, the Director D.J. Narain, and they were joined by members of the Deccan-based theatre group Swatantra Academy, the NGO Yugpath, the student body AISA, and, most valuably perhaps, representatives of the Pune Municipal Kamgar Union. Together, they marched over the Omkareshwar temple bridge, the site of Dabholkar's assassination, and stood there in silent respect. Solidarity marches were also held in Delhi by students of the National School of Drama, and in the universities of Hyderabad, Ahmedabad and Chandigarh.

The matter might have ended there. The ABVP however pressed on, making multiple public statements as they made the FTII, not for the first time, a soft target. Some members of the ABVP had gone peacefully to see *Jai Bhim Comrade*, said the city unit secretary, and had been deliberately provoked by 'a youth at the spot saying that he was proud to be a Naxal'. It was the involvement of another ABVP member that, while not attracting too much attention at that moment, would carry a long tail: that of its Maharashtra state president. A man named Narendra Pathak. A future nominee to Gajendra Chauhan's Governing Council.

Covert Publicness

In 1972, in perhaps the first modern instance of disruption of a Pune art event, a performance of Vijay Tendulkar's *Sakharam Binder* at the Bal Gandharva Rangamandir was stopped by a group of 'seven to ten men belonging to prominent political parties and socially conservative organizations'.[9] According to a witness, the disruption happened 'in the middle of its performance; the actors on stage were held up to have a discussion with the leaders of the group'. It is generally accepted that Manohar Joshi of the Shiv Sena, future Chief Minister of Maharashtra, was behind this attack. Some years later, reflecting on disruptions of stage performances mainly (though not only) by Shiv Sena activists, Tendulkar commented that there was nothing easier to interrupt than a play being staged.[10] You only need to tell the performers not to do it 'or else', and almost without exception you will succeed.

-9

Malavika Maheshwari, *Art Attacks: Violence and Offence-Taking in India*, New Delhi: Oxford University Press, 2018, p. 79.

-10

Vijay Tendulkar in conversation with Raju Parulekar, *Samvaad*, 2010.

This was true not only of theatre, it applied to all activity that was bound by time and place. Performances in infrastructure-heavy auditoria were static, in the way they were authored, starred, named, dated and placed. Such events were entirely reliant on the support of a hierarchical structure of authority that controlled those premises. It was rarely the audiences that caused the problem, said Tendulkar, disturbed as they might have been. The disruption was always by others, initiated by people who rarely saw the plays they attacked, who picked such events only because the venues were so completely fragile, the personnel so utterly vulnerable. 'As long as there is theatre,' Tendulkar mused, 'there will be someone to interfere with its performance.'

The turn in performance from the static to the mobile, from the scheduled to the unscheduled, from formal to informal, and from heavy infrastructure to none at all – eventually from the known to the anonymous, from *regisseur* to hacker – signified a larger millennial transformation of the public political event itself, from organized *morcha*s to spontaneous 'hits', and from Occupy protests to completely fluid movement (to 'be water', as the 2019 Hong Kong protests described it). Across the 1990s and early 2000s the fluid protest was in large measure a response to the growing dangers of a shrinking public sphere that offered few of the historical guarantees of public safety.

As theatre entered the street, it also entered multiple battles taking place on pavements, in neighbourhoods and maidans, over space and the right to space, to shelter and to 'occupy'. Moving in sync with street theatre was documentary film. Both forms took to the streets together with new lightweight equipment, to organize, to assemble and to disseminate. Both sets of actions occurred within an increasingly fugitive mode of informal public assembly.

Some years before this transition and long before *Jai Bhim Comrade*, Anand Patwardhan had already fundamentally redefined the public purpose of film. His first major film, *Waves of Revolution* – made on Super 8 with stock acquired off the black market and sound recorded on a cassette recorder – saw both technology and process inscribed into the record. Writing in 1981 about *Waves of Revolution* in a thesis titled 'The Guerrilla Film: Underground and in Exile', Patwardhan notes the 'poor quality of our sound equipment', most acutely felt when they 'attempted to do candid interviews by hiding the microphone in [their] clothing'.[11] Its technical poverty gave the filmmakers a 'perspective' as they recorded multiple conversations with 'students, teachers and middle-class youths who were enthusiastic supporters of the movement ... bureaucrats vehemently opposed to the creation of chaos and anarchy ... landlords and the urban rich who were too clever to speak their mind ... poor workers, rickshaw pullers, *hamals* and *chaprasis*', alongside recordings of 'songs popularized by the movement and sung by activists. These songs, some composed on the spot, varied from marching songs to a haunting melody sung by a single voice that called out as we crossed a river.'

The lightweight camera had a distinct role to play in this new public domain. It was both 'a weapon of self-defence' and a necessary 'eyewitness' to whatever occurred before it. For it to play these roles effectively, Patwardhan advocated the use of

> hand-held cameras ... grainy, imperfect, jerky, on-the-run, scratched images; interviews [with] persons in silhouette who do not wish to be identified ... using a whatever-is-necessary approach to what was hitherto a carefully upholstered, meticulously protected medium.

The shooting process included

> false identities, disguises, hidden cameras and tape recorders, surprise invasions of the film crew onto enemy property followed by strategic retreats, hiding the film once it has been shot, transporting it to safe processing labs.

And after the film was made there had to be a further process of 'reintroduc[ing] it into enemy territory wherever possible. ... The smuggling of the film outside this territory in order to win sympathy for the revolutionary cause from without becomes a further component.' By the early 1980s, Patwardhan had a six-plate Steenbeck 16 mm editing table in the bedroom of his house in Dadar. He had his own camera, and a projector and speakers, with which he would screen films in multiple informal locations, on streets and maidans. Even in this time, his cinema was as much about going to the streets with his Aaton and Photophone as it was a record *of* that movement.

Jai Bhim Comrade was of course made in a different era, and with different equipment. Started in 1997, it was filmed over a decade, but if it is seen – as Patwardhan wants it to be seen – as a sort

-11

Anand Patwardhan, 'The Guerrilla Film: Underground and in Exile: A Critique and Case Study of *Waves of Revolution*', reprinted In Thomas Waugh, ed., *'Show Us Life': Toward a History and Aesthetics of the Committed Documentary*, Metuchen, N.J.: Scarecrow Press, 1984, p. 451.

of sequel to his 1985 film *Hamara Shahar*, the larger project records an even longer millennial transformation, especially if we further add the epic *Reason* as the final part in a trilogy. *Hamara Shahar*, made on 16 mm film, began a chronicle of a war over space – at the time an essentially Mumbai-centred confrontation between a colonial elite desperately clinging on to their privileges and urban pavement dwellers fighting for their right to shelter.

Such public space, by the time *Jai Bhim Comrade* entered it, had become a riven, treacherous zone. It was a zone, a stage, for what Anand Teltumbde later named the 'macabre spectacle' of caste violence.[12] A new era arose in state-backed caste oppression when the wanton and unprovoked police firing upon residents of Ramabai Ambedkar Nagar in the Mumbai suburb of Ghatkopar on 11 July 1997 saw ten Dalits killed. As the film tracks the saga of legal and political retribution, it also reveals the growth of state oppression – of inquiry commissions going nowhere. Court rulings are delayed and subverted, video evidence is doctored. As it widens its canvas, *Jai Bhim Comrade* goes well beyond Mumbai, beyond *Hamara Shahar* in the wake of the killings of Khairlanji in 2006, to multiple locations in Maharashtra – notably to Vidarbha and thence the nation itself.

It starts with an end. *Hamara Shahar* tells its Mumbai story through the eyes of a small theatre group, the Aavhaan Natya Manch. The poet-singer Vilas Ghogre led a small group that wandered through the city's streets. Ghogre lived in Ramabai Nagar, and soon after the 1997 police violence, Patwardhan's old comrade-protagonist commited suicide in protest, chalking his suicide note on the wall of his *jhopdi*. *Jai Bhim Comrade* begins with Ghogre's death. In presenting its expansive saga of millennial India as a posthumous tribute to him, the film also seeks to re-ignite hope in the transformation it once chronicled in street performance, public poetry and documentary film, even as it records the massive political transformations that have taken place since the 1980s in the apparatus of the state.

The transformation appears vaster than anything its protagonists are able to contemplate. Some months before the FTII screening, on the eve of India's 63rd Republic Day, *Jai Bhim Comrade* was shown at Ramabai Nagar. As Javed Iqbal describes it, 'over three and a half hours, fifteen hundred people saw the film on a makeshift screen, many standing through its entire duration'.[13] Many watching the film

-12
Anand Teltumbde, 'The Political Economy: The Shaping of the Macabre Spectacle', in *The Persistence of Caste: The Khairlanji Murders and India's Hidden Apartheid*, London: Zed Books, 2010, pp. 54–76.

-13
Javed Iqbal, 'Where the Republic Still Lives', *DNA*, 2 February 2012.

had featured in it, but they now saw their stories as though framed within a new and unfamiliar canvas. The story went back in time, to the Dalit Panthers whose own poetics had defined Mumbai, to the killing of Bhagwat Jadhav by the Shiv Sena at a protest rally in 1974, and forward as Bhai Sangare, who was present at the early Ramabai Nagar agitations and is thus present in the film's opening section, lost his life in 1999 under strange circumstances at Mahad while literally re-enacting Ambedkar's 1927 *satyagraha* agitations. As the screening unfolded that evening, Ramabai Nagar gradually found itself placed as the uncomprehending centre of a vast national transformation.

Such a recognition may have been what led to the high point of the screening, the electrifying impact of the songs by Kabir Kala Manch with which the film ends. Music played a central role not just in the film, but across the entire spectrum of Dalit resistance. At one point in *Jai Bhim Comrade*, the poet Prabhakar Pokrikar marvels at the 'flood' of poets and singers that have emerged. There is now 'a poet in every lane, a singer in every hovel'. 'Protest songs sung in every *chawl*, *basti* and *galli* lead us to the newest generation of cultural activists ... whose songs are viewed as a threat by the state, that they're branded as Naxalites and forced to go underground', says Iqbal.

Political Realism, or the Macabre Spectacle Mediatized

Anand Teltumbde identifies a specific millennial development in Indian politics – the birth of a new form of public humiliation. It is a 'celebratory public spectacle ... of ghastly violence' performed with a specific intention, of putting a category of oppressed people 'in their place'. On the one hand, there is nothing new about such violence. 'Melavalavu's Murugesan was beheaded, and his head thrown into a well. Rape is not a private affair. ... Atrocities involve intricate and devious planning so that they constitute a lesson for the entire Dalit community. The worst crimes are planned meticulously to inflict maximum damage.'[14] The Dalit 'atrocity' includes numerous incidents such as Keezhvenmani (1968, when forty-four Dalits were burnt alive), Belchhi (1977, fourteen Dalits burnt alive), Morichjhanpi (1978, refugees from Bangladesh massacred during a government eviction drive in 1978), Karamchedu (1984, six murdered, three women raped), Chunduru (1991, nine Dalits killed), Melavalavu (1997, an elected Dalit panchayat leader and five

-14

Teltumbde, 'The Political Economy: The Shaping of the Macabre Spectacle', in *The Persistence of Caste*, p. 73.

Dalits murdered), Kambalapalli (2000, six Dalits burnt alive), and Jhajjar (2002, five Dalits lynched outside a police station).

On the other hand, when the Khairlanji massacre occurred in 2006 not too far from Nagpur, what was new was the media presence, both television and then electronic. Although 'Khairlanji is not unique', being an 'unconscious reenactment of the primordial punishment of the *shudra*s, and, by implication, of the untouchables, ordained in scripture', it heralds a 'new genre of atrocities' whose impunity would be wedded to actions happening in full public view and even performed in front of, and explicitly *for*, the cameras. Their extreme social visibility was only matched by their ubiquitous banality, leaving no one in doubt as to what had happened, who were involved and why.

Such visibility would be contrasted with a second stage of visuality politics, of a corresponding *in*visibility of what had occurred from official narratives. Reflecting on how 'television crime' turns crime first banal and then invisible, Teltumbde speaks of the 'naturalization' of violence to the extent that 'caste atrocities [have become] part of the Indian ecology. If a crime is committed against a dalit at such frequency as one every eighteen minutes – as per government records of reported crimes – what novelty does it hold?'[15]

Such visual ubiquity extends into a representational ambivalence, as any credible historical account of what happened in forms such as (most prominently, but not limited to) documentary film gets further linked to larger human rights questions. Are victims receiving legal, administrative or political justice? If they are not, how does the *representational confrontation* of the underlying challenges of exiting the system take place? How might recourse be found by other means? The protection a perpetrator receives that allows him to hide in plain sight can only be grasped, Teltumbde says, if it is framed within the radically new challenges posed by a neoliberal revolution that has seen the Indian Constitution move from an instrument of change to one that presents social inequality as 'natural and indeed the prime mover of progress. ... In essence, it reiterates in modern idiom the Hindu metaphysical doctrine.'[16]

Such a double-act of hypervisible impunity frames an equally visible/invisible counter-spectacle of an 'Ambedkarite' public domain of 'busts and statues, pictures and posters, songs and ballads,

-15

Anand Teltumbde, 'Mass Media Massive Prejudice', in *The Persistence of Caste*, p. 142.

-16

Anand Teltumbde, 'Introduction', in *The Persistence of Caste*, p. 32.

books and pamphlets, conferences, seminars and ... congregations'.[17] There is an element of both physical and moral self-preservation in the arrival of what Sharmila Rege once named a Dalit heterotopia that does not possess a fixed address or determinate physical space, but is based instead on mobility and elusiveness.[18] Its primary form is musical, performed by 'travelling troupes [that] move across regions and generations so that often ... the original composition is difficult to trace'. The music cannot be 'reduced to [an] organizing tool for politics or to something all too readily appropriated by market forces'. Rather, it reflects what Rege calls a 'distinctive social space through the reflexive circulation of the music; with texts not only asserting their own position, but also characterizing their relation to all other positions in the imagined horizons of circulation'.

> How do we understand the music as constituting a counterpublic – is it the claims to the oppositional that constitutes the counter? Or is it the host of alternate publishing and circulating institutions, practices and sites, that then make it counter? To some extent it is both ... but more importantly it is also in the awareness of the subordinate status – and of the conflict of ideas, the modes of address, and the speech genre.

The ambivalent image presents a whole set of new responsibilities to documentary cinema, as it does to street theatre. Among these are how to represent technologically produced subjects, 'biopolitical' beings inserting themselves into history through their bodily (as against other cultural) properties, whose very survival depends on how they can push the question of whether they are within or expelled from a skewed system into an 'excess', an 'overflowing of being and creativity that unbalances the relationship of force'.[19]

Hardt and Negri define excess in the context of Black Lives Matter and its subjective overproduction, but their 'political realism' as an immersive biopolitics – that forces 'the content of constituent power ... to become life itself [as] protesters and activists ... shine a light on the fact that ... life is subject to threat and exploitation' – might just as easily be applied to the theatre, music and documentary film that punctuate the recent Indian history of the macabre spectacle.

Both street theatre and documentary film in India have been closely linked to the rise of the political spectacle. In 1977

-17

Anand Teltumbde and Suraj Yengde, *The Radical in Ambedkar: Critical Reflections*, Penguin Books, 2018, p. 1.

-18

Sharmila Rege, 'Interrogating the Thesis of "Irrational Deification"', *Economic and Political Weekly*, vol. 43, no. 7, 16 February 2008, p. 17.

-19

Michael Hardt and Antonio Negri, 'Political Realism', in *Assembly*, New York: Oxford University Press, 2017, p. 234.

the Belchhi massacre provided the impetus for the famous street play *Belchhi*, which inaugurated the Bangalore-based Samudaya. Bhagalpur (both 1980 and 1989) saw major documentaries on both. The Bhopal gas disaster (1984) saw Suhasini Mulay and Tapan Bose's *Bhopal: Beyond Genocide*. The Malom massacre (2000) was referenced in Heisnam Kanhailal's iconic *Draupadi*. Godhra (2002) is known by Rakesh Sharma's *Final Solution*. And now Vilas Ghogre, the Kabir Kala Manch and the Ramabai Chawl firing are what define *Jai Bhim Comrade*. The whole purpose of 'documenting political battles is ... to make struggle visceral,' writes Jane Gaines, 'to go beyond the abstractly intellectual to produce a bodily swelling ... the radical film derives its power ... from the political events that it depicts'.[20]

The performative move in *Jai Bhim Comrade* from Aavhaan to Kabir Kala Manch directly maps on to the ideological tensions that pervade this counter-public. To Teltumbde it is a resurgent Ambedkarism 'channelled into slogans, poetry, flags, banners, Buddha viharas, congregations – the entire arsenal of symbolic displays'. It is a potent, dangerous form which could, he warns, find itself 'submerged within Hindu ritualism'. He points to how the Narendra Modi government announced in 2016 that five locations that defined Ambedkar's life, including Chaityabhoomi in central Mumbai, have been declared the '*panchteerth*' or five sites of pilgrimage. As 'Ambedkarism' becomes a 'free floating signifier', Ambedkar is himself reduced by the political class into an 'inert godhead ... or worse, a reactionary identity icon blocking any further enlightenment'.[21]

The process of building new solidarities around such Ambedkarism came at a cost. In the end it may have cost Ghogre his ideological integrity, musically and politically, as he struggled between Marxist and Ambedkarite pressures; cost him his membership of the Aavhaan Natya Manch (he was thrown out for what some in the group saw as his ideological compromises); and may eventually have cost him his life. Ghogre's suicide was itself a performance, as he died with a blue scarf over his forehead and a suicide note scribbled with a chalk on a wall behind him.[22] In a way, the entire point of *Jai Bhim Comrade* was (says Patwardhan) to try and figure out why Ghogre, 'an Ambedkarite who had become a

-20

Jane M. Gaines, 'Political Mimesis', in Jane M. Gaines and Michael Renov, eds, *Collecting Visible Evidence*, *Visible Evidence* series, vol. 6, Minneapolis: University of Minnesota Press, 1999, p. 91.

-21

Anand Teltumbde, 'Ambedkarites against Ambedkar', *Economic and Political Weekly*, vol. 48, no. 19, 11 May 2013.

-22

S. Anand, 'Between Red and Blue', *Outlook*, 16 April 2012.

Marxist, had ... at the moment of his death reasserted his Dalit rather than his Marxist identity'.[23]

When the Kabir Kala Manch was started in Pune in 2002, it was a musical group inspired to come together after Godhra to preach a liberal 'anti-caste, anti-communalism and democratic message', writes Teltumbde. Its musical lineage was similar to that of Aavhaan, influenced by Sambhaji Bhagat (and had behind it a very long tradition of poetry and music going back to Gawankar and Annabhau Sathe), but its radicalization occurred after Khairlanji. 'Ambedkar was now interwoven with Marx and I marvelled at how potent the combination was in the hands of young believers who challenged the selling out of an older generation that had settled for crumbs from the high table', says Anand Patwardhan, who first heard the Manch perform at Ramabai Nagar in 2007. Other accounts attribute a more explicitly Maoist turn to the influence of Sudhir Dhawale's *Vidrohi Sanskritik Chalwal*.

In 2007 began a cycle of political arrests under the draconian UAPA. That year Binayak Sen and lawyer–activist Arun Ferreira of the Chandrapur-based Deshbhakti Yuva Manch were arrested by the Anti-Terrorism Squad. Teltumbde outlines the sequel to Khairlanji, the agitations in Nagpur in the wake of the *Deeksha* ceremony commemorating Ambedkar's fiftieth death anniversary, followed by agitations in Yavatmal and Amravati and eventually across Vidarbha district. All of these were persistently presented by the state as 'naxalite', in part because it served as 'a convenient label for the Indian state to assume full authority to do whatever it pleases with ordinary people seeking space for dissent in their democratic republic'.[24]

In 2011 Sudhir Dhawale was imprisoned. When Deepak Dengle was arrested shortly after, the Kabir Kala Manch went underground. In 2012, Patwardhan used the money he had received for a National Award for *Jai Bhim Comrade* to start the Kabir Kala Manch Defence Committee. On 2 April 2013, shortly after Dengle was released on bail, Sheetal Sathe and Sachin Mali walked to the Maharashtra State Assembly. Along with them were Patwardhan, Prakash Ambedkar and other members of the Defence Committee. They spoke to the media, and then recited a song. They were, Patwardhan asserts, not surrendering but rather 'performing an

-23

Anand Patwardhan, 'Why We Defend the Kabir Kala Manch', 24 April 2013, patwardhan.com

-24

Anand Teltumbde, 'Post-Khairlanji: A Chronicle of Repression', in *The Persistence of Caste*, p. 123.

act of *satyagraha* for the freedom of expression'. The two were nevertheless arrested. Sheetal, who was pregnant, was given bail on humanitarian grounds on 28 June.

In August, a few short weeks after Sheetal Sathe and Sachin Mali's performative *satyagraha* outside the State Assembly, the FTII screening took place.

Your 'Cinema Rucksack': Tactical Media and Documentary

In July 2002, Neeraj Sahay, fresh out of the FTII and fresh also from his role in the late-90s strikes, outlined a radically new development in the career of community video. He had arrived in Ahmedabad that May along with another ex-FTII graduate, the filmmaker Gurpal Singh, to do whatever they could amid the increasingly horrifying escalation of targeting of the city's Muslim population. Gurpal had written a series of chilling accounts of the violence they had seen, such as on 5 July, where he spoke of people 'hesitant ... to disclose how they had to borrow money or eat at a relief camp or live on the charity of family or friends', how many 'could not earn their livelihood from 28th February until the middle of May', how surveys of burnt houses had not been done and when they had, they were being given token compensation cheques. Gurpal doubts that the man he was speaking to 'really expected me to offer anything more than moral support. All I could do was hold his hand and all he could do was cry silently.'[25]

Neeraj and Gurpal now set up the 'Shared Footage Group' as a community media project. In a 21 July note titled 'Gujarat Carnage – Documenting the Aftermath', Neeraj outlines the idea: 'a bank of footage' available for 'like-minded filmmakers' as well as to 'assist the legal effort by recording testimonies or visual evidence'.[26] In that note he is looking for help to shoot documents of 'police atrocities/ role of police in "riots", criminal injustice practised and supported by the state' and its many consequences. They have worked 'with cameras lent by people and often ... not in the best shape', spent 'a packet on repairs and servicing', and now need 'tapes (hi 8, minidv, vhs-c, vhs), mikes, batteries, blank CDs and any equipment that you think could be useful to us'. He is also looking for help in 'logging, with cross indexing etc. in some form which is easily accessible and open to data manipulation (in the sense of sorting by areas, or keywords, or incidents etc.)'. 'It is crucial for the whole thing to

-25 Gurpal Singh, 'Just another day in Ahmedabad', mail # 8, Onlinevolunteers.org, 5 July 2002.

-26 Neeraj Sahay, 'Gujarat Carnage – Documenting the Aftermath: Shared Footage Idea', Onlinevolunteers.org, 21 July 2002.

work,' he says, 'to have each and every interview/vox pop/group interview etc. transcripted and available in electronic form.' The Shared Footage Group made around 250 hours of footage between May 2002 and February 2003, mostly on DV and Hi-8.[27]

Among the numerous filmmakers who arrived in Gujarat with portable cameras and a backpack was former theatre activist and television journalist Shubhradeep Chakravorty. Turning to video documentary as a logical sequel to theatre (he had founded the IPTA wing in Faizabad) and television, he spent nearly a decade there racking up a cycle of films, starting with *Godhra Tak: The Terror Trail* (2003), followed by *Encountered on Saffron Agenda?* (2009), *After the Storm* and *Out of Court Settlement* (both 2012).

In September 2013, Chakravorty turned his attention to Muzaffarnagar, a month after the carnage that occurred in western Uttar Pradesh following clashes between Hindu Jat and Muslim communities centrally featuring caste honour and sexual violence. Widely considered the worst riots the state had ever seen, they lasted over a month with multiple deaths and nearly 50,000 Muslims forced into refugee camps.

Chakravorty shot and completed his documentary, titled *En Dino Muzaffarnagar*, over that winter. Six months later, on 28 April 2014, he and his partner Meera Chaudhary were invited to screen it at the Vikalp programme in Mumbai's Prithvi Theatre. It was an important invitation. Anand Patwardhan was in the audience, as were other filmmakers. Chakravorty's previous work had been viewed mostly as a form of video journalism, and, notwithstanding its admirable politics, had not been taken very seriously as cinema. At Prithvi his film received a good response. It encouraged him to make a more ambitious plan for wider screenings. This in turn meant that he needed to apply for a Censor Certificate. Perhaps, Chaudhary later mused, that had been a mistake.[28]

Two weeks after Prithvi, in June, *En Dino Muzaffarnagar* was officially banned. The ban was in short order upheld by the FCAT, which declared that the film had 'grave potential of creating communal disharmony' since it is 'highly and openly critical of one political party (BJP), names its top leadership and tends to give an impression of the said party's involvement in communal disturbances. This is a gross violation of the film certification guidelines.'[29]

-27

This was not the only instance of community media projects in Gujarat in 2002. Perhaps the best-known instance remains that of Video Volunteers, emerging from the Drishti Media Collective.

-28

Ashley Tellis, '"I will never stop making films": Meera Chaudhary', *Groundxero*, 2 May 2021.

-29

Tanul Thakur, 'The Long and Fruitless Struggle to Get a Censor Certificate for a Film on Muzaffarnagar', *The Wire*, 18 May 2016. Includes an actual copy of the order issued by the CBFC.

Chakravorty died on 25 August, a week after this announcement, at the age of 42 – just four months after his career-defining screening – of stress-related brain haemorrhage. The actual censorship saga began after he died, however, for Meera Chaudhary then ran a heroic campaign in his name, over multiple Supreme Court writ petitions and bureaucratic runarounds. In the end, she and her lawyer Prashant Bhushan forced the CBFC's Pahlaj Nihalani to disclose the contents of the Ministry's explicit 'opinion' on *En Dino Muzaffarnagar*, and to admit to the Supreme Court that they were working under direct Home Ministry instructions that the film be accused of creating 'disharmony' in the way it tries to 'defame a group of ... individuals and presents an *ex parte* view of rights'.

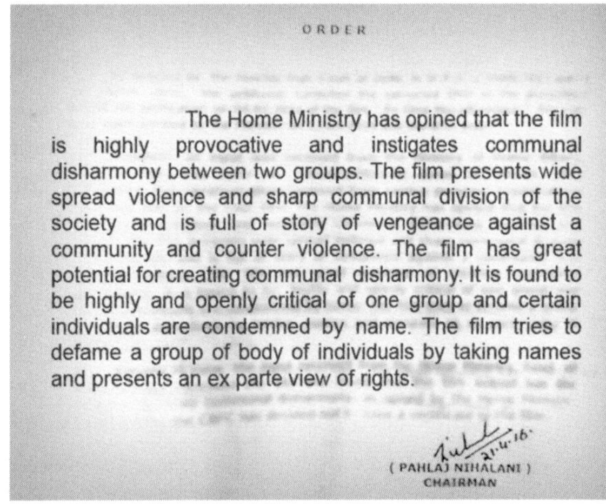

ORDER

The Home Ministry has opined that the film is highly provocative and instigates communal disharmony between two groups. The film presents wide spread violence and sharp communal division of the society and is full of story of vengeance against a community and counter violence. The film has great potential for creating communal disharmony. It is found to be highly and openly critical of one group and certain individuals are condemned by name. The film tries to defame a group of body of individuals by taking names and presents an ex parte view of rights.

(PAHLAJ NIHALANI)
CHAIRMAN

Summary and mash-up of order signed by Pahlaj Nihalani, Chairman of the Censor Board, in April 2016, acknowledging direct instructions from the Ministry of Home Affairs to CBFC on **En Dino Muzaffarnagar** (2014).

Legacies of Tactical Media

Some time in late 1979, in the aftermath of the Emergency, Safdar Hashmi wrote a 'Draft Paper on the Nature and Need for Street Theatre', from which Sudhanva Deshpande cites several excerpts in his book *Halla Bol*.[30] Hashmi was then already speaking of the need to be 'documentary and brief, shocking yet familiar', a sort of 'newspaper-in-action' looking at events 'from day to day'. There is a clear similarity between Patwardhan's turn to 16 mm documentary and Hashmi's parallel search for a new form (and a technology), which Deshpande defines as '(a) inexpensive (b) mobile and portable [and] (c) effective'.

Deshpande traces a genealogy to this move in Utpal Dutt's 1952 play, *Chargesheet*, that was part of the movement for the release of Communist prisoners (*bandimukti andolan*). He also underscores Hashmi's further tracking back of the form to the Bolshevik revolution, which curiously inserts Eisenstein, more than even in film, into the theatre, linked with inexpensive, mobile and effective media.[31]

Four years before Dutt's play, in November 1948, seven peasant activists were shot dead in the village of the Layalganj 'liberated free zone' in the Sundarbans while resisting the attacks of local landlords supported by hired goons and the police. They included a pregnant

-30

Sudhanva Deshpande, 'The 1980s: A Theory of Street Theatre', in *Halla Bol: The Death and Life of Safdar Hashmi*, New Delhi: Leftword Books, 2020, p. 89.

-31

Sudhanva Deshpande, 'The Inexhaustible Work of Criticism in Action: Street Theatre of the Left', *Seagull Theatre Quarterly*, Issue # 16, December 1997.

woman named Ahalya. The Communist Party of India was banned at the time. Ahalya's death led to an explosion of creative action. The IPTA (Indian People's Theatre Association) aimed to 'build upon spontaneous cultural responses to political events, to consciously bring aesthetics to bear on politics, in theatre, music, dance, art, and photography ... following the Telangana peasant movement in Andhra in 1948, the Kayyur peasant revolt in Malabar in 1940, the Hajong Tanka Adivasi rebellion in Assam in 1942, and the Tebhaga peasant revolt of 1946–47 in Bengal', writes Sumangala Damodaran.[32] The peasants' killing led to several famous songs being written, of which one, '*Hai Samhalo*' written and composed by Salil Choudhury, has become legendary. The ban caused 'IPTA's proscenium plays [to be] driven underground – and to the streets' says Samik Bandyopadhyay, as theatre went 'underground' to 'audiences prepared to share, with the performers, the risk of a police attack and prepared to give them necessary protection'.[33]

The shift in reaction to state terror from strategy to tactics, to the mobile, the provisional and the ephemeral – all aspects of future tactical media – was in evidence in a rather different reaction to the Ahalya incident, in a plan hatched in the immediate postwar years by a small group of filmmakers in Calcutta sitting in a dingy café known as Paradise, to smuggle a 16 mm film camera to Kakdwip, shoot the events there, develop their film clandestinely and then screen it in villages where the movement was going on. In the group were Ritwik Ghatak (aged 23), Salil Chowdhury (23), Mrinal Sen (25), Hrishikesh Mukherjee (26) and Tapas Sen (26). Chowdhury titled their proposed film *Jamir Ladai*, Sen wrote a screenplay, and Ghatak, nominated to be the cinematographer, managed to unearth a broken camera and 'learnt quite a bit about handling it, despite the fact that it was an ancient and rundown model', Sen later wrote in his obituary for Ghatak.[34] That film was never made, and the story – although Sen narrates it on more than one occasion – remains apocryphal. It is unclear how the group came to access a 16 mm camera (a rarity in 1946) or film stock (then still under rationing), which laboratory they planned to use or what projector they would take to the villages.

—

-32

Sumangala Damodaran, 'Situating the Rural in Musical Imaginaries of Nation, Region, and Identity', *Review of Agrarian Studies*, vol. 9, no. 1, January–June 2019.

-33

Samik Bandyopadhyay, 'Theatrescapes', *Seagull Theatre Quarterly*, Issue # 16, December 1997.

-34

As reconstructed by Sanghita Sen, the Paradise Cafe group started meeting around 1946. Sen wrote his first essay, 'Cinema and the People', that year, when he was arrested by the police near Kalighat Tram Depot. See Mrinal Sen, *Ami o Amar Cinema*, Kolkata: Banishilpa, 2015, pp. 30–31. It is unclear when exactly they started talking about the project, but by 1948 (when Ahalya and her comrades were killed) a complete plan for the film appears to have been in place. Sen burnt the script after a tip-off that police were looking for them. See Sen, *Ami o Amar Cinema*, pp. 214–15; and *Montage: Life, Politics, Cinema*, Kolkata: Seagull Books, 2002, pp. 18–20.

A little over six decades after Ghatak, Sen and others made their abortive plan of a cinematic raid on Kakdwip, Nakul Singh Sawhney took his camera and recorder to the *madrasas* in Loni, just outside Delhi, where many of Muzaffarnagar's refugees had found shelter. This was early September of 2013, and Nakul worked for the left–liberal online news portal Newsclick. News by this time had shifted increasingly to informal blogs and social media alongside more structured news aggregators. Newsclick was an early instance, started in 2009 by Prabir Purkayastha, and Nakul had helped to set up its video wing.

To Nakul, everything changed for documentary after Gujarat. Godhra in 2002 hammered in 'the last nail'.[35] This was a new era of the technologized spectacle, and it brought to documentary a radically new, post-celluloid, twenty-first-century purpose. While Rakesh Sharma's films are well known, other famous examples include Suma Josson – a former journalist working for the Press Trust of India (PTI) when making *Bombay's Blood Yatra* (1993) – who now made *Gujarat: A Laboratory of Hindu Rashtra, Fascism* (2002) as a campaign film for the State Assembly elections, and Gopal Menon's real-time documentary work *Hey Ram!! Genocide in the Land of Gandhi* (2002).

When Nakul went to Loni, it was mainly to check a political news angle, to see how this development figured in Narendra Modi's ambitions for the coming general election. It didn't take long for an entirely different picture to emerge. For one, what he saw was bigger than anything yet reported. The question was no longer whether or not Modi was going to win, for his rise was clearly unstoppable if western Uttar Pradesh was any evidence. The story was, rather, to do with the materials fuelling that rise. Nakul encountered radicalized grassroots, combining bias, rumour, news and public displays of violence into a lethal media spectacle. The film he needed to make was precisely *not* a counter-spectacle, *not* something within a news cycle or for immediate consumption. He had to slow it down, take longer over it, make something perhaps more reflective.

The slow cinema instinct ran counter to what Nakul had done so far, initially in street theatre and then in news media. At The Players, the street play *Khade Hain Lathi Taane* was followed by *Main Sachha Deshbhakt Nahin*, a play on patriotism that he

-35
Conversation with Nakul Singh Sawhney on Zoom, 9 March 2021.

co-directed in 2002, and a lot of acting with Jana Natya Manch, such as in the street play *Ek Mazdoor ki Swabhavik Maut* and the proscenium production *Shambuk Vadh*. It was when he saw Anand Patwardhan's *Ram ke Naam* that he – and he says, his entire generation – encountered the power and immediacy of documentary film, far greater, he felt, than anything theatre could ever manage. Theatre was in the end condemned to performance, to fiction. *This* was real.

The Other New Cinema

> 'Two–three pairs of clothes, a laptop, a set of hard disks, a white piece of cloth and a small projector.' – Sanjay Joshi, describing his Cinema Rucksack.[36]

In 2005 Nakul joined the FTII. He chose not to take the four-year film course but rather the shorter diploma in television production. He had heard about the militancy of the students there and friends had discouraged him from going, but he was more attracted than repelled by this reputation. On the other hand, he had his own decisions to make. Should he stay with street theatre or turn to documentary film? Or was there a way to combine the two into a mediatized amalgam?

Although Nakul's batch had their own minor skirmishes with the administration, the FTII campus was very much in a calm-before-the-storm moment, still negotiating the aftershocks of Agashe. Video had arrived, but the film wing was playing ostrich. In 2000, the dominant business-as-usual, nothing-to-see-here, everyday filmmaking approach had begun contrasting especially sharply with an evolving documentary scene in faraway Delhi. Documentary was undergoing a revolution there, and much of the action had shifted to graduates of the AJK Mass Communication Research Centre (MCRC) at Jamia Millia Islamia.

This was a history of communication that went back to Independence. Soon after the 1947 'Post War Educational Development Plan' and the founding of an audio-visual unit in the Ministry of Education to 'popularize the use of visual and aural aids as important tools for classroom instructional purposes', the Indian state explored social education programmes through merging 16 mm film with other media.[37]

-36

Quoted in Amit Sengupta and Ashfaque E.J., 'A film festival of the people, for the people, by the people', nationalheraldindia.com, 4 August 2019.

-37

A 1952 report of the Central Advisory Board of Education speaks of an 'Educational Caravan' going around villages with 'four vans fitted with various audio-visual aids and equipment like posters, gramophones, projectors, dramatic stage, musical instruments, library, merry-go-rounds, etc.'. Central Advisory Board of Education, Report of the 19th Meeting, 1952 (Appendix A e, Report on the Development of Audio-Visual Education in India). Much of this was the postwar turn of British Griersonism to what John Grierson himself named – after he was appointed as UNESCO's Director of Mass Communication – as 'fundamental education'.

Video – here understood as an intermediary, transitional technology between celluloid and digital – reveals a history specific to Delhi. If the New Indian Cinema rose to prominence in Kolkata, Thiruvananthapuram, Mumbai and Bangalore, through the 1970s it had an unstated video 'other' in Delhi (and Ahmedabad). In 1972, CENDIT was started in Delhi, and in its early days used several traditional media for social change including, says Rajive Jain, 'street theatre, puppets, posters and cartoons', before turning in the 1980s to video.[38] In 1975 Ahmedabad's SITE studios began production, often featuring filmmakers from the New Cinema in their early programming. In 1981 the Special Plan for Expansion of Television took off.

Video after the Emergency also saw the repurposing of an old 16 mm collective imagination. Yugantar was founded in 1980, Chandita Mukherjee and Anjali Monteiro contributed in 1981 to the AVEHI Audiovisual Resource Centre in Mumbai (ancestor to Mukherjee's own Comet Media Foundation), and organizations like SEWA and Abhivyakti too increasingly depended on community-based development. Mediastorm was started in 1984, the Prakrit Media Collective in 1987, Drishti in 1991. In part, this resurgence coincided with the post-Emergency entry of a vibrant if shortlived NGO sector, seeking to mitigate the totalitarian face of the state with some of its more beneficial developmental aspects. The arrival of 'participatory video' as an essential part of NGO work also saw the birth of an 'institutionally managed practice' of video, in order to promote what Shweta Kishore later called 'neoliberal values of individualism, self-interest and entrepreneurialism'.[39]

The MCRC's own legacy of postwar Griersonism, heightened by the considerable involvement of Canadian filmmaker James Beveridge in its early days, took a new turn in the 1980s as documentary video was increasingly merged with street theatre. Six women who were part of the second ever batch at MCRC formed Mediastorm in 1984 and made three documentaries clearly intended as tactical media interventions.[40] They too speak of Anand Patwardhan's documentaries as the game-changer (to them it was *Hamara Shahar*), as they do of their encounter with street theatre, where they credit Safdar Hashmi with being an integral part of their work, having contributed songs to two of their films and made

-38

Quoted in Giulia Battaglia, *Documentary Film in India: An Anthropological History*, Oxon: Routledge, 2018, p. 115.

-39

Shweta Kishore, *Indian Documentary Film and Filmmakers, Independence in Practice*, Edinburgh: Edinburgh University Press, 2018, p. 83.

-40

Mediastorm, 'Memories of a Collective', *The New Medium*, curated by Shaina Anand, MAMI, 2017.

the Jana Natya Manch available for their film *From the Burning Embers* on the Roop Kanwar sati incident in Deorala, Rajasthan. Mediastorm's films were shot on video and edited (they wrote later) in a friend's studio at night when the equipment was free, 'as the city slept', 'in shifts throughout the night, taking turns to work and sleep on the studio floor'.[41]

Such collaboration is in stark contrast to FTII's enduring cult of individualism that – for all FTII's links with Griersonism (Marie Seton, followed by Basil Wright and other UNESCO representatives, and indeed Beveridge himself[42]) – had remained largely impervious to documentary and would now be impervious to video, major exceptions over the years (Ramani, Pankaj Rishi Kumar, Avijit Mukul Kishore) notwithstanding. Indeed, it can be argued that in the early 2000s the reaction to video – a reaction defining the Shared Footage Group idea – as a blowback to Agashe had only deepened an older and larger chasm.

—

Inevitably then, despite his brief FTII interregnum, Nakul's explorations in video journalism were framed within a Delhi history of community media that had mostly bypassed the FTII's film (as against television) programme. News video had the immediacy of theatre alongside the slower, more reflective possibilities of documentary, such as what Rahul Roy or Lalit Vachani were practising. When Nakul returned to Delhi after his FTII stint (following the usual Mumbai intrerregnum, which he says he hated) to join Newsclick, an element of 'agit-prop' framed the immediacy of some of the documentary work he did there: for example, the short film he made in 2011 on the Maruti strike at Manesar. Alongside current affairs, he also made several slower documentaries for Newsclick – notably *Izzatnagari ki Asabhya Betiyan* (2012) on young women, honour killings and western Uttar Pradesh's notorious *khap* panchayats, which centrally features the street play *Dhyodi ke Paar*.

The media spectacle forced Nakul to consider, in *Muzaffarnagar Baaqi Hai*, a different strategy for negotiating the space into which he was entering with his camera and sound. Like Sanjay Kak's *Jashn-e-Azadi*, *Muzaffarnagar* is something of

-41

Both Rahul Roy and Amar Kanwar were part of a 'core group' that revived the street play *Ahsaas*, first done in 1979 at Miranda House, led by Ruth Vanita, following an incident of sexual harassment at St Stephen's College. Deepti Priya Mehrotra, 'Feminist Street Theatre: Plays as Contemporary History', *Indian Cultural Forum*, 9 July 2016.

Street theatre was very much a fellow traveller of the social communication documentary, often practised by the same people. See project by Sampurna Trust (India Foundation of the Arts) that looked at major street productions of the time, indiaifa.org, 2014–15.

-42

FTII's distance from documentary has been confusing, given its links to Films Division in the 1960s, Doordarshan in the 70s, its connection – via Marie Seton – to the British documentary movement, and its links to UNESCO. Film students complete a documentary as part of their course, and several are famous, but there is nothing that intrinsically links documentary to FTII as it does to MCRC.

Facing page and overleaf
Nationwide call for protest screenings of **Muzaffarnagar Baaqi Hai** (2015), following the 1 August 2015 attack on the screening of the film at Kirori Mal College.

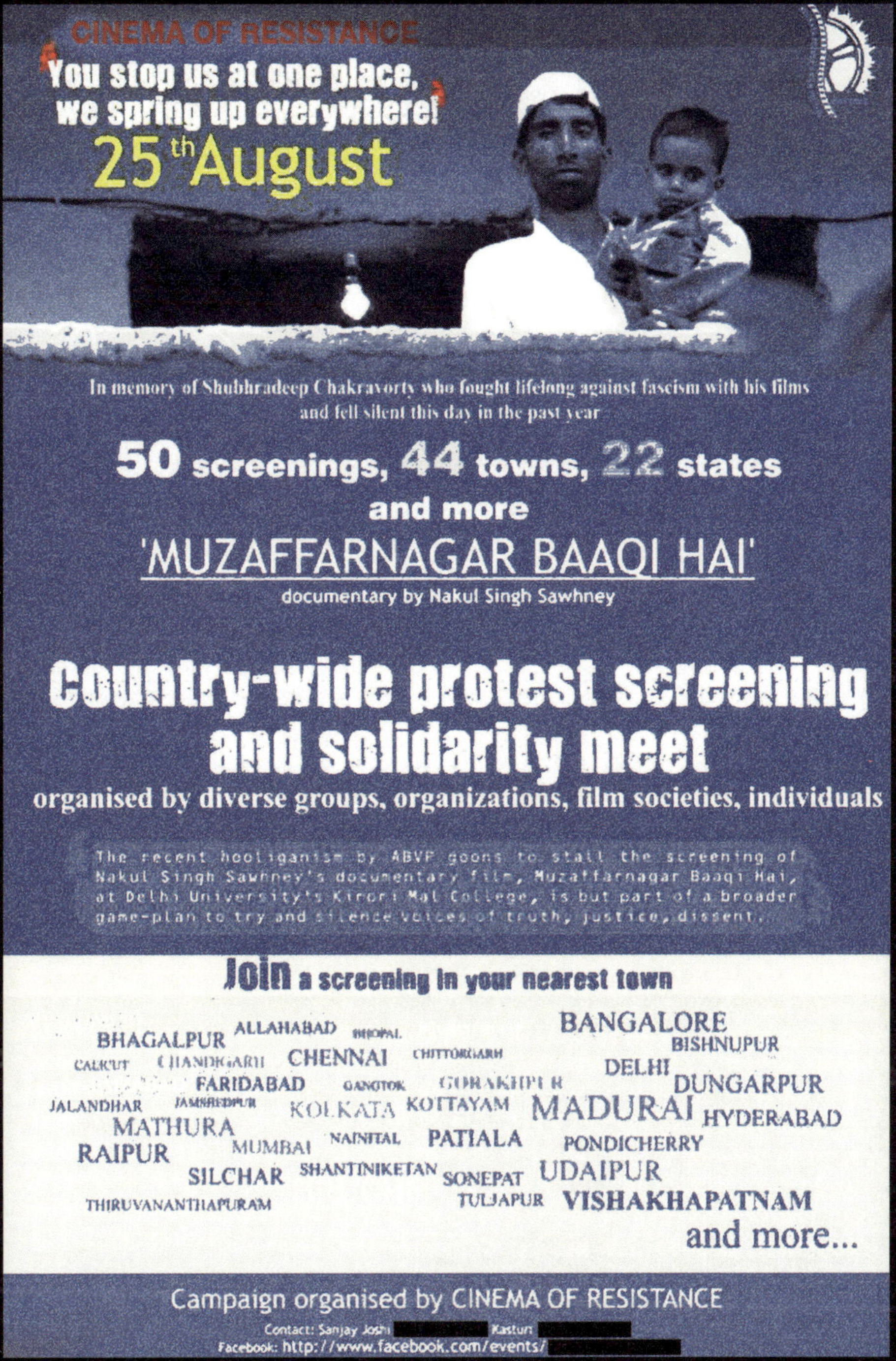
CINEMA OF RESISTANCE
"You stop us at one place, we spring up everywhere!"
25th August
In memory of Shubhradeep Chakravorty who fought lifelong against fascism with his films and fell silent this day in the past year
50 screenings, 44 towns, 22 states and more
'MUZAFFARNAGAR BAAQI HAI'
documentary by Nakul Singh Sawhney
Country-wide protest screening and solidarity meet
organised by diverse groups, organizations, film societies, individuals
The recent hooliganism by ABVP goons to stall the screening of Nakul Singh Sawhney's documentary film, Muzaffarnagar Baaqi Hai, at Delhi University's Kirori Mal College, is but part of a broader game-plan to try and silence voices of truth, justice, dissent.
Join a screening in your nearest town
BHAGALPUR ALLAHABAD BHOPAL BANGALORE BISHNUPUR
CALICUT CHANDIGARH CHENNAI CHITTORGARH DELHI
FARIDABAD GANGTOK GORAKHPUR DUNGARPUR
JALANDHAR JAMSHEDPUR KOLKATA KOTTAYAM MADURAI HYDERABAD
MATHURA MUMBAI NAINITAL PATIALA PONDICHERRY
RAIPUR SILCHAR SHANTINIKETAN SONEPAT UDAIPUR
THIRUVANANTHAPURAM TULJAPUR VISHAKHAPATNAM
and more...
Campaign organised by CINEMA OF RESISTANCE
Contact: Sanjay Joshi Kasturi
Facebook: http://www.facebook.com/events/

CINEMA JAARI HAI!

Cinema of resistance for freedom of expression

Country-wide screenings of 'Muzaffarnagar Baaqi Hai'

70+ screens, 50+ towns, 22 states

On August 1st 2015 members of the Akhil Bharatiya Vidyarthi Parishad exhibiting habitual hooliganism forcefully stopped the screening of Nakul Singh Sawhney-directed documentary, 'Muzaffarnagar Baaqi Hai..' at Delhi's Kirori Mal College. Videos witnessing this incidence of violent disruption of the screening can be seen in Facebook, Twitter and other social media.

'Muzaffarnagar Baaqi Hai...' is a documentary film that quite courageously reveals the conspiracy of the ruling class political parties which deliberated communal massacres to grab political power by-hook-or-by-crook, in their opportunist alliance with the new lumpen capitalist and feudal forces in the society during August-September 2013 in Uttar Pradesh. This documentary is significant in the times when the media, co-opted by the crony capitalist corporate forces, has turned into a fabrication machine than being the fourth pillar of democracy supposed to project truth and reality.

Narendra Dabholkar, veteran activist who fought vigorously against superstitions was brutally murdered in 2013. Artists of Kabir Kala Manch were put behind bars because their songs were considered seditious! In 2015, comrade Govind Pansare who ferociously blew away communal iconization of Shivaji, was assassinated in the daylight. Teesta Setalwad and Sanjeev Bhatt are continuously being framed and cornered by the state machinery. The same city of Pune where the innocent Mohsin Sheikh was lynched for wearing markers of his faith, also witnessed disruptions during the screening of documentary filmmaker Anand Patwardhan's iconic film, 'Ram ke Nam'. While the Ambedkar Periyar Study Circle faced a ban at IIT Madras; Tamil writer Murugan had to declare the 'writer' in him 'dead' under fascist pressures. Without any evidence an intellectual and teacher like G. N. Saibaba was incarcerated in Nagpur jail in precarious health conditions. FTII students struggling for their democratic rights were arrested at midnight and every force is used to try and crush their movement. And on the other side killers associated with the Ranveer Sena and Bajrang Dal - who boasted of massacres on camera - were let go scot free and let out on bail respectively. What do all these country-wide incidences suggest?

It appears that there has been a torrent of such incidences as mentioned above. Many a time we don't even get the information of prevalence of such repressions in different corners in India. It is possible to bring them in light only by building strong and united resistance against these dark times. This is precisely the reason why Cinema of Resistance does not look at incidence of muting 'Muzaffarnagar Baaqi Hai..' at Kirori Mal as an isolated incidence, rather it is observed as a dangerously fascist tendency that strangles the democratic spirit. Strong, committed resistance even by putting our lives at stake is the only possible mechanism to impede this trend. We take immense pleasure to share with you that this appeal of ours to respond by arranging countrywide protest screenings was welcomed from various corners of the country and **till this date we are informed that this protest will be organized in 22 states, 50 cities/towns and with more than 70 screenings.**

We dedicate the protest screenings to the memory of Shubhradeep Chakravorty who fought lifelong against fascism with his fims, and fell silent on this day the past year at a very young age, passing on his baton to us.

==

Circulated by People's Film Collective and Cinema of Resistance campaign, in public interest. Contact: cor.kolkata@gmail.com, 9163736863, corkolkata.wordpress.com, Facebook: Cinema of Resistance

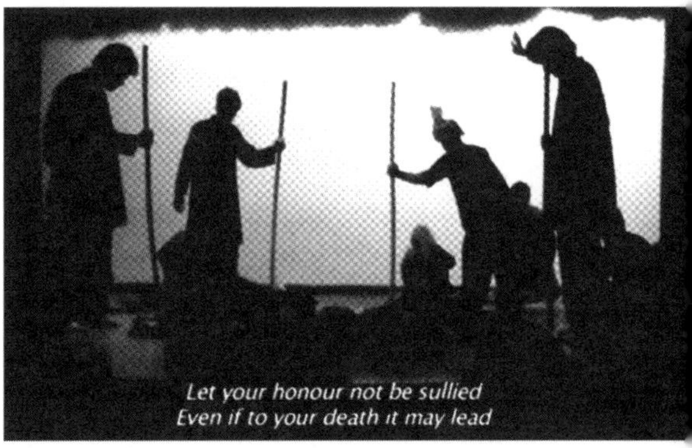

The street play **Dhyodi ke Paar** in Nakul Singh Sawhney's **Izzatnagari ki Asabhya Betiyan** (2012).

an epic cinematic work in the era of digital media. Unlike *Jashn-e-Azadi*, where amateur video and news recordings enter and become part of the film, *Muzaffarnagar* externalized the news aspect into other productions of community engagement on video that were made alongside but outside Nakul's film. This culminated in a larger community media project with a local office, library and screening space, that he named the Chalchitra Abhiyaan. The main film was allowed to be slowed down by the fact that the speeded-up 'immediacy effect' of documentary was handed over to other actions that took place parallel to but separate from the film he was making. All of Nakul's films since *Izzatnagari* have been co-productions with Chalchitra Abhiyaan and with other news portals – two of them with Newsclick, and one, his 2016 film *Kairana, After the Headlines*, with *The Wire*.

This twin strategy of combining filmmaking with organization follows Patwardhan's style of making a film in collaboration with social action (the best-known example being the mid-1980s work of the Nivara Hakk Suraksha Samiti alongside *Hamara Shahar*). However, the founding of Chalchitra Abhiyaan is different. *Muzaffarnagar Baaqi Hai* is an authored work, and therefore top–down, whereas the Abhiyaan, bringing news dissemination together with community video, is more horizontal. The first is slow, the second immediate. Chalchitra Abhiyaan now has a venue in the town of Kandhla in Shamli, a substantial screening schedule that includes both Indian and world cinema, a small staff, and an active programme in which townsfolk and villagers make and upload short films at the same time as Nakul makes his own.

'We Spring Up Everywhere'

Almost exactly two years after the ABVP attacked the FTII students in Pune, they attacked another film screening in Delhi. This was Nakul Sawhney showing *Muzaffarnagar Baaqi Hai* at his alma mater, Kirori Mal, for a Montage Film Society event. An audience of over a hundred and fifty students had gathered. Approximately 10 minutes into the film, a small number in the audience left, returning an hour later with around forty people who revealed themselves as

ABVP representatives. The event was invaded, threats were issued, and despite the overwhelming desire of those present to continue to see it, the rest of the screening was cancelled.

That evening has been well documented in several short videos showing men muscling into the auditorium, with faculty member (and principal organizer of the Montage Film Society) Dhananjay Kapse and his colleague Keval Arora trying to placate them, and young women screaming, 'You can't touch public property.'[43] There are also long interviews with ABVP-supporting students who explain why they did this, and why their feelings were hurt.

The 'horizontalist' steps that follow are of significance. Two days later the Ambedkar Students Association, Hyderabad, led by Rohith Vemula, staged a protest titled 'Curbing Academic Space and Lynching Democracy' in support of the FTII strike that was into its second month, Pondicherry University and the Montage Film Society. The following week the Cinema of Resistance put out a further call.

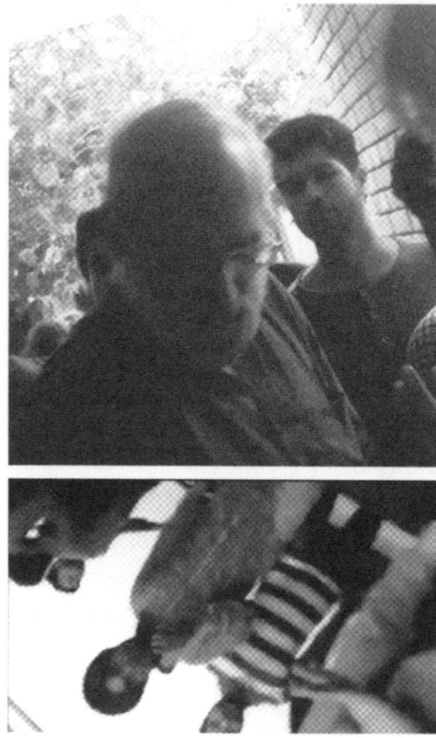

Nakul Singh Sawhney's concealed camera footage of the Kirori Mal attack on **Muzaffarnagar Baaqi Hai**, published on newsclick.in.

MCRC alumnus Sanjay Joshi, the primary organizer of Cinema of Resistance, is fascinated by what he calls the 'Cinema Rucksack' mode of film exhibition.[44] Joshi's project began when he successfully persuaded the venerated Jan Sanskriti Manch in Allahabad in 2005 to use their considerable networking expertise to do something innovative with cinema. The Manch, headquartered in Patna and with a significant Bihar presence, has multiple outreach programmes mostly across north India, and has been extraordinarily active in civic rights in the areas of literature, theatre and visual arts. Cinema of Resistance was founded the following year with its flagship Gorakhpur Film Festival, launched (it is said) when they screened Rahul Roy's *When Four Friends Meet* after the university refused to show it. Joshi has since then organized seventy-odd film festivals in Patna, Nainital, Allahabad, Varanasi, Lucknow, Azamgarh, Chittorgarh, Udaipur, Nagpur, Indore and Rohtak. They are entirely done with informal and site-specific means, writes Shweta Kishore.[45] The publicity is a 'blend of social

-43

Newsclick.in video, 3 August 2015.

-44

Sengupta and Ashfaque, 'A film festival of the people, for the people, by the people'.

-45

Kishore, *Indian Documentary Film and Filmmakers, Independence in Practice*, p. 124.

media, local small-media to rickshaw-mounted public address systems, handbills and word-of-mouth methods'.

The *Ghuspaithiya*

Nachi joined the FTII in 2012. His epic stint there ended in 2018. Over two of these crucial six years he represented the Students' Association. Included in these years were the 139 days of the great 2015 strike, when he was its president and its public face.

Nachi speaks in intensely emotional terms of this entire period, including but not limited to those 139 days, as a *yug* (an epoch) that led him more than once to something like breaking point.[46] This emotional intensity and the possibility of tipping over is found in different degrees in other students too, who had been immersed in this astonishing history and its flirting with the dark zones of power. Nachi however goes further in one respect. He maps this profoundly subjective journey – from Pollachi to Chennai and to Pune, and then to Delhi and places beyond – upon that of the nation, crisscrossing autobiography with the churnings in national space in this time. The encounter with the great masters, the theory of film and of swimming in a digital ocean of moving image data, go hand-in-hand with the art of political navigation that he learnt 'on the job', so to say, in real time.

What Nachi ends up describing is a journey as much through space as a movement within, a navigation into a very different, post-*regisseur*ial idea of a filmmaker. The filmmaker is now less of an awe-inspiring auteur and more a practitioner of what the Nair Committee called the 'unbelievably democratized' art of image-making playing out a deeply conflicted subjectivity on a new sort of national and even international canvas.

Five years and a month or, seen another way, half a lifetime after the 2013 attack, the inaugural campus screening of *Hora*, Nachi's student documentary on the Kabir Kala Manch, was officially cancelled. The reason put out was that it was a student evaluation and not a public event, and in any case the film didn't yet have a censor certificate. Informally, it was generally acknowledged that the FTII had caved in to police pressure. What also got cancelled as a domino effect was the screening of Nachi's student diploma film named *Famished Road* (2018).

-46
Conversation with Nachi, 2/3 March 2019, Chennai.

Hora wasn't exactly the film Nachi had hoped to make. He certainly wanted to do something that spoke for, or otherwise reflected, the past five years on the campus and in the country. He had in mind a film that would capture the astonishing moment of history into which the fates had conspired to insert him in 2015, and had multiple ideas for both what he wanted to do and, perhaps more relevantly, *didn't* want to do. It would be subjective, but it wouldn't be personal. He did not want it to fall 'into the trap of memory', a popular style (he says) at FTII, to 'create' an image and then to impose upon that image a subjective feeling. He says he trusted neither the image nor the feeling. Pankaj Rishi Kumar, who had once discussed this with him at a documentary workshop, had been encouraging, but Nachi realized at some point that the idea was bigger than what a student exercise could possibly manage.

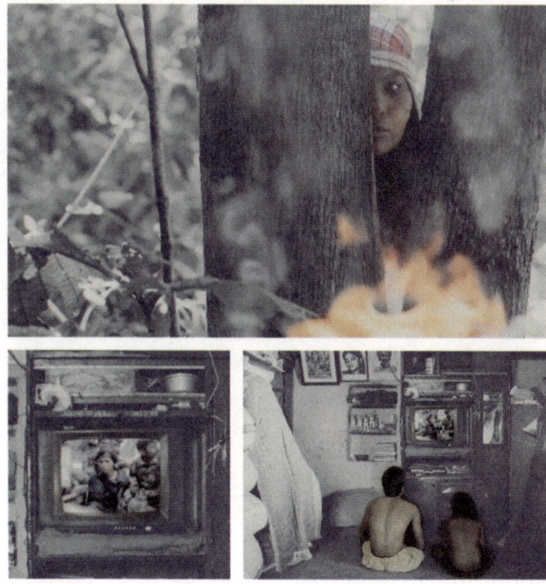

Scenes from Nachi's diploma film **Famished Road** (2018): the tribal 'witch' and the little boy.

As Nachi spoke of his imagined film, both space and the biopolitical subject took on the national hues of a post-celluloid horizontalism. His first year in Pune was defined by the Dabholkar assassination. In early 2014 his election as Students' Association president went alongside Narendra Modi's takeover of the Indian state. Nachi was further catapulted in 2015 into national space as the student body gave press conferences, negotiated with the central government. Now he shared space with nationally known student leaders like Kanhaiya Kumar, Shehla Rashid and others, part of a frontline of a national upsurge. He went everywhere – 'JNU, HCU, Aligarh, Ambedkar, yeah all of the institutes where I could meet other students.' He learned about national politics in Delhi – 'If you have to learn politics, I think you have to be in Delhi. ... I learned the language, Hindi, and also the political language.' And in his final year in 2018, Pune was simmering with the tension of Elgar Parishad at Shaniwar Wada, where the Kabir Kala Manch had performed and which now brought so much unwelcome police attention to his documentary screening and evaluation.

Moving to Pune and thence to destinations unknown, the politics of national space was inexorably linked to the campus challenges of the national–modern. The fields of Nachi's childhood shaded into those of *Pather Panchali* and *Ugetsu Monogatari*, developed a lifelessness – or perhaps a hopelessness, a *nirash* quality, he says – as they appeared in theory class. Surely, if what they told you in class was all there was, every one of his twelve batchmates would become cinematic masters overnight? This insight would also define the 48-hour 'Retracing Freedom' festival on Independence Day of 2015 during the strike. If it was not so easy, surely the filmmaker's answer must be in the way that navigating this jungle of ideas and theory links filmmaking directly to *political* navigability, on- and off-campus?

Now, how to make such a film? Issues developed with his cinematographer, a not unknown occurrence that was exacerbated by his search for a 'Ranjan Palit'-style cinematographic idiom. Might it have been better, he wondered later, for him to have shot the film himself? Indeed, his first preference had been cinematography, and he still intends, if he can manage it, to do his own shooting. The Ranjan Palit reference would be prescient for the biopolitical being. Not much later, Palit would release his own long-in-the-making autobiography, the extraordinary *Lord of the Orphans* (2020), where he speaks of himself with a strangely similar, barely conscious absent/present lens as both cinematographer and human being.

In the end, Nachi decided to keep *Hora* as a 'classical documentary' and to trust the camera to record where he went and what he saw. He had originally thought of a form in which three Dalit women would reveal their engagement with Ambedkar. Eventually, only Rupali Jadhav featured. Nachi hoped nevertheless to arrive at a kind of uncanny objectivity in his image. It would be an image distinct from the well-known 'observational mode'. His interest in this kind of an image, which he says he shared with fellow batchmates Mukul Haloi and Payal Kapadia, involved initiation, a ritual of *tapas* and perhaps of *riyaaz*, and in its relentless objectivity, it was perhaps the best way to address what everyone had been through in these years.

There was an unintended upside revealed by the cancellation imbroglio, however. When the two films were rescheduled – and shown, ironically, shortly (it appears) after a screening of Wong Kar-Wai's *In the Mood for Love* – they brought together the disparate protagonists of very different films in a way that might not have otherwise happened.

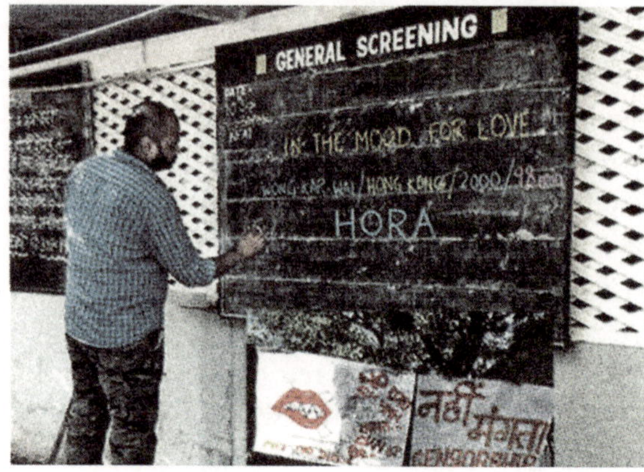

Nachi writing the **Hora** screening announcement on the FTII Main Theatre notice board, below the announcement of Wong Kar-Wai's **In the Mood for Love.**

Nachi thinks the controversy was created by police paranoia about Dalit activists flooding the campus. He feels sure that plainclothes police were present even among the tightly controlled list of invitees. What this paranoia resulted in, as happens always with paranoid censorship, was to imbue surreptitious meaning to everything, in a way that you think Wong Kar-Wai might have understood. The mysterious and unnamed tribal woman in *Famished Road* – who wafts through the forest which has once seen a labour contractor kill a young girl as a 'virgin sacrifice', and who is now believed to be out and about on full moon eclipses when the snake-demon Rahu is also at large – would have come along with the terrifying presence of the Kabir Kala Manch over whom the police had come to keep vigil.

In *Hora*, Rupali is followed by Nachi's camera over a few days in her home, her neighbourhood, in some of the local *basti*s and on stage as she and the troupe perform on Ambedkar Jayanti. In *Famished Road*, the tribal woman is being tracked by men in military uniform. The story is told through the eyes of a young boy, who discovers traces of the woman in the jungle, under the moonlight, while watching the drunken military men before they finally capture the woman, in a sequence the police would certainly have found harder to watch than anything in *Hora*. There is talk earlier of a 'witch', a *hadal*, in the village, whom the women in the village have sought to exorcise by various means. Every scene takes on a disconcerting meaning. One wonders what the plainclothes police made of it all.

Nachi's Facebook self-description of the filmmaker is of a *ghuspaithiya*, a complex term that a simple translation reveals as 'intruder' or one who 'enters without permission', and may also include elements of masquerade. Even as a child growing up in Pollachi he never found either children's films or superheroes interesting. He had been bedridden for a year, a traumatic memory that he reconstructs in his *plan-séquence* exercise, *Windows Wide Shut*. *Witchcraft*, a short film that he made in 2014 at a workshop run by iconic avant-garde filmmaker Jackie Reynal (the workshop required students to make a three-shot exercise on life at FTII) has its first shot taken in near-darkness, where a group of youths argue about mystical spirits over a drink. The second pans to a person winding a film spool and tilts down into the spinning reel. In the final section, the most intriguing of the three, we see Nachi himself, a ghostly presence, as though walking backwards past the images of V. Shantaram and the great Prabhat maestros on the FTII wall.

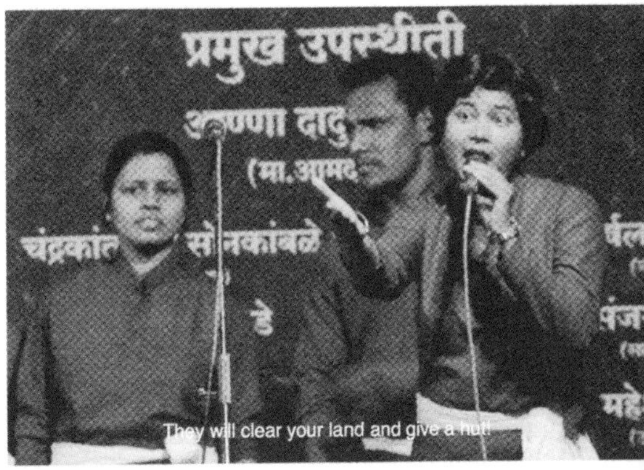

Rupali Jadhav and the Kabir Kala Manch in Nachi's documentary **Hora** (2018).

Static space, the space of the national, the terror of the great masters – and then the brief communitarian calm of the strike itself – all come together in his view that FTII can 'induce a fear of reality'. The feeling maps on to a 'there/not-there' condition, opening up from there into a part of the fugitive *regisseur* and tactical media.

—

In 2016, a second round of post-strike deep cleansing took place across the campus. On 1 June, at a meeting of the Academic Council of which Nachi was still a member, it was agreed that all exercises would be entirely digital. Indeed, one plan was to rename the FTII as a University of Cinema, Television and Allied Arts, also described in an official presentation as a 'Digital Media University'. Seven short-term courses would be introduced 'for mid-career professionals', and the syllabus would be revised into a 'choice-based credit system' over six semesters. The new 2015 batch was officially renamed the '2016 batch ... owing to the events on campus last year' and it was also agreed that students admitted had to be always 'in good standing'.

Students of the 2016 batch at least remembered the strike. By 2017 it had been entirely erased in the deep cleansing, and with it, the people who ran it.

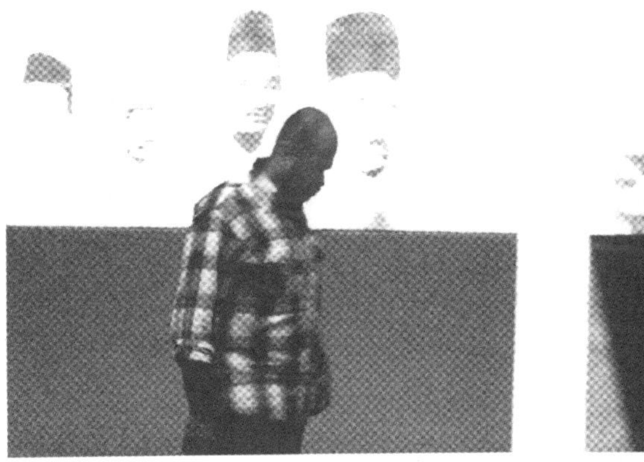

Nachi, in his short film **Witchcraft** (2014), walks past images of filmmakers from Prabhat Film Company.

> We almost, I think in one way, couldn't keep up to expectations. After that not much happened in the Institute, and I also was alone. The student body almost never functioned. Vikas and other people got busy with their projects and they were going. Also, after the strike, people start blaming you, 'because of you this is happening'. A lot of things happen to you, individual vindictive measures ... right from CCTV cameras and other things, and you are getting notices for everything then, being penalized. So, all that and you have a case, you have to go and appear in the court every time.

Vikas completed his diploma shoot in 2017 and left the campus soon after. He never got his diploma because he did not submit his thesis. He says he told his department head that he saw no purpose 'because none of you are really interested in what the student goes through in the process of learning, his craft and in the medium at large'. 'Personal fights like ... it mounted to the point where I am fighting with the admin every day. You are being singled out and you are being made not just guilty, guilty *to khair theek hai, woh to chhoti si baat hai* ['made to feel guilty is still fine, it is a small thing'], but you are not even supported in your final academic process. I was waiting there only to do my diploma film. I had no other reason [to be there].'[47]

-47 Conversation with Vikas Urs, 21 October 2021, Mumbai.

In mid-2018, Nachi trudges up the main road of the campus. He is getting his documentary done, but already he is as though a wraith, a ghostly remnant from another era that was 2015. He appears entirely alone now. What is happening is of course the inevitability of history. Another students' strike is going on around him, but he isn't a part of it. In August 2018, second year classes were literally in suspension even when Nachi's screenings got cancelled and rescheduled. A month later, in October 2018, a near-fatal accident took place at a field shoot when a hired crane fell and nearly killed two students. That saw yet another agitation. 'Every five years a strike has to happen irrespective of who is in the government', Nachi muses. 'I think it is because the place was designed like that.'

The Potato Eaters

Back in Chennai after the Pune screenings, in late 2018, Nachi plans to assist iconic Tamil filmmaker Pa. Ranjith in a project on the legend of Birsa Munda based on Mahasweta Devi's novel *Aranyer Adhikar*. (That film was shelved, but Nachi did assist on Ranjith's next, *Sarpatta Parambarai*, 2021.) Although Ranjith is best known for big productions, most notably ones with Rajnikanth (*Kabali*, 2016 and *Kaala*, 2018), it is his radical avatar that Nachi unveils before me, such as the ambitious Neelam Panpaatu Maiyam (or Neelam Cultural Centre), an arts organization associated with free events and public productions, and its subsidiary, the Koogai Thiraipada Iyakkam (or Koogai Film Movement), with which Nachi is specifically associated, and its online campaign titled *#VoteOutHate* that makes short films for YouTube. He is clearly enamoured of Ranjith's astonishing ability to work the system while keeping alive his Ambedkarite commitments.

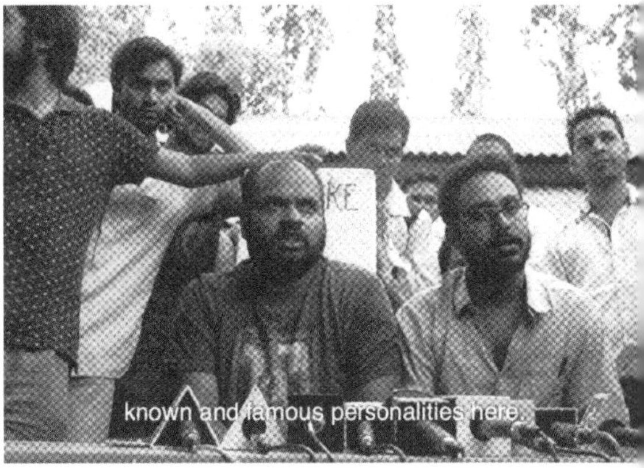

Nachi and Ranjit Nair after an early GBM, from Kshama Padalkar's **The Strike and I** (2019).

In 2019 Nachi launched his own Potato Eaters Collective. It is entirely social media-driven, a hyperactive presence with debates, premieres of independent productions and active file-sharing of films, a significant Facebook presence, several lively WhatsApp and Telegram groups, and a YouTube channel that shares rare, remastered films by Aravindan, John Abraham and others. The Collective takes its name from Nachi's longstanding fascination with the peasant painting by Van Gogh. That painting had appeared in his student dialogue exercise *Ghosts of Dead Rivers*, along with posters of Kiarostami's *Close-Up*, Ghatak's *Subarnarekha* and other films, in what seems to be a combination of film space and a library as a small group of friends have a meltdown on a rainy day. On his social media pages Nachi sometimes takes what many consider to be outrageous stands, and he often gets into scraps online. He insists on seeing films only in their pirate circuits and sometimes says he will never pay an OTT subscription. Whatever it is, Nachi sees all of this as a logical extension of a filmmaker's work.

CHAPTER 7

THE HOLLOW CENTRE

11 June 2016. On the first anniversary of the declaration of the great 2015 strike, editing student Shini J.K. cuts a cake under the Wisdom Tree. It has been a year since the start of what she calls the 'ruckus', and her feelings are, to say the least, mixed. Her main thought is the way they stayed together, survived the maelstrom, even when 'one or the other member of the community was hurt'.[1] 'Our emotion', she says 'became our politics.'

-1 Shini J.K., 'A Love Letter to FTII…', Countercurrents.org, 11 June 2016.

The Student Body

Shini speaks in short syllables, and doesn't especially care to explain further. It may be wrong of her to not provide answers, but then the students didn't really need to bother any more about 'being politically correct', for they had 'nobody to look at us from the top'. 'No mother-parties, no party lines.' They were, in the end,

Facing page
Letter signed by the ten members of the delegation that met with Arun Jaitley on 3 July 2015. They included Bina Paul, Resul Pookutty, Girish Kasaravalli, Paresh Kamdar, Fareeda Mehta, Prateek Vats, Reema Kaur, Nachi and Vikas Urs. Dharam Gulati, representing GraFTII, replaced the original nominee Umesh Gupta.

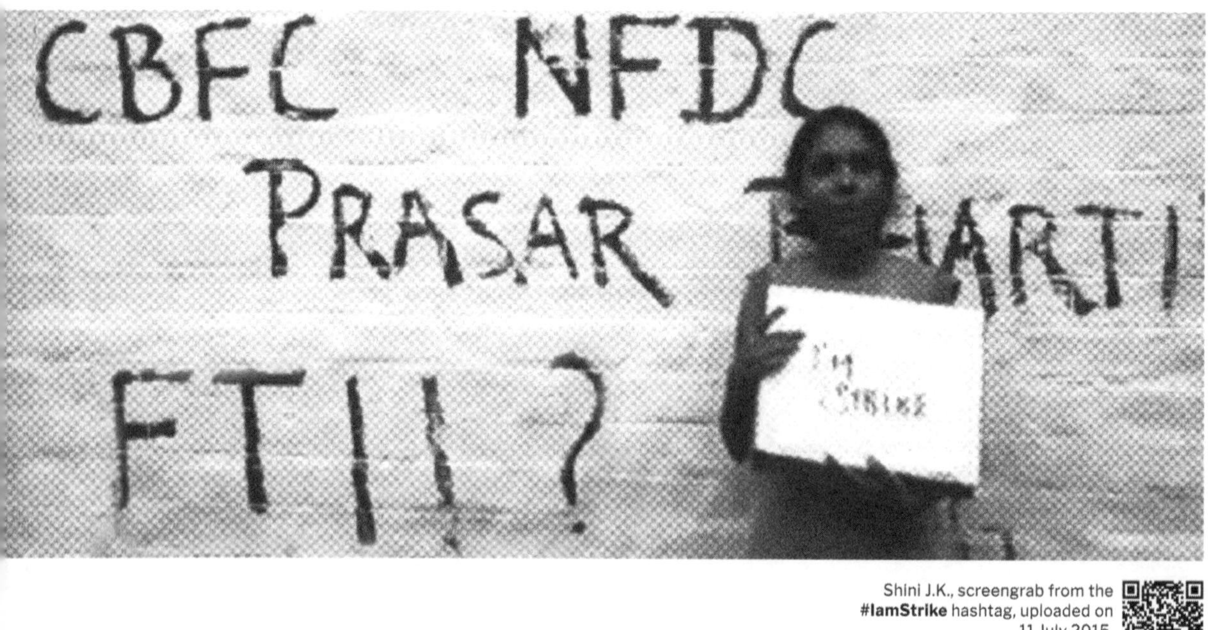

Shini J.K., screengrab from the **#IamStrike** hashtag, uploaded on 11 July 2015.

Submission and recommendations of the Panel

Setup to aid in the resolution of the current crisis at

FTII,Pune

To, 03/07/2015

Shri Arun Jaitley
Hon. Minister of Information & Broadcasting,
Government of India

We, the alumni of FTII, practitioners of the art of cinema and the representatives of the students, would like to humbly submit to you that we are very concerned with the recent developments in the governance of the Film and Television Institute of India (FTII), an institute of international and national repute. As you may be aware, this institute, since its inception in 1961, has enriched the Indian film industry, both technically and aesthetically, through the contribution of its graduates. We submit the following points and recommendations for your consideration:

1. **FTII Society:**
   In the past, the apex body, which comprised of filmmakers and academicians of national and international repute, have provided the vision and academic rigour essential for the art and pedagogy of cinema. Generations of students have been inspired by these individuals to enrich Indian cinematic practice.
   We are afraid, that the newly constituted society does not measure up to this tradition of academic and intellectual excellence of this premier institution.
   We recommend that the newly formed society shall not be operationalised. In the interim, an expert committee to suggest norms and guidelines for the setting up of a society shall be formulated and in this committee the Chairman and Vice Chairman of the outgoing Governing Council shall be included.

2. **Institute of National Importance:**
   The Hon. Minister's announcement in the Parliament to make this Institute an 'Institute of National Importance' brought great cheer to the entire cinema community. At this critical and exciting juncture of technological and aesthetic transformation, FTII is in acute need of upgradation. Granting the status of national importance will ensure that this transition is effected. To realise this transition a perceptive leadership is required.
   With due respect to the members of the newly constituted society we surmise that they do not have the necessary experience and academic expertise to spearhead this transition. We request the government to expedite the process of upgradation and provide able leadership. The Film and Television Institute of India has unique needs. We suggest that the government appoints a core committee, comprising of eminent film practitioners with pedagogical concerns and stakeholders from across India to formulate and oversee the setting up of the 'Institute of National Importance.'

F.M

AK

F.V

answerable only to themselves and to each other. If this made them look like elites to some, to numerous others they only looked 'weird and ugly'. If it appeared to be an 'absurd idea' to cut a cake to memorialize the first birthday of the strike, well, so be it, for that was how it had always been, given that 'everything had been absurd for us'. Survival was certainly not something you could take for granted in the deadly aftermath of 2015. 'We all were marked in the history', 'not as leaders or individuals, but as a community'. They were different individuals, separated in every way possible, by 'class, caste, gender, language, ethnicity, political inclinations'.

So what brought them together? Shini offers an enigmatic answer. 'Beyond everything', it was in the end about 'love, cinema and existence', a 'love in between, and for the space'.

On Day 31 of the strike, 12 July 2005, when Shini and several other students uploaded small clips under the *#IAmStrike* hashtag holding mock prison IDs, it wasn't *cinema mon amour* as much as another Godardian quote that appeared relevant: 'He who jumps into the void owes no explanation to those who stand and watch.'[2] If something of the ghost of the *regisseur*'s once-upon-a-time magnificence still existed in these frail bodies, the master of the enigmatic phrase would surely have approved of how they forced a crisis that the nation could hardly comprehend, let alone solve.

Some of Shini's monosyllabic responses were clearly due to exhaustion. Over the five months of the strike the students had interminably debated their positions, in marathon GBMs as well as outside them. They had assembled a strenuous outreach initiative on platforms and blogs, travelled across the country, made contact with universities, done press conferences and media appearances in multiple languages – so it wasn't like they hadn't tried. To many, it had ended badly, among differences over whether it had gone on too long or not long enough, and what, if anything, had been achieved. Several students were out of money, hounded by the police and the courts, as they struggled to keep personal and professional lives afloat. Most worrying of all, there was the hurt. Kundan Shah's gesture of slitting his throat in November 2015, when he held open his National Award, spoke for the disparate and ragtag student batches as much as for India's academic and art communities on campuses across the country.

-2

Jean-Luc Godard, 'Review of Jacques Becker's *Montparnasse 19*' (1958), in Tom Milne, trans. and ed., *Godard on Godard*, New York: Martin Secker and Warburg, 1972, p. 75.

June 2015: FTII campus.

Facing page
A burial ground – for film, for celluloid and for the artist. Details from Kshama Padalkar's **The Strike and I** (2019).

Overleaf
AirMacs humming around the Wisdom Tree.

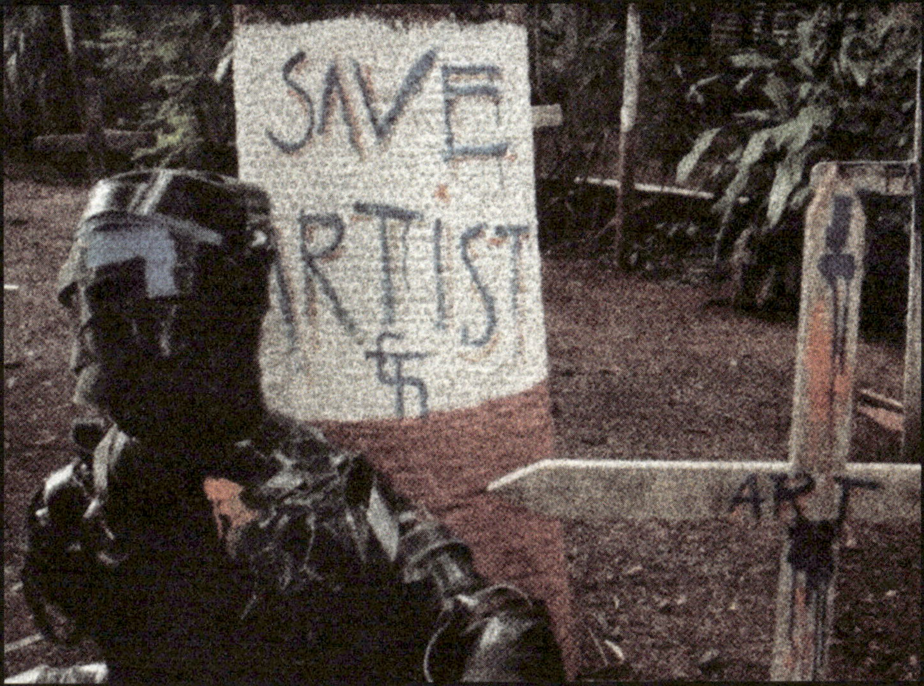
SAVE
ARTIST
ART
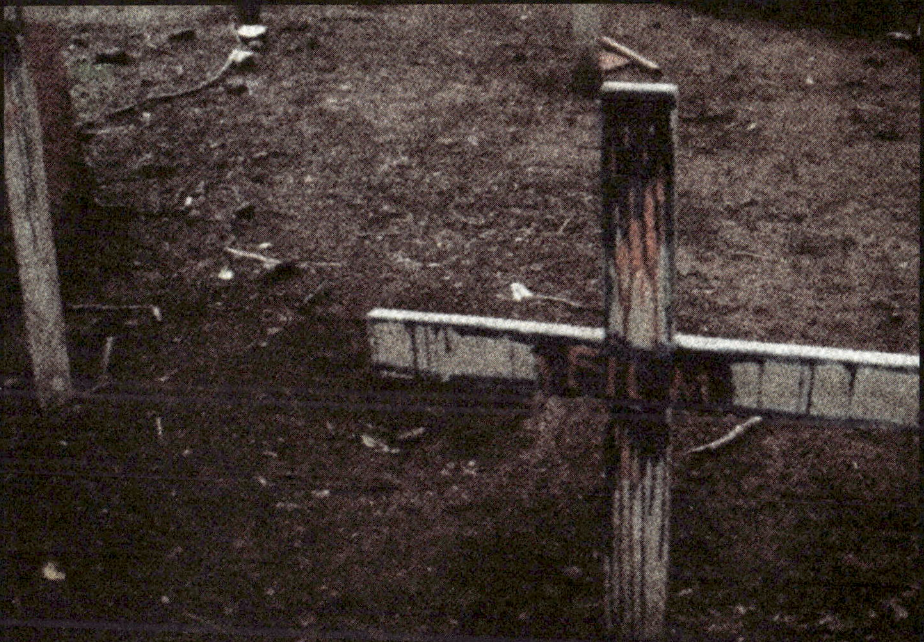
FILM

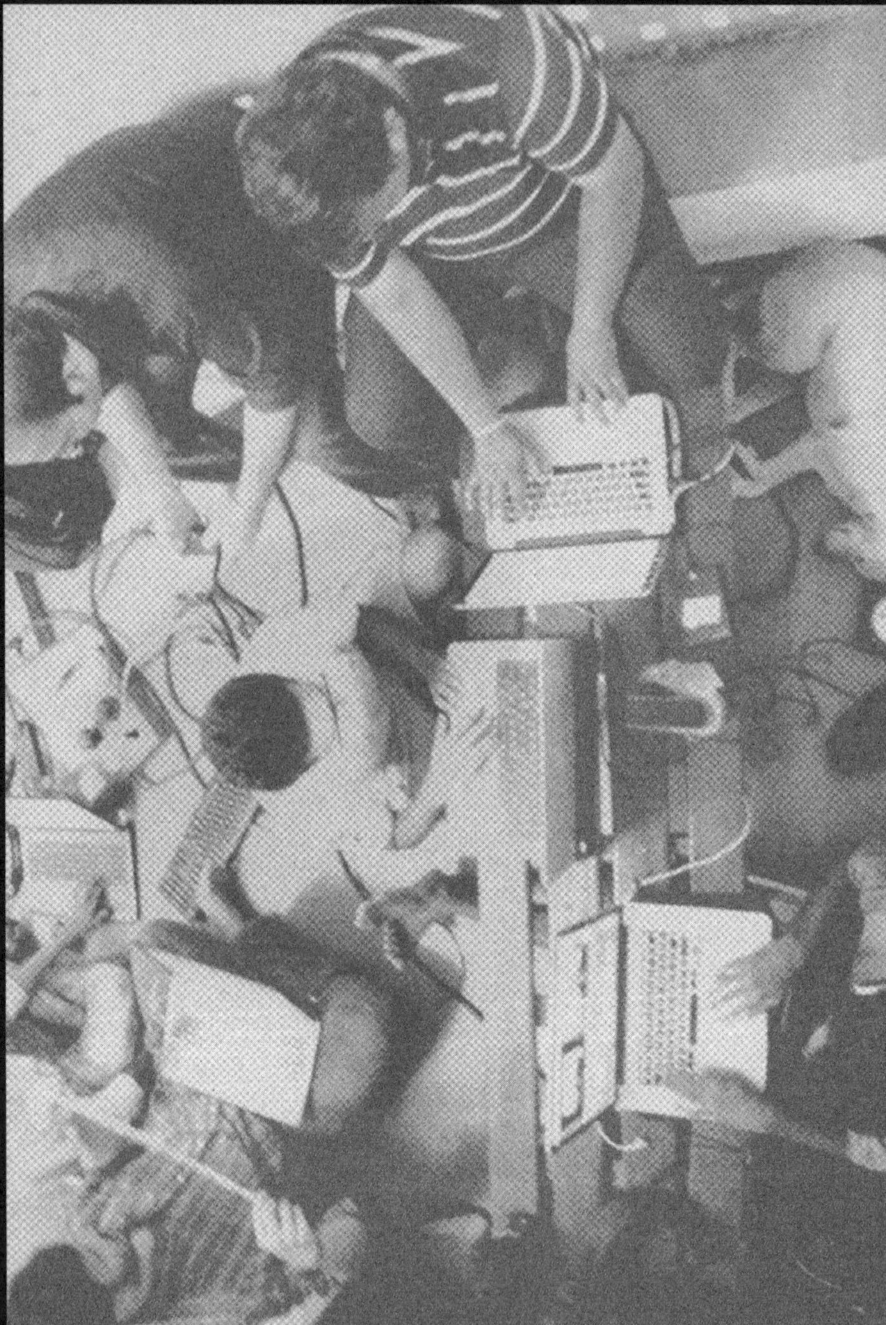

Whatever it was, all Shini wanted that night was a small ceremony to bring some closure to the chaos. 'This day and our gathering should bring back the normalcy in the campus, in every means, despite we all facing problems at multiple levels as individuals and as a community.'

The First Visitation

Shini's articulations aren't necessarily political in any conventional meaning of the term. 'It is the third day and ex-AAP member Yogendra Yadav is on campus', writes second year editing student Fatema Kagalwala in her strike blog at 8 p.m. on 14 June.[3] The consequences of bringing their struggle into a political mainstream are as terrifying as the political challenge of taking on the state. Subjective anxieties need to stand up to a very large cause that few can comprehend and few see as necessarily their own.

Yet another marathon GBM is about to start. Outsiders are usually not allowed. An all-night makeshift canteen is set up with a prominent *udhari nahi milegi* in black charcoal.[4] The tea bill is apparently being picked up by a senior faculty member who prefers to stay anonymous. Yadav's arrival at 7 p.m. causes enormous debate about how their struggle could – or should at all – connect to established ideological faultlines in Indian politics. That question would reach its crescendo on Day 50 with Rahul Gandhi's appearance.

> We are happy but also wary of the protest being politically hijacked. The head of the media team, a close friend, is sharing her concern with me about these dangers. She is worried. She is a natural leader, a born fighter and survivor and this is not her first fight against tough odds. She will also do this as many times as needed, but the memories of that one night refuse to leave her. When she was leading one such protest in her college. Where four men from a political party followed her at night. ... I see her still shaken from the old memory. I also see the courage that makes her go on.

Day 5, 16 June 2015, 10.30 p.m. At a quick dinner break before they regroup for another round of exhaustive meetings, Fatema speaks to her mother who tells her in an upbeat and encouraging voice, 'You kids go ahead! *Datt ke strike karo* and make sure you get what you want. The government can't do this!' This is in contrast to another student who, the following day, is asked by his mother to

-3 Fatema Kagalwala's blog-diary, 'FTII Strike Campus Diary – The turmoil of passion, the innocence of struggle', *Fight Club*, 20 June 2015.

-4 Ardhra Nair, 'FTII Row: Strike is to uphold things we stand for ... FTII's survival', *Indian Express*, 21 June 2015.

hang up 'because she was scared his phone is being tapped'. 'He has never ever heard such paranoia in his mother's voice.' Was the battle against an external enemy or was it also within?

In its first five days the strike rapidly gained momentum with support from JNUSU and AISA, filmmakers as diverse as Anand Patwardhan, Rakesh Sharma, Adoor Gopalakrishnan, Girish Kasaravalli, Subhash Ghai and Mahesh Bhatt. Protest marches were planned in Delhi in front of the I&B Ministry offices, and in Kolkata from SRFTI to Jadavpur University. As the apparatus of the strike gradually fell into place – with near-daily press releases and a social media strategy accompanying physical protests in different cities – the insistent question arose as to how to characterize, name, what they were up against.

Both Fareeda Mehta and Paresh Kamdar, on campus since April conducting workshops, are concerned by the rising tide of student militancy. In a way it appears to them as an inevitable consequence of the situation in which students had found themselves, yet the question remains – is this taking students away from why they are here or is it contributing to their practice? Back in April, Fareeda's main advice to Vikas had been '*Yeh jhagada-wagada chhodo* [Forget these battles], focus on making films.'[5] The same day (16 June) that the I&B Ministry's letter arrived inviting the students for talks, the normally apolitical Fareeda sends an email – even she has begun to accept the need for skills associated with a new era in what had once been called filmmaking, for (as she writes) 'who needs smart cities peopled by dumb humans?' It is time to hold the Ministry to its often-promised bill 'to upgrade the FTII, grant autonomy to it, put in place people of eminence and vision who would nurture an environment of questioning, of learning' – basically to say, 'Please Handle FTII with Care – Students at Work', for a government that neglects institutions of higher education is myopic.'[6]

Day 7, 18 June 2015. News comes in that Jahnu Barua, after he sent in his resignation from the Governing Council, has received what he interprets to be a threat from the I&B Ministry. A major meeting is happening between the strike representatives and a busload of GraFTII members who have arrived from Mumbai. GraFTII's own instincts has always been to stay away from confrontation, to see how to manage its many and diverse interests, and to somehow

-5

Conversation with Vikas Urs, 21 October 2021, Mumbai.

-6

Email from Fareeda Mehta to the students' body on 16 June 2015.

negotiate its way through the mess – and it is taking a serious hit.

Second year editing student Kshama Padalkar abruptly decides that she needs to film this if she is to see it through.[7] Kshama was in Mumbai when the strike broke and so first heard about it on Facebook. She assumed, as did most others including GraFTII representatives, that it would last at most a few days.

-7 Conversation with Kshama Padalkar on Zoom, 3 September 2020.

Kshama too, like Vikas and Koel, had been admitted in 2011, only to join almost a year later, and had thus seen something of the Hewitt agitations. Although she lived up the Prabhat road, she had never visited FTII. Film as a career option was a late choice (she was an MPhil in English from Hyderabad Central University), and when she joined, it was with a specific and very personal 'need' that she hoped the editing course would address. Student agitations were far from her mind. She too echoes the experiences of 2013 and 2014, the technological issues, the administrative indifference coupled with student appeasement in the hope that problems would somehow go away. She has however been a little bit outside it all, somewhat of a loner – with needs that didn't always map on to the student body. She has had a difficult time personally and, as with Fatema, the personal was turning political in disconcertingly complex ways.

This 'need' resurfaces, and the camera becomes an 'opportunity to stand firmly somewhere'. She borrows one from Ranjit Nair and begins filming all that is going on around her. She decides to do this independently of the strike media effort, and keeps her footage secluded from the central 3 TB pool. Shot over a hundred days with around sixty hours of footage, *The Strike and I* reveals the tensions, the anxieties and the resistance. The film begins with the first week and ends when Kshama's batchmates go on their hunger strike – it becomes too painful to shoot after that. She invites friends to speak to her on camera, but the only ones who have something to say are the women. The campus has historically had a scandalously skewed gender ratio, with the widespread view that women did not qualify for the rigours of cinema, especially cinematography.

'What are we really fighting and who?' Fatema asks on her blog on the 19th at 6 p.m., the classic question of all political struggle. 'Are we becoming what we are fighting?' She likens some questions to 'exploration trips [like] Enid Blyton's kids take into the forest' before the adventure turns dangerous. She worries that the students around her are 'beginning to play the same games we are fighting', censoring themselves when they should be fighting censorship. 'In our drive for a "purer" way of functioning, we are allowing ourselves to become corrupt. We are fighting, not standing up for anything we believed in, becoming totalitarian ourselves.'

There is nevertheless an 'alive-ness' on the campus in these days. 'We are waking up. To ourselves. We are faltering, falling too, picking ourselves up and others along with us, only to be met by the next seemingly unscaleable wall. But that's part of the process of growing up, no one promised it was going to be easy.' Through late June and July, Fatema blogged actively and enthusiastically. She wrote a long note on the pros and cons of Rahul Gandhi's visit,[8] and another titled 'Why we are doing what we are doing'. In a strident piece for *Outlook* titled 'My Freedom, My Pride', she wrote,

> ... editing studios are open 24/7 and my staff trusts me enough to hand them over without supervision, whenever I want to work. I can walk around the campus in the still of the night without any fear and that does wonders to my self-development. You haven't been able to provide me that kind of a world outside and now you want to take this away too. Nice.[9]

-8

Fatema Kagalwala, 'Rahul Gandhi at FTII: Of Democracy and Negotiations', *The Quint*, 1 August 2015.

-9

Fatema Kagalwala, 'My Freedom, My Pride', *Outlook India*, 9 July 2015.

—

What did they really have on the Indian state? Was there ever the likelihood of a credible solution to the problem – a problem named 'Gajendra Chauhan', that expanded into an omnibus container ranging from aesthetics to technology and from administration to pedagogy, in multiple locations on- and off-campus, across universities and in the streets and bureaucratic corridors of Delhi – or had things gotten to a point where conventional resolutions had been rendered impossible?

'Solidarity was our only hope', says Prateek. Building and sustaining a coalition of support across ideological and tactical divides was the only way forward. 'We could never have managed on our own.'[10] Could love and cinema provide anything remotely like a stable ideological foundation – especially when its twin embodiments, the *regisseur* and the cinephiliac, had morphed into unrecognizable avatars and memes? Could this thinnest of

-10

Conversation with Prateek Vats, 14 December 2018, Mumbai.

all beliefs overcome deep internal schisms that existed – schisms dividing students by batch, especially the controversial 2008 batch, by discipline, by region, and most strikingly in an overwhelmingly male-dominated student body, by gender? The crisis over solidarity being their only hope 'really kind of set the ball rolling for everyone', says Vikas, 'this doesn't seem like a choice made in vacuum'. 'There is a conscious effort to change the space in a certain way ... to look at new capitalism and its practices vis-à-vis filmmaking and how commercial viability of these spaces is more important [to campus authority] than the actual practice which will be slowly over a period of time left out.'

Fareeda's own challenge at this juncture is how to reconcile two different registers of reality, and perhaps, with it, also two registers of fear – one, a modest but crucial, incessantly significant register of never losing sight of who they are and why they are there; and two, to reconcile this standpoint with the elusive, terrifying phenomenon of state authority that confronted them.

Spanning these extremes, 'Gajendra Chauhan' remains an uncanny rendition of Walter Benjamin's Mickey Mouse. As contempt and derision fuse into real fear and the porn-star–joker too shades into bare-knuckled state totalitarianism, the students too come together – some out of conviction, others because they have no choice. This liminal figure would bind together multiple strategies, coalescing divides timelined by the elusive desire for cinema and what it meant to different people – and how such a desire could even begin to produce something resembling functional solidarity.

Screenplay writing student Vaidehi Sancheti is, like many students, initially sceptical. She has family commitments, things to do in life, she has taken a year off to finish the course and has no particular desire to interrupt that to take on a 'right-wing government'.[11] The original decision to strike appeared to her to have been overly sudden and perhaps even foolhardy. She didn't know if the students even understood what they were getting into. At the big GBM that followed the Delhi meeting, Sancheti states the issue. She has to find her own personal reasons for why she should support this. She remains unsure about the posturing going on with the strike leadership, worried that their bravado is 'fake'. She tells them plainly, 'I don't trust you.' They claim plurality as their core

-11

Vaidehi Sancheti, quoted from Kshama Padalkar's film, *The Strike and I* (2019).

value, but show none. 'TV is a handicap, screenplay does not even exist, so what plurality?'

More than the consensus-building efforts of the poetic and musical conviviality of the first two weeks, it is the chilling nature of the I&B Ministry rebuff on 3 July that shocks the 'undecided' students. (The meeting has been discussed earlier, in Chapter 1.) It had been short, eventful and eventually disastrous. Rathore, puppet master behind the Chauhan cutout, was absent. Arun Jaitley's position, as Vikas summarizes it, was (apart from the 'I have grand plans for you all' line) effectively that 'I am the boss, if you talk too much or if you cause more trouble, I am either going to shut this place or I'm going to sell it to the Bombay film industry who are waiting to buy it ... so you better mend your ways.' 'We questioned him on only one thing – we might have the best of the buildings and infrastructures, what we need are people who can teach. He just wound up the meeting on that.'

After 3 July, the cause has expanded. It is, says Sancheti into Kshama's camera, 'larger than you, larger than your egos or mine', so everyone had better 'up the ante' and rise to the occasion. 'They [the government] are not even willing to understand what we are trying to say.' 'We are asking for something that is right. We are not asking for anything very difficult or large ... we are asking for something which is very logical.'

Cinema's Burial Grounds

Day 18, 30 June. 'You don't have to walk far ... to see where all the action is', muses Manasi Nene.[12] Nene is a poet-performer and Pride organizer who started the Pune Poetry Slam while still a student at Fergusson College. 'There's a tree on the right, a stage set up on the left, and people all around. Lots of beards, lots of *kurtas* and graphic tees, lots of *chai* and *sutta*. Lots of spirit.' There are no classes going on, no student is obligated to be here. 'Still, they're here, and they're working. The headquarters is a small area under the Wisdom Tree, *chatai*s and bedsheets and cushions and laptops.'

Nene is here to take part on the second day of 'Roll the Humdrum', a multi-arts festival intended as a show of artists' strength.[13] It would also turn into something of a statement about expanded cinema as it relates to Article 15, to the public domain as a

-12 Manasi Nene, 'Inside the FTII Strike', manasinene.atavist.com.

-13 Among those present at 'Roll the Humdrum': theatre and film actor Piyush Mishra, lead singer of Swarathma Vasu Dixit, the rock bands Altered Theory and NuEdge, SIPA Dance Troupe, Indian Idol finalist and FTII alumnus Deepali Sahay, Indus Creed lead singer Uday Benegal, the Airplane Poetry Movement, and the fire art performer Arpit Singh. FTII Wisdom Tree Facebook page.

whole and especially, in these two weeks, to freedoms on the campus.

Several musicians and bands are taking part. The Pune-based Altered Theory are to perform 'alt-rock', Vasu Dixit of Swarathma and Uday Benegal of Indus Creed will be there, as will percussionist Sujat Ambedkar (great-grandson of Babasaheb) who was studying at Fergusson College. Nu-Edge plans a special rendition of Pink Floyd's 'Another brick in the wall'. Performance poetry is to feature the Airplane Poetry Movement, started by two college students, Nandini Varma and Shantanu Anand, along with Poetry Slam. The star turn shall be Ambedkarite poet and singer Sambhaji Bhagat.

Nene is also there for another reason. She wants to take in what appeared to her as an entirely new era in campus action. For all the heavy security process at the gate, she recognizes the 'vibe', the 'energy waiting in the air'. To her surprise, there is little evidence of 'loud gregarious protests and *morchas*'. Instead there are students everywhere doing 'what you came here for – to learn, to meet like-minded people', to 'do something that you believe is important', do all that you're supposed to do in an educational campus, the only difference being that 'they [are] not doing it inside a classroom'.

An unnamed striker animatedly explains the issues to Nene, using multiple philosophical references. If Paganism, says the student, is a 'polytheism spread out over many cultures and traditions' and Semitism is 'monotheistic', FTII needs to see itself as 'Paganist in that sense', in which students wholly devoted to their art have 'different gods, different heroes, different ways of worship'. So there can be no 'true god' or 'true form of expression', there has to be a diversity of devotion, of points of view, ideas, lifestyles and stories.

An organizer herself, Nene spends time figuring out how the students are achieving this enviable Pagan pluralism. The strike is run, she notes, by three student teams: Media, Logistics and Outreach. These teams 'report to a Core team, made of about 18 volunteers. Everyone involved is a student, and all the different programmes that FTII offers are represented here.' Everyone works from under this Wisdom Tree. It is 'close enough to the college *tapri*,

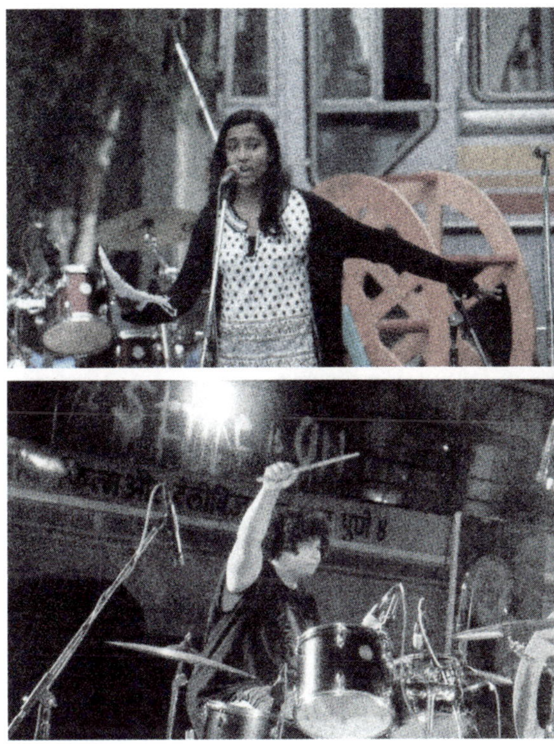

June 2015: **Roll the Humdrum. Above:** Manasi Nene, Pune Poetry Slam. **Below:** percussionist Sujat Ambedkar.

where everyone always has an open tab for *chai* and a friend carrying cigarettes'.

Day 32, 14 July. An official letter from Director D.J. Narain addressed to Nachi (as Students' Association president) appears on the notice board. It threatens mass rustication if they don't immediately stand down. It is one of the generally student-friendly Narain's last acts in office.

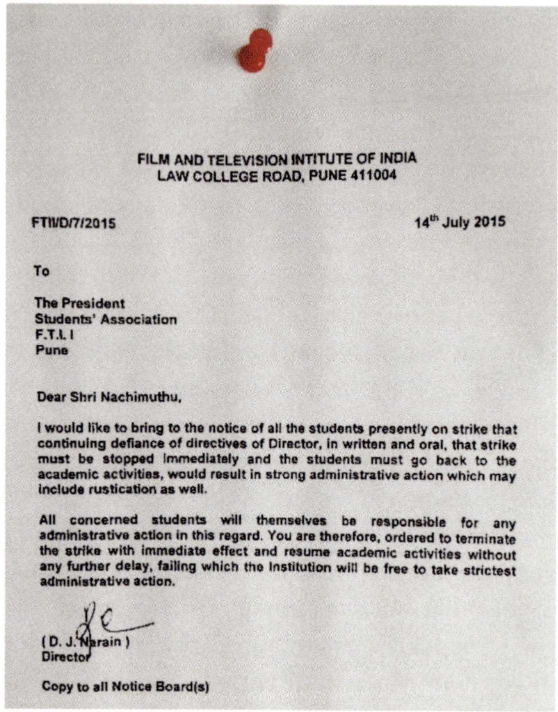

FILM AND TELEVISION INTITUTE OF INDIA
LAW COLLEGE ROAD, PUNE 411004

FTII/D/7/2015

14th July 2015

To

The President
Students' Association
F.T.I. I
Pune

Dear Shri Nachimuthu,

I would like to bring to the notice of all the students presently on strike that continuing defiance of directives of Director, in written and oral, that strike must be stopped immediately and the students must go back to the academic activities, would result in strong administrative action which may include rustication as well.

All concerned students will themselves be responsible for any administrative action in this regard. You are therefore, ordered to terminate the strike with immediate effect and resume academic activities without any further delay, failing which the Institution will be free to take strictest administrative action.

(D. J. Narain)
Director

Copy to all Notice Board(s)

Director D.J. Narain's 14 July 2015 letter to the Students' Association, threatening severe action if the strike is not withdrawn.

The pincer moves – on one hand a vandal attack and on the other, the use of that very attack to bring the police on the campus – are by then a well-known stratagem in the new Hindutva copybook. On the 19th, says a Students' Association letter to the new Director, Prashant Pathrabe, four men stood outside the gate and, in full view, destroyed the installation, shouting '*Yeh nahi chalega*' [This won't do] and threatening security guards with '*Baahar nahi aane ka, andar hi rehne ka*' [Don't step outside, stay inside].[14] As a direct consequence the police arrived to investigate, not the vandals but the campus.[15] Officers in civil dress began questioning students upon entering. According to another press release, the Joint Commissioner of Police claimed that there had been unsubstantiated complaints of narcotics usage, and that the police intended to investigate the premises within the next twenty-four to forty-eight hours.[16]

Day 39, 20 July. The big boys join the act. Vidhu Vinod Chopra, one of the 'filmmakers' Ghatak had addressed in 1974, releases an extended public statement of support on the WisdomTree YouTube channel as both he and Raju Hirani formally enter the picture to try and resolve a matter that, many within the Bollywood firmament had begun to feel, has slowly reached a tipping point.

The statement begins with Chopra's obligatory homage to his student days, reminiscing about his first steps beneath the big arch over the Main Gate, his first exposure to the CRT, his first encounter with Welles, Godard and Fellini, how life changed, how

-14

Students' Association letter to the Director, Prashant Pathrabe, 23 July 2015.

-15

Tensions rose after the 3 July meeting. '50–60 journalists [and] every media interaction videographed by one police officer.' 'Basically sedition. They were waiting *ki sedition ka mount karne ke liye proof mil jaye unko* [for some proof of sedition].' Conversation with Vikas Urs, 21 October 2021, Mumbai.

-16

Students' Association Day 43 press release, 24 July 2015.

he grew a beard, turned introvert. How he owes everything he is to the FTII. It was, he says, yet another small step for man and a giant leap for mankind – a transformational step in his life that appeared incomprehensible to the state.[17]

-17

'Vidhu Vinod Chopra Chips in to Support FTII', uploaded on 20 July 2015.

Two days earlier (18 July), GraFTII issues a press release that directly echoes Chopra.

The problem, as he speaks on, becomes this: how to quantify his debt, for it is two-way – what he has received from the institution and thus from the nation, but also what he has done in return, what *it* – institution/nation – owes *him*. Chopra had recently visited the film school at University of California, Los Angeles (UCLA). It was the sort of institution he could recognize, or perhaps one that could recognize him, in a way this politics-riddled and bureaucracy-controlled place appeared unable to do. He does not see why – if together with its several influential alumni, he were to lend a hand – FTII cannot aspire to the same standards of excellence. 'The students are asking for nothing ... they only want people on the campus who can inspire them.' He himself, if asked properly, just might agree to play such a role.

Chopra makes another point that is more complex than he may have meant it to be. He too has heard the often trotted-out line that the government is spending 'Rs 12 lakhs per person per year or some such figure'. So how much, really, is that? 'Please ask the government to compute, if they have spent Rs 50 lakh on Vidhu Vinod Chopra, how much he has paid them back in tax?' To take only one instance, of the Rs 350 crore that his Raju Hirani-directed production *PK* (2014) had made, says Chopra, as much as 300 crore had gone as entertainment tax. And that was just one film. Compute, then, his own financial outflow to the government and add to that the taxes paid by ex-student Bollywood producers, and you can see that 'FTII is a good business for the government.' And this does not even include his return gift of Gandhigiri to the nation with the *Munnabhai* series.

What Chopra did, unintentionally perhaps, was to lift the lid on a rather murky world of backdoor deal-making. It is where Bollywood, the state apparatus and informal political systems converge, recasting the FTII's own significance as a combination of income-generating cash cow and embodiment of the neoliberal promise of an institution of 'excellence'. Such significance is, to Chopra's mind, unique to the FTII, being a specifically cinematic question of value; it does not, for example, apply to graduates of the Indian Institute of Management who receive far greater subsidy while bearing no ostensible loyalty to the Indian ideal. It can only be comprehended by a rarefied zone of insiders to a nationalist coalition of financial, political and *regisseur*ial interests – interests that (and this was the true problem) the 'Gajendra Chauhan' effigy only inadequately represented. The striking students seemed incapable of comprehending this coalition of interests, even as their strike threatened to undermine the entire comfortable edifice. It isn't too late however. If Chopra does wade in, even now things might be salvaged. What is needed is for him to provide a rite of initiation into the rarefied zone where politics meets pleasure. It is after all the world that has historically defined GraFTII's agenda.

Chopra's view, in short, one that GraFTII largely shared, is that things have gone too far. This needs to be solved right now, and he doesn't see why it cannot be 'easily' solved if people like him enter the picture. And so, his offer. Half of it shall be a public patrician commitment to financially support all the students who needed money. The other half, more closed-door, a plan to mediate directly with Jaitley and Rathore (and, for some reason, L.K. Advani), and to crack the problem, hopefully once for all.

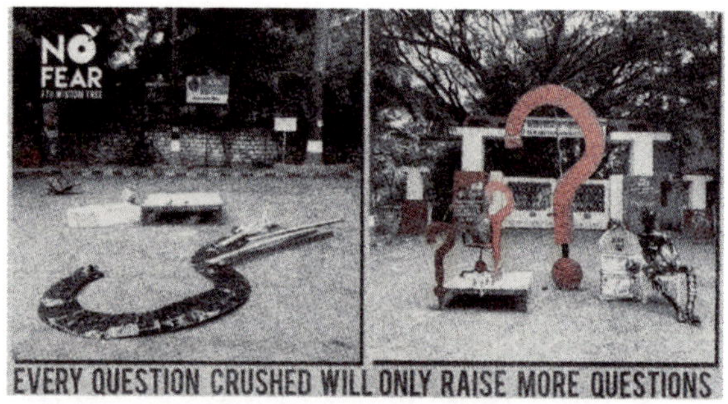

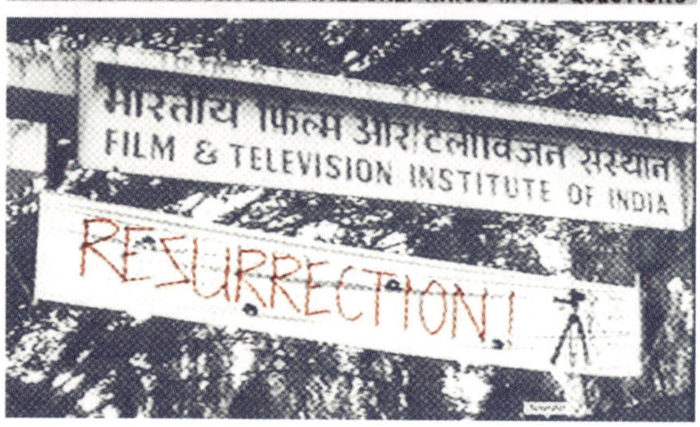

Above: Student poster the day after the 21 July 2015 destruction and resurrection of the 'question mark' outside the Main Gate. **Below:** The word **Resurrection!** strung out over the Main Gate in 2000, taken from strike footage shot by Satya Rai Nagpaul.

Day 40, 21 July. The iconic twenty-foot question mark outside the Main Gate lies on its side. The elaborate installation of an executive swivel chair with a stone on it and a milestone with the number of days since the strike began has been knocked to the ground by miscreants. Earlier that day, the Patit Pavan Sanghatana had demonstrated with banners supporting Chauhan, threatening students that they should either partake uncomplainingly of the state's gift of 'free' education and not do 'politics' – or else 'go home'.

RESURRECTION, as a day later the question mark is put up again with even more elaborate appendages, had been the word of choice in September 2000. Fifteen years later, the resurrected question mark becomes three, to illustrate the Facebook line on the *#NoFear* hashtag that 'every question crushed will only raise more questions'. A new figure has been added, a human effigy made from discarded 35 mm celluloid film, as though standing guard on the number-of-strike-days milestone.

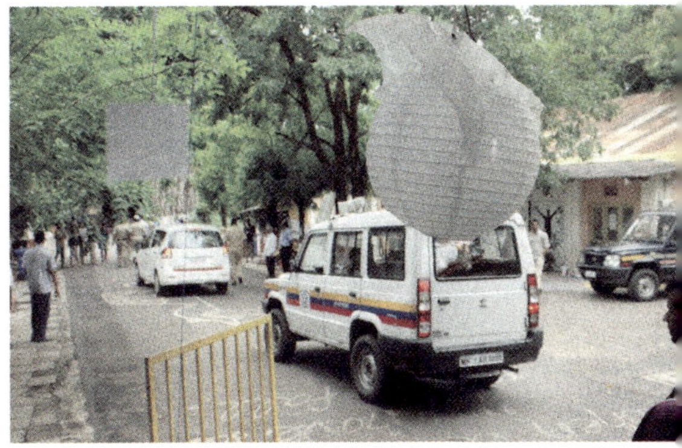

23 July 2015: The police convoy arrives with the Police Commissioner to review security on the invitation of the new Director.

Day 42, 23 July. At this *chhavni* or station around the Wisdom Tree, journalist and academic Aritra Bhattacharya watches the Pune Police Commissioner arrive in a convoy of three SUVs.[18] As the police contingent arrives, a floating population around the Wisdom Tree, involving 'students in transit within and outside the campus, faculty members and staffers who support the students but have not made official statements, and a trickle of journalists', is suddenly suffused with new energy. Students sing and begin playing the djembe and violin, as others from various streams pour in from the hostels.

Bhattacharya notes the seamless move from physical to digital spaces and back. Surrounding the Wisdom Tree is a hypermediatized space with laptops and multiple devices. A centralized repository, a 3 TB hard disk, has been made available into which everyone dumps their footage, and from where they take what they want for their edits and uploads. Poetry Slam's Manasi Nene is interested to see 'how the Logistics detail drills down to power outlets, WiFi connectivity, and food supplies'.[19] This is where media teams are running an active YouTube channel, administering a Facebook page, a Soundcloud account, a Twitter handle and several blogs, shooting, editing and uploading round the clock as they populate these different platforms. 'It isn't enough to go to the street with masks and painted chart paper, it isn't enough to sit outside your gate', Nene muses. 'The FTII students are fighting back with the weapons they know best.'

All of this formidable technology looks a little more vulnerable that day when viewed against the militarized muscle of the police convoy, or even the frenzied political demonstrations taking place just outside the Main Gate. One senses a distant Third Cinema echo in the futurist hum of AirMacs livestreaming and managing multiple hashtags and Twitter handles, of Fernando Solanas and Octavio

-18

Aritra Bhattacharya, 'Questions under the Wisdom Tree: Inside the FTII strike', *The Quint*, 31 July 2016.

-19

Manasi Nene, 'Inside the FTII Strike'. 'Ajayan, me, Ranjit, Nachi, Shini ... we became like the bigger group, the core group involved in the larger strategizing. And then we had the support groups for outreach, the media management, writing letters to the government; that me and Ranjit were doing. Prateek would participate in that because he was so used to writing letters during Hewitt that he said *ki mera toh haath itna pukka ho gaya hai ke* (my hand has become so sure) I can write. Prateek, Shubham and Kislay were among the scores of students working from outside campus. And Shubham was involved. So this larger group then had a really bigger number. So Lavanya, Sakshi, Fatima, Vaidehi, Shanet, Viraj ... initially everyone was in.' Conversation with Vikas Urs, 23 October 2021.

Getino's famous conception of cinema being an 'inexhaustible expropriator of image-weapons'.[20]

Drawing its own attention, however, to the irony of a Wisdom Tree buzzing with new media energy, is a resolutely old-media installation on a very analogue burial ground. There is nothing digital about the wooden crosses marking the graves of dead film, dead music and dead art. It is also the original resting place of the celluloid effigy. This contrasting burial-and-resurrection effect produces, Buñuel-like, a very twenty-first-century variation of the challenge Ritwik Ghatak had presented decades ago – at that exact spot, for all we know – to learn to 'be filmmakers'.

The Silent War, and the Second Visitation

Through much of late June and early July, a small but intensely mediatized cold war had taken place, and a slow-burn campaign had intensified after 3 July to cast the FTII as a den of rabble-rousing students who thrived on striking every few days. Two figures, '12-lakh-per-student' and '39 strikes', were routinely tossed around interminable television chat shows and debates. In late June, the question first came up in Parliament when five Rajya Sabha MPs 'condemned' the appointment of Gajendra Chauhan. On 14 July, when the Director sent his threatening note of 'strictest administrative action', the Students' Association wrote three letters directly addressed to Rathore, asking for a continuation of dialogue.[21] The same day they put out an exasperated statement to 'clarify their stand on every accusation', which began by spelling out the difference 'between a protest and a strike'.[22]

Whatever the fine-print squabbling, it was time, Chopra and Hirani agreed in late July, for the nonsense to end. And so they flew to Delhi to mastermind a confidential resolution with a handful of strike leaders in tow. It is said that Shatrughan Sinha too was involved in getting them the relevant appointments. Their first stop was Rathore's office at Shastri Bhavan and then, later in the day, a shorter meeting with Jaitley himself.

In both cases the story was the same – and both times the body language was pure Bollywood. The students were asked to sit outside while the big boys chatted in private. Familiarities were exchanged, backs slapped, a roadmap agreed, a deal struck. They

-20

Fernando Solanas and Octavio Getino. 'Towards a Third Cinema' (1968), *Cinéaste*, vol. 4, no. 3, 1970, p. 8.

-21

Letters dated 13, 15 and 16 July, 2015: the first thanking the Ministry for postponing the appointment of the new Director, and the second, after D.J. Narain's threatening letter of 14 July.

-22

The note gave a 'perspective' on the reasons for the strikes called in the past. The 1971 strike was 'to protest changes in course structure and syllabus'; 1979 was 'against the decision to discontinue the acting course which took another 28 years to restart'; 1984 was administrative issues; 1989 against syllabus change; 1994 about privatization; 2001 against fee hike and revised course structure. See 'FTII Students' Association Clarify Their Stand on Every Accusation', Fight Club, 14 July 2015

were then brought in and more or less instructed to immediately stand down their strike – that everything would be solved, and while nothing could be publicly promised, Chopra would stand guarantee that it would all work out. Much of it was in the domain of wink-and-nudge, a kind of real-time lesson in how these things were done in the big bad world. Rathore apparently said, in one of his multiple quotable quotes, that he was an army man, that he too smoked and drank – was, in short, one of the lads. Chopra airily promised to take direct responsibility to help with the academic mess, to conduct filmmaking workshops, smooth over the humps and petty disagreements.

The deal never happened. The GBM that convened on campus to discuss the meeting unanimously agreed to continue the strike until official on-paper promises were made by the government. They never were. Chopra made no further overtures, and along with some of the big-time Bollywood names, gradually distanced himself from the strike, helping students occasionally – as when the mass termination of contract labour took place in September, and during the October negotiations.

On Day 50, Rahul Gandhi arrived on campus with a personal entourage – his own homage to the cinema – of Chiranjeevi, Khushboo and Raj Babbar. Standing at the Main Theatre, jabbing his finger in the air, he asked, do you know why 'they' are 'scared of you?'[23] For all its barebones unsubtlety, it was a good question.

Hashtags

Day 11, 22 June. The first of a series of short comedies titled *Mann ki Baat*, directly riffing of Narendra Modi's radio broadcasts, is uploaded. Made by third-year student Raju Biswas, it features two country bumpkins named Bachha and Bholu Chacha. The first episode is titled 'Is Bimari ka Kya Hai Naam?' Viraj Tadwalkar, a student from the relatively new, one-year electronic cinematography course, is suffused with a manic obsessiveness. Online almost round the clock, to the extent that he says he began to lose weight, he becomes the uploading mastermind, timing how many images, which shorts would go up where, have what length – and how the look-and-feel of the strike would develop. 'It had to be distinct, away from clutter.'[24] Viraj had studied at the Xavier Institute of Communication and

-23
See in Kshama Padalkar's **The Strike and I** (2019).

-24
Conversation with Viraj Tadwalkar on Zoom, 16 January 2022.

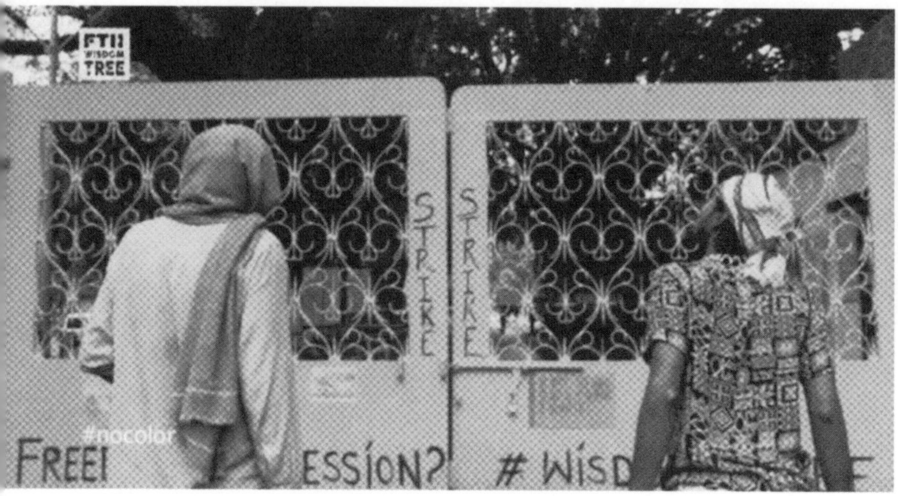

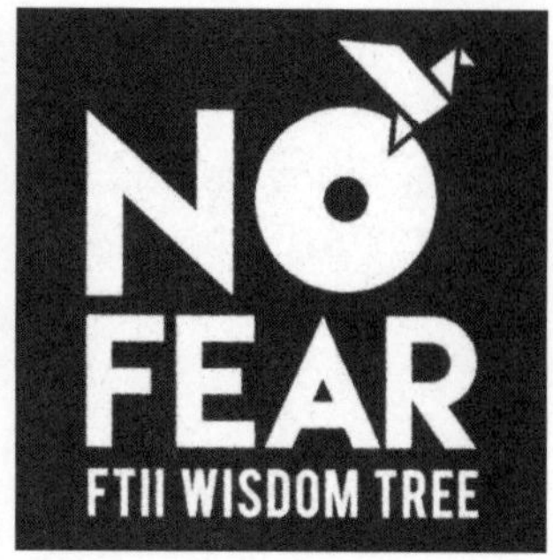

Left: 'Is Bimari ka Kya Hai Naam?', from a comedy series **Mann ki Baat** (Raju Biswas, 2015), featuring two country bumpkins, Bachha and Bholu Chacha, encountering and trying to make sense of the campus and the strike. **Right:** The **#NoFear** watermark, among the famous strike hashtags.

done the social media for its well-known Malhar college festival. Now he assembles several hashtags and adds them meticulously to all uploaded content. The decision is spontaneously taken to adopt a distinctive black-and-white visual look. *#NoFear*, *#NoColor*, *#FreeFTII*, *#StrikeIsOn* and *#WisdomTree* are created as edge-logos on all content, in line with multiple campaign hashtags and handles that powers protests in Delhi, Hyderabad and other cities between 2015 and 2016.

By mid-2015, the hashtag and Twitter handle had become key instruments for all political action. Hashtags had by then become clearing houses for aggregating and disseminating data. Themselves contentless, they approximated to their true content only when they got translated into analogue significance – as happened in Kolkata when the legendary *#hokkolorob* hashtag, first used on 10 September 2014, singlehandedly got a hundred thousand people on the streets ten days later, calling for Jadavpur University's Vice Chancellor to resign, which he eventually did on 12 January 2015.

—

Between *hokkolorob*-2014 and FTII-2015, a legal battle had also reached its pinnacle. That March, a second year law student named Shreya Singhal won a Supreme Court victory challenging a dreaded provision of the Information Technology Act directly targeting social media.[25] That provision (the notorious Section 66-

targeting social media.[25] That provision (the notorious Section 66-A) threatened imprisonment to anyone sending 'information that is grossly offensive', or 'causing annoyance, inconvenience, danger, obstruction, insult, injury, criminal intimidation, enmity, hatred or ill will' via 'a computer, computer system, computer resource or communication device including attachments in text, image, audio, video and any other electronic record'. It had been introduced the same month, February 2009, that saw the birth of Aadhaar, the heavy artillery in the battle over bodily individuation.

In that very month had also occurred another incident of a rather different kind, a high-visibility campaign against a Hindu right-wing organization's targeting of young people celebrating Valentine's Day, when a 'Consortium of Pub-Going, Loose and Forward Women' put out a call to send gifts of pink knickers to that organization as a satirical send-up of the khaki shorts that were the uniform of the RSS.[26] While there was no action against the women, not much later the police in different cities began knocking on doors with arrest warrants for actions like theirs – as they did when two young women from Palghar were arrested under 66-A, one for writing a Facebook post and the other for 'liking' it.

India's legal system would now take a major turn, and the cinema would have a role to play. Gautam Bhatia says (quoting Upendra Baxi) that Indian law has historically been constituted by two parallel regimes: one, the criminal justice system (CJS) characterized by elements of due process, personal rights and rigorous judicial review of state power, and a parallel 'preventive detention system' (PDS) in which none of these features obtain.[27] On this latter side has been the sedition law itself and sequel laws, TADA, POTA and now UAPA, all based on custodial detention and absolute executive (as against judicial) supremacy. The two halves are basically incompatible, and Indian law has got into numerous tangles trying to reconcile these opposites. Taking the example of the increasingly ubiquitous UAPA which defines an 'unlawful activity' to include anything that 'disclaims, questions, disrupts or is intended to disrupt the sovereignty and territorial integrity of India', Bhatia asks, how could the jurisprudence of the Supreme Court in Shreya Singhal coexist with a law that criminalizes 'questioning ... the sovereignty of India', and punishes a concept as fluid as 'membership'? He mentions a

-25

Supreme Court of India, *Shreya Singhal vs UOI* on 24 March 2015.

-26

This was the famous 'Pink Chaddi' campaign. See Nisha Susan, 'Valentine's Warriors: The Pink Chaddi Campaign, why it began and how', *Tehelka Magazine*, vol. 6, issue 8, 28 February 2009.

-27

Gautam Bhatia, *The Transformative Constitution: A Radical Biography in Nine Acts*, Noida: Harper Collins, 2019, p. 255.

Bombay High Court judgment (*Jyoti Chorge v. State of Maharashtra*, 2012, concerning the bail application of some members of the Kabir Kala Manch) to answer the question in two simple words: it can't.[28]

In tacit acknowledgment of the difficulty, the Information Technology Act had split the two domains of law into two separate clauses. One (66-A) was closer to free speech in the classical sense, while the second (69-A) was its opposite – where threats to the 'sovereignty and integrity of India' once again gave, as in the UAPA, summary rights to prior restraint. Singhal mainly challenged the former. She was directly inspired by the outrageous arrest of the two women in Palghar. Prosecuting these young women, she said in a blog, was a 'gag on the internet', and she asked for 66-A's abolition as contravening the basic right to free speech.[29] Most legal opinion saw Singhal's petition as easily provable. It was hard to believe that the police action of arresting the two women was defensible.[30]

Justice Rohinton Nariman too agreed. In what Bhatia later called a 'soaring judgment that dwelt upon the foundational importance of free speech', he asserted that the state's penalization of speech should be restricted to instances of 'incitement to violence'. Given that there was no evidence of any such incitement in the actions that led to the arrests under 66-A, that clause was clearly untenable.

But the judgment went further. Nariman agreed with Shreya Singhal *only* on Section 66-A – agreed, thus, with an old-fashioned free speech argument. He did not think there was a problem with the clause that brought the IT Act into what Bhatia calls a 'post-Emergency terrorism legislation'. Under this clause, 69-A, any perception of a threat to the hallowed Sovereignty and Integrity, or to public order, invested extraordinary powers in a controller who could legally 'intercept' any electronic information he wished on mere unfounded suspicion, to use prior restraint and otherwise prevent 'incitement to the commission of any cognizable offence'.

'We have information ...': Data without Content

Nariman presented an interesting reason for why he let 69-A go. He agreed that special legislation was perhaps needed for understanding speech on the internet. There was, he said, 'intelligible differentia between speech on the internet and other mediums of communication for which separate offences can certainly be created by

-28

Ibid., p. 252.

-29

Shreya Singhal, 'Why I, Shreya Singhal, Challenged Section 66(a)', *NDTV*, 25 March 2015.

-30

As legal scholar Pranesh Prakash wrote, it would 'take a highly clever lawyer and a highly credulous judge to make "liking" of a Facebook status update an act capable of being charged with electronically "sending ... any information that is grossly offensive or has menacing character" or "causing annoyance or inconvenience".' See Pranesh Prakash, 'Social Media regulation vs Suppression of Freedom of Speech', *Kafila*, 19 November 2012.

legislation'. The main charge was this. Across the dimensions of the Information Technology Act, information was being only described by its *medium*. Information is (says Section 2.1)

> data, message, text, images, sound, voice, codes, computer programmes, software and databases or microfilm or computer-generated micro fiche.

Although 69-A had the flaw of being overly inclusive, its inclusiveness actually arises from a strange feature of information technology itself, one that has created a second and more serious problem – namely, that at no time does the IT Act even try to view the *information* it claims to have in all these devices as possessing any significant *content*.

> ... the definition does not refer to what the *content of information* can be. In fact, it refers only to the *medium through which such information is disseminated.* ... Information of all kinds is roped in – such information may have scientific, literary or artistic value, it may refer to current events, [it may] be obscene or seditious. [N]o distinction is made (any longer) between mere discussion or advocacy of a particular point of view, which may be annoying or inconvenient or grossly offensive to some, and incitement by which such words lead to an imminent causal connection with public disorder, security of State etc.[31]

Nariman took the debate beyond the relatively settled domain of the content of protected free speech and into a far more ambiguous and contested space – namely, the legal nature and the properties of data itself. In seeking to regulate speech, the specific amendment to the IT Act that was now being challenged sought to define speech as *all* forms of digital storage and movement. 'Section 66-A', Nariman said, 'casts the net very wide.' But even that wasn't the real problem.

The real problem was the 'medium' through which such information is disseminated. It was, reversing the famous McLuhan dictum, as though the *message was now the medium*. If the celluloid auteur had fashioned the means by which the dangerous right to free speech could actually work in the public domain – from the organization of the movie theatre to the narrative organization of a filmic narrative – *both* speaker and speech had now morphed into perilous new avatars.

For the Khosla Committee, the filmmaker was at least still a person – someone who could be named, identified, charged with specific

-31 Supreme Court of India, *Shreya Singhal vs UOI* on 24 March 2015, Section 20.

authorial responsibilities and held to account if he failed them. Now, even as every action had by default become a form of filmmaking and as everyone turned filmmaker, the actual *regisseur*, once the formal guarantor who said, 'trust me, I promise the system will work', was everywhere and nowhere. If, once upon a time, the very act of making a film had been viewed as a politically dangerous act in the late silent cinema of colonial India, a century later, in a startlingly similar way, all usage of the internet had become potentially threatening, obscene and seditious, for since data existed without either author or content, its very *existence* on someone's hard disk – or even the existence of your digital avatar within its chain of its circulation – had become sufficient evidence of 'disaffection' and 'disloyalty'.

All that Khosla had once feared had come to pass. A threat to the 'sovereignty and integrity of India' was from there but a step.

Fumigation

The reconstitution of the lived space of the analogue campus – its Article 15 form, so to say – into a social media ecosystem brought an added dimension to the documentary mode. The necessity of a narrative space–time mash-up between the online and the offline for political survival returned Anand Patwardhan's old adage, of the camera being both eyewitness and instrument of self-defence, into a new era of participatory democracy. By the time of Singhal, both speech and authorship had become contentious concepts. While the author of the Facebook post – who was expressing her personal opinion, wondering (when Shiv Sena supremo Bal Thackeray died) whether he was a martyr of the stature of Bhagat Singh and Sukhdev – was clearly working within classical free speech norms, the 'like' emoji was necessarily more complicated, for she wasn't saying anything of her own but merely endorsing another's speech. Other post-authorial interventions raised further questions when a chemistry professor from Calcutta's well-known Jadavpur University was briefly arrested for uploading cartoons of Bengal's Chief Minister Mamata Banerjee,[32] and a debate occurred in Parliament on forwards, morphed images, memes, retweets, embeds and 'likes'.

—

-32 The case has only recently been withdrawn. See Himadri Ghosh, 'Professor Who Forwarded Mamata Banerjee Cartoon Is Still Facing Charges Under a Scrapped Law', *The Wire*, 18 June 2021.

Day 26, 7 July. Theatre director Sunil Shanbag brings over his play *Blank Page* as a gesture of solidarity with the strike, and unintentionally gives documentary on the Wisdom Tree channel an additional, post-authorial, experimental aspect. The Tamasha Theatre performs the play on the studio floor rather than in the Main Theatre, to an audience seated on three sides. The performance has an unusual mash-up style, combining phrases from famous poems in multiple Indian languages as they are recited in syncopated rhythms by walking, sitting and pirouetting actors, that directly echo much of the multi-arts spirit of 'Roll the Humdrum'.

A week later, second year direction student Himanshu Prajapati uploads a film version of *Blank Page*, calling it *Feel in the Blanks*.[33] In his rendition, the play itself goes entirely missing. The action happens on the campus, either offstage, or before or after the performance of the play. Actors warm up, Shanbag walks around getting his act together, sits in the wings watching his actors perform as he recites the lines with them. The film cuts to the end of the play as Yashaswi Mishra thanks everyone for coming, and students mill around before they leave.

There is an inversion of centre and periphery that is in part a sly invocation to the *regisseur* bossing his screen. More than that, it is a filmmaker's response to the way Shanbag's play acknowledged the expanded-cinema campus. The theatre is the action that *surrounds* the performance. A new kind of cinematic spectator-cum-protestor is inserted into the absent centre where the play once was.

In early August, Mukul Haloi – now well known for his extraordinary Assamese film, *Loralir Sadhukatha* (Tales from Our Childhood), set during his childhood amid ULFA rebels – uploads a collaborative short film titled *Level Zero*. Mukul and Himanshu are, with Payal Kapadia, 2012 batchmates who had already announced themselves with some accomplished second-year exercises – such as Himanshu's *Hello! Tiwari*, Payal's *Watermelon, Fish and Half-Ghost,* and Mukul's tour de force single-shot long-take film *Sand Dune and a Lullaby*. *Level Zero* is as though made by nobody, or perhaps by everybody: Mukul says it 'all came together magically'.[34] Set up as a sci-fi film about a sleeping sickness that has descended upon the city, it is an assemblage of shots that were either taken by Mukul or contributed by his batchmates. We see a window in a haze,

-33
Available on Prajapati's YouTube channel.

-34
Email from Mukul Haloi dated 21 January 2019.

We then see buildings gradually enveloped by smoke. After a fade to black, we have a contrasting shot of lush greenery. In the midst of the greenery a giant film screen is raised and then brought down. The film ends when the screen comes down. There is an overall Apichatpong Weerasethakul-like effect that has been central to Mukul's student work. The smoke shots were taken when the campus was being fumigated for mosquitoes, he says, mostly by his cinema-tographer Sandeep Yadav, although Payal contributed a few shots and the fumigation metaphor would later take full form in her acclaimed *Dopahar ke Badal*.

Day 40, 21 July. Rather like the fumigation smoke in Mukul's film, the moving image is at once everywhere and nowhere on campus, ubiquitous and form-less. The art of 'being' a filmmaker is by now as though split into two halves: one, sleek and new media-friendly; the other, an older, gnarled, celluloid incarnation. The student body, although unified and straddling pre- and post-digital batches, seems unable to produce a vision sufficiently unified as to be able to stage a full-on cinematic resurrection myth, and there seems to be no clue as to how the cinema could possibly itself turn into a political *cause célèbre*. They do not have the same courses, nor the same issues, nor even the same ambitions. Beyond a shared animosity to Gajendra Chauhan lies an ocean of anxieties surrounding the question, 'what is cinema/who are you?', reappearing with renewed malevolence in an increasingly post-authorial era. It goes to the heart of the strike itself and its reigning purpose.

Five days later, on **26 July, Day 45**, the ABVP finally arrive at the gates.[35] Kshama, who had been in the audience at the *Jai Bhim Comrade* screening and Kabir Kala Manch performance, and had seen that attack – she echoes the sentiment that something on the campus changed fundamentally after that – now walks out of the Main Gate

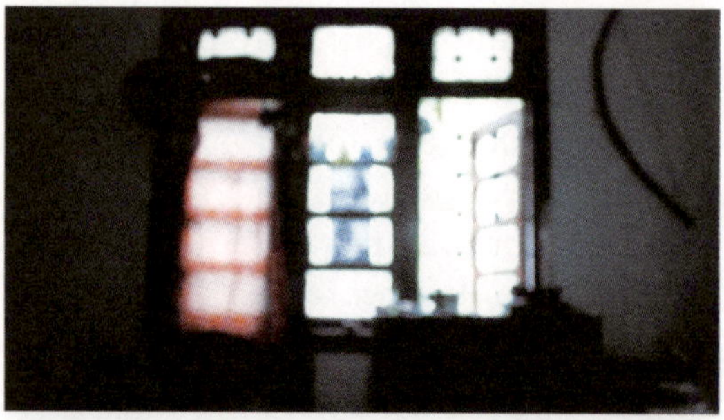

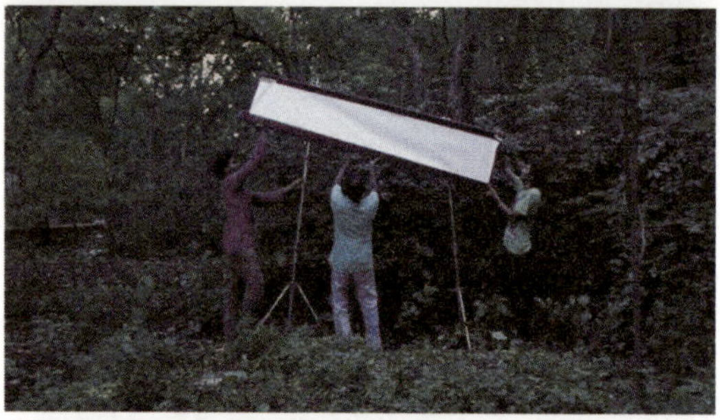

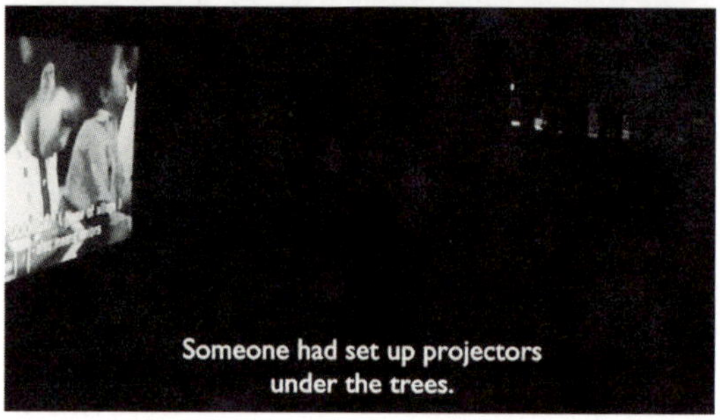

Improvised screens

Above and centre: From Mukul Haloi's **Level Zero** (2015).
Below: From Payal Kapadia's **A Night of Knowing Nothing** (2021).

-35 Asseem Shaikh, 'ABVP muscles into FTII row: wants strike to end', *Times of India*, 26 July 2015.

changed fundamentally after that – now walks out of the Main Gate against advice, stands camera in hand next to the mob and shoots their frenzied sloganeering. From here she cuts to a shaven-headed Fatema speaking directly into her camera. The strike had become polarizing. Her old anxieties have resurfaced. The students too appear to have turned increasingly authoritarian, notwithstanding their avowed anti-authority stance. The 'methodology of the strike, the wording of the strike, everything – the structure of the strike', nothing seems clear. She speaks of her feeling of terror at one point as she hears the slogan-shouting just outside.

> I could have cracked it if I had wanted to. I could have made a point, I could have impacted things. But for me it was like, *yahaan main kya prove karne ki koshish kar rahi hoon*? [what am I trying to prove here?] Do I want to get into that space and prove myself ... on those parameters? You know, then I am saying those parameters are right. When I am saying those parameters are not right, why should I jump into that space and try to prove myself right in that space? And I think that's what all the women who had a problem with the strike also realized, *ke, yaar* if it is a male space and if I am going to make myself, what do you say, heard or seen or whatever, then I have to live by those male rules. I have to shout louder than them.[36]

-36

Fatema Kagalwala, quoted from Kshama Padalkar's film, *The Strike and I* (2019).

'The Language of Politics Speaks Hindi'

On the afternoon of 3 August 2015, for the first time in its history, FTII's students formally positioned their protest within a larger national cause. They did it in perhaps the only place where such a national claim could be made – Delhi's Jantar Mantar. Soon after the disastrous meeting with the Information and Broadcasting Ministry, the decision was taken to take the strike beyond the campus. 'Small teams of students were made, who went to Delhi, Aligarh, Meerut, Chandigarh and addressed students there. People who were teaching in Ambedkar. From DU to Punjab University, to Aligarh Muslim University to Pune University, Mumbai University. Then we connected with left bodies, AISA, SFI', says an ex-student. 'And then a whole chain was activated.'

This was an ambitious undertaking. It was not something they had tried before, and it meant many things. Principally, that its specificities – all the many issues that the Nair Committee had spent so much time worrying over – had to take second place as saffronization of education became front and centre its sole public cause. To do so, the FTII had to be entirely repositioned, placed alongside universities like Nalanda and institutions like the ICHR, ICCR, NBT, IIAS, IIMS (to quote the strike poster), to which it had no previous connection. Chauhan now was placed alongside an obscure historian named Y. Sudarshan Rao, selected to head the ICHR (Indian Council of Historical Research), along with the more familiar Pahlaj Nihalani, head of CBFC – all as Modi-era *sarkari* appointees.

Most of all, for the issue to turn 'national', the strike had to uproot itself from its familiar environs and substantially relocate to Delhi. Previous strikes had held demonstrations, meetings, rallies, hunger strikes and press conferences in Delhi. The problem in the past had always been that Agashe's 'Conceptual Proposals', the '1+1+1' restructuring or Hewitt were never going to be prime-time national news. 'Gajendra Chauhan' was different. Here was direct state interference with significant autonomy and free speech implications; the *Khuli Khidki* metaphor was easily transmissible, and it all signalled a common need to explore the limits of creative and intellectual freedom. On 3 August, Delhi turned up in strength.

The day also saw the first public encounter with a 'national political language'.[37] This language was not only about organization. It was about self-representation, and about whether film students speaking of freedom of expression on the campus could bring a perspective that didn't simply subsume their cause into the political mainstream. In Delhi, the young filmmakers produced an attractive figure of artist–*regisseur* with revolutionary intent, and they were welcomed everywhere they went. 'JNU, Ambedkar University, LSR, Kirori Mal College, you're just being accepted. ... It was very good energy.' There were extensive conversations with Shehla Rashid and other student leaders who pointed out to them that not being part of the fractious student movements in Delhi – not being 'super articulate' on national television, welcoming support from wherever they got it, working in multiple languages from Malayalam to Marathi to Bengali – they were a refreshingly new presence on the national landscape. The big student unions – AISA, NSUI and SFI – rolled up, the Aam Aadmi Party extended support, as did the Congress. The academics Apoorvanand and Mukul Manglik spoke,

Facing page and overleaf
Student posters announcing the 3 August 2015 Delhi march, from Jantar Mantar to Parliament.

-37

'Actually a lot of things I learnt about national politics ... in Delhi, because I think if you have to learn politics, I think you have to be in Delhi ... every day you have something happening and you will learn, and you will learn both the good and bad. I also learned the language, Hindi, and also the political language.' Verbatim conversation with Nachi, 2/3 March 2019, Chennai.

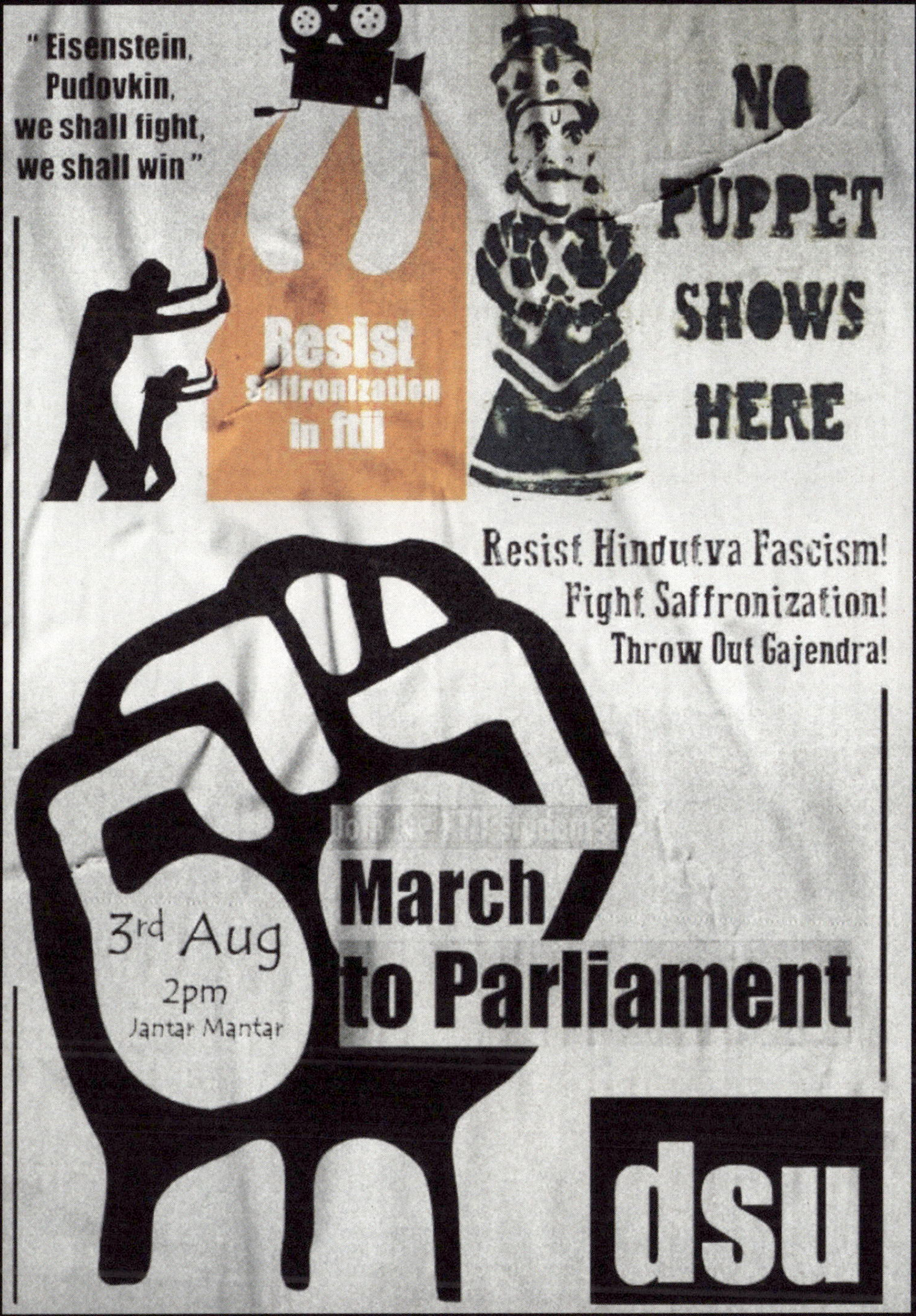
" Eisenstein,
Pudovkin,
we shall fight,
we shall win "
Resist
Saffronization
in ftii
NO
PUPPET
SHOWS
HERE
Resist Hindutva Fascism!
Fight Saffronization!
Throw Out Gajendra!
March
to Parliament
3rd Aug
2pm
Jantar Mantar
dsu

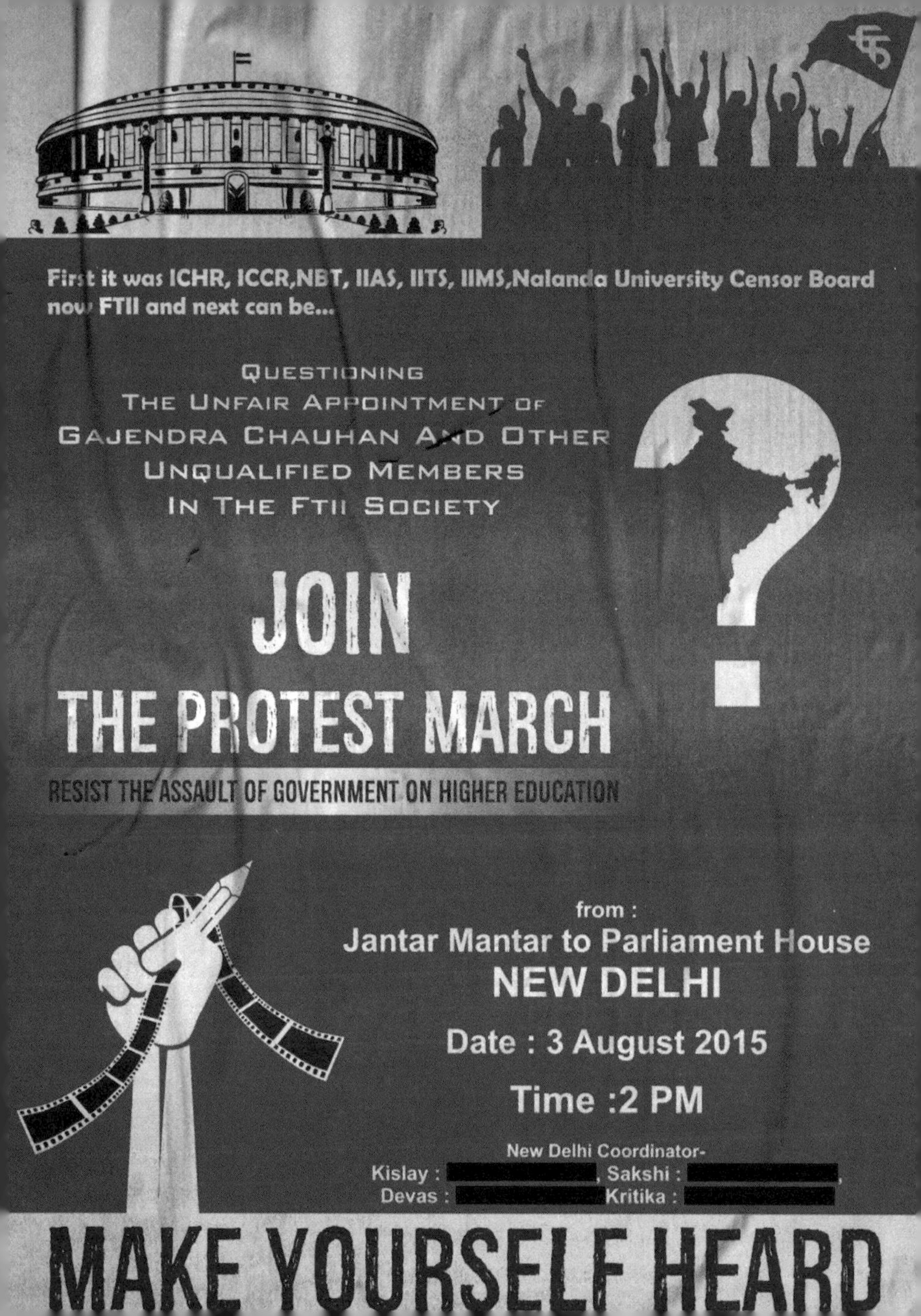
First it was ICHR, ICCR,NBT, IIAS, IITS, IIMS,Nalanda University Censor Board
now FTII and next can be...
Questioning
The Unfair Appointment of
Gajendra Chauhan And Other
Unqualified Members
In The FTII Society
JOIN
THE PROTEST MARCH
RESIST THE ASSAULT OF GOVERNMENT ON HIGHER EDUCATION
from :
Jantar Mantar to Parliament House
NEW DELHI
Date : 3 August 2015
Time :2 PM
New Delhi Coordinator-
Kislay : , Sakshi : ,
Devas : Kritika :
MAKE YOURSELF HEARD

as did political activist Kavita Krishnan, and filmmakers Sanjay Kak and Rahul Roy. Roy congratulated 'one small Institute' for taking on 'such a large government'.[38] As the protest turned festive with music and theatre, the protesters declared that they would not leave Parliament Street until an authorized Ministry representative came down to meet them.[39]

It wasn't always evident what political language would sound like when film students began to speak it, or how they might reverse-engineer that language back into campus cinepolitics. To do that, they had to speak for more than just themselves. They then needed to bring the cinema out of the closet of Khosla-era exceptionalism – to overcome the historical dread of its 'impact on society' that by 2015 had made the cinema closer to social media than to the usual exemplars of free speech such as poetry or painting – and make it stand for freedom in the arts as a whole. None of this would prove to be easy.

-38

Aradhna Wal, 'Glimmer of hope as FTII students take protests to Delhi', *DNA*, 4 August 2015.

-39

'We were stopped. *Dhakka mukki hui bahut samay tak* [there were scuffles for a long time] and eventually they agreed that we will meet the student representatives. Me and Nachi went and met [K. Sanjay Murthy, the Joint Secretary]. He was sitting in his room watching live television, *TV pe*, the march. ... "Look, this is getting way beyond control and we do not want things to go out of hand" [he said]. "And I am not going to have any conversation vis-à-vis, any negotiation with respect to the appointments. Those are decisions made by the ministers and I have no say in it. But don't push us to the point where this becomes a law-and-order issue." We said, "It is our fundamental right to protest, and we are not making it a law-and-order issue, so you take a call that when we head back to campus we [can be] heard." Because we again sent letters. We were sending letters every other day and they were just sidestepping everything because they had figured out this entire thing about *hum* media *ke* counter-narrative *se inko sambhaal lenge* [we'll take care of them with a media counter-narrative].' Verbatim conversation with Vikas Urs, 21 October 2021, Mumbai.

CHAPTER 8

GROTESQUE BODIES

Day 68, 18 August. The police arrive in four jeeps and two trucks at half past midnight. They are in full riot gear.

Cops had been a presence for around three weeks on campus, indeed ever since the Police Commissioner's visit on 23 July. The day after that visit, a press release had 'already made known [that] the presence of police on campus for the last two days are making [students] feel vulnerable and threatened ... the Joint Commissioner of Police [had] unexpectedly announced to the media that an investigation could be conducted on the campus premises within the next 24–48 hours.'[1]

-1 Students' Association Day 43 press release, 24 July 2015.

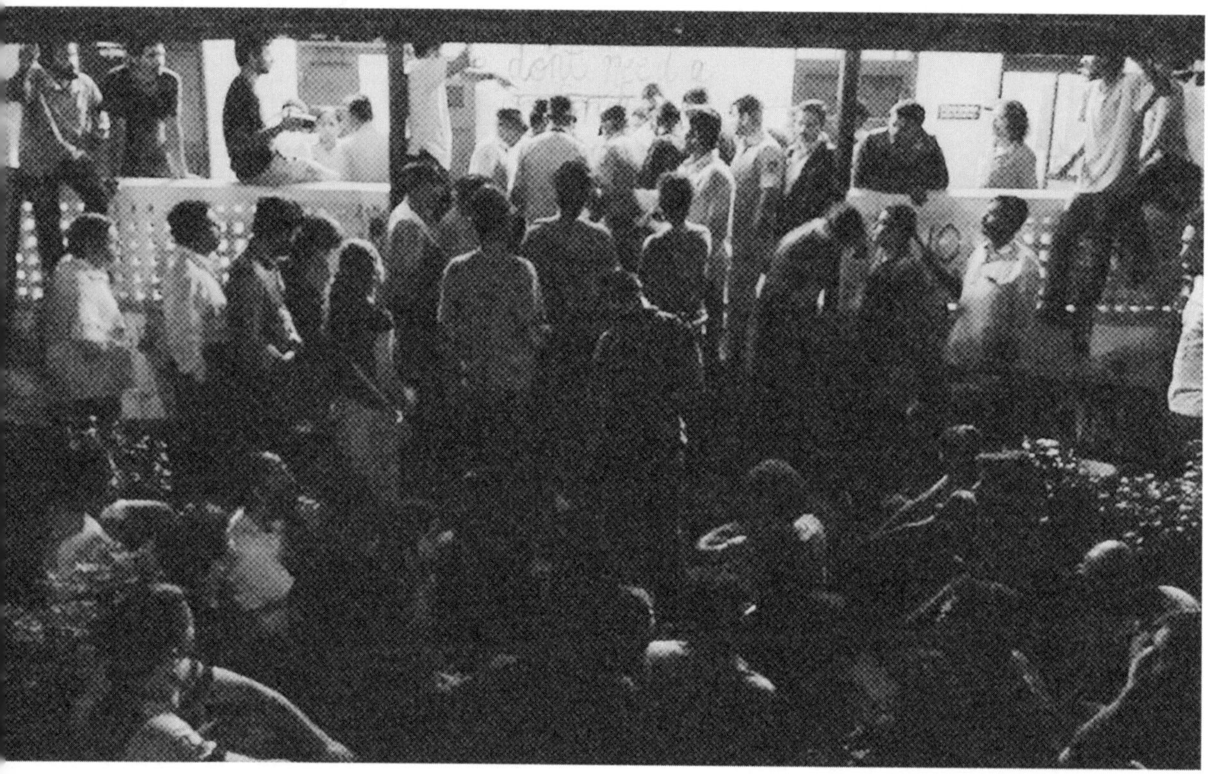

'They came at midnight.'
The night of 17 August 2015, outside the Director's office.

The previous week, on 5 August, two days after the Jantar Mantar march, the new Director Prashant Pathrabe had put up a retaliatory notice. He announced that academic assessments of a batch of students who had been on campus since 2008 would take place in a week on an 'as is basis' – in other words, in whatever condition their work existed. Hostel wardens had been informed that some thirty students who had 'overstayed' were going to be kicked out. On the 17th, a students' discussion with Pathrabe extended into an indefinite *gherao*. It was largely peaceful, for everyone remembered how on a previous occasion, in October 2000, another Director, Mohan Agashe, had accused *gherao*ing students of attempting murder. The events of 17 August were extensively filmed, by both students and the administration, and amid the arguments there was also occasional laughter – like once when the students asked Pathrabe who he voted for in the general elections and he replied, 'I won't say, but whoever I voted for didn't win.'

This night, however, the police appear to have arrived with specific intent. Their arrival seems anticipated. The Registrar, a man named U.C. Bodake who ought to have been present at a time like this, cannot be contacted; his house is locked. The police have some kind of a list of who they are after. The timing of the assault, just past midnight, is clearly a signal of some kind. Twenty-two students are rounded up, charged with unlawful assembly, rioting, causing non-fatal hurt, deterring public servants from discharging their duty and criminal intimidation. Seventeen get anticipatory bail but five students are taken away, formally arrested and jailed at the Deccan Gymkhana police *thana*.[2]

Grotesque Bodies

The loss of faith in the state apparatus and the increasingly invisible nature of authority now have an unexpected cinepolitical consequence. Through the second week of August the strike turns darker, the celebratory mood of July replaced by a rather less attractive, more familiar, but also more *exhausted* political body lashed to its mast. Such a body lies in stark contrast to the infinitely more attractive amalgam of artist–*regisseur*–student on show in Delhi a scant two weeks earlier.

On 12 August, students wrote a letter directly to Prime

2 'The students have been charged under sections 143, 149 (unlawful assembly), 147 (rioting), 323 (voluntarily causing hurt), 341 (wrongful restraint) and 353 (obstructing public servant from discharging duty) of the IPC. The students also questioned the university registrar U.C. Bodake's absence, after they found his house [opposite the main gate] locked when the police were making the arrests.' *The News Minute*, 19 August 2015.

Minister Narendra Modi, launching a series of missives addressed at different points to Rathore, to Jaitley, to Modi himself and to the President of India. None of them are easy to read. Some sound like political *naïveté*, or perhaps an obscure tactical purpose. This particular letter reminded Modi that if India 'is a nation representing hope, tolerance and peace' with 'a rich heritage of arts, culture and cinema, where the largest number of films are made', then it surely follows that such a nation needs to 'engage with the students ... over the ongoing crisis and initiate a dialogue with an open mind', to recognize that their concerns 'are most pertinent and serious and they are waiting to be addressed by your government'.

Facing page and overleaf
The response of the 2008 batch to the Director's notice of 5 August 2015 calling for immediate assessment of their diploma films.

Belief in such a view of the nation, however held, had to balance out with an alternative history of freedom on the campus, of abstract power translated into the petty authoritarianism of everyday functioning. It was all some version, says a former student, of 'don't make your film, we will cancel your diploma, punitive actions – a death penalty mode'. '*Phaansi chadha do,* expel *kar do, isko nikaal do, usko* de-bar *kar do*, a climate of fear, so *ek ko dekhenge to dusre log chup rahenge* [Hang them, expel them, remove him, de-bar her, a climate of fear, so if you make an example of one, others will be quietened].' Security personnel became armed, somebody was 'always watching us, you have a guard who is saying *ki raat ko kaun baitha hai* note *karo* [keep a watch on who is present at night].'

Three days earlier, on Independence Day (Day 65 of the strike), a second arts festival named 'Retracing Freedom' had sought to redefine the strike in similarly sunny language, as an attempt to rediscover 'the genesis of the art and cinema of our nation'. Cinema was, in their hands, to be a way to 'unit[e] the masses', reveal itself as 'not ... indulgence but a basic need of a society' that might even give human beings 'reasons to feel alive'. An independence that could 'ignore citizens' interests, stifle their voices' was, said 'Retracing Freedom', no independence at all.[3]

Over the first two weeks of August, in contrast, it became clear that Pathrabe had received his orders from an authority with very different views on independence. Perhaps, on 17 August, the police crackdown of the following day was already on Pathrabe's mind, for the tactic had clearly changed. The target now was twofold. One, to hit students in the batch that had joined in 2008 and were, seven

-3
FTII WisdomTree Facebook post, 'Retracing Freedom at FTII', 14 August 2015.

Students' Association
Film and Television Institute of India,
Law College Road,
Pune: 411004

Pune
07-08-2015

To,
The Director,
FTII

Subject: 2008 batch hostel eviction notice

Sir,
This letter is in response to the notice served by the Warden to some 2008 batch students, asking them to vacate their hostel with immediate effect, on the grounds of an assumption that their academic activities are over.
The Students Association would like to strongly raise an objection to such an action by the administration. No project is deemed complete till the final film is officially submitted to the institution. Hence the crew members of a diploma team working in their respective specialization, cannot be asked to leave till their respective diploma films are complete and officially submitted.

FTII has a tradition where a director, camera person, editor and sound designer work together in the pre-production and production stages of their projects and should continue to work in the same spirit in the post production stages as well. In the light of such a healthy and collaborative practice of filmmaking, a notice of this effect, only comes across as unnecessary meddling and interference in our academic activities by the administration and the government, validating our fears of threat to the institution's autonomy under this government.

This notice is also seen as one of many tactics used to arm-twist us by reducing the strength of students on strike, forcing them to leave the campus when their projects are not yet complete.

We appeal to you to not use these tyrannical tactics as it will only further hamper our dialogue with the ministry to resolve our issues and leave foul impressions amongst students about the FTII administration and the ministry.

We expect you to respond to our concerns immediately.

Thank you.

Students' Association, FTII

FOR NACHIMUTHU
PRESIDENT,
STUDENT'S ASSOCIATION

(RANJIT NAIR).

7/8/15

To
The Director,
FTII, Pune.

7th August 2015

Subject: **Regarding the letter of assessment of 2008 Diploma films**

Respected Sir,

We the students of 2008 batch have received an unexpected notice by email that the assessment for our Diploma films will be held on 11/08/2015 in as is where is basis.

In this regard, we want to let you know that we did not receive any prior notice regarding the dates of assessment. Furthermore it is important to elaborate the delay which is now looked at as a sole responsibility of the 2008 batch overlooking the scenarios the batch has managed to work without creating any official complaints from our side.

Institute not ready for intake of a new batch, 2008:
Our batch came in the year September 2008 when the institute was not at all ready infrastructurally- hostel, classrooms, equipment, studio space, faculty and staff- to take in a new batch. Students from 2004 batch were still shooting their Diplomas when we came in the institute, which got over around 2009-10. There were no faculties in the department of Direction and there was no HOD in Direction and Sound department.

No hostel rooms to accommodate 2008 batch:
Lack of hostel rooms had forced us to accommodate upto 6-8 students in one room and in a few cases we were even accommodated in store rooms of FTII. This battle for hostels ran till 2011 when the new hostel came up and the senior batches had vacated their rooms. It is very important to mention that we used to sleep in shifts, as there were no beds available- one person would sleep for a few hours and then another would sleep on the same bed!!

Swine Flu:
Immediately after our first year, the Direction students were made to wait for almost a period of 5 months as there was no classrooms and faculty available for 2008 Direction batch; because 2006 and 2007 batches were respectively doing their second and third year classes/ workshops. In the mean time Swine flu hit Pune, and the institute like other educational institutes of India came to a standstill- delaying the start of our second year.

Lack of academic planning:
There was no planning in place for different departments to work in sync. For example, the cinematography batch students often finished their workshops well before the workshops of any other departments would start, and hence, would have to wait for the projects to begin. This is a clear case of ignorance in academic planning.

Refusal of zero year in 2009:
Furthermore, the students of FTII had requested to declare a zero year in 2009 owing to the infrastructural impossibilities, which was overruled. So, the 2009 batch had arrived and immediately after their first year they were given a priority by the administration to start their second year. So, we became the scapegoats of the delay of the institute as well as the hurry to run our junior batch on time, ignoring the need to run our batch on time. Under the same light, we were made to wait for our seniors to finish their shoot/ classes and practicals before we could use the same equipment and studio space for our practicals and projects.

Less number of sound students and overload in sound post production:
There was an intake of fewer sound students in the 2008 batch. Only 10 students in the sound batch as opposed to 14 projects. Many sound students had to double up for multiple projects which caused cumulative delays in completion of the projects of the 2008 batch as a whole.

1 ISFF, 2 NSFA, Golden Jubilee celebration during our academic year:
It is important to mention that one International Students Film Festival (ISFF) and two National Students Film Awards (NSFA) were organized during our academic schedule. The golden jubilee celebration of FTII took place during our academic year. Each time during the above events all the academic activities had come to a stand still for more than a month. This created a domino effect in academics and projects across the batches, and our batch was time and again given the second priority while the institute would try to regulate its activities and get back to normal functioning.

Mumbai labs stopped processing films:
The film processing of our projects of sound and picture was done in Mumbai and the film processing labs in were shutting down around the year 2012-13. A few labs in Mumbai, still working with married prints were overloaded with industry's work. So, we had to wait in line to get each of our projects processed at these labs.

Shift from Film to Digital:
The whole infrastructural shift of screening projects on DCP (Digital Cinema Package) in the institute happened during our time. It is important to mention that 2008 was the first batch who shot playbacks, or any other project on Alexa, a the institute. At that point in time, even the institute was undergoing a process of figuring out and actualizing the new process. There were no trained staff to carry out the new functions and follow up the process. Even the newer equipments needed new faculty to teach. New subsidized contracts had to be made with the labs in Mumbai for the Digital processing of sound and picture. We quietly supported the institute during this process at the cost of delay of our academic schedule.

As is where is basis assessment:
It is highly unethical to organize the assessment of our Diploma films in as is where is basis, without any intimation and or consultation, after what we have been through during the last six years. We all are working through various personal difficulties of family and economy in the hope to complete our work and exit the institute. The assessment is therefore the last collective academic input we will receive from the experts in the presence of all our batchmates; and this undue assessment will hamper that process.

So, we request you to kindly postpone the assessment and cooperate with individual students of our batch and help them complete their projects and ceremoniously organize an assessment of our completed Diploma films together.

Thaking you,

For students of 2008 batch.

years later, still completing courses that they should have finished in three. And two, to terminate the employment of several contractual employees using the strike as the excuse.

There was a lot of ink, much fine print and many explanations for how this delay had come to pass. It was, said students, partly due to the chaos of the technological transition from celluloid to digital – the collapse of support from film laboratories in Mumbai, the move to DCP screening packages. It was also to do with the long-term legacies of the Agashe era.

Whatever. The news mainstream glazed over the fine argumentation. For the political right wing, undeserving students exploiting 'elite' privileges and state-subsidized facilities was as potent an image as the Bad Guy they claimed to oppose. To much of the media, this batch was no different from the FTII student body as a whole. Together they were each spending 12 lakhs annually of taxpayers' money. They represented all that was wrong, not only with that particular institution but with Indian education in general. *They* were the reason why meritocracy and privatization had to be the principles running higher education in India. It was an exhausted Mandal-era cliché that went back on the campus to 1977 and the obscene-rabble-entering-pristine-institution image that the Satish Candra report had created, and which had perhaps received an influential visual definition in *Holi*.

That August, however, the cliché developed further consequences. It formalized the split in the narrative. One half of the story retained the futurist elegance of first-order anti-Chauhanism that had made the FTII strike so utterly compelling to so many. The other half was resolutely directed at the messy twenty-year saga of the afterlife of the Agashe years.

In a way, the divide reproduced, yet again, the metaphorical divides of clean digital versus dirty celluloid. To stay with liberal anti-Chauhanism was to risk throwing the 2008 batch under the bus – not entirely inconceivable for at least some of the post-2012 'digital' batches who did not quite see why their futures needed to be nailed so tightly to those of their celluloid seniors.[4] To make that batch not an exception but the *norm*, to introduce that body of students centre stage, was to depart from something that the strike had actively worked to achieve through much of July, and which

-4

For Vikas, the knowledge of how the place ran literally changed by batch. 'Even students who were on strike from the 2013 batch, or the TV batch ... were unable to accept this' (i.e. the narrative of the 2008 students). 'My batch knew it, because we were by then in the third year. *Humko pata hai ki yeh jagah kaisi chalti hai* [we know how this place runs], *hum kaise chal rahein hain pichle 4–5 saal se* [how we have run over the past 4–5 years]. *Humko pata hai ki yeh hamara saath bhi hone wala hai* [We know this will happen to us too].' 'We were a lot more accommodative and understanding of what crisis they have gone through ... that furthered the polarization, but that polarization within the student community did not lead to a situation where students wanted to not be a part of the strike. And a lot of people did not want to be a part of the strike at least in person, in private was because of the scale at which it was mounted and where it was heading. They were really scared of that, more than the issue of the 2008 batch. Because eventually *jab gherao hua* [when the *gherao* happened] that was because of the 2008 batch's assessment where everyone landed.' Verbatim conversation with Vikas Urs, 21 October 2021, Mumbai.

had culminated in the astonishing public display of solidarity at Delhi's Jantar Mantar.

As these grotesque bodies merge with other ghosts on the campus a familiar feeling of the uncanny returns, of having seen all this before. In 2000, the strikers had rejected multiple carrots – Bobby Bedi is explicitly seen in Nagpaul's footage offering one – with a familiar hue: one, immediate and temporary workarounds for this specific batch; two, on condition that they withdraw their demand for structural change; three, on further condition that they withdraw their strike immediately. The 2000 strikers had gone against the advice of seniors who had extended conditional support, convinced that they were arguing in the long-term interests of the FTII. Both Nagpaul's material of 2000 and Kshama Padalkar's *The Strike and I* in 2015 show students arguing, pleading with their respective Directors, warning them of the lasting consequences of their ill-judged actions. Across fifteen years, both Directors remained unmoved.

Both pleas nevertheless proved chillingly prescient. Now we see, in *The Strike and I*, the Institute's faculty shuffling in: Kedarnath Awati, Sandeep Chatterjee, Debkamal Ganguly and others. Awati says to the camera that assessments could have waited until the strike was called off, then turns to Pathrabe and directly suggests that an appeal be made to 'JS' (Joint Secretary-Film). Pathrabe is unflinching. The issue is soon joined by another: the termination of staff contracts.

As in 2000, when friendly ex-students (such as Naseeruddin Shah) had withheld support for the larger cause – with a 'we'll support your specific batch, but not your larger demands for systemic change'-type position – now too, several senior alumni who had been otherwise supportive of the strike became anxious about what solidarity with the 2008 batch would do. Many read it as intransigence. The previous month, in a meeting held in the

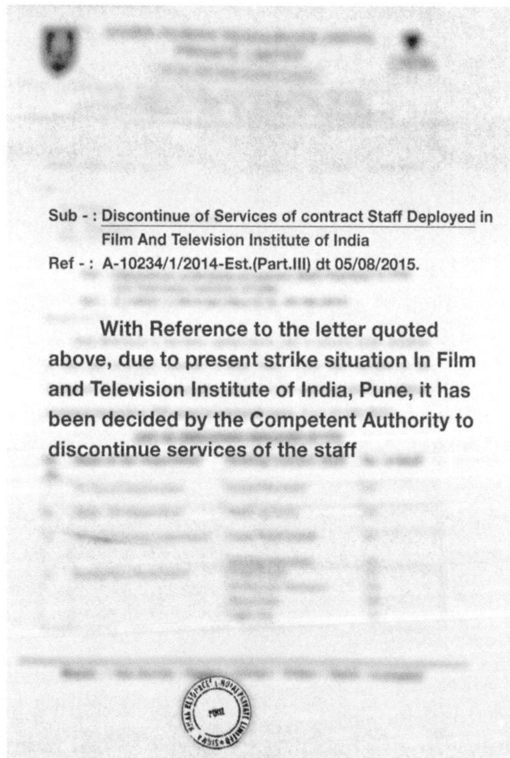
Sub - : Discontinue of Services of contract Staff Deployed in Film And Television Institute of India
Ref - : A-10234/1/2014-Est.(Part.III) dt 05/08/2015.

With Reference to the letter quoted above, due to present strike situation In Film and Television Institute of India, Pune, it has been decided by the Competent Authority to discontinue services of the staff

10 August 2015: summary and mash-up of formal notice to terminate staff using the strike as an excuse.

Main Theatre, Jahnu Barua, one of the candidates touted as either Deputy or Co-Chair, had warned students to beware, for the strike had gotten to a point where the next steps, if not taken carefully, could be disastrous. The government, he said, knew that it had made a mistake, but would never admit it. There was an opportunity here, but great political wisdom needed to be shown if the students were to navigate this critical phase in a way that didn't hurt them even more. Any false step would be fatal, not only for the student body but for the FTII's very future.[5]

Girish Kasaravalli too warned that mistakes were being made. He had, he would say later, organized 'many strikes' in his time, and the essential feature in the art of striking is negotiation. *You must know when to back off.* 'When you are organizing a strike you also know how many extra demands to place, so that those demands will be sort of face-saving for the government.' This did not happen here.[6]

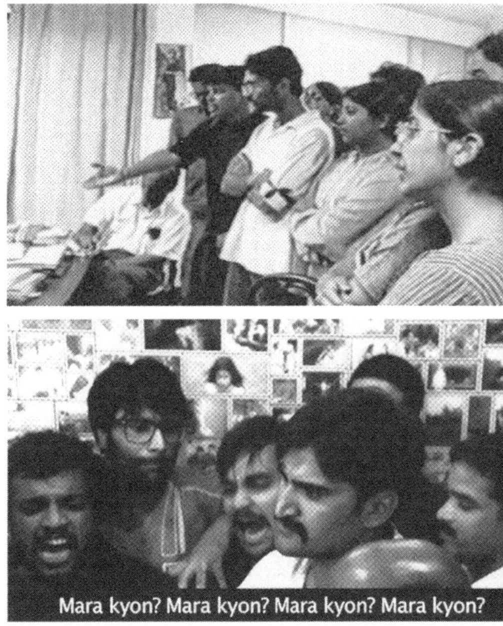

Confrontations with Directors. Above: Agashe in 2000, shot by Satya Rai Nagpaul. **Below:** Pathrabe in 2015 (from Kshama Padalkar's **The Strike and I**, 2019)

—

The following week, in a passionate and game-changing piece in the *Times of India*, Resul Pookutty threw his influential support unambiguously behind the 2008 batch. He too took the problem beyond its immediate referents and returned it to 2000. To him it had been self-evident 'that the incoming batch of students would not be able to complete their studies in three years', that this batch had been admitted 'at the Ministry's insistence' despite recommendations to convert 2008 into a zero admission year.[7] This very batch would be once again scapegoated, and once again at the Ministry's insistence (as Pathrabe all but admitted), with the clear plan to break up the student body.

The problem wasn't only a matter of the 2008 batch, just as in 2000 it hadn't been only a matter of the students admitted that year. Then as now, there were two ways to look at it, two irreconcilable imaginations – just as there had been when Nair had clashed with Hewitt. The first anti-Chauhan story was by implication progressive–liberal anti-Modi outrage. It had major support but one downside:

-5

Extrapolated from Jahnu Barua's speech to students, in Kshama Padalkar's *The Strike and I* (2019).

-6

Conversation with Girish Kasaravalli, 4 October 2018, Bangalore.

-7

Resul Pookutty, 'Students Suffered for FTII's Random Academic Decisions', *Times of India*, 23 August 2015.

it tended to absolve previous governments. It did, for example, allow Rahul Gandhi to garner his bit of political capital without taking any historic responsibility for the situation they were in.[8]

The second story was messier. But it was also more historically accurate. It was the one that panned out on 18 August and the days to follow. For one, it was the larger narrative; for another, it had a cinepolitical pedigree. It was about the cinema, and it mapped the transition from celluloid to digital on to a larger story of India. It implicated the Modi government as much as it did the UPA and NDA regimes that preceded it. It necessarily went back to 1996, to privatization and the onset of neoliberal governance, and to transformations in the apparatus of the moving image and of cinematic authorship. It perhaps, who knows, even went back to the Emergency.

The first story blanked out the 2008 batch. The second made the batch central to the saga. Indeed, it gave the strike its historical memory.

The Hollow Centre in Expanded Cinema

> 'Frame first, act later. Does life begin when film ends? Or is there no life after film?' – Ranjan Palit in voiceover, *In Camera*, 2009

As July turned to August, John–Ghatak–Tarkovsky began to yield a coded cinematic language. It was a language in the tradition of *Jaane Bhi Do Yaaron*'s Antonioni Park – a treacherous zone of mystery signposted by covert references shared between filmmakers and insider–spectators who were in the know.

Such a language dominated 'Retracing Freedom', a forty-eight-hour film festival at the Classroom Theatre on Independence Day. The organization of the festival had been assigned mainly to those who were (says Mukul Haloi) 'not in the forefront of the strike'. They selected titles that were, putting it mildly, eclectic – Day 65, for example, saw back-to-back screenings of Godard's *Le Petit Soldat* (1963) and Samuel Fuller's *Shock Corridor* (1963).

To Mukul, film history was at the time a 'very personal thing'.[9] In class he had learnt about 'Eisenstein and all those cuts' but it had been a 'completely useless kind of process'. Now, in contrast, the canonical language of cinema began unexpectedly to share its secrets. You could see, as though with unprecedented clarity, the

-8

Both Rahul Gandhi's visit to the FTII and his support have been controversial, but it does need to be said that he was perhaps the only major opposition figure in Parliament who raised the FTII issue in public on multiple occasions.

-9

Conversation with Mukul Haloi on Zoom, 7 September 2020.

‘kind of situation the filmmakers had been in’, as they revealed to you and you alone why, and under what conditions, they had made their films. To Mukul, then in his second year of the direction course, this had been the missing point: the ‘point of connection with film, to fit yourself [and] your time and history and past [into it]’.

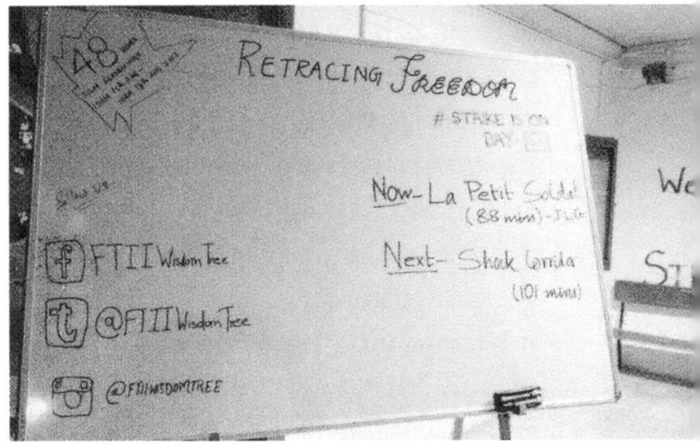

15 August 2015: Day 66 – notice board of the Classroom Theatre announcing the day’s screenings at ‘Retracing Freedom’: Jean-Luc Godard’s **Le Petit Soldat** (1963) and Samuel Fuller’s **Shock Corridor** (1963).

Perhaps the defining characteristic of the cinema that emerged on campus was an enduring fascination with *sensory absence*. In contrast to protagonists exuding main character energy (a Salim Langda, let’s say), who could orchestrate the moral logic for motivated action around them, now – even as the state lost its ethical moorings – traditional narratorial authority found itself compromised. What we got as a consequence were absent protagonists. Various narrative symbols began taking the place of offscreen terror, replacing any conventional protagonist with an insecure, hollowed-out emotional–sensory centre. The real actors were those behind the camera, and we were invited to self-insert our gaze to fill this absence, thus to *re-occupy* absent narrative agency.

This is perhaps most explicit in the best-known film to emerge from the 2015 strike, Payal Kapadia’s *A Night of Knowing Nothing* (2021). Her absent protagonist ‘L’ is a dreamlike assemblage of fiction and documentary, original and found footage, interspersed with still images, news clippings, wall graffiti and line drawings.

L’s story, such as it is, unravels through a series of letters purportedly found in a student hostel room at FTII. These letters, spoken over the soundtrack, tell of a heady romance that flowered between two students during the early days of the strike. As the protests turn darker and state totalitarianism grows, the love story too turns tragic, as L’s individual saga finds itself mapped on to the transformation of the Indian state that she sees around her, as though in real time, on the campus, in her relationship and on the street.

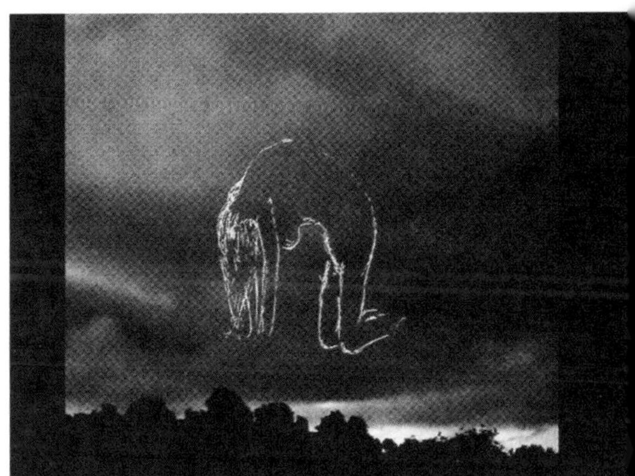

Payal Kapadia’s **A Night of Knowing Nothing** (2021).

Now the lovelorn L becomes an omniscient presence. Her all-seeing gaze reprises – and invites her spectator to look at – a distinct history of expanded cinema. Gene Youngblood has described his ‘expanded cinema' as pivoted around 'extra-objective' synaesthesia. It is where the cinema grows beyond its limits. 'The only films capable of supporting multiple viewing ... are synaesthetic films in which the viewer is free to *insert himself into the experience differently* each time.'[10] Youngblood's big example is Michael Snow's famous *Wavelength*, which he names a 'pure drama [with] no "meaning" in the conventional sense', only developing meaning in the way it sets up 'the relationship between the film and the viewer'.

In 2019, four years after the strike, Prateek Vats completed his surreal testament film *Eeb Allay Ooo!* All of Delhi's corridors of power, its high-security buildings on Rajpath and Shastri Bhavan, have become infested by monkeys. The entire authority of the state devolves upon a contract worker who has to make strange sounds to scare them away.

Many saw it as a direct metaphor of the 2015 strike.[11] They also saw possible links with the increasingly grim descent into cynicism that followed the heady celebrations of June and July, and the way the film's monkey-chasing protagonist, Anjani (the name of Hanuman's mother in the Ramayana) too gradually descends into the subaltern muck and mire of simian irrationality.

As the hollow centre leaks out inexorably into everything around it, it reveals other properties. If some of its characteristics are explicitly political, others are suffused with mystical, primitive, sometimes aboriginal nature – in student films ranging from Sanyukta Sharma's *A Dream Animal* (2013) to Payal Kapadia's *Dopahar ke Badal* (2018), Koel Sen's *Valay* (2018), Nachi's *Famished Road* (2018) and, most recently, Ashmita Guha Niyogi's *Catdog* (2019). Characters become either single-point condensations, like the tribal girl in Nachi's *Famished Road* or the policewoman inside the Deccan Gymkhana Police Station in Himanshu Prajapati's *Three–Two–One* (2018), or character relays, as in Pranjal Dua's stunning 2013 short *Chidiya Udh*, wound tightly around a boy on a chicken farm and a woman working in a hotel.

Such presences teeter at the edge of a realism-effect, always threatening to fall over into uncharted symbolic territory. When they do fall over, the film typically moves into surrealism proper – commonly in pre-diploma exercises, such as Payal's digital video exercise, *Watermelon, Fish and Half-Ghost*. The perpetual threat that

-10

Youngblood, 'Image-Exchange and the Post-Mass Audience Age', p. 130.

-11

Sankhayan Ghosh, 'How Prateek Vats' *Eeb Allay Ooo!* Was Born Out of the FTII Students' Strike', *Film Companion*, 20 February 2021.

everything onscreen faces creates an unnameable offscreen materiality that is emplotted as nature, sci-fi, or totalitarian forces. Audio in general, and 'effects' in particular, remain a driving presence.

Eeb Allay Ooo! is – as John Abraham's and Kundan Shah's first films were, as *A Night of Knowing Nothing* too would be – a 'batch' production. Most of its key participants had graduated from the FTII within a short window of six years: Prateek, Shubham who wrote the film, its sound recordist Bigyna Bhushan Dahal, and some of the actors (Shashi Bhushan, Nutan Sinha, Nitin Goel) were from 2006; editor Tanushree Das was from 2005; cinematographer Samyananda Sahi from 2009; producer Shwetaabh Singh from 2012; and lead actors Shardul Bharadwaj and Naina Sareen from 2013.[12] The 'batch' tradition inaugurated by *Jaane Bhi Do Yaaron* typically was to create leaky ensembles, moving from one to many makers, from fiction to documentary, from studio to street and finally into unmediated street action. Anjani too in this regard, like L, misses motivational purpose. He is a lost, absent or delegitimized protagonist whose absence invites spectatorial insertion even as the film itself moves centripetally, spills beyond itself.

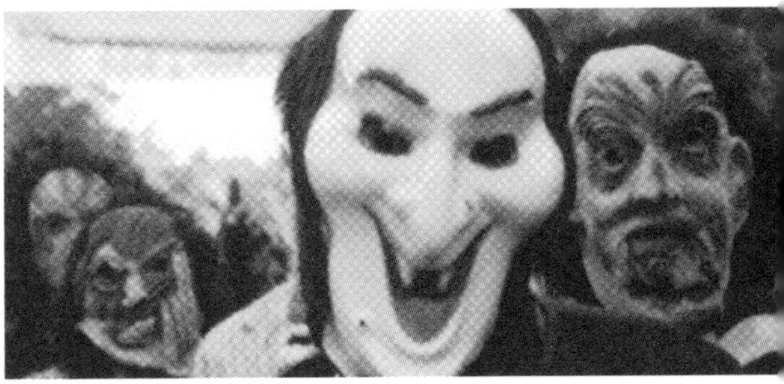

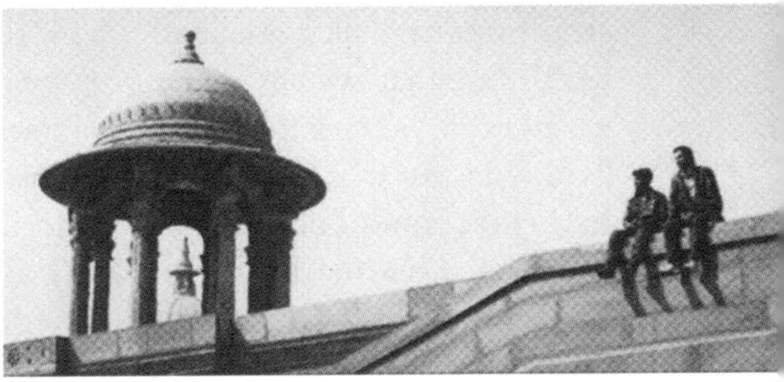

Above and below: The descent into simian hell and the ramparts of Lutyens' Delhi in Prateek Vats' **Eeb Allay Ooo!** (2019).

A year later, in 2020, Ranjan Palit completed his testament film, *Lord of the Orphans.* Palit is a cinematographer of legendary dimensions. His early work produces a storied history of the Indian documentary. He shot for Anand Patwardhan, Sanjay Kak and Amar Kanwar, together with such classics as Manjira Dutta's *The Sacrifice of Babulal Bhuiya* (1988) and Reena Mohan's *Kamalabai* (1991), in addition to his own collaborations with Vasudha Joshi (*Voices from Baliapal,* 1988 and other films). His characteristic immersive, tactile, close-to-the-subject intensity was in this time definitive in bringing to independent documentary much of its basic handheld grammar.

Some time in 2009, Palit began converting this distinctive cinematographic style into a subjective witness statement. That year he made his own film, *In Camera*, in part because, as he says in it, 'I realized that my own life is passing me by. Maybe it is time to

-12

Eeb Allay Ooo!, in addition to being an 'FTII' film, was also in many ways a 'Players' film, as many members of the crew had been a part of it before joining – Prateek, Shubham, Abhishek Bhardwaj, Shardul, Shwetaabh and others who helped in measures big and small proudly trace themselves to that wonderful theatre group which encouraged independent thought, stressed rigour of one's craft and pushed all of us to produce work embodying the zeitgeist of our times. Email from Prateek Vats, 11 September, 2022.

start telling my own story.' This story is that of a cinematographer–eyewitness. The eyewitness sees things, the cinematographer records some of what he sees, haunted by questions like: 'How do I frame something personal like this? What am I trying to do? Should I be doing *this*? Or is *this* more evocative?' 'Have I lost my sense of real incidents, events, people?' 'Has the world turned to a maze of images?' (All quotations from the voiceover of *In Camera.*)

Lord of the Orphans produces an epic autobiography of the absent subject. Palit made it after he withstood a personal mental health crisis that saw him do no work for three years. It is made as a mash-up of documentary and fiction, memory, history, dream and lived reality. In the film he encounters his daughter Maya, last seen leaving the family home in the 2009 documentary, now returning. Much of the first half of the film, including his own personal breakdown, is told through actors. Over time, however, the actors disappear and the actual people he is depicting enter, culminating in the almost on-screen death of his first wife, the painter Rumi Ray, who comes into the film literally on her deathbed and actually dies in the process of the shooting.

—

In 2015, such a cinematic invitation to enter a hollow narrative container would play a direct role in cementing the collective as July turned to August, and the strike turned more confrontational. In early September 2015, Payal sought to capture some of this history in a curated package for Films Division's FDZone in Mumbai. Her idea was to speak from within the strike but, like Pookutty, she too cast a wider net. FTII had, Payal wrote in her short programme note, 'resisted market forces for so many years' – and the reasons for such resistance were in the films she wanted to show, which 'deal specifically with' what she simply named 'a state of transformation'.

The experimental films in her list, such as *Feel in the Blanks* or *Level Zero*, shaded into the more explicitly protest films that had been uploaded through June and July on *#Wisdomtree*, such as the *Mann ki Baat* comedy series. It takes a strange gaze to recognize anything overtly 'political' here – until you start seeing what is not there. Only one film in the FDZone list was in any way overtly *about* the strike: Simanthini Dhuru and Anand Patwardhan's *Strike Day 70*. It was also the only one not made by a student or former student.

As Payal's list expanded and went back in time, a rather different cinematic logic emerged. First she returned to 2015, to Jessica Sadanah's *Water's Childhood* and Aman Wadhan's *Letters from Korlai*, then to 2014 (Arun Kuppuswamy's *Vijay*), then 2012, by which time the cinema began revealing a distinct mode of both making and showing film. Both Prantik Basu's *Makara* (2012), a remarkable folk story from Maharashtra about a crocodile beneath the clouds, and Dua's *Chidiya Udh* reveal such a mode. They also reveal a legacy – both films acknowledge Kamal Swaroop, and as we move on, we see the names of Fareeda Mehta and R.V. Ramani among the acknowledgments. Included in Payal's list was Naveen Padmanabha's *Open Café* ode to Kamal Swaroop.

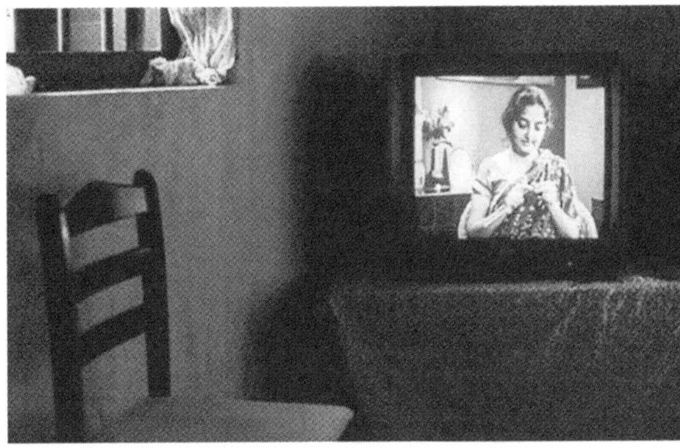

Detail from Renu Savant's **Airavat** (2011). Hansa Thapliyal is shown on a television monitor talking about the invention of a camera that can capture ghosts.

Outside of Payal's list, other clear departures too were seen. Renu Savant's mythical story *Airavat* (2011) shows everyday life unfolding in a middle-class chawl even as news comes of an elephant trying to squeeze itself into the courtyard, Squadron Leader Rakesh Sharma enters outer space, and on television, set alongside Tagore's *Tobu mone rekho* and Gandhi's speech in 1931, we have a story (narrated by Hansa Thapliyal) of a man who has invented a camera that can capture ghosts. Savant's later work, both her project for the Yokohama Triennale and her major documentary *Many Months in Mirya,* reveal a fascination with stories that are not told, images that conceal as much as they reveal.[13]

In September, however, this covert shared language of the cinema was just sufficiently political to keep students together, and also for the Films Division to cancel their FDZone event. One representative said, off the record, that they weren't 'comfortable' screening Payal's selections.[14]

The Absent State

As August further shaded into September, the strike turned increasingly dark. Prateek had seen Hewitt first-hand, and the difference between then and now was especially vivid.[15] What was new was the indifference. On previous occasions the Ministry would

-13

See especially Renu Savant's collaboration with Kush Bhadwar, titled *Brave Revolutionary: Redubbed* (2020), which re-edits Nana Patekar's famous 'revolutionary' soliloquy from *Krantiveer* (1994).

-14

Rupali Shukla, 'Films Division cancels screening of FTII students' films', *Times of India*, 3 September 2015.

-15

'Our experience was qualitatively different. I am not saying they were better but it had never happened earlier, in the most bitter of fights, that your film would be prevented from being made ... the daily campus fights were around, like, you didn't get the lenses you want, or something.' Verbatim conversation with Prateek Vats, 14 December 2018, Mumbai.

have 'tried to engage you into a process, the Joint Secretary would have been on campus within a week of something like this ... and at least give[n] an illusion that [they were] listening and placating the students. *Kaam nahi ruka is tarah se* [Work never stopped like this].'

Day 70, 20 August. One day after the police arrived on the campus, the Ministry of Information and Broadcasting announced a three-person review panel comprising S.M. Khan, Registrar of Newspapers of India, Anshu Sinha, Director (Films), and S. Naganathan, Under-Secretary (Films), to do an onsite assessment. The significance of this announcement, coinciding as it did with the police action, was not missed by anybody. It was hardly conceivable that talking could lead anywhere.

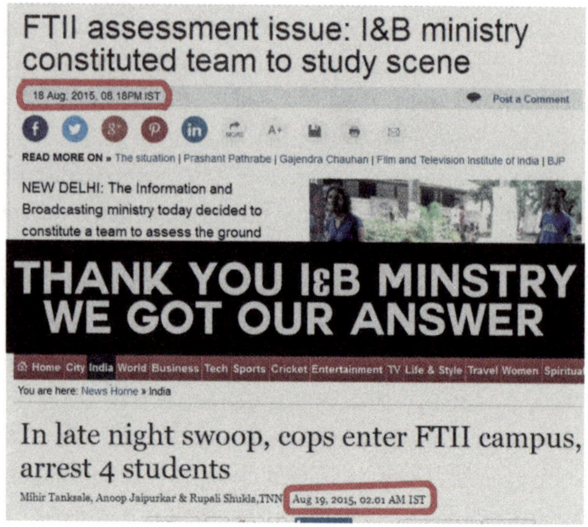

Student poster on 20 August 2015, two days after the midnight police raid on campus, pointing to the coincidence between the raid and the announcement of the Khan Committee.

By now authority had turned into an absent shape-shifter. Its only presence was uniformed, that of the police and armed security. Nobody appeared able to speak any more for those in power, either for themselves or for their position. Senior bureaucracy spoke in Chinese whispers. They were supportive and even sympathetic. They declared their desire to help, they gave lots of informal off-the-record do-this-do-that advice, and then found multiple ways to say that this was beyond them, that instructions were being issued from higher up – '*secretary-level* people saying "[we] can't do anything, it isn't in our hands, it isn't our decision".'

So it was part of the pattern when Khan and his team arrived, that the conversation was pleasant. Khan appeared to be a nice man with a genuine desire to work things out. Both the students and the faculty spent time with the team. Naganathan specifically asked to see Awati's 23 August letter to the I&B Ministry which outlined his reasons for why the 2008 batch had found themselves in the crisis they were in, and insisted that whatever the larger reasons, it was certainly not the fault of that batch.

Much rode on the report being a step towards a solution. When it did come out, however, it was a disaster. Nobody ever saw the original version, only newspaper summaries of it. It was evident that Mr Khan had been fed. He said his findings showed that the 2008 batch was solely responsible for delay in completing projects, which had happened because they had not been 'ready with their scripts'. Infrastructure, said Khan, was plentiful and entirely adequate.

What was surprising perhaps was the extent to which the campus *faculty* got torpedoed by Khan. The faculty, whose position had by now become completely untenable, was accused of 'populism', rapped for failing to assess incomplete projects, disparaged for their promise to complete assessments after the strike was over, since 'in the light of previous extensions, the Institute could ill-afford to grant such concessions at the cost of a fresh batch of students'. The Director, on the other hand, came off smelling of roses. He was entirely excused for the 'unfortunate incidents' that had culminated in the FIR against students, for it was the 'perpetually shifting conduct of the faculty' that was deemed the real culprit. Pathrabe, Khan found, was 'well within his rights to call security personnel and lodge the FIR'.[16]

Gradually, the dark arts of negotiation got called into question as the proverbial back channels gleamed like mirages in the desert. 'We did not know how to respond to it, we are not used to negotiations [of this kind]', says Prateek. '*Matlab, saaf-saaf kaho na* [Meaning, why don't you speak clearly].' It was always '*Tum log* strike *wapas lo, phir hum aisa karenge, hum waisa karenge* [First take back your strike, then we will do this or that]. Nothing in writing.' This was not how Hewitt had happened. Student strikes are anyway not very popular, but now, '*Unka toh* narrative *aaj hi shuru hua*, 12 crore *rupiya* student *pe kharcha hota hai* [That was the only narrative, that 12 crores were being spent on each student]', the relentless new language of '*yeh* tax payer, tax payer, tax payer'.[17]

—

Three weeks after the great-nation-in-distress letter to Narendra Modi, a second letter went out, this time to Rathore. The language of desperation was now increasingly apparent: both a practical desperation following the collapse of the Khan initiative on which

-16

Shoumiojit Bannerjee, 'Khan Panel report comes as a blow to FTII students', *The Hindu*, 3 October 2015.

-17

Conversation with Prateek Vats, 14 December 2018, Mumbai.

the students had wagered everything, and more a conceptual and even aesthetic crisis at the utter absence of a contending other and the collapse of the narrative apparatus itself. 'We write this letter to bring attention to the fact that *this crisis has now reached an extreme* that we could have never imagined', it goes. 'The students had placed their complete trust in the 3 member committee ... we have not gotten any clarity on the outcome of what we felt was a positive step to resolve the crisis. And in fact, *the step taken to lay off the lowest economic rung of the contractual staff* has thrust escalation upon us and has now put in the motives of the committee led by Mr Khan itself in question' (all emphases in the original).[18]

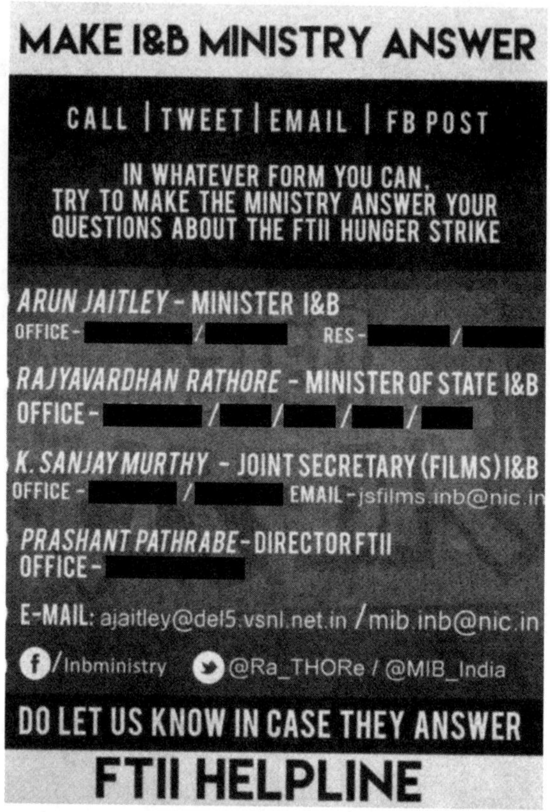

Student poster in September 2015 in the midst of the hunger strike, revealing the increasing desperation of the students.

Five days later, a signature campaign was mounted to get filmmakers, and indeed anyone interested, to write to the President of India and to express distress at the 'ongoing mishandling of affairs at the Film and Television Institute of India ... by the Ministry of Information and Broadcasting'.[19] The same day, the students wrote yet another letter to Prime Minister Modi with the same complaint (about the way the I&B Ministry 'had miserably failed to address and resolve the fundamental issues raised by the students of FTII for more than 2 months'), but also asserting their right to complain since they were 'the major stakeholders, whose careers would be jeopardized by such arbitrary actions of the government'.

Day 90, 9 September. The startling absence of authority, the hollow centre, brought a new and poignant significance when three students – Hilal Savad, Alok Arora and Himanshu Shekhar – literally inserted their bodies into the narrative with a relay hunger strike as a last-ditch effort to get the government to produce themselves before the student gaze. Earlier, on 5 September, Abhijit Das, a contract employee teaching in the Art Direction department, had begun his own hunger strike, which lasted 66 hours. They now listed eight

-18
Letter to Rajyavardhan Singh Rathore, Minister of State, I&B Ministry, dated 1 September 2015.

-19
One such, written on 5 September 2015, by the Concerned Citizens of India for the Integrity of National Institutions, saw 190 teachers conveying their own 'Mann ki Baat', on the occasion of Teachers' Day.

issues they wanted to discuss, and said they would not call off their hunger strike until the authorities came to the table.[20] Chauhan was first on the list, the FIRs and court cases against students was next. Academic timelines had to be discussed, as well as infrastructure issues. A major issue was contract staff.

On 11 September, in another letter, Arun Jaitley was informed that 'just minutes ago, an FTII student [has been] transferred to the ICU after he was shifted to the hospital because his blood sugar levels drastically fell after 30 hours of hunger strike'. Yet another letter which followed three days later to Jaitley sounded increasingly desperate. The crisis was now 'in its most extreme and perilous stage'. It had become 'dangerous for the students' and placed 'the entire institute, students, teachers, and staff alike under inexplicable emotional, physical and mental duress'. There was a 'breakdown of communication between students and their own government'. Everyone had to face the 'reality that is the most unfortunate fact of this now-almost 100 day long agitation'.[21]

The breakdown would have serial consequences. Paresh Kamdar, one of the visiting faculty regulars since 2013 along with Fareeda Mehta and Kamal Swaroop, testified to the extent to which conversations with in-house faculty, always barring exceptions, had ground to a halt.[22] Kamdar had been invited by the editing, direction and even cinematography batches to come and teach. He had sensed this crisis with in-house faculty brewing from as far back as 2013. As Awati too had written in his letter to the I&B Ministry, in-house faculty possessed 'no power at all'. Many had lost credibility, faced with new technology they didn't always understand, several were on contract, underpaid and undervalued by a Ministry that had no qualifications to run an academic establishment, and their jobs were now actively under threat.

On 14 September, the hunger strike saw solidarity action in Delhi University, Jamia and JNU in Delhi, Jadavpur, SRFTI, Presidency and Calcutta Medical College in Kolkata. What was startling, and in sharp contrast to a stonewalling, absent authority, was the unprecedented groundswell of popular support from the unlikeliest of places across the country. There were the film, arts and humanities students. There were their unions. On this support, the strike relied.

-20

Express News Service, 'FTII students end hunger strike; talks to resume on Tuesday', *The Indian Express*, 28 September 2015.

-21

Letters from the Students' Association to Arun Jaitley, I&B Minister, dated 11 and 14 September 2015.

-22

Conversation with Paresh Kamdar, 15 December 2018, Mumbai.

Facing page
Letter of solidarity from Students Federation of India, Aligarh Muslim University, 27 August 2015.

Overleaf
'The international community can't help noticing ...'. A stinging rebuke addressed directly to the Indian Prime Minister from Alberto Barbera, Director of the Venice Film Festival, on 1 October 2015.

What wasn't expected was the flood of public support. 'Everybody began coming in, students from Hyderabad, Lucknow, Patna, Bhopal, Delhi, Chandigarh ... all sorts of people started coming on board.' Workers from the Maruti-Suzuki union turned up because 'one friend had fought their case in Delhi', and they said, '*Bahut suna tha, ek baar aake milna chahte the*' [We had heard a lot about you, we wanted to meet you once].'[23] Demonstrations in support took place across several cities, initiated by groups of diverse political persuasion.

Day 108, 27 September. An invitation for talks finally arrived and the hunger strike was called off in response. The student representatives met senior I&B Ministry officials. The Secretary of the Ministry, Sanjay Gupta, presided over the discussions. He was accompanied by Joint Secretary K. Sanjay Murthy and Deputy Secretary Deepak Kumar. The top administrative brass of the Ministry and seven students were present: Ajayan, Ranjit, Nachi, Vikas, Reema Kaur, Shini and Malyaj Awasthi. They met over four sessions in the first ten days of October. They met only to find – yet again – that nothing had changed. Yet again, for all the earnestness displayed on all sides, it was as though pre-ordained that this too would end in failure. Once again the familiar 'Centre of Excellence'

-23
Conversation with Prateek Vats, 14 December 2018, Mumbai.

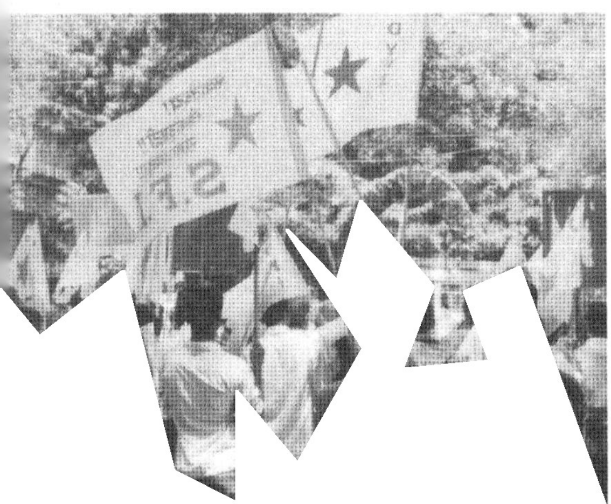

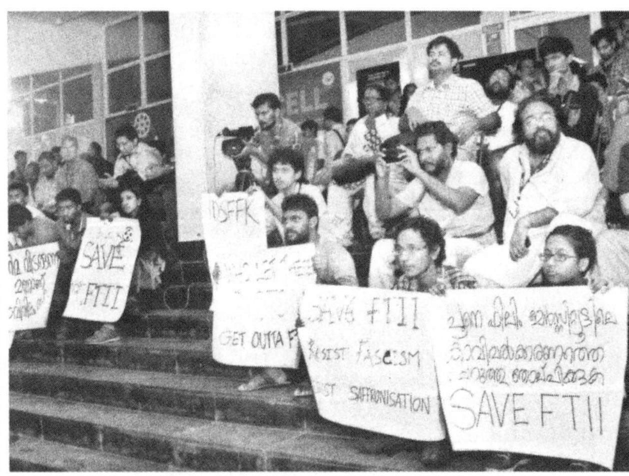

Expansion of political support.
Left: Students Federation of India rally on 20/22 August, 2015.
Right: Potest at the International Documentary and Short Film Festival of Kerala on 28 June 2015.

Students' Federation of India (SFI)

AMU Unit Committee
Aligarh Muslim University
Aligarh, U.P.-202002

Dated 27.08.2015

Dear friends at FTII,

The Students' Federation of India, AMU Unit committee expresses its solidarity with your continued struggle and your spirited resistance. The police action in the FTII campus depicts the intensity of your struggle which forced the state mechanism to resort to such third party arbitration from the police in order to curb the voices of dissent.

The administration by reacting in this way and paving ways so that the students of an educational institute be treated as criminals depicts the complete control of state over the affairs of an institute and poses serious questions over the autonomous structure of the institute. An institute, like that of yours should not be subject to vicious agendas of the Right-wing Government at centre and should be made free as regards the decision making pertaining to affairs of institute is concerned. The mediation should be done between the administration and the students with a mature outlook giving due consideration to the concerns of the students.

The 80+ day strike by the student fraternity of FTII have indeed, served as an inspiration to the youth of entire country to fight for their rights and against oppression which is so rampant in the entire country. We extend our full support to the cause in pursuit of which we have intensified our movement at Aligarh Muslim University Campus in gathering support and solidarity for your cause. We hope that the struggle succeeds.

BHAVYA SUDHIR
(PRESIDENT)

JAVED IKBAL
(SECRETARY)

la Biennale di Venezia

72. Mostra Internazionale d'Arte Cinematografica

To:
Shri. Narendra Modi
The Hon. Prime Minister,
Government of India

Copy to: Shri. Arun Jaitley
Minister of Information and Broadcasting

Venezia, October 1, 2015

Sir,

India, the world's largest democracy has always been to the world a country of stunning cultural and racial diversity. For us, it is a nation representing hope, tolerance and peace, a country of limitless potential as a rapidly growing economic super power, a land with a rich heritage of arts, culture and cinema, where the largest number of films are made. This image and adoration derive from the plurality and ingenuity of your spiritual vision and artistic expressions as well as from your values of tolerance, exemplified by Mahatma Gandhi, a figure uniquely respected around the world.

It is in that light that we sincerely urge you to engage with the students of the Film and Television of India over the ongoing crisis and initiate a dialogue with an open mind. We do feel that the students' concerns are most pertinent and serious and they are waiting to be addressed by your government.

The Film and Television Institute of India, the premier film school of your country, has been invaluable not only to your film industry but also to the cultural sphere of the Indian sub-continent and other Afro-Asian countries whose students have studied there. Many students from Europe and Latin America who have been there cherish fond memories of that Institute. For half a century it has continued to produce film makers who are renowned the world over.

The international community of film makers can't help noticing the dire crisis that FTII is going through. We feel sad that the students of one of the best film schools in the world are struggling to get their legitimate concerns addressed.

We hope that you will be able to engage with the students with an open mind, and be able to arrive at a solution that shows the level of seriousness and commitment you have towards the future of India's cinema and its' cultural stature as a modern nation.

Sincerely,

Alberto Barbera
Director
Venice Film Festival
alberto.barbera@labiennale.org
www.labiennale.org

carrot was dangled, almost as a reflex action. There was nothing on the core issues. And nothing on Chauhan.

Meanwhile more protest festivals were held. The Queer Film Festival took place on the campus on 30 August. Through September and October, letters of support kept pouring in. There was an especially stinging message from Alberto Barbera, Director of the Venice Film Festival, who wrote directly to Narendra Modi asking him to show 'seriousness and commitment ... towards the future of India's cinema and its cultural status as a modern nation'. On the hundredth day of the strike, a second major march was organized in Delhi.

The Third Visitation: 'I have killed ...'

There would nevertheless be one final, profoundly cinematic twist as this particular act closed and another began – one final exit line, by none other than our shadow protagonist, Rajyavardhan Singh Rathore. In late October, soon after the Films Divisions talks came to nought, Aruna Raje called offering to mediate and managed to get a meeting with Rathore. All seven students who had taken part in the Films Division negotiations were there. It became somewhat theatrical as Rathore, apparently anxious about something, had the event video-recorded, perhaps as self-protection. The footage isn't available in the public domain.

Rathore was full of bluster. The carrot was dangled again: he wanted an FTII whose students could send their films to the 'Oscars and to Cannes'. Rathore was faced with a barrage of questions, and even Raje, although there as an interlocutor, began to question him. For all the many letters, the pleas and confessions to all those in authority, Rathore came up with perhaps the final chilling line, which shall be his own epilogue to the role of the state as a *parens patriae*. Turning to one of those present, he said to the group, 'Tell him not to look at me like that. At Kargil I killed men who looked at me.'

In the end, and yet again, Rathore walked away. From the talks, and from our narrative.

To Prateek, the elusive, whispered, forked-tongue approach incessantly evoked longer histories. It gave him, for example, a retrospective way of looking at how, in hindsight, Hewitt might have panned out. In 2011 he had thought they'd won a victory. Now he could see how the authorities had nibbled at the sides of the Nair Report and cherry-picked whatever suited them. 'Lots of new construction, trees [were] being hacked, contracts issued, and the overdetermined mantra, outsource, outsource, outsource. What about what [Nair] said about fees or costs or teachers or how to take teachers?'

The real wonder, as Prateek thinks back, was how – given this shadow-boxing – they had been able to stretch the action of 2015 for so long. 'By mid-August it was clear *ke bahut kuch ho nahi raha hai* [nothing much was happening], but what *was* happening was that students were connecting to something – it was becoming big! Very big and very exciting. And that energy was there.'

As students reconciled to the fact that nothing more could now be done, as they decided to widen their struggle even as they returned to class, the toll proved heavy. Might it have been better to have called it off after the hundredth day? 'The students might have preserved themselves a bit better' had that happened, says Prateek. 'That extra 40 days ... really drained all energy. And then bitterness stepped in, and cynicism.' Once the strike finished, 'something just flipped'.

Thinking back, Vikas sees it as a kind of strange majoritarian idea of change:

> ... a blatant desire to change, change *matlab* change completely, change radically, change with a desire to make money out of everything. Fundamentally, their pursuit is that every f***ing resource should generate revenue. Nothing should lie quiet. Everything, *matlab paani*, land, air, *sab kuch* ... has to eventually serve a larger purpose according to their idea of what that larger purpose is. ...
>
> They are turning everyone into a filmmaker. *Woh karenge kya uska*? Critical insight *kya hai*? *Kuch nahi*. *Sab ko* camera *sikha do,* sound *sikha do,* editing *sikha do, aur unko* filmmaker *banao raton raat.* [What will they do with that? Where is the critical insight? Teach everyone camera, sound, editing, make them filmmakers overnight.] They get the branding.[24]

It was on the evening of Day 138 that a major GBM was finally held and the decision finally taken to return to class – Vikas and Ranjit sat in forlorn solitude. Vikas had wanted the strike to go on. The

-24
Conversation with Vikas Urs, 21 October 2021, Mumbai.

andolan ka josh [revolutionary energy] was still alive for him and he had become 'addicted' to the energy.

—

By then the writing was on the wall. What was needed was a way to find an exit at the same time that its cause got inscribed into a national domain. As it worked out, eight filmmakers announced that they were returning their awards. Meanwhile, on campus, the students announced that they were returning to class.

On 28 October, Day 139, four students – Nachi, Yashaswi, Vikas, Rakesh – sat behind a microphone-studded table. The picture they presented, front and centre, was the big one – that of incipient state fascism. Kalburgi was mentioned, as were the atrocities at Dadri and Sonped (in Faridabad, where children of a Dalit family were burnt alive), and the public threat of violence to Kannada filmmaker

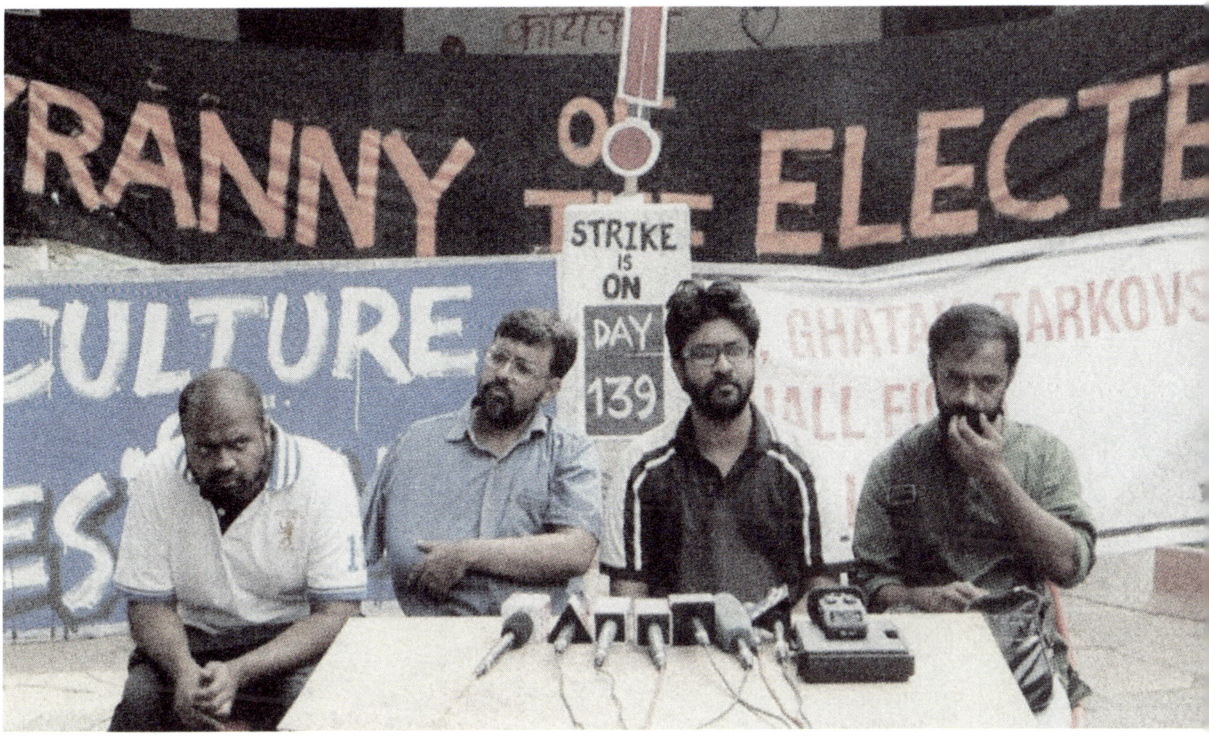

28 October 2015, Day 139: students return to class, but the protest will take other forms. (From left) Nachi, Rakesh, Vikas and Yashaswi.

Chetana Thirthalli after she participated in a rally supporting the eating of beef.

There were three prominent texts behind them. One was *Tyranny of the Elected*; the second, *Culture of Resistance*. Vikas had seen Arun Jaitley the previous evening on television railing against Supreme Court judges and what Jaitley called the 'tyranny of the unelected'. 'Art direction students quickly got it together', says Vikas. 'It stayed for a while before we were asked to bring it down, but that was enough to get it on the national media.'

The third: *John–Ghatak–Tarkovsky/We shall fight, we shall win*.

CHAPTER 9

THE TOTALITARIAN PLEASURE GARDEN

They had hung in there for 139 days. When the strike ended, the solidarities did too, as students, ex-students, supporters and bystanders moved on to different destinations. The FTII, in its ongoing search for relevance, produced yet another vision plan for its future in 2016. Other movements were more complicated, such as the explosion and fragmentation of several keywords of the strike.

The *cinema*, as we see in a small number of examples and stories below, exploded into multiple sequel directions, and with it went the attendant concepts of *filmmaker*, of *publicness* and indeed of *freedom* itself.

Cut-Pasting Freedom: Section 144 and the Pleasure Garden

Ever since it made Goa its permanent home, the International Film Festival of India (or IFFI, India's oldest 'official' film festival) has tried hard to be all things to all people. It markets itself as a kind of eastern Riviera, bringing together art, entertainment and tourism in equal measure. There is plenty of nostalgia for cinema in screenings, exhibitions and lifetime awards for ageing greats. There is a hard-nosed film bazaar where filmmakers look for completion monies, coproduction opportunities and distribution possibilities, where a 'creative' post-celluloid economy thrives. There are numerous watering holes surrounding the festival venues on Panaji's famous Campala Avenue, where glitzy art- and fashion-loving upmarket Bollywood schmoozes with European and American festival representatives. And there are the crowds gathered to see European and Asian art-house 'titles with buzz' doing the festival rounds.

Something else was unique that November of 2015 to IFFI's 46th edition. It was the spectre of young people haunting its venues with a strange and evil aura. All youth, bearded males especially, were being stopped, even those with valid identity cards, their wallets searched, their devices opened. Security personnel were everywhere. Lists were being used to check identity documents.

A major agitation was going on not far from the festival venue, protesting the suspicious death of a Catholic priest.[1]

Whatever its rationale, Section 144 of the Code of Criminal Procedure was in force across all the screening venues of IFFI #46, covering the watering holes, the riverfront and the landscaped walkways of the Kala Akademi. You were not permitted to gather in groups of more than five. You could not perform any public action, could not distribute a leaflet or make a speech.

Soon the only film students left at India's premier film festival were a few solitary and isolated presences on the street. Some were dressed as clowns in full make-up. They gave away free balloons. On Campala Avenue, alongside the Mandovi river, was a small installation, a combination altarpiece and memorial. Famous film stills lay on the ground or were propped up alongside candles, strewn with balloons and rose petals. Covering them was the legend JOHN–GHATAK–TARKOVSKY. People were invited to place flowers in the cinema's memory. Many did.

Since 2010 IFFI has had a small but well-regarded 'Talent Hub', which screens student films from FTII, SRFTI, AJK-MCRC and other film schools. Their students are invited to attend major domestic film festivals, and they are usually granted leave of absence and even a small travel and stay allowance. To show their films there and to see world cinema is part of their education, and student-filmmakers are among the liveliest of its participant-audiences, offering the most vociferous opinions on everything showing.

That year the Talent Hub had been summarily cancelled. The reason, said the organizers, was the festival's 'tight schedule'.[2] Seventeen FTII students were anyway unable to be present, having been charged with various crimes and forbidden to leave Pune. Others who had been scheduled to go suddenly found their travel support withdrawn.[3] Only a small number actually made it there on 20 November, the date on which the inaugural ceremony was to take place amid high security at Goa University's Shyama Prasad Mukherjee stadium. At the inauguration, the chief guest Anil Kapoor quoted Jean-Luc Godard's 'the cinema is truth 24 frames a second' line, and danced to songs from *Ram Lakhan*.[4] Other shades of the Godardian truth were unveiled at varying camera speeds. Laxmikant Parsekar, Chief Minister of Goa, mispronounced

-1

On 7 November, a Roman Catholic priest named Father Bismarck Dias, well known for his radical activism and for drawing attention to scams and controversies in land-intensive projects ranging from a new greenfield airport, a golf course and an electronic city being conceived by the state government, was found mysteriously dead in Panaji. Protests alleging foul play by the police raged across the state around the same time as the Film Festival. See Mayabhushan Nagvenkar, 'Curious case of Father Dias: Beer, ghost-busting, mystery, murder and a dead Goan priest', *Firstpost*, 18 November 2015.

-2

Atikh Rashid, 'Dropped during FTII protests, event showcasing students' films set to return to IFFI this year', *The Indian Express*, 5 September 2018.

-3

Rupali Shukla, 'Fearing protests, FTII refuses to sponsor students for Goa fest', *Times of India*, 9 November 2015.

-4

'Glitz & glamour: IFFI blockbuster opens', *The Goan*, 21 November 2015.

Facing page, top to bottom
The public memorial to the cinema on the banks of the Mandovi; students dress up as clowns outside the main Festival entrance to beat Section 144 (the ban on public assembly).

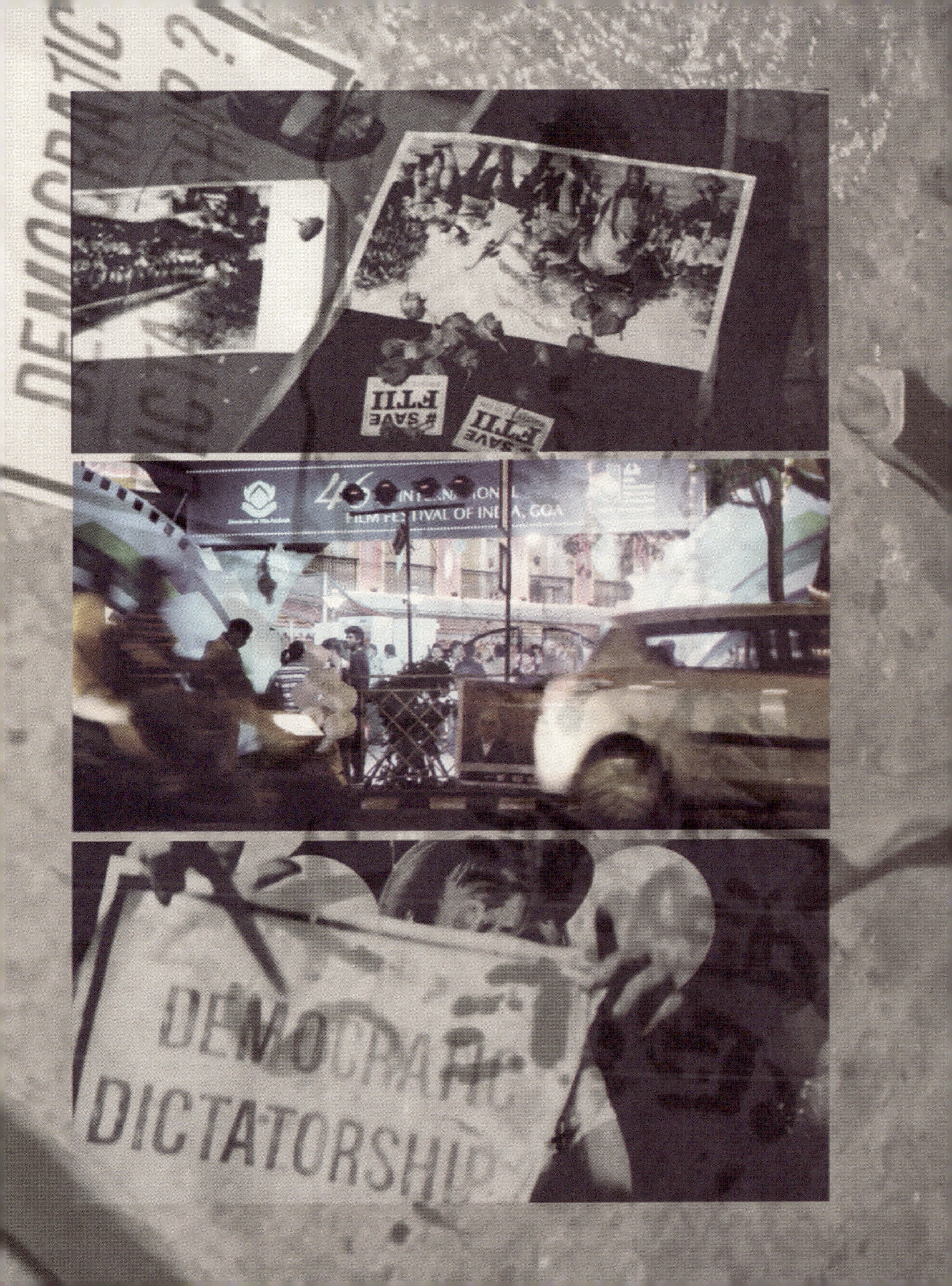

FILM FESTIVAL OF INDIA, GOA
DEMOCRATIC

the names of both Shyam Benegal and Sahir Ludhianvi even as he complained that Goa, host of the event, had made only ten films that year. Ilaiyaraja was given a special award. Clips from early Amitabh Bachchan, Rajnikant and Kamal Haasan films were shown alongside scenes of Shahrukh Khan with Kajol and Salman Khan with Madhuri Dixit. It was when I&B Minister Arun Jaitley rose to speak that cinematic truth took on another, perhaps darker, shade. Two young men sitting on the top tier suddenly got up holding large placards, shouting, '*Jawab do, Jaitley saab, jawab do* [Give us an answer, Mr Jaitley, give us an answer]'.[5]

They were Kislay and Shubham. There was consternation as live television cameras swung round and zoomed to the upper balcony. The comperes, Ayushman Khurana 'dressed in a tuxedo and a pouf' and Aditi Rao Hydari, tried to drown them out by playing IFFI's theme song, even as the security detail rapidly overpowered the two young filmmakers.

—

Kislay and Shubham's arrest made local headlines. Occurring amid heightened tensions in the state, an information blackout on where they had been taken and what had happened to them (their abandoned scooter was found outside the stadium) created a moment of sheer panic and real fear of the worst. Nobody had known in advance what the two had planned – they themselves didn't know until a short while earlier, Kislay says – nor how they had managed to get past the security to pull this off.[6]

It was a long night. The human rights lawyer Albertina Almeida eventually traced them to the Agacaim police station and found out that they had not been hurt. They were however charged, says North Goa SP Umesh Gaonkar, with the non-bailable charges of 'criminal conspiracy, trespassing ... and assaulting government servants on duty'.[7]

Much of what happened next, after they were produced in court and eventually released, reprises parts of the old Vikalp action at MIFF in 2004. Along with the cancelled film package, other recent films by them and several always-present cinematic masterpieces, the students went up Campala Avenue to the Institute Piedad near

-5
Pamela D'Mello, 'Two More FTII Students Hassled in Goa as IFFI Attempts to Prevent Further Protests', *Scroll*, 22 November 2015

-6
Conversation with Kislay, 2 September 2018, Delhi.

-7
'Goa police charge striking FTII students with serious offences', *Goa News*, 21 November 2015.

Mandovi Hotel – around ten minutes away from the IFFI venues. This was technically church property, and so notionally off-limits to the police. Here, 'Retracing Freedom' found a second iteration, with screenings, talks and live events. The Goa administration made a determined attempt to stop even this. When Section 144 didn't work, given that they were in a protected space, they took it to the District Magistrate of North Goa who declared that the event was in violation of the Cinematograph Act, 1952 since they were presumed to be showing uncensored films.

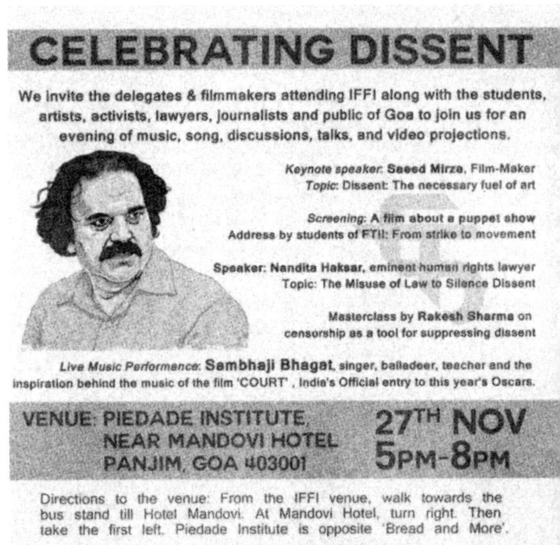

The dissenting festival. Saeed Mirza, Nandita Haksar, Rakesh Sharma and Sambhaji Bhagat at Piedade Institute, close to the IFFI venue.

The event went ahead anyway. Police were present in strength on the first day, but then got so bored with the slow cinema that they dropped the surveillance, only keeping occasional watch from the outside. Saeed Mirza was a constant and major support. R.V. Ramani, Rakesh Sharma and Nandita Haksar were also there to participate and help. Like Bhupesh Gupta Bhavan in Vikalp 2004, the Piedade turned into a combination of assembly, screening venue-cum-rebel film festival and live performance space. The events at 'Retracing Freedom' spooked the IFFI as students testified to their harassment at the festival venue. A second year editing student intern was asked to leave the film bazaar shortly after he was introduced to NFDC Director Nina Lath Gupta.[8] Students everywhere with an FTII connection were having their IDs summarily confiscated, their wallets searched, their devices examined. Copies of *In Defence of Our Present* with statements by twenty-four filmmakers who had surrendered their national awards had been piled up for free distribution. The booklet was meant for festival delegates, but to distribute it at the venue was to break the law.

Both Kislay and Shubham spoke. Kislay gestured towards the 'farce' going on up the road. People at the Inox were, he said, right now watching Jia Zhangke's *Mountains May Depart* and Julia Vargas-Weise's *Sealed Cargo*, even while Section 144 had been enforced outside. Having seen these films, Kislay presumed, people were discussing them. Which meant they were discussing Chinese society, the economic crisis of Greece and Bolivian politics inside a space that was stopping them from seeing Indian films, preventing

-8 Shoumojit Banerjee, 'FTII student branded as "potential threat", made to leave Goa film fest', *The Hindu*, 21 November 2015.

them from receiving local publications, and thus preventing Indian audiences from talking about *India's* social realities.[9]

What this also meant, Kislay appeared to suggest, was that an *Indian* filmmaker in an *Indian* film festival could no longer do what filmmakers usually do on such occasions – namely, show your film and talk about it. Putting on a clown's make-up, performing a street play, distributing balloons and gatecrashing the inaugural to interrupt the Minister was a logical and necessary expansion of a filmmaker's work in today's India.

-9

Quoted from a sequence in Prateek Vats' *Retracing Freedom: Goa* (2015). The film is however unsigned and undated.

-10

Gautam Bhatia, 'Film and Internet Censorship', in *Offend, Shock or Disturb: Free Speech under the Indian Constitution*, New Delhi: Oxford University Press, 2016.

From Abbas to Kislay

Both Kislay's action at that IFFI inauguration and his explication of it at the Piedade evoke a history – of new meanings being accrued to the concept of public order, and the new ways in which they were defining the legal restrictions on free speech. If once upon a time, that of K.A. Abbas' celebrated Supreme Court battle of 1970, restrictions to the *regisseur*'s right had been defined by decency, morality, contempt of court and defamation – against which free speech at least could have a defence – now, Article 19 (2) restrictions on free speech had come to be defined primarily by their threat to the sovereignty and integrity of India and the security of the state, governed by concepts like disaffection, disloyalty and the omnibus threat to public order. Unlike the former, these latter offences – as the North Goa police station took pains to assert – were non-bailable.

The Indian cinema has its own unique law on free speech: Section 5B of the Indian Cinematograph Act, 1952. The Act itself, in contrast to multiple judgments following Hidayatullah on Abbas – on *Tamas*, *Bandit Queen* and *Fire* – makes no mention of the *filmmaker's* right to speech. Its central purpose is to reinvent in post-Independence India what Gautam Bhatia calls the 'heavy-handed British approach ... reflect[ing] a larger worry [a]bout the ... impact that the new medium would have upon the allegedly excitable, irrational, and underdeveloped natives because of its direct appeal to the senses and the way it bypassed "reasoned judgment" for the emotions'.[10]

5B's basic purpose is not to defend the filmmaker. It is to defend the *public* from the *filmmaker's* excesses. Eminent members of the public sit in judgment, in a variation of a trial in a city square, not on a film's content, meaning, desirability or significance, but purely on its 'suitability' for public exhibition. Filmmakers stand before them and receive instructions on how they should have done their work.

In 1970, 5B revealed a bug in the system. 'It appears', Justice Hidayatullah wrote in the Abbas judgment, 'that the draftsman [of the Cinematograph Act] used a copy of the Constitution ... and fell into the error of copying [an] obsolete clause' of Article 19 (2). This obsolete clause was the version that existed before the First Amendment to the Constitution in 1951. A key word – the all-important word 'reasonable' – was thus found missing. Abbas had noticed this erasure, and argued that the slippage was clearly intentional. Hidayatullah, however, was not impressed. This surely couldn't be a big issue. 'The argument that S. 5-B of the Cinematograph Act does not reproduce the full effect of the second clause of Art. 19 need not detain us', he writes. 'The Constitution has to be read first and the section next', and the draftsman's error 'can neither take away nor add to what the Constitution has said on the subject ... it cannot mean that the restrictions can be unreasonable.'[11]

'Reasonable' was not the only word missing in the original Cinematograph Act. Also significant was the pivotal lead phrase of 19 (2), 'Sovereignty and Integrity of India'. This was added to 5B only in 1983. In 1951 the Constitution was itself amended and the word 'reasonable' was added before 'restrictions' – and, more foundationally, the phrase 'undermines the security of, or tends to overthrow, the State' was replaced with the words 'public order'. The original draft had assumed that threats to national security would come from outside the country, says Gautam Bhatia. After 1951, the threats were increasingly seen to be coming from within. 'The citizen's right to freedom of speech ... has been held by some courts to be so comprehensive as not to render a person culpable even if he advocates murder and other crimes of violence', complained the First Amendment, adding that 'in other countries ... freedom of speech and of the press is not regarded as debarring the State from punishing or preventing abuse of this freedom'.[12] It was griping at the government's inability to ban newspapers 'in the interests of public order'.

-11

Supreme Court of India, *K. A. Abbas vs The Union of India & Anr* on 24 September 1970.

-12

Gautam Bhatia, 'Free Speech and Public Order–I: Before the Amendment, and the Idea of Responsibility', *Indian Constitutional Law and Philosophy*, 8 August 2013.

By the time Kislay and Shubham stood up before Arun Jaitley that November, a new state populism had completed a shift – one that Abbas may have argued as having existed in Article 19 (2) itself, and certainly in its cinematic 5B iteration. The shift is one where the classic instruments of censorship – morality, decency, etc. – are entirely placed aside, and public order becomes the sole defining principle for Article 19 (2). In what follows, the entire domain of 'reasonable restriction' moves from being a *justiceable* right, with some due process, into the domain of *preventive detention* with no due process. Seventy years after Justice Fazl Ali expressed his apprehensions in his famous dissenting opinion in 1950 – when Communist leader A.K. Gopalan challenged his detention – that if the First Amendment had its way, 'public order', 'public tranquility', 'security of the State' and 'sedition' would effectively come to mean the same thing, his concerns were graphically in evidence.

By 2015, India's state executive had entirely usurped the concept of 'public' – which, like 'people', had become an abstraction, their 'interest' becoming what the state said it was. Free speech too got pushed out of the criminal justice system and into the domain of prior restraint. Filmmakers were no longer being threatened merely with censorship. The more likely charge was 'threat to public order', and the more likely instrument of censorial choice, a jail term.

As multiple legislations cut-pasted the constitutional provision of Article 19 (2), the distortions took a specific turn. The 'Sovereignty and Integrity of India', absent in the original 5B, rose to become the major virtue to be protected from the dangers of free speech. 'India' became more important than the people who lived in it, its sovereignty and integrity more valuable than that of the increasingly elusive speaker in whose defence the right originally existed, or even the equally elusive public whose interest gave the speaker this right in the first place or who may have actually needed protection from it.

As sister phrases, like 'disloyalty' (in 124A of the IPC, on sedition) and 'disaffection' (Citizenship Act, 1955 and of course the dreaded UAPA), were added, the Censor Board was both expanded and superseded by multiple new instruments. The growing distortions to the original constitutional provision – in (to take only two recent examples) the Information Technology Act, 2000, and the Personal Data Protection Bill, 2019 – lead to a major question as to whether Hidayatullah's confidence in the Constitution's emphasis on 'reasonableness' to remain the ruling principle can any longer be sustained.[13]

-13 Gautam Bhatia, 'The Striking Down of Section 66A: How Indian Free Speech Jurisprudence Found its Soul Again', *Indian Constitutional Law and Philosophy*, 26 March 2015.

A couple of years later, Kislay produced a graphic illustration of this shift of freedom in his first feature, *Aise Hee* (2019). The absent narrative centre is in full display in its protagonist, an old woman who simply wants to exist, for whatever is left of her life, in the ways she has known or now wants to know. She has, she thinks, a reasonably simple concept of freedom. It soon proves to be not so simple as she starts becoming a threat to her family, to the community, and even to the political character of her neighbourhood. As her benign freedom begins to threaten various fragile familial and social arrangements, a shift takes place in the very concept. Her assertion of her free will and her right to choose what she can and cannot do at home and on the street, whom she is permitted to meet and talk to, is gradually replaced by her primary responsibility of maintaining the veneer of public order. She doesn't accept this.

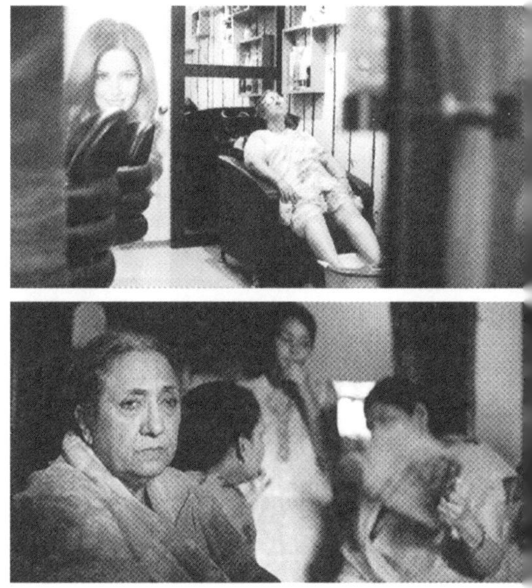

Kislay's 'absent' narrative protagonist in **Aise Hee** (2019).

Her refusal to surrender her right of subjective choice before a social good defined by others causes a crisis that, in a strange way, chronicles the shift in how Article 19 (2) is now applied – and how it was applied that day in Goa when Kislay and Shubham stood up and threatened public order and, with it, the Indian nation's sovereignty and integrity.

A 'Corporate–Military' Approach

Police returned to the campus on 10 March 2016. Seven months after the 2015 *gherao* and arrests, another eighteen names were added to the seventeen already chargesheeted. This meant that now thirty-five of FTII's students – their best and brightest, many already making international reputations in prestigious festivals that the FTII's official annual report of 2016–17 proudly listed among its achievements of the year – were formally charged with criminal offences and were out on bail with their travel restricted, the legal harassment in full flow.

That May, a mysterious parcel was delivered at the campus gate. It came, officials said, by ordinary mail addressed to the Director. Its contents were announced to be a 'bomb-like substance', a live detonator, and a letter threatening the FTII with dire consequences if, of all things, JNUSU president Kanhaiya Kumar did not stop his activities.[14] The perpetrators were never found.

The incident, whatever its credibility, added to the incipient tension growing on the campus.[15] Although FTII's intense political links of mid-2015 with the city of Pune had by now more or less dried up, there remained some connection between this internal tension, the response of the authorities, and what the city itself was going through in 2016 and 2017.

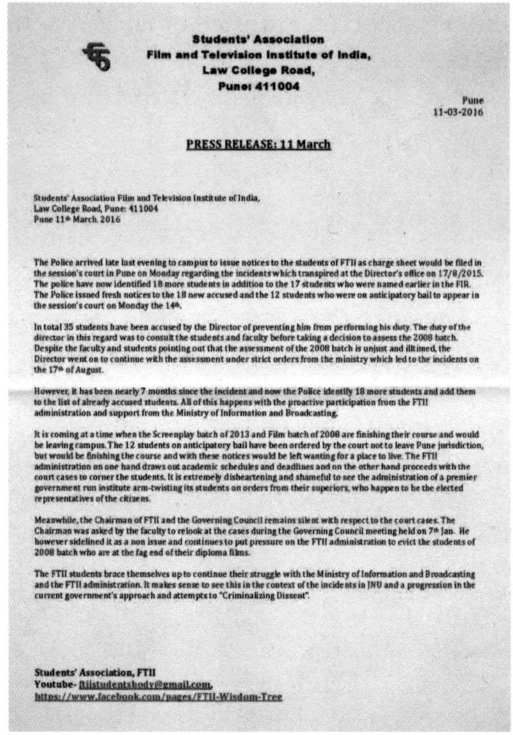
Students' Association
Film and Television Institute of India,
Law College Road,
Pune: 411004

Pune
11-03-2016

PRESS RELEASE: 11 March

Students' Association Film and Television Institute of India,
Law College Road, Pune: 411004
Pune 11th March. 2016

The Police arrived late last evening to campus to issue notices to the students of FTII as charge sheet would be filed in the session's court in Pune on Monday regarding the incidents which transpired at the Director's office on 17/8/2015. The police have now identified 18 more students in addition to the 17 students who were named earlier in the FIR. The Police issued fresh notices to the 18 new accused and the 12 students who were on anticipatory bail to appear in the session's court on Monday the 14th.

In total 35 students have been accused by the Director of preventing him from performing his duty. The duty of the director in this regard was to consult the students and faculty before taking a decision to assess the 2008 batch. Despite the faculty and students pointing out that the assessment of the 2008 batch is unjust and illtimed, the Director went on to continue with the assessment under strict orders from the ministry which led to the incidents on the 17th of August.

However, it has been nearly 7 months since the incident and now the Police identify 18 more students and add them to the list of already accused students. All of this happens with the proactive participation from the FTII administration and support from the Ministry of Information and Broadcasting.

It is coming at a time when the Screenplay batch of 2013 and Film batch of 2008 are finishing their course and would be leaving campus. The 12 students on anticipatory bail have been ordered by the court not to leave Pune jurisdiction, but would be finishing the course and with these notices would be left wanting for a place to live. The FTII administration on one hand draws out academic schedules and deadlines and on the other hand proceeds with the court cases to corner the students. It is extremely disheartening and shameful to see the administration of a premier government run institute arm-twisting its students on orders from their superiors, who happen to be the elected representatives of the citizens.

Meanwhile, the Chairman of FTII and the Governing Council remains silent with respect to the court cases. The Chairman was asked by the faculty to relook at the cases during the Governing Council meeting held on 7th Jan. He however sidelined it as a non issue and continues to put pressure on the FTII administration to evict the students of 2008 batch who are at the fag end of their diploma films.

The FTII students brace themselves up to continue their struggle with the Ministry of Information and Broadcasting and the FTII administration. It makes sense to see this in the context of the incidents in JNU and a progression in the current government's approach and attempts to "Criminalizing Dissent".

Students' Association, FTII
Youtube- ftiistudentsbody@gmail.com,
https://www.facebook.com/pages/FTII-Wisdom-Tree

Police return with chargesheets. Students' Association press release, March 2016.

Sanatan Sanstha, the organization responsible for the 2013 killing of Narendra Dabholkar, had since then spread its wings across much of western Maharashtra and Goa. Numerous other organizations had also sprouted, and a distinct, visible alternative to official state-Hindutva appeared to be growing through multiple networks in western Maharashtra and coastal Karnataka.

—

On 1 June, the 74th meeting of FTII's Academic Council took place with television producer B.P. Singh as chair. It was a strange event. It began by noting that one of the reasons for the growing 'ad-hocism' on campus was the absence of 'basic statutes', and so it was repeated in words of one syllable what these statutes were. The Director was, it was unambiguously reasserted, the Executive Head. The Deans, Proctor and Faculty reported to him. Students were required to be at all times 'in good standing' – no effort was made to hide the clear

-14 'Letter threatening JNU's Kanhaiya triggers bomb scare at FTII campus', *Hindustan Times*, 8 May 2016.

-15 'Full-fledged security system with everything, armed police, armed soldiers, CCTVs, lights everywhere … like this one military camp.' The new Director, Bhupendra Kainthola, 'personally would agree or disagree on the film that would be screened in the main theatre or an invited filmmaker who would come'. Conversation with Vikas Urs, 23 October 2021, Mumbai.

threat in those words. The meeting further adjudged that the revised syllabus introduced just before the 2015 strike was 'not ... doable'. 'Given the recent events at the FTII and subsequent spotlight ... on its activities, it was incumbent on the faculty to come up with a curriculum that would conclude within three academic years.' It was also decided that 'in the interests of smoother workflow and in keeping with the current practices in the industry ... all exercises [would be henceforth moved] to a digital platform'.

Then B.P. Singh stood up and made a powerpoint presentation of what he called a brand-new 'Vision Document' for the FTII. The very first slide changed the name and even the character of the place. It would no longer be dedicated to film, or indeed even to television – it should instead be reinvented as a 'Digital Media University'. This university should offer some twenty-five disciplines, ranging from the familiar ones of Direction, Cinematography, Editing, Sound and Acting, to new courses in Broadcast Journalism and Advertising, and even entirely new areas like 'Make up and Hair Styling', 'Voicing and Dubbing' and 'Video Games'. All of these would be housed within a School for Cinema, Television and Audio, which would oversee eight other Schools ranging from Media Management to Advertising to Visual Design. As early as the following year, he wanted to launch a Media Business Management and Administration programme, alongside courses in music composing and screenwriting. They would be credit-based, and would culminate in the award of a Master's degree in addition to the post-graduate diploma that was on offer.

In part this was a loose laundry-list of industry fantasies, in part an assemblage of vanilla media and communication syllabi taken off the internet. But it was more than all that, with its classy pleasure garden feel of verdant totalitarianism set amidst a fenced-in and policed perimeter. It also had an intense feeling of *déjà vu,* its ambition an exhaustingly familiar remix of earlier FTII classics – a mash-up, you could say, of Agashe-plus and Hewitt-extra. Given that the original cause for those earlier debacles still remained – namely, the infrastructural problems that the place had seen since at least the early 2000s – it was possible to predict where this would go.

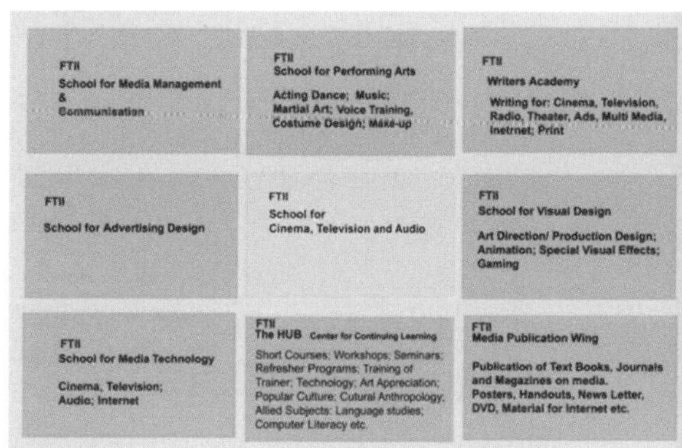

June 2016: Academic Council Chairman B.P. Singh's powerpoint presentation outlining the new vision for restructuring FTII into a 'School of Cinema, Television and Audio' and a 'Digital Media University'.

Times *had* changed, however. For all its yesterday-once-more feel, new issues were brewing as the old privatization mantra – the dominant charge in the Agashe era – had mutated.

Robin and the Keys to the Classroom Theatre

Robin Joy was on a train from Kerala to Pune when he heard of Gajendra Chauhan's appointment. He was to assist on a film, a short four- or five-day shoot in and around the city. Although it was an independent production, some students were informally involved and he planned to stay on the campus. That film never happened. What *did* happen was that he found himself on campus and plumb in the middle of the events of June 2015. Robin stayed on for a month. He thus saw the celebratory melee of June and July, took part in the intense debates and the expanded cinema-effect of the moment.

By now Robin had become an old hand at this, having developed, long before he formally enrolled, an uncanny *Forrest Gump*-like ability to be at FTII whenever momentous events occured. He had also, for example, been among those present at the screening of *Jai Bhim Comrade* in August 2013, having arrived, again coincidentally, to informally assist on a student diploma.[16]

Robin had been a cinephile from high school. He had experimented with a DV-Cam, been in a theatre group named Natyashastra outside Palakkad, acted in amateur theatre and film, been 'floored' by *Aguirre, The Wrath of God*, and knew his Godard – had, in short, done the route. Although he had an engineering degree, the cinema beckoned. He had wanted to apply to the FTII since 2013, but it was only when he finally did so in 2016 that he saw film in its expanded avatar, saw what it now took to call yourself a filmmaker. He would also see, first hand, the transition of authorship on campus into the management of public order.

Although he had seen some of the strike for himself, what Robin and his batch experienced was its grim aftermath – a year after it was supposedly over. His story begins in August 2016, on the anniversary of 'Retracing Freedom'. It was his second semester (the Syllabus Review Committee had imposed the CBCS, or choice-based credit system, that May), and his batch had had a few skirmishes with authority, including one action of supporting a member of the

-16
Conversation with Robin Joy, 16 December 2018, Pune.

cleaning staff who they felt had been unfairly terminated. On Independence Day they held their sequel event. Along with classics that 'celebrated dissent', this time they also showed several of the WisdomTree uploads and other strike films made by students and others over the past year.

Their screenathon took place at the famous old Classroom Theatre, or CRT, where the earlier version too had happened. A relic of the Prabhat days, the CRT is central to all of FTII's institutional pedagogy and, just as importantly, has historically been open for screenings, often selected by students (who have their own screening committee), that go on into the night.

The fallout occurred shortly after. Initially there were murmurings – along the lines of 'You have come here to learn about film, what's all this got to do with it?' – followed by the withdrawal of a previously simple system of collecting the key to the CRT from the security detail. It was symbolically a significant little gesture, but it snapped an important historical link.

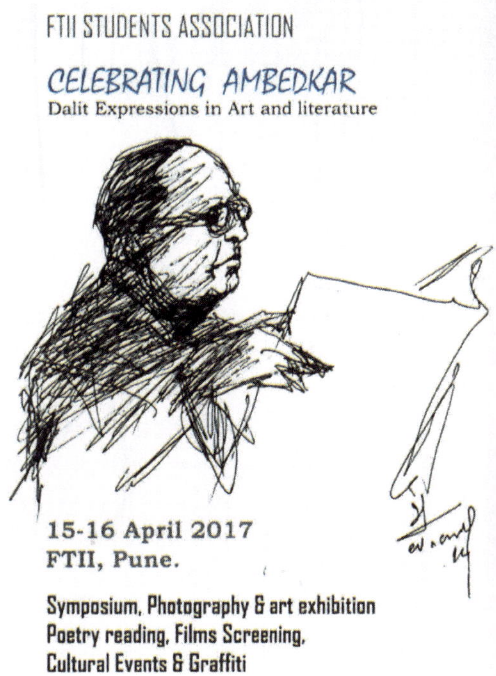

Celebrating Ambedkar festival poster at the Classroom Theatre, April 2017,

Permissions became harder for everything. An invitation to the ska band Delhi Sultanate fell through over permission to use electricity supply. In February 2017, the Students' Association was officially informed that its representatives would from now on no longer sit in the Academic Council's discussions 'pertaining to issues such as academics, syllabus, discipline, fee structure, staff and faculties and administration'.[17]

That April, they planned to commemorate Ambedkar Jayanti – an event celebrated on campus usually with a blood donation drive. To make sure everything went fine, they covered every permission loophole. They applied for clearance weeks earlier. Various names were suggested, and official clearance was obtained after some negotiation for inviting the photographer Sudharak Olwe and the filmmaker Nagaraj Manjule. A two-day symposium and screening programme was planned that they called 'Celebrating Ambedkar: Dalit Expressions in Art and Literature' – because government policy apparently forbade the use of the word 'Dalit' in the main title.

The CRT was booked for 15 and 16 April. A few days before,

17 Conversation with Robin Joy, 16 December 2018, Pune.

they were suddenly told to compress their two-day event into an hour; but they ignored the order and went ahead with the original plan. Somnath Waghmare's *The Battle of Bhima Koregaon* and Renjith Kuzhur's *18 feet* were among the films screened. Olwe spoke at length. That night he stayed over on campus and the intense discussion went on.

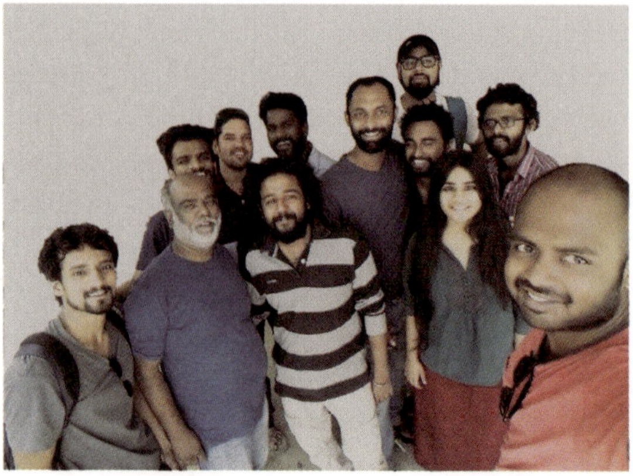

Celebrating Ambedkar. Sudharak Olwe with Robin, Prachee, Nachi and other students.

The next week students were served formal notices for having organized an event without permission. That, says Robin, wasn't true, but his point was rather different – they had self-evidently held a debate in the CRT that was *meant* for such things. Events such as theirs *needed* to be organized as part of their curriculum. They were integral to how filmmakers were formed.

Shortly after, the hallowed history of access to the CRT was formally terminated. Night screenings were prohibited and a new law instituted by which 'special permission' was required from 'the Dean, the Director, the Registrar and the Security, to watch a movie', says Robin, with 'the name of the film, the synopsis, everything'.[18]

Six months after 'Celebrating Ambedkar', Robin, now the president of the Students' Association, wrote a letter to Chauhan's replacement, Anupam Kher.[19] He pointed to the numerous courses on offer – just one example being a 'Short Course in Fiction Writing for Television', run for twenty days for a fee of Rs 20,000 – even as severe infrastructure shortages remained.

Robin had discovered that it was the Seventh Pay Commission's Performance-Related Incentive Schemes, offering incentives on the condition that government departments raise some portion of their income from commercial ventures, that were driving these expensive short-term courses at FTII, often at the cost of its core programmes. More complicatedly, several of the faculty and staff implementing these fund-raising courses had been hired on short-term contracts or even as casual labour, which disqualified them from the very benefits they were accruing to the institution. A related issue was the rampant outsourcing of both equipment and labour.

Meanwhile, the punishing mandatory twelve-hour shifts were placing 'exhausting and inhuman expectations on light men,

-18

Ankur Pathak, 'How the BJP Is Using Censorship and Surveillance to Destroy FTII', *Huffpost*, 18 September 2018.

-19

'An Open Letter from FTII Students to Anupam Kher', *The Wire*, 12 October 2017.

carpenters, painters, make-up artists and actors', wrote Robin to Kher. The unseemly speed with which courses were being completed negated their basic academic and pedagogic purpose. Practicals were being either cut down or cut out entirely. Both the length and shooting ratios of diploma films had been reduced. Faculty was in short supply, overworked and on contract, in 'constant fear of being sacked ... if they [didn't] follow the administration'. Students were being forced to sign 'undertakings to finish their courses on time'.

Prachee, the 'Chilling Effect'

In December 2015, at the 4th Mumbai Shorts International Film Festival (MSIFF), Adwaita Das presented her student film, *Doctor Mandela Kaise Pagal Hua*, completed earlier in the year. The film is made in high-absurdist mode, adapting Grant Morrison's graphic novel, *Arkham Asylum: A Serious House on Serious Earth*, but it asserts a claim that it is 'based on true events and real people'.

It has a mental asylum peopled by lunatics who clearly resemble – and were played by – students. They are being oppressed and controlled by a rampantly corrupt and sadistic nexus of medical authority and the police. Incidents of violence occur and even a rape is shown, depicted entirely through stylized performance. Into this morass enters a 'Doctor Mandela', who is hounded, driven insane by the authorities and eventually framed for everything that's wrong. His descent is shown through a series of song picturizations as inmates dance to Hindi song hits.

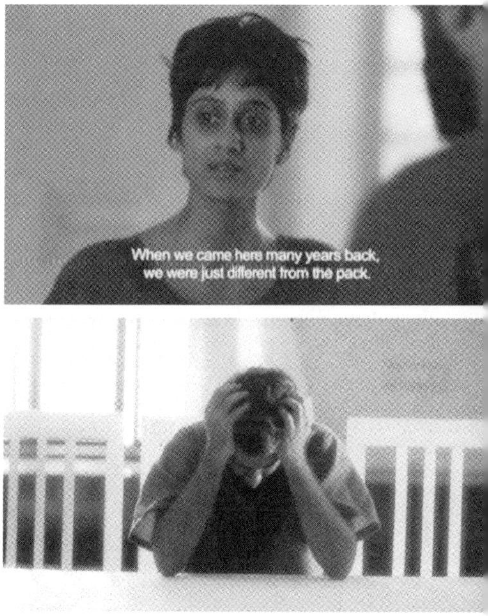

Inside the mental asylum. Adwaita Das' **Doctor Mandela Kaise Pagal Hua** (2015).

This was the film for which Adwaita Das stood up to receive a best editing award at the 4th MSIFF. It was to be presented to her by Assamese editor–filmmaker Nilanjan Dutta – ex-student of FTII, participant in the 2000 strike and now FTII faculty member. As Das went up to the stage, she placed her mobile phone so as to record her speech.

On the stage, lit by the projector's beam, she publicly accused Dutta of having done something to her that formed a part of the very film for which she was now being awarded. 'This is my story of FTII', she says in the video of her speech that she later put on YouTube; it is the story of 'all those who have seen it and what happens in that film'. There is 'also a sexual harassment case in it'.

> And here I am standing with Nilanjan Dutta, who was the person who told me and a batchmate to sexually manipulate people so that they can come to the ragging session, and to please sexually take favours. It has been a long time, it has been seven years and I have really tried to put it behind me. I needed to speak up today and I would love to hear it from you [pointing at Dutta] that you would not do this again to any student, anymore ever again.

(Adwaita Das had, in the original incident of 2008, accused Dutta of being drunk and, using the excuse of the controversial *satsang* or informal ragging system, of speaking in explicit language about Nagisa Oshima's *In the Realm of the Senses*, telling her what she needed to do to batchmates to better understand the film.)

Dutta appears amused. 'It's interesting', he says judicially, 'that you opened up.' He reminds her that he is 'still a faculty member at FTII'. And he blames the entire 'misunderstanding' on the cinema. 'When you teach cinema,' he says, 'unfortunately there's an element of sexuality in it which is even what we are talking about in cinema.'

Adwaita Das vehemently shakes her head, turns to the audience and asks if he should be allowed to use the cinema as an excuse 'to get away with this'.[20]

Six months after Adwaita Das' startling public statement at MSIFF, in August 2016, Prachee Bajania joined FTII. Prachee had previously studied at the National Institute of Design, Ahmedabad and worked at the Srishti School of Design in Bangalore. Both those places had a vastly larger female population, and she was now concerned about FTII's notoriously skewed gender ratio both at the student and the faculty level. She had however been reassured by female ex-students, told not to worry too much and take things as they come.

It appeared to her – and this was a feeling not uncommon to women who are often in a minority of one or two in a batch of ten or more – that she had, almost from the moment she entered the place, been elected to carry the 'gender' burden. Initially, this was not personal. It affected all women equally, however they chose to respond. This would soon change.

-20 *The Video* (2015) by Adwaita Das.

Nilanjan Dutta had left (or had been asked to leave) the FTII in 2009, soon after the incident to which Adwaita Das referred, but had rejoined in 2013, to the consternation of many. By 2016, when Prachee entered the programme, he had become Academic Coordinator, and there existed several new complaints against him with no evidence of any official action. That October, the FTII Students' Forum wrote a public letter protesting this inaction, copied to the Information and Broadcasting Ministry, the Social Justice, Women's Welfare and other Ministries.[21]

A year later, when an Internal Complaints Committee was finally formed, on 27 November 2017, twenty-seven female students, comprising the bulk of the female student contingent on campus, signed a joint letter. Despite two formal rounds of complaints against Dutta, one in 2009 and a second in 2014 when Shabnam Sukhdev headed the Gender Sensitization Committee, there existed no paper trail, no evidence of this history for the ICC to consider. The entire past record had been, the students' letter claimed, effectively erased.

Things soon turned more personal when Prachee faced a production crisis with her dialogue exercise in 2017, the short film *Vacchat*. She had had a falling out with her sound recordist and designer (and batchmate). Such occurrences are not uncommon when 'teams' are formed among batches, and there are well-worn protocols to deal with them where the teams are either reconfigured and the assignment handed to another student or, if necessary, taken over by a faculty member. Prachee sought to solve the problem, she says, with the knowledge of all concerned and only to save time, by using friendly outside help – again not uncommon (as the interim Nair Committee pointed out). She did however eventually agree to use the designated recordist's work, since he too would be assessed for it, however unsatisfactory it was to her. Some of this spoke to authorial filmmaking practices and would link to an old problem of how conventions that defined the filmmaker's role rubbed up against institutional protocols.

What tipped it over and sent it spinning out of control was a second crisis Prachee faced, this time specifically gender-related and specifically personal. This was a straight allegation of sexual harassment by a batchmate, but it took a new turn at a location shoot in Aurangabad in 2018 while she was making her documentary *Makhfi*. Once again Prachee encountered a situation that was not uncommon on campus, one she was expected – even

-21 Priyanka Dasgupta, 'FTII students' forum points at institute's dubious stance towards sexual harassment complaints', *Times of India*, 4 October 2016.

by several fellow students – to quietly tolerate. When she chose not to do so and formally complained, an internal Inquiry Committee held under the Sexual Harassment of Women at the Workplace Act of 2013 eventually found her harasser guilty.

A few days later, however, on 2 August, the FTII issued two sets of formal notices on the earlier sound issue. One was to the errant recordist who was given a 'stern warning' for having 'breached the trust by taking a sound session out of the department without the permission of the Sound Department authority'.[22] The second was to Prachee. She was accused of an 'unsuccessful, unethical attempt' to 'replace the sound mix by an unauthorized sound work'. In an astonishingly harsh punishment clearly exceeding the alleged crime, she was to be 'expelled', allowed to make, instead of her diploma film, only a 'ten minute film' with a team 'comprising only staff' and no students. None of her films, she was told, would be allowed to be entered into film festivals. If they were sent, they should only go to festivals 'where award of the [film] director is not involved'.[23]

—

'It's not much of a difference, interestingly, between ... national politics and what is happening in FTII', Robin muses in late 2018.[24] He speaks of the hyper-centralization of the 'statutes'. 'The Director is the only lord of the place.' 'Everything comes from there. No power to Dean. No power to HODs.'

Which increasingly meant that 'anything can happen at any moment'. Prachee discovered this when the FTII Director Bhupendra Kainthola and Chairman Anupam Kher revealed her name to the media against all protocol, Kainthola even claiming, unbelievably, that he was only retaliating against a Facebook post in which she had mentioned him.[25] As the Dean wrote to her a day after the formal expulsion letter, 'in FTII, for everything Director is the final authority, please write to him'.

Both Prachee and Robin were still learning the slow art of what India's courts would call the 'chilling effect' of the law and permanent threat, when, in December 2016, seven months after the alleged mail bomb was received, a full detail of some forty members of the elite Maharashtra State Security Corporation – a

-22

Order signed by Dean Films, dated 2 August 2018. Copy with author.

-23

Order signed by Dean Films, dated 2 August 2018, with the Enquiry Committee's report on 'anomalies in Dialogue Exercise of Prachee Bajania'. Copy with author.

-24

Conversation with Robin Joy, 16 December 2018, Pune.

-25

Kainthola is quoted as saying this in his defence in a press statement, and had mentioned the name of the student in it. Speaking to the *Times of India* earlier, he said he had done this because the student had mentioned his name on her Facebook profile, and he was only retaliating. 'Women Against Sexual Harassment (WASH) writes to Maneka Gandhi against director Bhupendra Kainthola', *Fenil and Bollywood*, 29 October 2018.

professional security force with access to arms – was deployed on the campus.[26] 'The entire system got updated to a central security system', Koel Sen recalls. 'So, all those uniformed guards which are the Delhi kind of guards ... with those guns and things walking inside the campus till Shantaram Pond where we used to just chill. Now we couldn't do that.'[27]

—

Over these two years, Pune too was transformed. Fringe militancy swept across western Maharashtra, Goa and coastal Karnataka. 'This was the part of Maharashtra which the RSS could not penetrate for a long time', writes Sanghamitra Prabal while discussing the Sanatan Sanstha,[28] perhaps the most visible of numerous organizations set up, often by former RSS members, with aggressively terrorist agendas.

Prominent among these were the Shiv Pratishthan Hindustan, originally started in Sangli in 1984 by an ex-RSS member named Manohar alias Sambhaji Bhide, and the Hindu Ekta Aghadi, founded more recently, in 2007, by a former BJP Corporator in Pune named Milind Ekbote, after he lost the civic election that year.[29] Ekbote had developed a track record of rioting, trespassing and criminal intimidation, and had been convicted five times while still a Corporator.

By the second decade this movement had spread to coastal Karnataka, so that in June 2017, when the Hindu Janajagruti Samiti (founded in 2002 by a psychiatrist named Jayant Balaji Athavale) convened a conclave in the Sanatan Sanstha's headquarters in Goa to work towards a Hindu Rashtra by 2023, no less than 150 mostly new organizations were present, despite the BJP itself and its affiliated Sangh Parivar outfits staying away.[30]

On 5 September, the journalist Gauri Lankesh was assassinated in Bangalore. Her killing, like that of Dabholkar and Communist leader Govind Pansare, was directly ascribed to this burgeoning coastal threat of 'Hindu terror'. Two weeks later, in a related development on 21 September, senior civil society representatives including retired judges and police officers met in Bombay's Ambedkar Bhavan to discuss the alarming situation in Maharashtra. It was, says the lawyer Nihalsing Rathod, whose

-26 Anuraag Bende, 'FTII guns for more security', *Pune Mirror, Times of India*, 17 December 2016.

-27 Conversation with Koel Sen on Zoom, 20 July 2016.

-28 Sanghamitra Prabal, 'Sanatan Sanstha and its Hindutva Designs', *Economic and Political Weekly*, vol. LIII, no. 41, 23 October 2018, p. 19.

-29 Anand Teltumbde, 'On the Urban Maoists', *Economic and Political Weekly*, vol. 53, no. 26–27, 30 June 2018.

-30 Naresh Kamat, '150 Hindu outfits to meet in Goa to discuss "Hindu Rashtra" by 2023, BJP, RSS to stay away', *Hindustan Times*, 11 June 2017.

report in *The Leaflet* offers the most detailed report of the events to follow, 'everyone's opinion that some steps had to be taken to ease out the tension between communities', and it was suggested that a 'public programme ... be organized' in Pune as a reply and perhaps a show of strength.[31]

The coming bicentenary of the Bhima Koregaon battle was agreed as a suitable occasion. Meetings were held, hosted by retired Justices P.B. Sawant and B.G. Kolse-Patil, plans were firmed up to hold an 'Elgar Parishad' – a kind of public 'call' – on 31 December. A Pune Coordination Committee was formed with Justice Sawant as its chair, that would be run with contributions of Rs 3,000 from each of 260 social organizations working in and around the city. It was planned to invite Jignesh Mevani, Radhika Vemula, Prakash Ambedkar and others, and to ask the Kabir Kala Manch to perform. On 15 October, a Facebook page was started in the name of the Bhima Koregaon Shourya Din Prerna Abhiyan, and – given that the plan was to overthrow the 'new Peshwai', it was decided that the programme would be held at the Shaniwar Wada ground 'as a bitter-sweet gesture of historical irony'.

The event itself occurred on 31 December 2017 between 2 p.m. and 10 p.m. It went peacefully and, given what was to follow, detailed descriptions have been written up of what took place, the songs sung, the speeches given.

The following morning the Bhima Koregaon site was attacked, with all the hallmarks of impunity – in the sense in which Anand Teltumbde uses the term. The perpetrators were not arrested even though they made no attempt to hide either their identity, which was listed in the first of the two FIRs registered, or their intentions. There were counter-FIRs, 'stock witnesses', the usual tricks of the trade.[32] A *bandh* was declared, but things soon more or less returned to normal. Except that they didn't.

What next happened was a statewide police crackdown that blamed the Parishad organizers for having incited the riots. They first went after individuals who had spoken, or sung, or even merely been present at the Parishad itself, accusing *them* of having instigated the violence. They then followed up with an ever-widening list of people, activists, academics and lawyers of diverse ideological affiliations, first in Maharashtra and then across the country. They

-31

Nihalsing B. Rathod, 'One year of Bhima-Koregaon case: Part II – Why Elgar Parishad spooked Sambhaji Bhide and Milind Ekbote, the alleged architects of January 1, 2018 anti-Dalit violence', *The Leaflet*, 6 January 2019.

-32

Supreme Court of India, *Romila Thapar vs Union of India* on 28 September 2018.

claimed to possess, usually on various hard disks, laptops and other devices, evidence that had characteristics similar to what Justice Nariman, in the 2015 Shreya Singhal judgment, had described as 'data without content'.

The 2018 judgment on the writ petition filed by Romila Thapar and other noted academics in the Supreme Court mentioned multiple 'leaked documents' by the police making multiple and ever-more bizarre accusations.[33] They had, the police said, unearthed evidence of 'senior comrades proposing concrete steps to end the Modi-era by planning a Rajiv Gandhi-style incident to assassinate the Prime Minister'. They claimed to have found evidence that 'selection and purchase of arms' was going on, that the 'rates of such arms' were being worked out, and the 'routes and ways of smuggling such arms into India for its onward distribution amongst the cadres' were being designed. They said they had evidence of 'training', including how to lay 'booby traps and directional mines'. All of this was in the nature of digital evidence on 'computers/laptops/pen drives/memory cards', which showed that the arrested were 'planning and prepar[ing] ... large scale violence and destruction of property, resulting into chaos in the society'. 'Each of them', said the counter-affidavit, 'is part of a well thought out criminal conspiracy and had supported the event arranged at Pune by the Elgar Parishad through a frontal organization called Kabir Kala Manch.' There was an 'ongoing sinister design of ... criminal offences having the potential of destabilizing the society'.

In his dissenting judgment, Justice Chandrachud questioned the basic 'fairness of the manner in which the police have approached this investigation'.[34] He pointed to how, within a few hours of the Supreme Court issuing notices to the state of Maharashtra and to the others impleaded as respondents to the proceedings, a press conference had been held by the Joint Commissioner of Police proclaiming that the Pune police 'had more than sufficient evidence against the five individuals', despite the fact that a 'transit remand [had been] stayed by this Court while ordering them to be placed under house arrest'. Chandrachud spoke of the 'disconcerting behaviour' of the Joint Commissioner in this 'oblique manner [of responding] to the interim order of this Court by recourse to the electronic media'.

-33
Ibid.

-34
Justice D.Y. Chandrachud's dissenting judgment, No. 22, in ibid.

A major reason for the violence, the police alleged, was an inflammatory speech that Sudhir Dhawale was said to have given. That speech, '*Jab julum ho to bagawat honi chahiye shahar mein* [When tyranny happens, there has to be rebellion in the city]', has been widely cited and was reproduced in the judgment in its entirety, in particular the words, '*Ye nayi Peshwai ko hamko shamshan ghat mein, kabrastaan mein dafnana hai* [This new Peshwai has to be buried, cremated].' The *nayi Peshwai* was of course an explicit reference to incipient militant brahminism, but the specific lines – which the police said incited a mob to attack the site – turned out to be, according to a Supreme Court submission, from Brecht's *The Good Person of Szechwan*. (A few minutes of digging reveals their source as the lines in the play that the prostitute Shen Teh says to the poor water-seller after the influential local barber smashes his arm: 'What a city this is, what people you are! When an injustice is done in a city, there must be an uproar/It would be better for the city/to perish in flames before the night falls.'[35])

-35

Quoted from Bertolt Brecht, *The Good Person of Szechwan*, in *Collected Plays*, Volume 6, edited by Ralph Mannheim and John Willett, New York: Vintage Books Edition/ Random House, 1976, p. 43.

History of a Political Vanguard

Dhawale's rhetorical insertion of Brecht into the heart of a confrontation that has defined an ethical and legal watershed moment for India is befuddling and confusing – but it also reveals an unusual genealogy for India's avant-garde arts, especially as it played out in the Bombay of the late 1990s and changed yet again in 2017. Dhawale is of course known for the Vidrohi Sanskritik Chalwal, started after his landmark convening of the rebel literary conference in 1999 in Dharavi, and for the journal *Vidrohi* (launched in 2002). That conference had a specific political target, namely, the official state literary *sammelan* going on at Shivaji Park, chaired by a popular romantic poet named Vasant Bapat and dominated by the BJP–Shiv Sena. Vidrohi was a direct challenge, then, to the effete modernisms that dominated a largely brahminical literary establishment – marking its battle lines with the presence of Baburao Bagul, the *éminence grise* of Dalit writing in Marathi, as chair of their rebel event.

To such a rebel view, Brecht may well have appeared as a figure favoured in the 1980s by the art-house Chhabildas Theatre movement, a European fashion to be mocked rather than quoted.

(More than Dhawale it was *Vidrohi*'s co-editor Vira Sathidar, known for his performance of the radical folk singer Narayan Kamble in Chaitanya Tamhane's 2014 film *Court*, who had a direct theatre connection.[36]) Over three decades, however, the faultlines had shifted, as the institutions and practitioners of aesthetic modernism moved between being uneasy bedfellows working cheek-by-jowl,[37] to attempts at aesthetic coalitions[38] and occasionally, as in 1999, outright confrontation. *Vidrohi*'s own coalitions were on display that day in 2017 at the Elgar Parishad, and they directly invoked, if not exactly Brecht, a larger history of radical music, poetry and theatre, recalling the avant-garde front influentially inaugurated by the short-lived, poet-led Dalit Panther movement (founded 1972, disbanded 1977).

A broad arts coalition was also implicit in the founding, in April 1977 (shortly after the Emergency ended), of the Committee for the Protection of Democratic Rights (CPDR). Started by Anuradha and Kobad Ghandy with the playwright Vijay Tendulkar as its *de jure* president, headquartered in the Ghandys' tiny apartment in Colaba's First Pasta Lane, it also signalled an era dominated by

> ... the days of 'parallel' cinema. Marathi amateur theatre was blossoming at Dadar's Chhabildas Hall. The Dalit Panthers had exploded onto the Marathi literary scene. Adil Jussawala's *New Writing in India* was still making waves. Forum Against Rape, Mumbai's first feminist group, had just been founded.[39]

'The Bangladesh war was just over, drought and famine stalked Maharashtra', writes Jyoti Punwani, co-founder. For CPDR itself this lineage was in part inherited from PROYOM, a youth movement started by Dev Nathan and Kiran Kasbekar, and which included at different times the artists Altaf and Navjot, the poet Adil Jussawala and the journalist Darryl D'Monte (writes Nancy Adajania in her book, *Navjot Altaf: the Thirteenth Place*[40]). Anuradha Ghandy, majoring in Sociology at the Elphinstone College, 'was everywhere, inviting Mumbai's leading radicals to talk about the reasons for the drought, putting up posters that proclaimed *Beyond Pity* and urging students to get involved with the crisis in the countryside, defending this stand against those who felt a student's role must be limited to academics and at the most, social work'.[41]

Cyrus Mistry's well-known debut novel *The Radiance of Ashes*,

-36
Sathidar founded the Nagpur chapter of the Indian People's Theatre Association (IPTA) in 2017.

-37
In the mid-1970s, different movements in theatre, literature and poetry took place in a fairly tight location of central Bombay, between Shivaji Park, the Chhabildas School and the Mumbai Marathi Granthasangrahalay.

-38
You get the flavour of the conversations in Vijay Tendulkar's introduction to Namdeo Dhasal's poetry anthology, *Golpitha*. See 'Prastavana', in Namdeo Dhasal, *Golpitha*, Pune: Neelkanth Prakashan, 1975, pp. 5–11.

-39
Jyoti Punwani, 'Memories of a Naxalite Friend', *Times of India*, 20 April 2008.

-40
Nancy Adajania, *Navjot Altaf: The Thirteenth Place*, Mumbai: The Guild, 2016, p. 31.

-41
Punwani, 'Memories of a Naxalite Friend'.

also set in this time, has numerous characters easily identifiable with real-life referents, for, as he says on his flypage, 'any resemblance to recent historical events is entirely deliberate'. Its prologue, first published in the magazine *Debonair* in 1983, invented his protagonist Jingo, or Jehangir, a young graduate trying to write his first novel even as he hangs out with Bombay's radical upper class of former collegemates, in a low-end speakeasy and in the *charas* dens – both venues familiar to the Panther poets – alongside radicals like Gurdeep who work for a slum-dwellers' organization named the Committee for the Protection of Slumdwellers' Rights, a direct reference to CPDR which also began its political work in the slums of Worli, in Nehrunagar, a slum *basti* in Ambavali that is being threatened with demolition. Jingo, forced to take refuge in the *basti*, thinks he can join the movement, but is immediately filled with a 'supressed hysteria in their fervid preoccupations which immediately made him want to exclude himself from their missionary embrace'.[42]

It was in 1981 that the uneasy, if still manageable, combination of elite aesthetics with occasional warfare first changed into something altogether harder and grimmer. In his autobiography *Fractured Freedom: A Prison Memoir*, Kobad Ghandy lists four major moments in Maharashtra's recent political history.[43] One is the 1988 *Riddles in Hinduism* protest. Two, the 1994 agitation to rename Marathwada University. Three, the Ramabai Nagar killings of 1997. Finally, closest to Nagpur, the Khairlanji massacre of 2006. A year after Khairlanji and shortly before she died of cerebral malaria, Anuradha Ghandy wrote one of her last major essays, 'Dalit Fury Scorches Maharashtra'. It had her leaving us with this warning:

> The Maharashtra government has unleashed its repression on the masses. Hundreds have been arrested, the police have resorted to firings and lathi-charges at innumerable places [It is] as if protesting against casteist violence [has become] equal to an attempt to overthrow the state.[44]

It took less than a decade for Anuradha's prescient warnings to come true.

—

-42

Cyrus Mistry, *The Radiance of Ashes*, London: Picador, 2005, pp. 136–37.

-43

Kobad Ghandy, *Fractured Freedom: A Prison Memoir*, New Delhi: Roli Books, 2021.

-44

Anuradha Ghandy, 'Dalit Fury Scorches Maharashtra', in Anand Teltumbde and Shoma Sen, eds, *Scripting the Change: Selected Writings of Anuradha Ghandy*, New Delhi: Anuradha Ghandy Memorial Committee and Daanish Books, 2011, p. 126.

Spectres of Time

Koel Sen's choices of what to do has often lain between extremes. In 2006, as she was planning her future, the alternatives were far apart – between a classical art degree at the J.J. School of Art and a degree in Information Technology from Elphinstone College. What brought the two institutions and the two choices together was a longer history being played out in the immediate moment. She would be in the art district that had sprung up around Kala Ghoda, the National Gallery of Modern Art, the Jehangir Art Gallery, the Chhatrapati Shivaji Maharaj Vastu Sangrahalaya Museum and other big arts venues. Koel chose Elphinstone, where she joined a Computer Science programme which had 'one module where we could understand graphics and animation'.[45]

Koel fractured her foot just before the June 2015 strike call at FTII. She was in her third year, part of the batch that was at the very centre of the action. The fracture, however, meant that she missed the events of June and all of July convalescing in Nagpur. Although she was around in August, she was not in the frontline of the agitation and wasn't there when the August *gherao* happened.

Koel too thus encountered the aftermath of the 2015 strike rather than the events themselves. (She remembers far more vividly the 7 January 2016 incident when she was among the students arrested overnight for protesting Gajendra Chauhan's first visit to the campus.) By mid-2017, in her final year at the FTII, Koel had returned to Mumbai, having by then 'had it' with the campus. 'We lived there for more than six and a half years. So, it was time to leave.' She remains ambivalent about the FTII, the strike, and indeed this entire history. She has seen political action around her from her infancy, and it wasn't something that necessarily attracted her. 'I will do what I want to do', she says she told her parents. 'My politics, whatever it is, will come out through my work and my films.'[46]

Koel's cinema came to be, if anything, profoundly *about* ambivalence. Her first work at FTII, the dialogue exercise *Adhar*, was an autobiographical portrait of a young girl who goes with her mother to meet her father, a radical activist. The father tells her a story. We see her drawings of him in the jungles, on her wall. The film ends with a closed door, from which emerges its dominant image – her doll hanging from a doorknob as though expelled from the house.

-45

It was a stone's throw from the house of Koel's local guardian, Sanober Keshwaar, lawyer, human rights activist and something of an iconic Mumbai figure. On the other hand was the very Bandra-based 'Bollywood–NGO' mindset that Koel had developed following stints with Bharat Bala Productions (legendary for having fabricated the enormously influential popular iconography of patriotism with films typically titled *Jana Gana Mana, Vande Mataram* and *Maa Tujhe Salaam*) and perhaps its polar opposite in every way, the edgy feminist digital media organization Point of View, run by the filmmaker and media activist Bishakha Dutta.

-46

Conversation with Koel Sen on Zoom, 23 June 2021.

Like her cinematic protagonists, Koel too struggles, generationally, politically, historically – and in her case, also technologically – between the old and the new, split between the long histories that frame her analogue life and her digital-native adherences. Different settings return with renewed significance and past history is relentlessly revealed as defining the present. Her student documentary *Bahava*, on the Ravi Varma Press at Malavali, is 'as though a printing press had died and after its death its parts had disintegrated into people's homes in the village'. It has spectral lithographic prints of famous images embedded in the floors and walls or floating over remote houses often shot in dusky light. Gaubai Sabale sits on the Varma Press lithographs as she sings *ovi*s. Kashinath Bhosle, a former worker at the press before it closed, explains the lithographs within a local *varkari* tradition.

Several of the iconic tropes – the ghostly isolated house, the rural well seen from top-angle, the dusky forest walks – reappear in Koel's *Valay*, as does the ambiguous mother figure. In *Valay*, this woman is one of three characters set inside and around an ancient house on a remote hilltop that itself becomes something like a character in the fiction. She is a widow in late middle age living alone, and has apparently adopted two Adivasi youths (their relationship remains unclear). The boy helps out in the house while playing the drums in a band, the girl is studying. There is a suggestion of an amorous liaison between the two. There is both dependence and alienation in an expansive and remote setting

A part of Koel's commitment to the moving image is its engagement with live musical performance, the tech-heavy world of live video art, Resolume Arena and Touch Designer on a MIDI interface. As a filmmaker she has worked in real-time performance almost like a DJ might do. What she likes to do, she says, is to 'disintegrate what is seen on a two-dimensional surface ... into its core pixels' by adding 'layers of video noise and pixel movements'.

She is at the same time committed to extreme slow cinema. 'I bounce back and forth between the skeleton and the body [of the original image], generating something new, something completely different.'

Robin completed his student diploma film *Goonj Khamoshi Ki* and left the campus immediately after, in 2019. He says he had no energy left to remain in the place a day longer than necessary. His film features a young couple living in a house struggling to retain their normalcy in an unnamed city that has become increasingly rife with terror. The man goes to work, the woman appears to be building a career as an artist. They debate what to do, whether to abandon everything and leave. They finally decide to escape, unable to cope with the tension, only to find themselves facing a mob asking, 'Where do you think you're going?'

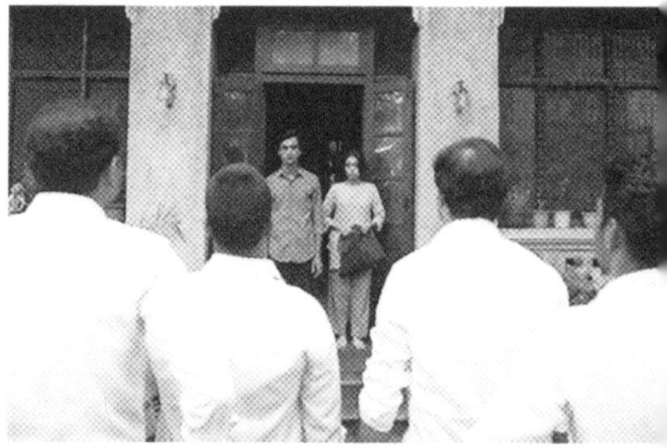

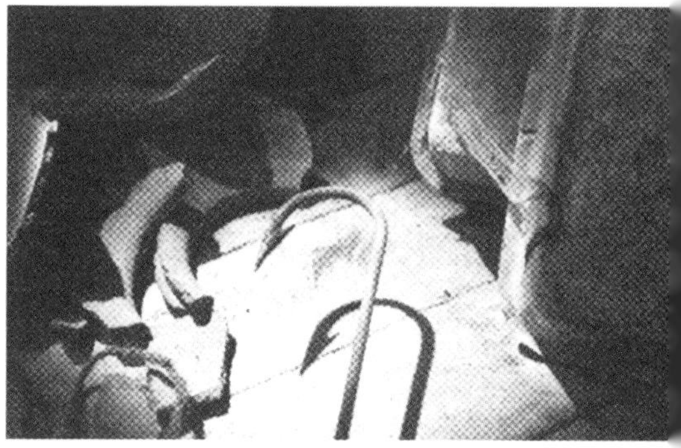

Above: Robin Joy's **Goonj Khamoshi Ki** (2019).
Below: Robin Joy's **Ootha** (2018).

There was something of Robin's hard-won realization of what freedom of speech had come to mean in the cinema, in the way the opening line of his film – 'All characters in this story are fictitious, or maybe not' – was followed by an invitation to viewers to ponder over whether they had sensed similarities with any other events. If they did, it surely wasn't 'mere coincidence'. On the other hand, if they didn't, the viewers were invited to 'forget this film after seeing it, just as they do the stuff printed on the back pages of [their] newspaper'.

Prachee too completed *Makhfi*. The film, whose making coincided with her sexual harassment inquiry, is about the elusive Mughal princess Zebunissa who had the pen name Makhfi or the 'hidden one'. It is set in and around the Qila-e-Ark or Zanana Mahal in Aurangabad. The space had been used as a government art college, and otherwise reduced to ruin.

Prachee reads into Zebunissa's poetry a coded sense of pain, love, loss and longing, presented, she says, in a deliberately subversive metaphysical language.[47] She also reads into the palace wings a metaphor for her words. The totalitarian pleasure garden metaphor returns, once again, for our consideration.

The walls have gigantic pop-art images on its walls, presumably the legacy of the art college, over which the camera pans as the voiceover recites in Persian from Zebunissa's *Diwan-e-Makhfi*. One caved-in floor has the rotting corpse of a dead dog. Several mysterious denizens, human and animal, appear to occupy a space largely believed to be abandoned. Spaces produce other spaces around and beneath in a series of endless rooms.

-47
From Prachee Bajania's 2019–20 project at the India Foundation for the Arts.

Yesterday Once More

Three years and four days after the *gherao* of 2015 and three months after the first Bhima Koregaon arrests, the campus was again on strike. It was led by a batch that had been as though twice removed. They had been admitted after a zero year had been enforced, after the 2008 batch had safely departed and the place digitally scrubbed with the near-complete purge of celluloid from the curriculum. By the time the 2017 batch was admitted, few students knew of or had any connection left with past history on the campus or with the city of Pune.

Which meant that, in contrast to the Vision Document's *déjà vu* yesterday-once-more effect, this strike had all the freshness of the belief that it was happening for the first time, that their problems were as though new to the campus. Studios that were to be completed by June 2018 hadn't happened. Most of the teaching was taking place through workshops, often conducted with outside help. There appeared to be a disconnect of both space and time.[48] Several of their arguments, about shortage of studio space, cameras, lenses and human resources, cutting down or even abolishing of student exercises, non-delivery of promises, had a strong if sometimes unconscious 2008-era recall.

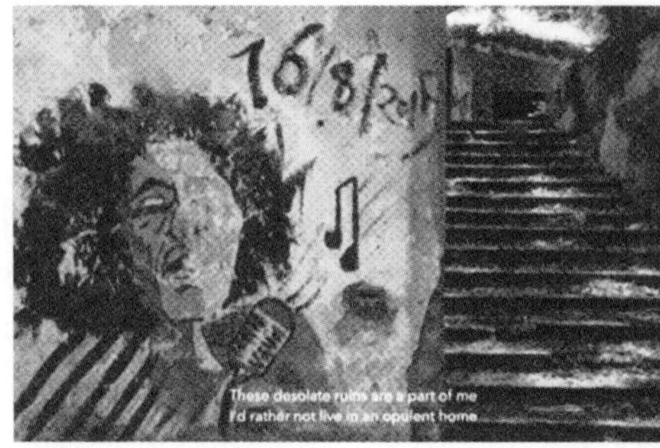

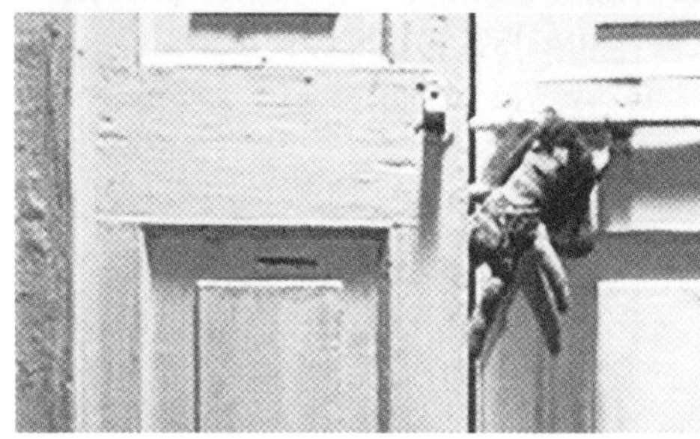

Above: The Zanana Mahal in Prachee Bajania's **Makhfi** (2019). **Below:** The expelled doll in Koel Sen's **Adhar** (2016).

—

Even as this was going on, on 30 September 2018, an accident occurred at a location shoot when a 22 foot crane crashed down injuring two students, Anuj Ujawane and Satish Kumar. The injuries might have been fatal. Outsourced substandard equipment, often at what were claimed to be higher rates than it might have cost to acquire the equipment, had been a topic of contention since the past year, and the accident inevitably saw further agitation protesting against poor equipment, dereliction of duty and endangerment of students.[49]

—

-48

Conversation with Aadhith V. Sathvin, 19 December 2018, Pune.

-49

'Detailed letter to FTII director lists problems, hints at mass protest', *Pune Mirror*, *Times of India*, 10 September 2018.

Perhaps the only incident over the 83 days that opened a larger political frame beyond the FTII cocoon was the sudden cancellation, on 6 September (or two weeks before the crane disaster) of Nachi's student documentary *Hora*, featuring Kabir Kala Manch's Rupali Jadhav. Of all the incidents that defined the last five months of 2018, Nachi's screening was the only one that brought in the fraught atmosphere that had engulfed Pune after the incidents of Bhima Koregaon. The Students' Association alleged pressure from the ABVP.[50] The FTII authorities said this wasn't a public screening and outsiders weren't conventionally allowed. When the film was eventually shown to a closed door, strictly invited audience, Nachi claimed that plainclothes police were present.

-50 Varsha Torgalkar, 'FTII Refuses to Screen Film on Kabir Kala Manch Made by Ex Students' Union President', *The Wire*, 7 September 2018.

—

The 2018 strike ended after 83 days on 12 November. It was nearly as long as the 2015 strike, and on several occasions almost as bitter. No attempt was made this time round to cast their action within a larger political frame, to take on the state, or to discuss issues beyond those limited to the campus.

This time there was little news coverage. This time FTII's news value had been exhausted; its relevance dimmed.

ANNEXURE - I

No. M-14016/4/2018-DO(FA)
Government of India
Ministry of Information & Broadcasting
'A' Wing, Shastri Bhawan, New Delhi-110001.

*****

Dated: 04.06.2019

MEETING NOTICE

Subject: Rationalization/Closure/Merger of Film Media Units namely National Film Development Corporation (NFDC), Children's Film Society, India (CFSI), Films Division (FD), National Film Archives of India (NFAI) and Directorate of Film Festivals (DFF)-regarding.

Reference this Ministry's Office Order of even No. dated 29.01.2019 (copy enclosed).

It has been decided to convene the 1st meeting under the Chairmanship of Shri Bimal Julka (Information Commissioner) on the subject on 14.06.2019 at 11.00 am in Films Division Complex, 24-Dr. Gopalrao Deshmukh Marg, Mumbai-400026. A brief on the matter for the members of the Expert Committee has been enclosed at **ANNEXURE-I.**

2. Expert Committee members are requested to kindly make it convenient to attend the aforementioned meeting at the scheduled date, time and venue.

3. The Competent Authority in this Ministry has decided to appoint Films Division as the nodal agency to facilitate the convening of the meetings of the said Expert Committee. Films Division is requested to co-ordinate with the members of the Committee for their ticketing, transportation, hotel accommodation, sitting fee etc. as per T&Cs stipulated in this Ministry's Office Order of even No. dated 29.01.2019.

Encl: A/a.

(S. B. Pandey)
Under Secretary to the Govt. of India
Tel: 011-23385221

To,

1. Sh. Bimal Julka, Information Commissioner, Room No. 304, CIC Bhawan, Baba Ganganath Marg, New Delhi-110067.
2. Shri T.S. Nagabharana, Keshava Krupa, No.61, 3rd cross, Mysore bank colony, Banashankari 1st stage, Bangalore, Karnataka-560050.
3. Shri Shyama Prasad, 9-D, Windsor Mansion, Kuravankonam, Tiruvananthapuram-695003.
4. Shri A.K. Bir, Film Maker, B-9, Flat No.32/33, 3rd Floor, Khira nagar, SV Road, Santacruz (W), Mumbai-400054.
5. Shri Rahul Rawail, 300/c, Vaz banglow, Off. Turner Road, Bandra (W), Mumbai-400050.
6. The Additional Secretary & Financial Advisor, M/o I&B.
7. The Joint Secretary (Films), M/o I&B.
8. The Director General, Films Division, 24-Dr. G. Deshmukh Marg, Mumbai-400026.
9. The Managing Director, NFDC, 6th Floor, Discovery of India Building, Nehru Centre, Dr. Annie Besant Road, Worli, Mumbai-400018.
10. The Additional Director General, DFF, August Kranti Marg, New Delhi-110049.
11. The Director, NFAI India, Law College Rd, Deccan Gymkhana, Pune-411004.
12. The Chief Executive Officer, CFSI, 24-Dr. G. Deshmukh Marg, Mumbai-400026.

'THE ONLY FORM OF ART ...'

> History shows that films have sparked off political debate and threatened governments, heralded social change and ... sent real-life lovers to their death. It is perhaps in salute to such impelling powers of persuasion that [cinema] is the only form of art deemed fit to be regulated by an Act of Parliament.
>
> – Justice Mukul Mudgal[1]

A Thing Called Cinema

In July 2021, filmmakers Shilpi Gulati and Prateek Vats, academic Bhargav Rani, and lawyers Sahana Manjesh and Mani Chander responded to a Ministry of Information and Broadcasting call for public comments on their proposed amendments to the Indian Cinematograph Act, 1952.[2] A key amendment being proposed was to create what was widely dubbed as a 'super-censor' – a new rule that would effectively allow the I&B Ministry to override the decisions of the Censor Board. Four months earlier, the Film Certification Appellate Tribunal (FCAT), which had allowed filmmakers to appeal Censor Board decisions, had been scrapped.

Gulati, Manjesh, Vats, Rani and Chander wrote up a twelve-page submission and passed it around for signatures. The submission was intended as a coalition-builder around an issue that clearly affected them all. It was also a rallying cry around the cause of the cinema itself, and it worked. They received an astonishing 9,000 signatures as film producers, directors and actors across nine film industries joined hands with documentary filmmakers, film collectives and representatives from theatre, visual arts and academia.

Such a coalition crossed diverse and sometimes even conflicting interests. The 2021 Cinematograph Amendment Bill campaign (hereafter referred to as 'the campaign') focused its submission on four demands that its authors felt captured all concerns, were both inclusive as well as acceptable to all stakeholders.

The first was a longstanding industry requirement endorsed by the Shyam Benegal Committee of 2016, that the CBFC be limited to certification rather than censoring of films. Second, that

-1

Justice Mukul Mudgal (Chair), 'Report of The Committee of Experts to Examine Issues of Certification Under the Cinematograph Act 1952', 28 September 2013, chapter 1, n. 1.

-2

'Cinematograph Amendment Bill: Film-makers decry paternalistic censorship laws', Free Speech Collective, 28 June 2021.

Facing page

Meeting notice by the Ministry of Information and Broadcasting announcing the rationalization, closure or merger of the National Film Development Corporation, Children's Film Society, National Film Archive of India and Directorate of Film Festivals.

the controversial super-censor clause be dropped. Third, that a draconian new clause on piracy also be dropped. And fourth, that FCAT be reinstated. All of these, the authors hoped, were wide enough to capture the interests of filmmakers and spectators alike.

Many of the signatories were members of the film industry who clearly had an interest in *favour* of a Censor Board, but one that could be rejigged to protect *their* interests – such as, for example, with a sacrosanct certification process that would protect certified films from the courts, from the police or from any vandalism perpetrated by a loony fringe that the law delicately calls 'aggrieved parties'. Among them were producers who also wanted protection from another (and to them, equally malevolent) threat – of 'pirates' who would steal their IP and their commodity.

Among the documentary filmmakers who signed, on the other hand, were many who had faced rather different kinds of threats from 'aggrieved' groups, and whose concerns with censorship were somewhat different – a difference that recalled K.A. Abbas' original impetus for challenging the CBFC, between those who were only concerned with the ban on 'dancing, singing and hip-swinging', and had little conception of 'social or political themes to which anyone might object'.[3]

Then there were archivists, hackers and academics who also signed, who weren't directly affected by mobs and the 'religious sentiment' lobby, but who definitely feared being equated with those very mobs, or getting hurt in the war on piracy that threatened the fair use provisions of the copyright law on which their work so crucially relied.

It was to support this final category that the campaign made its fifth, and perhaps most daring, submission, which went as follows:

> The Cinematograph Act must be amended to include a clear definition of 'public' exhibition and bring under its purview only commercial films with substantive capital investment and revenue models tied to theatrical exhibitions.

Specifically, they wanted the Act to be limited only to 'mass publics' and the venues that catered to them, and so to leave out

> private cultural centres, exhibitions for scientific purposes, research seminars, neighborhood film clubs, film festivals, archives, libraries, classrooms and outreach programs organized by NGOs.

-3

K.A. Abbas, 'The Short and Long of It!', *Close-Up*, vol. 3, no. 5–6, 1970, pp. 110–11.

Alongside this they also argued that there should be an 'exempting [of] non-commercial use of copyrighted material'.

With this last demand, they were naming a new and previously unknown category of stakeholders, a growing non-commercial online space of sharing, forwarding, clipping, copying and meme-making, alongside academic research and NGO activism. They wanted to have this entire category of work on the moving image excluded, in its own interest, from the definition of the term 'cinematograph'.

What such a coalition of interests did was to throw into sharp relief a basic question: Was there any overarching definition of the cinematograph sufficiently friendly to all these interests? Could there even be an idea of cinema that could bring them together, speak for them all?

Already in 2013, the Mukul Mudgal Committee appointed to propose amendments to the old Act had asserted, none too originally, that the cinema had changed fundamentally and that the old Act was obsolete. This was patently unarguable. What remained unclear was whether the change had been such as to make any overarching Act redundant.

What to regulate, if the object of its censorious attention was no longer the cinema as we had known it?

Or could there be a rather darker story here? Could it be that the new draft Cinematograph Act, precisely in recognizing the technological obsolescence of film and the gradual dissolution of the moving image into the digital public domain, was also morphing into a rather different 'cinema' as its actual target? Could we read a more sinister *inclusive* ambition behind this action? Might not the forcing of a vaster, more all-inclusive definition of the cinema (such as what Mudgal wanted) lead to this elusive, so-called non-commercial, digital space to be brought into an omnibus censor and draconian piracy provision, rather than be left out of it?

Over Eighteen Months, in Two Epochs

The story had begun eighteen months earlier. In a seemingly disconnected intervention, in 2019, an 'Expert Committee on Rationalization of Film Media Units and Review of Autonomous Bodies' was announced by the Ministry of Information and Broadcasting with the intention to 'rationalize' the National

Film Development Corporation (NFDC), close the Children's Film Society of India (CFSI), and merge the Films Division (FD), Directorate of Film Festivals (DFF) and National Film Archives of India (NFAI) into a single 'umbrella organization'.[4]

-4
Ministry of Information and Broadcasting meeting notice sent by S.B. Panday, Undersecretary, dated 4 June 2019. The NFAI was set up in February 1964.

All these institutions had been created over roughly a decade, beginning with the founding of the International Film Festival of India (IFFI) in January 1952 and culminating in the NFAI in 1964. All of them, across this time, nevertheless traced back to a unified, often controversial vision that had also been built, coincidentally, over another eighteen-month period.

The events between January 1951 and July 1952 produce a curious moment of origin for 2019–20. In January 1951, independent India set up its first film Censor Board under the chairmanship of a man named C.S. Agarwal. Eight months later, in October 1951, the S.K. Patil Film Inquiry Committee published its findings on the Indian cinema – outlining a plan to set up precisely the institutions now being sought to be closed/rationalized/merged. In July the following year, 1952, the Indian Cinematograph Act was passed. All three events – the founding of the CBFC, the Patil Report and the Cinematograph Act itself – were within the prevailing spirit of high state interventionism pervading the planned economy launched in April 1951 by the first Five Year Plan. Coming together, they added up to a bizarre statement of what independent India saw to be wrong with Indian cinema, and what needed to be done.

Such an imagination of a single overarching umbrella organization for regulating cinema was therefore not new, and was always controversial. It was for a while graphically on display in Mumbai, in Walkeshwar's White House Annexe, where the Censor Board existed cheek-by-jowl alongside the 'reformist' Film Federation of India and the 'developmental' NFDC. What had then brought these institutions together, apart from common premises and a common cafeteria, was a single, immersive idea of cinematic 'decline'. The narrative had been pre-programmed to attack a certain type of cinema and to privilege another. Both 'types' were at best hazy descriptions. To be regulated and brought under control was a 'low' cinema, usually made with financier capital, typically with connections across the new border created by the Partition. To be supported, subsidized or made tax-exempt was a state-sponsored industry, ideally represented by films in the genre of the reformist social. Such reformist cinema had its origins in the genre of British war propaganda known then as the 'approved film', soon to be simply dubbed 'good' cinema.

Central to that umbrella imagination was a film-industrial policy to make a cinema more worthy of the new state, one that might better incarnate its model citizen/filmgoing subject. Industrial production (including taxation, infrastructure, tariffs over raw stock import and critical control over investment subsidy) needed to come together with a new capacity to show how production practices impacted film form. Industrial and textual reform (represented by the FFI) had to coalesce into a reformist agenda (the work of the CBFC) in which the film industry could at once undergo self-improvement together with internal restructuring (the role of the NFDC).

All three initiatives, then, came together propelled by a project of *spectatorial reform*. If only the state could nudge industry in that direction, the project believed, the market would do the rest. Of special interest therefore was the pedagogic, policy-incarnating variant of the reformist initiative. It even had an entire academic discipline that it named 'film appreciation',[5] which oversaw the proposed collaboration between a postwar Department of Education and the new institutions envisaged for regulating the film industry.

Seventy years later, in June 2020, the Expert Committee on the 'rationalization' of these film institutions stated its findings. It saw enormous overlap between different units of the government. It therefore recommended that all these be integrated into 'an umbrella configuration with 4 broad verticals', named 'Production, Festival, Heritage and Knowledge'.[6] Each would be headed by 'professionals'. For all the separation of time, the idea was not too different from what Patil had once envisaged.

In 2021, when the Cinematograph Bill Amendment campaign assembled its coalition of signatories, it was working within a very large historical canvas. The campaign came as though at the tail end of an aeon of battles that the Indian cinema has seen over censorship, as several new battles saw the return of a very old concept mobilized yet again – of a gullible public in whose name the censorship apparatus could be defined, and whose interest was being served by its often draconian provisions.

-5

Film appreciation has a complicated history. In 1932, Britain's seminal *Film in National Life* Report described the teacher-archivist of film as a *'skilled investigator'* who could indicate 'the main lines for development [for filmmaking], and [who] might save considerable expense in producing films which might later prove unsuitable, or suitable only for small sections of population' (pp. 135, 202). In many ways the 1928 Indian Cinematograph Committee's mammoth five-volume evidence and conclusions need to be read alongside the *Report of the Colonial Films Committee* (1930) and *Film in National Life*, and all three in turn read alongside, e.g. Paul Rotha's classic *Celluloid: The Film Today* (London: Longmans, 1931). Rotha saw two genres of film as being central to Commonwealth (and future nationalist) governance. The first was the *propaganda film*, and the second – England's explicit contribution to the cause – the influential *approved 'masterpiece'*. Rotha predicted that 'cinematic geniuses of the future' would soon make possible a 'film of direct intention', to impact the 'produce and welfare of Great Britain, its Dominions and Colonies' (ibid., pp. 60–62). The discipline takes root in India with publications of the NCERT (National Council of Educational Research and Training) such as Marie Seton's *Film as an Art and Film Appreciation* and *Film Appreciation: The Art of Five Directors* (both 1964), H.S. Bhola's *Effective Use of Display Material in Schools* (1963), and H.S. Bhola and S.L. Ahluwalia's *AV in Aids and Development* (1964). These were also among the earliest Film Appreciation textbooks at the FTII.

-6

Press Information Bureau, Press Note, 'Expert Committees on Rationalization of Film Media Units and Review of Autonomous Bodies submit report', 2 June 2020.

The 2021 campaign thus shows how the original Cinematograph Act was premised 'on the perception that Indian masses were illiterate, unruly, and prone to be incited into passion by the influence of cinema'. And how, after all these decades, even under the proposed revisions that the conception of the public remains unchanged, still viewed through the same 'paternalistic lens' and still providing the main rationale to 'exert tight control over our cinematic practices'.

There were, however, several new anxieties. Was the public of 2021, for all of its definitional sameness over the century, the same as it had been after, say, the Second World War? Perhaps the true question that now emerged was not how much the public had changed, but whether a single definition existed any longer for the film spectator. Or had this category too, like the diversified and fragmented filmmaker, become an abstraction – a ghostly spectator everywhere and nowhere, both hypervisible and *in*visible?

The 'People' Once More

In 1966, the same year as Mani Kaul and Kumar Shahani completed their graduation films *Yatrik* and *The Glass Pane*, a lesser known FTII student also graduated with an unremarkable documentary named *Water in the Tap*. Five years later, at the height of the Kannada 'new wave', this ex-student, K.M. Sankarappa, made his only major film, *Madi Madidavaru*. Like much of the New Cinema in that language, the film was better known for the novel it adapted, a landmark text by the Pragatishila writer Basavaraja Kattimani set in the Quit India movement. Sankarappa did nothing else of note in the cinema, limiting his work to newsreels and state government documentaries, while occasionally teaching in Bangalore University's Communication Department.

In 1990, this filmmaker took the Indian state to court.[7] He filed a petition in the Karnataka High Court that threw the kitchen sink at the state. Sankarappa premised his argument on his basic, blanket contention that the Indian Parliament was not qualified to have passed the Cinematograph Act in the first place. He followed this bazooka hit with multiple shots at its Sections 3, 4, 5D, 6 and 7, all of which he considered variously either unconstitutional or bad in law. His action seemed not to stem from any individual grievance. Indeed, the Standing Counsel even argued that since he

-7
Karnataka High Court, *K.M. Shankarappa vs Union Of India* on 2 April 1990

didn't appear to have been individually affected, he 'could not be considered to be an aggrieved person' and was therefore 'not entitled to challenge the validity of the provisions of the Act'. This didn't work because, said the court, Sankarappa was a filmmaker, a film teacher and, most important, a citizen of India – all of which gave him enough standing for his petition.

Sankarappa was – as indeed the students' strike of 2015 too would realize – neither the first filmmaker or film student, nor the last, to tangle with the strange and bizarre turf maelstrom involving India's judiciary and its executive, or to figure out what the cinema was doing in the very eye of that storm between two arms of the Indian state. He would realize, as Abbas had before him and others since then, that the Cinematograph Act was not built to support the interests of the filmmaker. It was there to ostensibly protect the *people* – in other words, the state, the *parens patriae* that uniquely claims the sole right to care for and to represent them – from the *filmmaker's* excesses.

Necessarily, Sankarappa trod a thin line, as the 2021 campaign too did, between arguing, like Abbas, against the very validity of the Cinematograph Act – even as also asserting its virtues, as possessing *some* form of legally recognized procedure, however broken, that gave at least a fig-leaf right of appeal against arbitrary executive action. Like Abbas two decades earlier, Sankarappa's arguments were mounted essentially on a freedom of speech platform. Unlike Abbas, however, most of them didn't get by. The High Court was able to read them down, reduce them to procedural issues and dispose of them.

Only one argument hit home, and it did so for interesting reasons. This was his challenge to the original Section 6.1 of the Act, by which the central government, having created a Censor Board and an Appellate Tribunal, nevertheless sought to retain the right to ask for the record of 'any proceeding in relation to any film' and make any order 'as it thinks fit' for a previously censored film.

Sankarappa made a straightforward argument. Having set up a judicially recognized infrastructure, the executive could hardly bypass that infrastructure with whimsical decisions of its own. The High Court endorsed this view entirely. 'If the exercise of the power of judicial review can be set at naught by the State Government by overriding the decision given against it,' it said, 'this would sound the death knell of the Rule of Law'.

In 1991, appalled by the possibility that it might lose its extra-judicial prerogatives, the central government yet again invoked the trope that had unfailingly worked for it. It challenged Sankarappa in the Supreme Court, saying that it was essential for the state to retain the right to override the Censor Board since there was widespread 'public resentment' against films people didn't like, and that 'law and order situations [often] arose' even in films cleared by the CBFC and FCAT.[8] Once again the government lost.

Two decades later, a rather different kind of filmmaker made the same argument in the Supreme Court. In August 2011, Prakash Jha's mega-budget *Aarakshan*, featuring Amitabh Bachchan and Saif Ali Khan leading a major star cast, was considered by the National Commission for Scheduled Castes and Scheduled Tribes to be 'casteist' and potentially anti-Dalit. Once again, a populist argument allowed first Mayawati's Uttar Pradesh government to ban the film, and then the Punjab and Andhra Pradesh governments to follow suit – with Punjab further claiming that they had 'Intelligence Reports that the movie has certain scenes and dialogues, which may upset some communities in the state'.[9] All the states used the 6.1 clause, claiming that it was potentially likely to cause law and order problems.

Jha repeated the argument that Section 6.1 was unconstitutional, but he added another issue. You couldn't, he said, withdraw an already censored film and claim that it presents a threat to law and order even *before* the film had been released. Surely the film had to first enter the public domain to even pose such a problem. This was an important argument since it evoked some rather different legal provisions that the Censor Board didn't yet have – laws that argued (as for example 69-A of the Information Technology Act) for the right to take preventive action in order to avoid *future* incitement to the commission of a cognizable offence. Yet again the Supreme Court agreed with the filmmaker.

The Faceless People, the Mob, and the State

By 2013, the old colonial concept of an unruly mob threatening films existed mostly in the imagination of the state and sometimes the law. It was, as William Mazzarella says, a concept of public

-8

Supreme Court of India, *Union of India vs K. M. Sankarappa* on 28 November 2000.

-9

'Andhra bans Prakash Jha's Aarakshan after Punjab, UP', *India Today*, 12 August 2011.

'affect' to be invoked and then disavowed – essentially an *abstraction* that always provided a shock whenever it was physically manifested in the cinema. It was an 'affectively evacuated bourgeois conception of public reason', and as a 'public affect' – a provocation attributed to the cinema to which 'uneducated people' are in the censorial imagination uniquely vulnerable – it has dissipated into practically everything. It exists everywhere as a 'potential', says Mazzarella, to be triggered at will, from the banal to the elaborately performed, 'whether on screen, on the stage, in the streets'.[10]

In 2013, the Mudgal Committee created its own version of expanded cinema – alongside an expanded public – asking for the legal definition of 'film' to include all kinds of material that existed entirely outside of the film itself. Its direction was clearly to include an ancillary industry that has grown around the cinema, or significant parts of what the Confederation of Indian Industry names the 'media & entertainment sector', into its conception of the amended Act. Such an expansion of the cinema well beyond the object 'film' would necessarily lead to a corresponding rise in the number of 'aggrieved' people, as Mazzarella's 'public affect' too had to be brought into the ambit of censorship.

To deal with *this* expansion, Mudgal recommended a significantly scaled-up, quasi-judicial FCAT. It would be a dedicated court purely to deal with the cinema, a 'specialized Tribunal' that knew how to 'filter out busybody and unscrupulous elements' who only wanted 'rabble rousing or publicity'.

In 2021, the central government went in a seemingly opposite direction. Fifty years after Justice Hidayatullah had paved the way for its introduction in the Abbas judgment, FCAT was formally abolished. It was, on the face of it, the very opposite of what Mudgal had recommended. It also caught the film industry entirely unprepared. For one, it came seemingly out of the blue; for another, it did not appear possible, apparently being in direct violation of the Supreme Court's ruling.[11] In fact, however, the government had just found another way to do what Mudgal had wanted.

Two months before the abolition of FCAT, the Digital Media Ethics Code was released, introduced to directly target social media and OTT. From Twitter to all social media platforms, messaging platforms, web publishers and OTT platforms, it required extreme

-10

William Mazzarella, *Censorium: Cinema and the Open Edge of Mass Publicity*, Durham: Duke University Press, 2013, p. 25.

-11

The ostensible reason was that this fell within the Tribunals Reforms (Rationalization and Conditions of Service) Ordinance, 2021.

conditions that made them responsible to anybody with a 'grievance'. The guidelines were framed 'keeping in mind the difference between viewership in a theatre and television as compared to watching it on Internet', said a publicity statement, and were designed to 'empower ordinary users'[12] – no doubt users who, returning us to the G.D. Khosla Committee on Censorship in 1969, did nothing, saw nothing, and only communicated their displeasure in 'references' to concerned authority.

This raised a parallel question. Was digitization raising a bigger picture for state intervention than anyone had conceived? Should the new anti-piracy law of the proposed Act not be read alongside the Digital Media Ethics Code? In fact, should large parts of the cinema not come under the Information Technology Act, 2000, rather than the Cinematograph Act?

FCAT had constituted a specific hurdle, given that two objections of the Supreme Court had been specifically that extra-judicial powers could not be allowed when a 'quasi-judicial body' existed. It had to be done away with if the old 6.1 clause was to be reinforced, given new teeth. The double movement that took place, of eliminating FCAT and bringing in 6.1 (triple, if you include the Ethics Code), potentially gave the Information and Broadcasting Ministry vast unilateral 'revisionary powers' by which it could 'on receipt of any reference ... direct the CBFC to re-examine a film that has already been approved for public exhibition', writes Shilpi Gulati.[13] Who, Gulati wants to know, was authorized to send this 'reference' to the government? Clearly anybody could, in what appeared to her to be direct encouragement to 'vigilante groups to ... use it as a way of threatening filmmakers for allegedly hurting "religious sentiments"'.

Expanded cinema thus saw rather new battle lines. On one side was the entire filmmaker's legacy – from Abbas to Sankarappa to Prakash Jha, to the many filmmakers who signed the rejoinder. On the other, there was a more amorphous practice of the digital moving image. As this divide opened up, the 'people' too split.

There were, on the one hand, the people as seen through the paternalistic lens of the government – a benevolent, somewhat indulgent view of innocent citizens whose hurt sentiments could be assuaged by any member of the public sending a simple 'reference'

-12

Government notifies Information Technology (Intermediary Guidelines and Digital Media Ethics Code) Rules 2021, Ministry of Electronics and IT, posted on 25 February 2021.

-13

Shilpi Gulati, 'Super Censorship of Cinema?', *Economic and Political Weekly*, vol. 56, no. 31, 21 July 2021.

to the I&B Ministry, which would be sufficient for the Ministry to recall any film for censor re-examination.

In sharp contrast was another public – far less benevolently viewed – of pirates and hackers. They merited no patrician indulgence. They were directly targeted with the other truly draconian clause being proposed, 6AA: that 'without the written authorization of the author', nobody – and it literally meant *nobody* – would be permitted 'to use any audiovisual recording device in a place to knowingly make or transmit ... a copy of a film or a part thereof', no exceptions. This clause hit directly at fair use. Here no simple letter to the I&B Ministry sufficed – it would be heavy fines ('not less than three lakh rupees but which may extend to 5% of the audited gross production cost') or, very likely, jail time.

'The Kid Taking Trophy Shots': Another Kind of People

> You have raised the issue of fair use and what happens if a kid is taking a trophy shot of the screen and how do you deal with that. The dilemma is this. The reverse case is that if you allow them to do that, then they will take small parts of it and stitch it outside. Even today, Sir, some of it will come as an offence under the IT Act ... he has to see what misery is to be done.
>
> – Secretary, Ministry of Information and Broadcasting, 2019[14]

In 2019, a Standing Committee on Information Technology of the Lok Sabha came out with its recommendations on the Cinematograph Amendment Bill. Like Mudgal, this Committee too noted the 'dramatic transformation of the information and cinematography landscape in the present time', but said that the draft Bill was 'not ambitious enough to cover wide range of issues concerning the general public'.

Among its central concerns was that the Bill did not have a provision for fair use, and in its absence, there was 'no protection provided ... to someone who forwards a film clip/short extract of movies as memes, jokes etc., for non-commercial purposes'.

The I&B Ministry showed no indulgence here – they fought this recommendation ferociously, tooth and nail. '*Even one minute*', said the Ministry with feral intensity, 'as an exception would create the possibility of stitching of smaller clips and creating a commercially useable content online'. Any exception *at all* would 'defeat the purpose of having an absolute anti-camcording provision'.

-14

Standing Committee on Information Technology (2019–20), Chairman: Shashi Tharoor, The Cinematograph (Amendment) Bill, Ninth Report, New Delhi: Seventeenth Lok Sabha Ministry of Information and Broadcasting, 2019, Section 55.

The Ministry went on. It simply saw no merit in the idea that 'making copies of the work' could in any way 'contribute towards creating a narration or events in consequence'. After all, it said, 'access to cinematograph works for educational purpose can be obtained by legalized channels as well, such as purchasing a DVD', and 'making infringing copies is not the only option'.

What about the word 'knowingly'? What happens if someone unknowingly breaks the law, such as a child taking a 'trophy shot' of the screen? Not even then, said the Ministry. Let the smallest detail go by, and the entire system was doomed.

> We do not know whether a small part of five or three minutes is really not going to be a dangerous way of stitching smaller pieces which can be recorded. There are evidences in the past that it is difficult for anyone to record the entire two hour long film but a film can be recorded by 50 different people, part of that group for 10 minutes each and they stitch the film. They are told that you record from this time to this time, then it shifts to the next person.

There were no 'aggrieved' publics here and no indulgent approach. This was the fear of the apparatus now come full circle.

In a curious slip, one that the 2021 campaign caught and reproduced, the Standing Committee on Information Technology may have had the last word. Urging the I&B Ministry one last time to reconsider, to bring fair use back into the Bill, it requested that there at least be 'adequate safeguards to innocent viewers' who were either doing their work or simply expressing their creativity. There was the definite threat of a 'misuse of the proposed provision in the Bill and related harassment of innocent people'. What the amended Cinematograph Bill threatened to do was, said the Standing Committee, 'make criminals out of ordinary citizens'.

In the Ministry's take-no-prisoners approach, however, there were no innocents. Everybody had become a filmmaker and so everybody had to be in the know. Perhaps this was where the cinematic ideal had ended, the circle inexorably complete – where the old Patil Committee imagination of 1951 finally bit the dust, and with it, what was once a national project. Where the cinema – having, under state control, first criminalized film students – had now made criminals of us all.

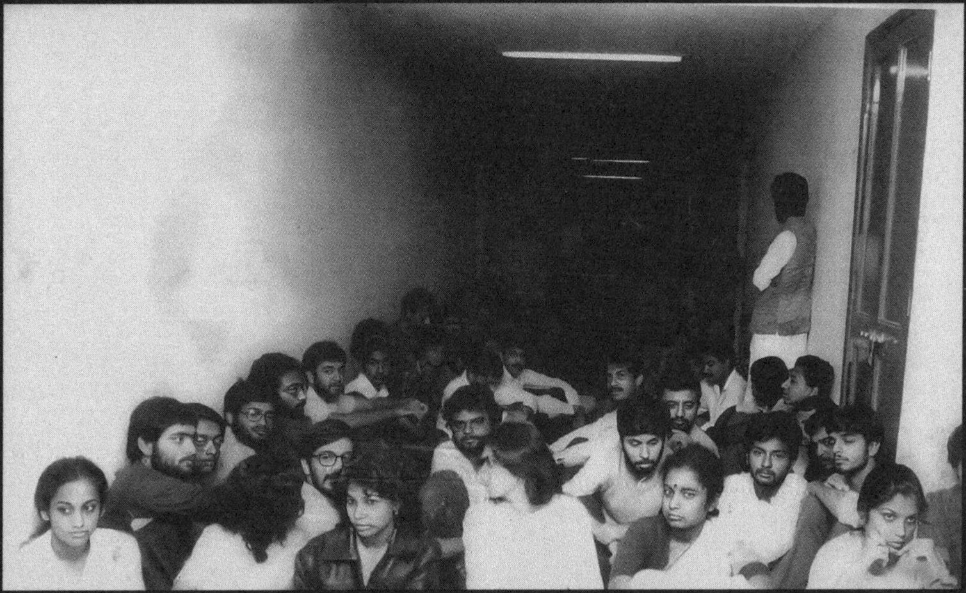

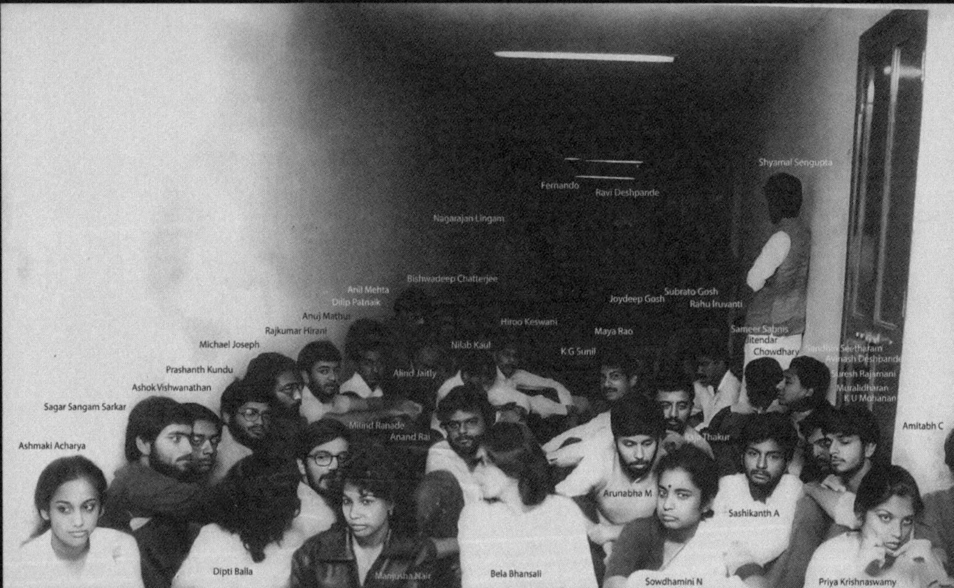

R.V. Ramani's photograph of the 1984 strike: students sitting in the corridor obstruct the venue of the FTII Governing Council (chaired by Mrinal Sen) meeting. Identification and image enhancement by Nagarajan Lingam. The all-women frontline, created to hold back the police, includes – one realizes only now – Priya Krishnaswamy, S. Soudhamini and Ashmaki Acharya. There is some ambiguity about the identification. Several figures in silhouette at the back create what Ramani has called a 'wishlist of people who one imagines were there'. The author was, he believes, present when this photograph was taken (before being thrown out by the Students' Association), and would have been standing just behind the photographer in an appropriately liminal zone.

ACKNOWLEDGEMENTS

It was on 15 June 2015 that I got first-hand news about the strike. Surabhi Sharma was standing in the corridors of Mumbai's Films Division, her phone buzzing. An FDZone screening curated by her had just ended and she was outlining developments taking place even then on the FTII campus to a small group of avid listeners. It was early days yet, but Surabhi sounded deeply worried. She was convinced it would be larger than what its protagonists imagined. To her, the dangers were palpable and immediate, but they also involved larger histories.

'Someone', she said in passing, 'should really write about this.' A short while later, when I offered to try (in what proved to be the origin of this book), Surabhi spoke to me at greater length. She had multiple practical anxieties, but more often her worries were how to escalate her role and that of everyone involved into a larger cinematic legacy. It was the cinema that brought everyone together and rendered palpable the many intellectual and creative freedoms that were now under threat. It was the only legacy at hand that might enable the widespread solidarity they so desperately needed to keep their struggle going.

Since the early 2000s, Surabhi has worked with other film-makers, many of them her seniors and peers, to create a structure of informal and largely extra-institutional support that has at key moments turned into a fully formed political practice – as it did, for instance, during the Vikalp initiative of independent documentary filmmakers in 2004. In her description, however, this involvement goes back to at least the mid-1990s, and the cycle of agitations that she had seen as a student. As she spoke on, her canvas kept expanding concentrically, returning to the early '80s, to the mid-'70s, and eventually to the very origins of the FTII and to founding documents about the cinema conceived by the independent Indian state.

Such an expanded definition of the strike, of cinema itself and of political action became a repeated refrain as the months of 2015 unfolded, and a small off-campus collective of alumni, friends and supporters mobilized an increasingly vital moving centre for the strike – organizing, lobbying, networking, helping, mentoring, counselling, advising students and other young filmmakers. Soon enough an infrastructure of informal support opened for my own project, allowing me to reach out and make contact, to navigate in real time all that was happening. There was an enduring discussion on the interpretative possibilities, the rights and wrongs, the roads taken and not taken, to work out what could happen and where the barriers lay. For all the usual caveats, this book would have been impossible to realize without Surabhi Sharma and the environment of support she created for it.

—

Another longer and more personal history merges into this one. Some time in the mid-1970s, the patent attorney R.S. Amladi, my maternal uncle, bought an apartment in Kanchan Galli, two streets away from the FTII, in part for my grandmother and other aged relatives, in part because my cousin Parag Amladi (and to some extent I) had begun getting interested in the cinema. Over the next decade, sneaking into screenings at the Main and Classroom Theatres effectively became my film education, but it also forged an identity that has lasted down the years, as an interested if sometimes illegitimate *bystander*, as against an active participant, an eyewitness and eventually historian, of what I saw, heard and learned both on and off that particular campus. It enabled friendships with students, many of which have endured. It led to longstanding and close associations with senior filmmakers, especially with my own mentor Kumar Shahani, and then with Mani Kaul, Kamal Swaroop, and less intensely, Saeed Akhtar Mirza, Kundan Shah, Girish Kasaravalli and, over a bizarre few days, John Abraham. It was this legacy that returned in conversations with Saeed Mirza, and framed the Foreword he so generously agreed to write for this book. Other associations grew and flowered in locations in Mumbai, in screenings and events at Screen Unit (my first publisher), at the Xavier Institute of Communication where Parag Amladi worked and which regularly hosted conversations with filmmakers like Kumar Shahani, Saeed Mirza and Arun Khopkar, and several other places, formal and informal. Khopkar especially remained through this time a close friend and key interlocutor. In the early 1980s I came into rather more intense contact with a peer group, a generation of filmmakers either of my age or only slightly younger than me – among them R.V. Ramani, Anup Singh, Vikram Joglekar, Paresh Kamdar, Piyush Shah, Fareeda Mehta and Rajat Kapoor – and to conversations, arguments, laughter and breakdown, extravagant claim and wild ambition, as I received multiple insights into how films are made, how they can be seen and how they come to mean something.

—

This book would not have been possible without the support of Vikas Urs. He was the first leading figure in the 2015 strike with whom I had extended conversations, including granular and detailed discussions on how the campus changed in the years leading up to 2015. An entire second round saw Vikas return to his personal archives and the Students' Association's email account to produce an astonishing archive, literally by the day, of the 139 days. Equally important was Nachi, Harishankar Nachimuthu. He has been generous with his time, first in Pune, then over several days in Chennai, and continuously thereafter on WhatsApp. This is also a shoutout to Nachi's Potato Eaters, my major source these days of keeping abreast of news in the independent cinema circuit.

Where I turned to more concrete events in the period after the Hewitt agitation, I sought out more focused discussion. Prateek Vats took me in some detail through almost a decade of history, from 2006–07 through to December 2015, and helped in multiple ways, most recently inviting me into the inner debates around the campaign to resist the amendments to the Cinematograph Act, which also led to significant conversations with the lawyer Sahana Manjesh and the film researcher and filmmaker Shilpi Gulati. I have received a rich description of the late 1970s from Ashok Ahuja, Anil Zankar and Sanjiv Shah. Padmaja Shaw contributed a great deal of useful information on the period when Kundan Shah, Rajendra Shaw, Ravi Ojha and Gopal Singh Golan started their commune in Hyderabad, the origins of what would become *Jaane Bhi Do Yaaron.* Ramani filled me in on the early 1980s (especially the 1984 strike, which I personally witnessed and marginally helped with – including one meeting between the students and Mani Kaul, Saeed

Mirza and Ketan Mehta that took place in my house in Mumbai). Jabeen Merchant read and shared her comments on this book, and also spoke at length about the early 1990s and then about her stellar role in the Nair Committee report of 2010–11. Kavita Pai talked me through the 1996–97 strikes. Manoj Lobo, Amit Dutta and Ganga Mukhi spoke to me at length about the 2000 strike – Manoj, in addition, excavated three utterly invaluable old CDs with almost twelve hours of astonishing footage of that time. Over an intense evening Kamal K.M. gave me his take on this time and the way it has determined his life-choices ever since. Gurvinder Singh spoke to me about his involvement and then his distance from the place that was once close to his home. Neeraj Sahay read through and gave multiple, detailed comments, and several astonishing insights into this history and most particularly the moment of the millennial turn, from FTII to Godhra and the Shared Footage Group, when he was at the centre of it all. Naveen Padmanabha was both a major support and a key source of information on the Hewitt agitations and their immediate aftermath. Kislay gave me a thick and complex description of the years that followed, the strike itself as he understood it, and its aftermath in Goa. I spoke to Prabhati Gharat and Kshama Padalkar – Kshama especially in the context of her feature-length film *The Strike and I*. I met and spoke to Sakshi Gulati in Delhi, and then Rima Kaur and Shashank Walia in Chandigarh. Shini J.K. read through the text, for which I remain grateful. Koel Sen gave me, over extended discussion, the frame with which it ends. Fatema Kagalwala also read through the book. I had one early conversation with Payal Kapadia in Pune, a few with Vijaya Singh during the strike, longer ones with Mukul Haloi and Viraj Tadwalkar, and of the later batches, with Robin Joy, Prachee Bajania, V. Aadhith, Rachit Pandey and Vinod Bangari.

A special thanks to Keval Arora, who spoke and shared material on The Players and the early 2000s, through which passed so many future filmmakers including key figures in the story told here. Nakul Singh Sawhney also spoke at length about this period, leading into his own work in documentary film. Among the FTII's current and former faculty, I have spoken to Sandeep Chatterjee, corresponded with Kedarnath Awati, spoken to Anjum Rajabali and had a brief conversation with Amit Tyagi. I also received comments on my text from Indranil Bhattacharya. My deep gratitude to all of them.

As ever, my academic community, of both old and sometimes young friends, has remained my bedrock: I remain indebted for their extensive responses to Madhava Prasad, Lawrence Liang, Valentina Vitali, Rochona Majumdar, Ratheesh Radhakrishnan, Teresa Braggs and Ila Ananya. A special thanks to Ashish Avikuntak for conversations on the larger career of celluloid film, a central part of this story, and of course their specific manifestations on the campus in 1997. As always, I remain grateful to my comrades at the School of Arts and Aesthetics, JNU, in particular Ira Bhaskar, Ranjani Mazumdar and Kaushik Bhaumik.

—

In the end, however, for all the support I received, this remains a personal account. It is an argument primarily about the cinema, but now told within a fundamentally transformed political framework in India. It is certainly the first time I have tried to write so directly about other people, many of them students and young filmmakers just starting their careers, belonging to a technologically and politically informed generation a third my age. Given that much of this history is in the era of social media, I have (like all of us) had unprecedented access to an unexpected treasure trove of personal and official positions, arguments and real-time debates, some fierce and even vituperative, all in the public domain – in documentary footage uploaded with hashtags and handles, on blogs, and on numerous Facebook, YouTube, Twitter and Instagram postings. My actual conversations with people have often thus been spliced with quotations, frame-grabs and material recycled from such sources.

Such a citational strategy is a first for me. It has been made possible primarily by the subjective nature of the narrative itself and by my own standpoint in this history. I am grateful for extended legal advice from Jawahar Raja and Sahana Manjesh, and for support, both practical and conceptual, from Shaina Anand, Ashok Sukumaran, Zinnia Ambapardiwala and Jan Gerber, my old colleagues at indiancine.ma.

Notwithstanding the extraordinary support I have received from my many interlocutors, it is especially worth asserting that they should not be considered either necessarily in agreement with its content or responsible in any way for it. I have tried to check back with everyone cited here, and done, as far as I could, the necessary fact-checking to ensure that there are no misrepresentations or misquotation. (In the event of errors, corrections will be carried out in future editions.) In the end, however, the book remains essentially a personal, argumentative and thus inevitably selective account. For this, I must take sole responsibility.

—

John–Ghatak–Tarkovsky is published as part of a collaboration between the Sher-Gil Sundaram Arts Foundation (SSAF) and Tulika Books. I remain as always indebted to old comrades Geeta Kapur, Vivan Sundaram and Indira Chandrasekhar, and now am delighted to also acknowledge the other Trustees of SSAF and the staff of both organizations in what is a growing and vibrant institutional context for practice in the arts and academics.

An important moment in this history was in early 2020 when Gautam Das, then working at the Kochi-Muziris Biennale, invited Surabhi Sharma and me to assemble a package of films to do with protest in India. Unfortunately the Biennale itself did not happen because of the pandemic, but its unintended consequence was to give me time to attempt a more ambitious text than I had planned. An even more significant development was the translation of this book into Malayalam by Gautam Das, and its publication by the Kerala State Chalachitra Academy. I am grateful to C. Ajoy, Secretary of the Academy, and N.P. Sajeesh, Deputy Director (Programmes), for all their courtesies in making this happen. For returning the idea back to the Kochi-Muziris Biennale, thanks to Bose Krishnamachari and Mario D'Souza. And for friendship, advice and support in making all of this happen, raising a cheer for C.S. Venkiteswaran and Bina Paul.

Research for this book was supported by the Centre for the Study of Culture and Society's faculty research fund. For the pragmatics of the actual research, I need to specially mention Achal Vohra's help in more ways than I can name. I thank Shonali Gajwani for handling the transcription of many hours of audio recordings and Sanghita Sen for filling in details of Ghatak's time at the FTII.

Kinshuk Rawat's insightful, deeply involved and always painstaking design brought an entirely different dynamic to the process, as we struggled sitting in Bangalore's coffee shops with the lowest of low resolutions, seeking to fabricate and sometimes montage a design solution for intractable problems both technical and (occasionally) legal.

As always, Tejaswini Niranjana – for being my first reader, for holding things together, to tell me when it's not done and when it is.

Ashish Rajadhyaksha
Bangalore, October 2022

INDEX